D0175128

MARITAL RELATIONS, BIRTH CONTROL, AND ABORTION IN JEWISH LAW

MARITAL RELATIONS, BIRTH CONTROL, AND ABORTION IN JEWISH LAW

by David M. Feldman

SCHOCKEN BOOKS · NEW YORK

First SCHOCKEN PAPERBACK edition 1974
10 9 8 7 6   85 86 87 88

Copyright © 1968 by New York University
Library of Congress Catalog Card No. 68-15338
Published by arrangement with New York University Press
All rights reserved

Manufactured in the United States of America

ISBN 0-8052-0438-5

Preface

The Jewish tradition offers precious insights and helpful value judgments in the areas of human concern touched upon in this book, insights which can be of substantial enlightenment to a generation beset by confusion and reappraisal.

Despite the intrinsic importance of our subject, its various phases have until now been left virtually untreated in any systematic sense. The areas of marriage, procreation, marital sex, sexual pleasure, as well as the themes of Chapters 6, 7, and 8, and even of Chapters 9, 10, 11, and 12, have hardly been explored at all. As to the central theme of contraception itself, or the related problem of abortion, most statements of the Jewish view available in primary or secondary works are based on a handful, so to speak, of Responsa decisions, and on a one-dimensional citation thereof. The present effort draws on several hundreds of Responsa, assimilating not only their conclusions, but their analyses of the factors involved as well. As a result, a totally new picture emerges, breaking new ground in terms of definitions, principles, and a unifying view.

The volume at hand affords an important contribution on another level. This consists in its mustering of otherwise inaccessible classic and contemporary sources, some hitherto unknown to scholars in any language, and of collating these sources in a sequential pattern. The texts are allowed to speak for themselves; the interpretation offered is consistent with and documented by the processes of legal and literary development in Codes, Commentaries, and Responsa.

It must be pointed out, in the cautious spirit of the writers of Responsa, that the decisions of "case law" in many of these Responsa were addressed to specific individuals in specific circumstances and, strictly speaking, are not transferrable as legal determinations. Inferrable, nonetheless, are some highly significant generalizations, and these I offer in pride and enthusiasm to the interested reader everywhere.

The "Jewish law" of the title refers, of course, to the classic legal tradition that begins with Bible and Talmud and courses through to the most recent Responsum, as sketched in Chapter 1. The extent to which this law is operative today differs among the three alignments of modern Judaism — Orthodox, Conservative, and Reform. The law [halakhah] itself is traced here through the works of its historic spokesmen, in a manner seeking to transcend the position of any one group. For, all three are heirs to the culture, outlook, and values of Judaism's legal-moral tradition reflected in these pages.

The various libraries utilized in the preparation of this work have been graciously accommodating, and it is a pleasant duty to record my thanks to Mrs. Gertrude Serata of the Library of the Jewish Theological Seminary of America, as well as to the staffs of the Mendel Gottesman Library of Yeshiva University, the Jewish Division of the New York Public Library, the Klau Library of Hebrew Union College in Cincinnati, and the National Library of the Hebrew University in Jerusalem. I am thankful, too, to the staff of New York University Press for the attractive format which this book has assumed.

For academic training and inspiration, I am grateful to the faculties of the first two institutions of learning mentioned above. For this and much more, I owe a special debt of gratitude to my father, Rabbi Moses J. Feldman of Los Angeles. While a Hebrew version of Chapter 11 was duly accepted by the Seminary as a doctoral thesis in 1966, and a recension of the manuscript was read by my learned father, I assume sole responsibility for both the material and its interpretation in that as well as all other chapters in this volume.

I wish I could adequately accord thanks to the leaders and members of my beloved congregation, the Bay Ridge Jewish Center. They have been most generous in their encouragement and understanding during the past few years when research and composition kept me from a fuller involvement in community affairs. I express my appreciation to each individual among the officers, trustees, and membership, and hope they will find the present offering worthy of their affectionate confidence.

DAVID M. FELDMAN

Brooklyn, New York

November, 1967

Prefatory Note to Second Printing

In the short span of time since this book's first printing (October, 1968), the issues it treats have been the subject of much public discussion. Yet, no significant rabbinic Responsa or related literature have appeared in the interim. It was, accordingly, deemed unnecessary to recast or update the footnote references, much less the text's frame of reference.

There is one exception. Responsa from the pen of the revered Abraham Issac Kuk, Chief Rabbi of the Holy Land until his death in 1935, were not published until 1969. His decisions are included in this edition (see p. 226), not only because of his singular eminence and their consequential bearing on our subject, but also because his conclusions constitute—I make bold to say—a gratifying endorsement of this book's central thesis.

D. M. F.

September, 1970

Preface to Schocken Paperback Edition

The reception accorded this book in its various hard-cover printings has, of course, been deeply gratifying. Since the book's initial publication, the sexual revolution, the feminist movement, and population control are far more pronounced as themes in our society. Nevertheless, the passage of time has not diminished the adequacy of the halakhic material presented here as a response to the perennial questions it addresses, and the reader will find no less value and substance in this unaltered presentation.

I am grateful for the wider distribution made possible by soft-cover publication. A larger audience can then come to know this example of halakhic method, as well as of moral concern, spiritual insight, and humane compassion reflected in Rabbinic teaching.

D. M. F.

January, 1974

Contents

Part 1. Introductory

Chapter 1. The Structure of Jewish Law   3

The Talmud
Post-Talmudic Codes
Rashi and Tosafot
Maimonides' Code
The Thirteenth-Century Talmudists and Asheri's Code
The Tur Code
The Shulhan Arukh
The Later Authorities
The Extralegal Tributaries
The Responsa Literature

Part 2. The Positive Factors

Chapter 2. Marriage—Independent of Procreation . . .   21

Marriage in the Christian Tradition
Marriage in the Jewish Tradition

Part 5.   Abortion

Part 6.   Postscript

Note on Transliteration of Hebrew and Aramaic Terms

The system of transliteration here follows that of the *Jewish Encyclopedia*, with some important variations:

(1)   The nonconsonantal *yod* is restored (*Ba'alei* instead of *Ba'ale*).

(2)   An apostrophe is used instead of an *e* for *sh'va na* (*Y'vamot* instead of *Yevamot*). This has the advantage that a distinction may be made between *zera* and *z'ra*, both of which would be *zera* in the conventional system. Exceptions are made where the word is part of an accepted phrase or title (*Menorat HaMaor; Geonim*). An apostrophe is also used for *sh'va na* where no letter at all is customarily used (*Av'nei Nezer; Igg'rot Mosheh*), although not consistently.

(3)   A double letter is used when the Hebrew has a *dagesh forte*, or *dagesh hazak* (*Niddah; kavvanah*), but not where the English pronunciation may suffer (*ubar* instead of *ubbar*), or after prefixes (*HaGadol; mi-bifnim*).

(4)   An *h* is written where a Hebrew word ends in *heh*, although this differs from well-accepted usage (*Y'shivah; Mosheh*).

(5)   An *h* is also used to represent the gutteral *het*, the dot usually written underneath that distinguishes it from ordinary *heh* being omitted and assumed. The other gutteral sound, *khaf*, is rendered *kh* (*Tokhahat Hayyim; Halakhah*).

(6)   *Beit* without *dagesh lene* [*kal*] is *v* instead of *b* or *bh* (*Even HaEzer; Yom Tov*), and *peh* without this *dagesh* is *f* instead of *ph* (*Tosefta*).

(7)   *Tzaddi* is *tz* instead of *z* (*Tzemah Tzedek, Yitzhak*).

Part I

INTRODUCTORY

I

The Structure of Jewish Law

The present study is based on classic texts of Jewish law, from the Talmud to the most recent of Responsa. So that the authorities and sources do not become a meaningless roster of names to the uninitiated reader, the following sketch of the structure of Jewish law is offered. It affords something of a background against which the relative authority of one text-citation over another can be appreciated and by which the framework of the subject's development may be perceived.

The Talmud

Supreme in authority, of course—the "fundamental law"—is the Torah in its narrower sense, which means the Pentateuch, the Five Books of Moses. In its broader sense, the "Torah" encompasses all of developed Jewish religious law and lore. From the legal standpoint, even the remainder of the Bible serves as an auxiliary basis; when the Rabbis speak of a "biblical law," they are referring to commandments or ordinances that derive from the Pentateuch alone. The word "derive" here is used advisedly, for ordinances not found literally in the Pentateuchal text but which the Rabbis deduced therefrom by agreed-upon rules of interpretation are also called *d'oraita* [from the Torah]. Amplification of biblical law to include safeguards—a "fence around the law"—or ordinances, observances, or even new enactments (*takkanot*) instituted by classic rabbinical authority, are called *d'rabbanan* [from the Rabbis].[1]

The conventional division is between *Torah shebikh'tav,* the Written Torah, and *Torah sheb'al peh,* the Oral Law. "By the side of Scripture there had always gone an unwritten tradition, in part interpreting and applying the written Torah, in part supplementing it," says George Foot Moore in his study of Talmudic Judaism.[2] This oral interpretation is, in turn, divisible into two essential forms: In defining what the Torah requires in the matter of practice ("the way wherein they should walk and the thing which they should do" [Exodus 18:20]), the *halakhah* (from *halokh,* to go, to walk) was devised. The detailed application of Torah law was systematically formulated, and the ordinances and observances were defined and regulated in accordance, again, with agreed-upon rules or canons of legal decision. Hence, *halakhah* is the law or a particular law. Where, on the other hand, the oral law yielded extralegal teaching such as moral maxims, legends, philosophical and historical speculation, theological observations, and the like, these became known as *aggadah* [the narrative]. *Halakhah* and *aggadah* are the two great currents in the oral tradition.[3]

The earliest widely accepted reduction to writing of the legal matter of the oral law was the work of R. Judah the Patriarch (*HaNasi,* known simply as "Rabbi," d. 219) and was called the *Mishnah* [the *disciplina,* or manual of study]. Before his time, R. Akiva (d. 132) and his pupil R. Meir had essayed earlier compositions of the *Mishnah,* but that of "Rabbi" promptly became the canonical one. The word *Mishnah* derives from a root meaning "to study"; hence its definition as a manual or the repository of relayed teaching. It is indeed the cornerstone of all later law, for the Talmud, with all its vast size, is primarily a commentary and exposition of the Mishnaic nucleus. Traditional material formally omitted from the Mishnah, moreover, is given due consideration by the Talmud. Described by the general term *baraita* [outside], this material becomes an aid to explaining the Mishnah and stands alongside it in the Talmud's discussions. The word *baraita* covers other definitive corpora of law as well, though they have individual names, such as the *Tosefta*

[1] In Maimonides' Introduction to his *Commentary on the Mishnah,* he defines biblical laws as (1) laws expressly stated in the Torah; (2) laws derived from the Torah by interpretation; and (3) certain laws not derived from the Torah but regarded as *"halakhot* to Moses from Sinai." This last phrase is understood by Asheri (in *Rosh* to *Hilkhot Mikvaot,* Ch. 1) to include laws as clearly accepted or as anciently established as if they were derived from Moses on Sinai.

[2] G. F. Moore, *Judaism* (Cambridge, 1927), I, 251. The tradition is referred to in the New Testament as *paradosis ton presbyteron,* the "tradition of the Elders." Mark 7:2–13. See also Hermann L. Strack, *Introduction to the Talmud and Midrash* (Philadelphia, 1931), Part I, Ch. 2.

[3] See, e.g., Strack, *op. cit.,* Part I, Ch. 1.

[Supplement], which is now a separately printed collection of remnants of earlier compilations of halakhah that found no place in Rabbi's official *disciplina*. Also, the *Mekhilta*, *Sifra*, and *Sifrei* are included in this general term, although they are works of *Midrash* rather than Mishnah.

Midrash is an important term for our purposes: The word means "exposition" and refers to large extra-Talmudic collections of biblical interpretation. Like the Oral Law itself and unlike the Mishnah, there are Midrash collections of both halakhah and aggadah. The three mentioned above are halakhic *Midrashim* on books of the Pentateuch and are largely contemporaneous with the Mishnah. On the other hand, the *Rabbah* collection of Midrash comprises aggadic elaboration of, and homilies upon, the Five Books of Moses as well as the Books of Ruth, Song of Songs, Ecclesiastes, and so on, which date anywhere from the sixth century to the eleventh. But these, like the *Tanhuma*, another cycle of *aggadic* Midrash, are based on material of much earlier vintage.

Since the Mishnah is the fundament of the Talmud, its six divisions, called Orders, are the divisions of the Talmud itself. The Six Orders are further divided into sixty-three tractates called *massekhtot*. The word's root is akin to that of the Latin *textus*, both meaning a weaving together, hence a text or treatise. [4] The third of the Six Orders, for example, is *Nashim*, meaning Women, and contains seven tractates, the first of which is *Y'vamot*, literally "Sisters-in-law" or Levirate Wives. Because this tractate contains the pivotal *baraita* about contraception, as well as references to the duty of procreation, it is referred to frequently in this study. Other tractates in the Order *Nashim*, such as *Kiddushin* [Betrothals] and *K'tubot* and *Gittin* [Writs of Marriage and of Divorce] also contain much material relevant to our subject, as does *Niddah* [The Menstruant] from the sixth Order *Tohorot* which deals with ritual purities. Since the Talmudic discussion of any subject within the tractates, however, follows not a logical but an organic sequence, and since all of Jewish law is interconnected, with analogies adduced from one sphere to the other, references from the whole of the Talmud are brought to bear on the subject at hand in the relevant literature. Source texts from tractate *Shabbat* of the second Order [*Moed*, "Appointed Times"], or from tractate *Sanhedrin* [The High Court] of the fourth Order [*N' zikim*, "Torts"], or from any number of other tractates, necessarily figure in our discussion as well.

Infinitely more voluminous than the Mishnah itself, the large body of

---

[4] See, e.g., George Horowitz, *The Spirit of Jewish Law* (New York, 1953), Appendix I, for contents of the Six Orders of the Mishnah; also Ben Zion Bokser, *The Wisdom of the Talmud* (New York, 1951) for much informative material.

analysis, discussion, dissection, and commentary on the Mishnah is called *G'mara*, meaning, in Aramaic, "the study."[5] In Hebrew "the study" is the "Talmud." By usage, Talmud refers to both Mishnah and *G'mara* together and hence, leaving to one side the great collections of Midrash, "the Talmud" is the comprehensive term for the large corpus of official formulations of oral law and lore. The Talmudic period, if it is said to begin with early Mishnaic times, comprises a span of at least six centuries. The ongoing argumentation, commentary, and refinement continued for at least three centuries after the redaction of the Mishnah and was brought to a close about the year 500. This scholastic activity took place primarily in the academies of Babylonia—Sura, Nehardea, and Pumbedita—where the Sages lived under Zoroastrian rule. Back in Palestine, a parallel development was taking place: the comments and interpretive teaching of the Sages there were sifted and set down in writing about a century earlier than was the case in Babylonia. The Talmud of Babylonia is much more exhaustive than the Palestinian Talmud and, for many and various reasons, predominated throughout subsequent Jewish history as the object of intensive study and as the reigning authority in Jewish law.[6] Hence, "the Talmud" means the Babylonian recension thereof, although *TB* as opposed to *TP* is used for accurate footnote reference.

Post-Talmudic Codes

The first important stratum of interpretation after the period of the Talmud is that of the Geonim. With Babylonia still the center of the Jewish world, the heads of its higher academies bore the title of *Gaon* [Excellency] and taught the Torah to students from near and far. In addition to the Responsa which they wrote as answers to queries in matters of law and faith, they were the first to compose systematic codes of halakhah by summing up in logical arrangement the conclusions of Talmudic discussion. The first of these is the *She'iltot* of R. Ahai Gaon (d. 760), a leading scholar of Pumbedita. The book contains 191 discourses, arranged according to the sections of the Torah as read in the synagogue, and seeking to explain the commandments therein in the light of the Talmud and other halakhic works.[7] The *Halakhot G'dolot* by R. Simon Kaira of the ninth century is another early example of an ambitious

[5] Strack, *op. cit.*, p. 5.

[6] See Ch. 1, "An Introduction to the Palestinian Talmud," in Louis Ginzberg, *On Jewish Law and Lore* (Philadelphia, 1962).

[7] See, e.g., Meyer Waxman, *A History of Jewish Literature* (second ed.), I, 281 ff. S.K. Mirsky, in the Introduction to his edition of *She'iltot d'Rav Ahai Gaon*, maintains that this work incorporates material of Talmudic times.

attempt to arrange topically the material of Jewish law and offer the decisions. After him, the estimable R. Hai Gaon and others produced some important partial codes in the next century and a half.

The scene shifts to North Africa where Talmudic studies flourished at the beginning of the second millenium. Chief among the commentators of this school was R. Hananel of Kairawan, who combined three convergent streams of learning: the Palestinian, the Babylonian, and the European. His annotations are of the greatest importance and appear alongside the text in printed editions of the Talmud.

For our purposes, the important product of the North African school is the work of R. Isaac of Fez, Isaac Al Fasi (1013–1073). Like the *Halakhot G'dolot* on which it was modeled, this "Alfasi" is a codex which closely follows the Talmud but which omits when it can all the discussion leading up to the legal conclusions. By including an opinion of one of the Sages, Al Fasi stamps it as the norm (halakhah); by simply ignoring another opinion he shows it to be rejected. His greatest influence lies in this, his role as decisor [*posek*] of the halakhah, for in the Talmud the debates on doubtful points often leave a matter undetermined. Al Fasi helps us to understand the meaning of the text as well: "We have, therefore, in the Alfasi, a work which is a commentary and a code at the same time. The commentary is implied; the code is manifest. And both are in the form of an abridged Talmud."[8]

Rashi and Tosafot

The commentary par excellence on the Talmud was, however, being composed by Al Fasi's younger contemporary on a different continent. Rashi, the acronym for R. Sh'lomo Yitzhaki (1040–1105) of the French province of Champagne, lived in an era of thriving Talmudic study in Europe after its decline in Babylonia. It was the century when R. Samuel HaNaggid of Granada in Spain had composed his systematic *Introduction to the Talmud* and when the pupils of the illustrious Rabbenu Gershom of Mayence—among whom Rashi's teacher is to be counted—founded many schools. From his teacher Rashi had learned the value of keeping written notes. Out of his classroom explanations to his disciples, there came the great Commentary on the Talmud. Based on earlier notes of R. Gershom's school, his Commentary is largely the result of his own keen insight, comprehensive mastery of all of

---

[8] Samuel Daiches, *The Study of the Talmud in Spain* (London, 1921), quoted by Horowitz, *op. cit.*, p. 50. See also Ch. 5, "The Codification of Jewish Law," in Ginzberg, *op. cit.* On medieval rabbinic studies generally, see S. W. Baron, "The Reign of Law" in *A Social and Religious History of the Jews*, second ed. (Philadelphia, 1958), VI, Ch. XXVII.

Talmudic literature, awareness of the pupils' difficulty, and an unrivaled felicity of style. Here, too, however, we deal not with a "dictionary," with commentation which merely explains obscure passages—although that it does magnificently—but with a legally decisive presentation of the essence and applicability of the Talmudic argument. [9]

In the several schools that rose up under the influence of Rashi's popular intellectual activity, his notebook came to serve as a text. Known as the *konteros*, after the Latin *commentarius*, it was and is formally studied along with the Talmud and has opened to great numbers what had been virtually a sealed book.

Among the most eminent teachers of the next generation utilizing this companion text, were members of Rashi's own family. The central debate on the birth control *baraita* in this study has as its principals Rashi on one side and his grandson, R. Jacob ben Meir of Rameru on the other. The latter is known as *Rabbenu Yaakov Tam*, "Our Rabbi Jacob the Unblemished," after the biblical description of Jacob as *tam*, meaning whole, simple, unblemished. To Rabbenu Tam pupils flocked in large numbers, some from countries as distant as Bohemia and Russia, and he was consulted by Rabbis from near and far. Rabbenu Tam "possessed a remarkably original, broad yet subtle intellect, and his writings display keen penetration and singular vigor of thought." [10] These words apply as well to the other masters of the new species of Talmudic literature initiated by Rabbenu Tam. Under the general heading of *Tosafot* (literally, "Supplements"), this type of commentation does much more than supplement the *konteros*, which served as its point of departure. The *Tosafot* aim at profounder depths, dissecting a Talmudic passage or Rashi's accepted commentary with the scalpel of subtle and forceful logic, against the background of an all embracing mastery of the principles and content of the Talmud. Rabbenu Tam in particular "took pleasure," a modern biographer of Rashi puts it, "in raising ingenious objections to Rashi's explanations and in proposing original solutions," as did the other Tosafists. He continues,

> Yet, it would be a mistake to see in the *Tosafot* nothing but the taste for controversy or the love of discussion . . . the Tosafists even more than Rashi sought to deduce the Halakhah . . . and to discover analogies permitting the solution of new cases. [11]

A large part of Rabbenu Tam's contribution is contained in his *Sefer HaYashar*, but his pupils quote him in the *Tosafot* on just about every other page of the

[9] See the fine biography by M. Liber, *Rashi* (Philadelphia, 1926).

[10] Liber, *op. cit.*, p. 188.

[11] *Ibid.*, pp. 191–92.

Talmud. Another prolific writer of Tosafot, a nephew of Rabbenu Tam, was R. Isaac of Dampierre, known as "Ri." In all standard editions of the Talmud since the first Bomberg (printed) edition of 1523, the text is flanked by Rashi and Tosafot facing one another and lending it their respective modes of illumination. Many Tosafot, other than those appearing in editions of the Talmud, were composed during this time and later published separately. The Tosafot of R. Isaiah da Trani of thirteenth-century Italy—known as *Tos'fot RiD*— is an important example.

Maimonides' Code

While such commentation proceeded apace, the work of proper and systematic codification awaited a successor to Al Fasi. It found one in the son of a disciple of his disciple—R. Moses ben Maimon, "Rambam" (1135–1204) of Cordova in Spain, deservedly the most famous Jew of the Middle Ages. Not the least of many achievements of Maimonides was the greatest single work of halakhah ever produced—a monumental code of Jewish law. He called it the *Mishneh Torah*, the "Second Torah," because thenceforth no other book "would be needed" in determining the law. He states his purpose in the Introduction as that of offering the student the developed law conveniently accessible, making it unnecessary to consult any intervening work. Arranged in architectural orderliness and written with brilliant lucidity, the Code comprises all of Talmudic and Geonic law in fourteen grand divisions, or books, which total one thousand chapters. (In the Hebrew numerical system, 14 is *Yad*, which gave the book its more popular name *Yad HaHazakah*, the "Strong Hand.") This marvel of structure, scope, and clarity commands the awesome respect of scholars to this day and must be reckoned with in any analysis of the halakhah. Yet it suffered from the defects of its virtues: Intending it as a single, complete, practical handbook, Maimonides chose to exclude even the minimum of Talmudic discussion and, of course, to omit the citation of authorities for his decisions. Less understandable is his omission of the views of the Franco-German scholars. Dogmatically, in clean but categoric propositions, Maimonides laid down the law. His work thus became the target of the strictures of R. Abraham ben David of Posquieres in Southern France, and subsequent editions of the Code have Ben David's demurrals printed on the margin or as a kind of inset within the text. Other scholars of that and later generations endeavor to supply the missing source references (as in the Commentary, *Maggid Mishneh*) and the Franco-German material (*Hagahot Maimuniyot*), as well as to meet the objections of Ben David (*Migdal Oz*), or elucidate the material generally (*Mishneh LaMelekh*). Several of these commentaries are likewise printed with the Code itself, so that the regal masterpiece, with *nos'ei kelav*, its "armament bearers," now reigns supreme, unique and impregnable.

Ben David himself, despite his opposition to Maimonides' method of code-making, contributes a small work to this genre—a partial code. He collected the laws of *Niddah*, the treatment of which he concluded with a compact discourse on proper marital relations; hence the importance to our subject of this work, which he called *Ba'alei HaNefesh*. An earlier work of Maimonides, his *Commentary to the Mishnah*, is also relevant.

The Thirteenth Century Scholars and Asheri's Code

Some sort of a union between the Spanish and the French-German schools is exemplified by the mid-thirteenth-century Code, called *Sefer Mitzvot Gadol* (*SMaG*). Here the material is grouped around the 613 biblical commands, divided into positive and negative ones, under which are given the Talmudic deductions therefrom and other material less closely connected. The views of the Tosafists of the Rhineland are given a hearing along with those of Maimonides, serving as a bridge of acquaintance between the two. A generation later Rabbi Isaac of Corbeil wrote his compendium called *Sefer Mitzvot Katan* [*SMaK*], which proved highly popular among laymen and scholars alike and which, too, figures in our treatment here. So does an important thirteenth-century Code called the *Mord'khai* by R. Mordecai ben Hillel of Nuremberg (d. 1298). Actually less of a code in the usual sense than a digest of opinions, decisions, and Responsa, the *Mord'khai* is held in high esteem by scholars to whom it served as a comprehensive source book.

Another code-like commentary from this period, or commentary that offers a digest of Talmudic debate, is the *Beit HaB'hirah* of R. Menahem HaMeiri (1249–1315) of Perpignan, Southern France. Written in the lucid style of his model Maimonides, this work is a running commentary to most of the tractates of the Talmud, many of which, unfortunately, were not published until the nineteenth century when the work quickly became a popular study companion. His ability to interpret, distill, and set forth the essence of the Talmud and of other authorities had instant appeal among students. His own newly coined phrases in referring to these authorities became well known: Al Fasi was the "Greatest of Decisors"; Rashi, the "Greatest of Teachers," and Maimonides the "Greatest of Systematizers." [12]

The "great reconciler" between the two schools was the foremost Talmudic scholar of his age, R. Moses ben Nahman—Nahmanides, ("Ramban,"

[12] He refers to them respectively as *g'dolei ha-pos'kim, g'dolei ha-rabbanim, g'dolei ha-m'habb'rim.*

1195–1270) who lived in Spain but who had learned his Talmud from French masters. He esteemed their method, the analytic method of subtle dialectic, and blended it with the local Spanish approach, the method of synthesis, of erudite systematization. Much more important than his partial Code, *Torat HaAdam*, on mourning customs, are Nahmanides' analytic commentaries and *novellae* on the tractates of the Talmud, where his genius yields new insights and resolutions of difficulties. Of course, his superb Commentary to the Bible itself, which is ample in both erudition and keenness, must be mentioned. Also, a small tract, important for our study, the *Iggeret HaKodesh* on the subject of sexual relations, has been ascribed to him as well.[13]

Nahmanides' most outstanding pupil was R. Solomon ben Adret ("Rashba," 1215–1310), who compiled codes of particular sections of the halakhah and who, too, is better known for his incisive *novellae* on the Talmud, to say nothing of his Responsa. Three thousand of his Responsa have been published.

As the famous Rabbi of Barcelona, Ben Adret was host one day to R. Asher ben Yehiel (1250–1327), who had fled there from the pillage and persecution visited upon the Jews of medieval Germany. Rabbenu Asher (Asheri or, better, "Rosh") was appointed Rabbi at Toledo and achieved renown as a scholar, teacher, and judge. His fame for our purposes rests upon his Abstract of the Talmud which followed the example of Al Fasi (and like it, was called "*Halakhot*"), but was enriched by the opinions of the later authorities, Maimonides and the Tosafists. His Abstract was marked by scholastic acumen and met with a ready reception in his old and new homes. Some parts of the Talmud itself were the object of a running commentary by Asheri; he has, moreover, authored separate Tosafot of his own to many tractates. All of these, together with one of his Responsa, figure prominently in our study. Rabbenu Y'ruham (d. 1340), author of a significant code not infrequently consulted, is reckoned among the pupils of Asheri.

The Tur Code

The next landmark code was that of Asheri's son, Jacob, who, next to Maimonides, is the most resourceful of all codifiers. He took the *Mishneh Torah* as his model, but his work is the independent creation of an original mind. He gives neither sources nor proof but generally cites the post-Talmudic authorities by name. Rabbinic studies had developed rapidly since the period of Maimonides two centuries earlier and, as R. Jacob says in the

---

[13] On the question of the authorship of *Iggeret HaKodesh*, see Ch. 4, Note 89.

Introduction to his work, there was then hardly a point of law on which there were no differences of opinion.

Like that of his father and Nahmanides, the work of R. Jacob combined the French-German dialectics with Spanish systematics, and answered all the requirements of a code for the next two centuries. Even then, the new codices adopted his system and arrangement, about which more must be said: His book is called *Tur*, short for *Arba'ah Turim*, the Four Rows (after Exodus 28:17, the four rows of stones on the High Priest's breastplate). The first of the Four is called *Orah Hayyim* [Way of Life] and comprises the laws of Sabbath, festivals, daily prayers, and so on. The second is *Yoreh Deah* and deals with forbidden and permitted foods, as well as vows and purity regulations. The third is *Even HaEzer*, which treats of marriage, divorce, sexual relations, and the like. The fourth is *Hoshen HaMishpat*, collating civil and criminal law, inheritance, property, etc. The name of the third of the Four Rows, that of *Even HaEzer*, alludes to the phrase *ezer k'negdo* in Genesis, where the woman is called man's "helpmeet." Later codes adopted this highly serviceable arrangement, and even the section numbers within each of the Four Rows became standard. Hence, *E.H.* appears frequently in our footnotes, with *E.H.* 1 and *E.H.* 23 signifying the same relevant section in either the *Tur* or the later codes or commentaries thereon. Responsa books, too, have designated either sections or entire volumes accordingly: Vol. *E.H.*, Vol. *O.H.*, etc. R. Jacob's *Tur* succeeded as the standard Code even in his own lifetime and, on account of its conciliatory yet definitive nature, displaced many similar works of before and after.

The two centuries that elapsed between the *Tur* and the *Shulhan Arukh* saw little that was novel in the field of complete codes. Some partial efforts, such as a work on the liturgy alone, called *Sefer Abudarham*, of R. David Abudarham of Seville (d. 1345) may be mentioned, as well as *Maharil*, the custom compilation on the authority of R. Jacob Halevi Mollin of the Rhineland (d. 1427). A highly popular work, translated into many European languages, was the *Sefer HaHinnukh* of R. Aaron Halevy of thirteenth- and fourteenth-century Barcelona. This is a catalog of the commandments according to the weekly Torah reading, accompanied by much legal definition and moral edification. While significant new codes may not have been produced, the study of Talmud was far from neglected. This was the period of the great *Rishonim*, the Early Authorities, so called because they date from before the *Shulhan Arukh*. In addition to Nahmanides, Ben Adret, and Asheri mentioned above, these include R. Nissim, Ritva, R. Aaron Halevi, R. Isaac bar Sheshet—even R. Yosef Habib, whose *Nimmukei Yosef* Commentary to Al Fasi's Abstract is an important source—and many others. A work called *Shittah M'kubetzet* of the seventeenth century preserves some of the literary fruit of these *Rishonim,* much of it not otherwise available in their volumes of *novellae.*

The Shulhan Arukh

After the expulsion of the Jews from Spain and Portugal towards the end of the fifteenth century, they found themselves scattered throughout many lands —Turkey, Holland, Asia Minor, Palestine, and so on. This upheaval undermined the power of the "custom of the country"; in some places mixed communities arose, made up of Spanish, Italian, German, and other Jews. Only one who had mastered the immense material gathered since the *Tur* and whose prestige was commensurate could meet the challenge of dislocation and reestablish legal and customary order. R. Joseph Karo, scholar and mystic of Safed, qualified; moreover, he possessed the literary capacity necessary to reduce the existing codices to one Code. He began by writing his *Beit Yosef,* ostensibly a commentary to the *Tur,* but actually an independent, self-contained work. This was the result of twenty years of painstaking examination and study of every line and phrase in the *Tur,* supplying analysis and sources. After spending twelve more years in revision, he set out the conclusions of *Beit Yosef in* brief and called them the *Shulhan Arukh* [the "Set Table"], where the student could find what he wanted prepared and accessible. His ranking pillars of authority are Al Fasi, Maimonides, and Asheri; he usually adopts an opinion held by any two of the three. Some determination independent of antecedent authority is also evident in his great Code. Along with an insufficient acquaintance with the Ashkenazi (Polish-German) practice, this feature invited opposition—which might very well have been fatal to his Code were it not that the lack was overcome by R. Moses Isserles of Poland. The latter's *Glosses,* reflecting Ashkenazic differences in accepted practice, became the *Mappah* ["the Table Cloth"] to the *Shulhan Arukh.* Still, acceptance was far from won. It took a while before Karo's Code, even thus augmented, could triumph over another code of that time, or overcome the criticism of R. Solomon Luria.

Luria found much to criticize in the *Shulhan Arukh* and brought forth his own competing Code-Commentary in its place. He maintains that his own is closer to the original Talmud and, therefore, more authoritative. Since, after all, the Talmud is the final "court of appeal" and all subsequent literature must be judged in terms of its faithfulness to the original Talmudic law,[14] his claim could not be ignored. The other competing Code was that of R. Mordecai Jaffe, who had been preparing a comprehensive code before the *Beit Yosef,*

---

[14] See I. H. Weiss, *Dor Dor V'Dor'shav,* III, 215 ff. See also *infra,* Ch. 11, p. 213, on Luria's *Introduction* to *Bava Kamma.* Cf. Note 17, below.

then the *Shulhan Arukh,* and then the *Mappah* had appeared. In each case, he welcomed news of these efforts only to find them lacking as far as he was concerned. His own Code, called *L'vush,* paraphrases rather than quotes the earlier authorities, which makes for a highly readable work. It follows the divisions of the *Tur* and *Shulhan Arukh,* except that the first of the Four Rows, *Orah Hayyim,* is divided into two. Also contemporaneous is a small code-like tract, emanating from Karo's circle of mystics in Safed, called the *Sefer Haredim,* described and drawn upon in Chapters 4 and 8.

The Later Authorities

The commentators and decisors after the *Shulhan Arukh* are known by the inclusive term *Aharonim,* the Later Authorities. Some of them helped make the *Shulhan Arukh* the accepted standard work it became. R. David ben Samuel HaLevy (author of *Turei Zahav,* the *"Taz"*) and R. Shabb'tai ben Meir HaKohen (*Siftei Kohen,* the *"Shakh"*) offered their Commentaries to Karo's Code, in the middle of the seventeenth century, questioning or defending its decisions and adding refinements and new "case law."

In keeping, however, with what was stated above, that the Talmud is really the final authority, the *Aharonim* are formally considered inferior to the earlier masters. In the Talmud itself, none of the Amoraim (Sages of the *G'mara*) may contradict the words of the *Tannaim* (Mishnaic Sages). Every exponent of the Law is—in the phrase of a medieval Commentator to the Mishnah—superior "as a matter of assumption" (*min ha-s'tam*) to those of succeeding generations.[15] Where faithful transmission of authentic tradition is involved, such retrospective deference is proper. Less proper but quite understandable is the sentiment expressed by a contemporary of the above two expositors of the Shulhan Arukh. R. Aaron Kaidanover (d. 1676) wrote to a colleague:

> You have given attention to the later authorities (*Shakh* and *Taz*). My studies are limited, thank God, to the Talmud and older authorities. Why should we nibble at the bones of later teachers when we can feast on the meat spread upon the golden tables of Talmud, Al Fasi, Maimonides, Asheri . . . on which everything depends. The later writers confuse a man's mind and memory. You would, therefore, do better to sell their books and buy an edition of the *Tur* with Joseph Karo's commentary.[16]

[15] *Tos'fot Yom Tov to Eduyot,* I, 5. Cf. *TB Shabbat* 112b: "If the Early ones were as angels, we are as humans, etc."
[16] *Resp. Nahalat Shivah* (Warsaw, 1884), No. 50. See N. H. Dembitzer, *K'lilat Yofi,* p. 62.

But the hierarchy here is one of learning, rather than of authority. According to the canons of rabbinic decision, the latter-day master—assuming his awareness of earlier rulings which he may show to be inadequate or inapplicable—is, by virtue of that cumulative knowledge, to be deferred to. The principle is then *halakhah k'batra'ei*—the law follows the latest ruling.[17]

Competent in logic and learning and cumulative in legal precedent and refinement, the writings of "Shakh" and "Taz" gained their merited acceptance and were printed alongside the text of the Shulhan Arukh. So were many others—such as *Beit Sh'muel* of R. Samuel ben Uri on the *Even HaEzer* section —far too numerous to mention; they will be identified as they enter our discussion. The result was that Karo's Code became the new citadel, after Talmud, Maimonides and Tur, around which there clustered commentaries and glosses. The incomparable Elijah, "Gaon" of Vilna in the eighteenth century, chose the medium of commentation upon the Shulhan Arukh for his magnum opus in rabbinical writing.

In 1863, R. Solomon Ganzfried compiled a laymen's handbook of some everyday laws; he called it the *Kitzur* (abridged) *Shulhan Arukh*. It remains in wide use and high usefulness, and has been translated into English—but under the extravagant title, "Code of Jewish Law." For the purposes of our subject, the availability of just this work in English is regrettable; it betrays a relatively austere and forbidding view of sexual matters.[18] Unabridged digests of one or more of the Four Rows of the Shulhan Arukh also were composed, distilling again the continuing legal development. The overarching achievement in this realm is the *Arokh HaShulhan,* a grand restatement of the entire Code and of subsequent legislation, not without independent judgments, in most felicitous language. The work of R. Yehiel M. Epstein at the turn of this century, it enjoys widespread popularity and esteem.

Works based on the Shulhan Arukh, or even volumes of Responsa, were not at all the only literary media for the *Aharonim.* Some have their say, in the present treatment, through the instrumentality of Commentaries to the Talmud, which continue to be authored up to the present time. Some, such as the colorful R. Jacob Emden (d. 1776), utilize all three of these categories and several more as well; we shall meet him often in these pages.

The Extralegal Tributaries

Our subject draws heavily on the mainstream of Codes and Code Commentaries, of course. But if the authoritativeness of works in the legal com-

---

[17] The principle is Geonic (see *Iggeret R. Sh'rira Gaon,* ed. Levin, p. 38); it is explained by, e.g., Alfasi to *Eiruvin* (end); Asheri to *Sanhedrin* (IV, 6); and by R. Joseph Kolon (d. 1480) in his *Responsa,* Nos. 84 and 94, the latter relayed by Isserles to *Hoshen Mishpat,* 25,2 (end). See also *Pri M'gadim, K'lalim* No. 8, Preface to *Yoreh Deah.*
[18] For significant variations in phraseology, with respect to sexual matters, in *Shulhan Arukh,* the *Kitzur,* and their antecedents, see below, pp. 70ff.

plex is a function of their sequence or position in a framework, or of their fidelity to basic Talmud law, such is not the case with the extralegal tributaries. Even the Bible Commentaries, so many of which contribute to the picture presented in this study, would not, by the mere fact of being attached to the Bible, be able to overrule official interpretation of scripture. The latter properly finds its elaboration in Commentaries to the Talmud and to the Codes. Philosophic works of the Middle Ages partake of the same status: they are extralegal and, as elements in the "Jewish mind," help shape the picture, but are only auxiliary to the legal process. They require no sequential sketch at this time; when introduced in this study, they are briefly characterized in the body or the footnotes.

Some are in a special category and do merit mention here. The *Sefer Hasidim*, for one, contains the literary testament of three leading spirits of Hasidism (Pietism) in medieval Germany (five centuries before the Hasidic movement of R. Israel Ba'al Shem Tov, in the eighteenth century), and, in particular, of the writings of R. Judah the Hasid. The book often resembles a mass of casual jottings, with numbered paragraphs, yet is

> ... undoubtedly one of the most important and remarkable products of Jewish literature. No other work of the period provides us with so deep an insight into the real life of the Jewish community ... in the most intimate connection with every day life.[19]

The author's "historical position," according to a modern scholar, is akin to that of Francis of Assisi.[20] The book became popular in many circles and is even quoted in legal contexts by some Responsa.

Menorat HaMaor ["The Lamp of Light"] is the name of two separate but similar books, both worthy of special mention here. The first is by R. Israel Ibn Al Nekawa of Toledo, who died in 1391. The book is a fine example of popular ethico-philosophic writing, although not very original. It is primarily a compilation of hundreds of beautiful maxims regarding the practice of virtue and of various virtues, garnered from all corners of Talmudic literature and skillfully woven together. The second is by R. Isaac Aboab of the same city, who died in 1492. It resembles the method and content of its namesake work but surpasses it in intellectual level and narrative competence. Both of these frequently reprinted classics contain a section on proper conjugal relations.

---

[19] Gershom Scholem, *Major Trends In Jewish Mysticism* (Schocken, 1941), p. 83.

[20] F. I. Baer, quoted by Scholem, *loc. cit.* The two men lived at about the same time and had similar pietistic influences upon their communities.

Another literary creation in a special category is the Zohar, which book, or group of books by that name, is the Bible of Kabbalah, of Jewish mysticism. It is the very cornerstone of the entire mystic movement, which became a substantial factor in Jewish life for six centuries after the Zohar's appearance in the thirteenth century. All later mystical works merely use its passages as a basis for further development.

Its mode of appearance was rather quaint and is still a matter of debate: The Zohar is ascribed to the Tanna (of the Mishnah) R. Simon ben Yohai with the assistance of an assembly of Sages initiated into the secrets of mysticism. It made its appearance at the end of the thirteenth century through the Kabbalist, Moses De Leon. This "Book of Splendor" was accepted by his contemporaries, though it did not lack for those who doubted its antiquity. After the Zohar's authority grew, voices of challenge to its antiquity or genuineness became louder, and, by the nineteenth century, a fair-sized literature on the subject had grown up with scholars taking various positions as to how much and which, if any, elements were of ancient origin.[21]

The mystic orientation was a dominant influence in the lives of many. The term mystic in this connection refers to a wide gamut of attitudes or motifs: from a dark, theurgic occultism to an enlightened, romantic suprarationalism, or an inwardness of religious experience. The author of the *Shulhan Arukh* was a mystic, but he intended his Code to be a bare statement of the inherited law, uninfluenced and unadorned.[22] Something of the role that mysticism did play in the development of our subject will become evident, especially in Chapters 6 and 8. This includes the contribution of the Zohar's spiritual descendants as well, such as *Sefer Haredim*, already mentioned, and the estimable *Sh'nei Luhot HaB'rit* (The "*ShLaH*") of R. Isaiah Hurwitz (d. 1628).

The Responsa Literature

Because the pivotal baraita on the birth control question was not included by the major Codes the door was opened to its extensive consideration by another body of literature. The Responsa are formal replies to legal queries addressed to the scholars of all generations. We have already referred to some, from as soon after the Talmud as the Geonic period. As Jewish life developed in the various countries of sojourn, historical, political, and economic changes raised many new legal problems. The Tosafists and *Rishonim*, too, had au-

---

21 See Scholem, *op. cit.* Chs. 5 and 6; Waxman, *op. cit.*, II, 392 ff.
22 See "The Shulhan Arukh: Enduring Code of Jewish Law," by Isadore Twersky, in *Judaism: A Quarterly Journal* (Spring, 1967), pp. 146, 149, 153.

thored Responsa and, after the dislocation caused by the Spanish expulsion, much literature of this type emanated from Turkey, Poland, and Palestine. Most of the great codifiers and commentators mentioned above are also authors of Responsa. The period of the *Aharonim* saw the issuance of a huge number of Responsa, and the process continues to this very moment.

In the main, Responsa are replies to queries submitted by Rabbis to their more learned colleagues concerning questions not specifically dealt with in the *Shulhan Arukh* or other Codes. They are characterized by personal attention to a specific case at hand. The data are given and the Respondent analyzes the legal literature bearing upon the case, cites analogies and the rulings of previous authorities, and comes up with an answer of "forbidden" or "permitted" or with advice on steps to be taken to resolve the issue or problem.[23] Highly individual, the question and the answer appertain primarily to the person involved, although they become part of "case law" and enter the legal mainstream as precedent authority. But further characterization of this unique literature, or even identification of the leading Respondents, is best not undertaken at this time.[24] These will emerge more accurately from the examples cited and excerpted throughout this study.

The bulk of the source material on which our subject's treatment is based is indeed the Responsa literature. Since the Codes left the matter untreated in its essentials, it was this genre that became the vehicle for analysis of and ruling upon the hundreds of separate cases of necessary contraception that were submitted for rabbinic decision. The different methods of contraception, different reasons for asking, different circumstances of pregnancy hazards, and different interpretation of available Responsa, all kept the question open and the number of Responsa growing. For our purposes, the vastness of the literature is an advantage: since each Responsum is actually an essay, the accompanying value judgments with respect to marital relations, procreation, human welfare, and the like, afford us a unified picture—and an inspiring one—of a vital but hitherto unappreciated facet of Jewish law, tradition, and life.

---

[23] Partial collections of references to the Responsa have been appended to the *Tur* or to the *Shulhan Arukh* in the form of Commentaries thereto. The *K'neset HaG'dolah* of 17th-century R. Hayyim Benvenisti is an example of the first; *Sha'arei T'shuvah* to *Sh. Ar. Orah Hayyim* and *Pit'hei T'shuvah* to the other three sections, the latter by 19th-century R. Zvi Hirsch Eisenstadt, are examples of the second. Far more exhaustive is *Otzar HaPoskim*, a monumental project recently undertaken by a collegium of scholars in Jerusalem. The initial volumes, on the opening *simanim* of *Even HaEzer*, have already appeared.

[24] See Solomon Freehof, *The Responsa Literature* (Philadelphia, 1955), esp. Chs. 1 and 2.

Part 2

THE POSITIVE FACTORS

2

Marriage—
Independent of Procreation

No single biblical passage, Talmudic precept, or rabbinic Responsum can convey the attitude of Judaism toward birth control. Nor can birth control itself be viewed in isolation; it is necessarily but one facet of a broader complex of related issues. Among these, the role of marriage, of procreation, and of marital sex in the Jewish scheme of things must be considered.

Marriage—to begin with the first of the relevant factors—is, in Judaism, a *mitzvah*, a religious duty. Moreover, the particular constellation of values in the Jewish concept of marriage—procreation, companionship, etc.—is a unique one and can more clearly be understood against the background of the classic Christian view. Attitudes toward marriage, considered independently of procreation or marital sex, represent an area of sharp contrast between the two traditions, and the extent of early Christianity's reaction to or divergence from the Jewish example helps define the latter.

Marriage In The Christian Tradition

It would, of course, hardly be fair to describe the attitude even of early Christianity as that recorded in Paul's reply to the Corinthians (I Cor. 7:9): "If they cannot contain, let them marry; for it is better to marry than to burn." The circumstances of this utterance, namely the anticipation of the imminent Endtime, were rather special. Paul, furthermore, was replying to specific inquiries from the recent converts at Corinth, not presenting a discourse on the subject as a whole. In other texts (such as Ephesians 5:22 ff.) something of the affirmative biblical (Old Testament) view does find expression, notably Genesis 2:18: "It is not good for man to be alone; I shall make him a help-meet"; Genesis 2:24 "Therefore shall a man leave his father and mother and cleave unto his wife and they shall become as one flesh"; as well as the biblical passages wherein the husband-wife relation becomes a sublime symbol of the mystic bond between God and Israel. Regardless, however, of the weight given to one text over the other or to differences in interpretation, one fact is objectively true of the developing Christian tradition: celibacy became the ideal, and marriage was treated as an unworthy concession to the weakness of the human will.

Several factors may have accounted for this turn of events, not the least of which was the intrusion of dualistic philosophies proclaiming the inherent evil of the body and of sexuality. Perhaps the finest treatment of the entire subject comes from the pen of Dr. Derrick S. Bailey, an Anglican scholar, who analyzes the elements making up the normative Christian position.[1] On the one hand, he writes, the Greek populace had no notion of moral purity in sexual matters, and their hedonism and sensuality would often degenerate into licentiousness. Gradually infiltrating into Roman society, the baser elements of Greek sexual life there became "the coarse, brutal, and calculated vice for which the imperial city has ever since remained notorious." Against this laxity of moral standards and depravity in sexual behavior, the philosophers of the age proclaimed an ideal of asceticism which expressed itself primarily in renunciation of sex, wedlock, and the family. Stoicism, for example, tended to reject matrimonial and domestic ties, while Neo-Pythagoreanism inclined towards a dualism which regarded coitus as a defilement and which inculcated the ideal of abstinence.

Upon the sexual thought and life of the primitive Church, each of these attitudes left its mark, writes Dr. Bailey, who then pays tribute to the contribution of Judaism:

> The Jewish respect for marriage and the family was continued in the ideal of the Christian home as, in some sense, a "religious institution" in which natural relationships were elevated and strengthened by the sharing of a common faith. . . . In the spirit of the old Israel, the new upheld the divine ordinance of the moral value of wedlock but . . . the virgin state was accorded a supremacy which

[1] Derrick Sherwin Bailey, *Sexual Relation In Christian Thought* (New York, 1959).

the Orthodox Jew would have repudiated as an impious frustration of the purposes of God.[2]

"It is the teaching on virginity which was a radical break from the Old Testament," Professor John Noonan of Notre Dame writes, "and which put marriage in a place where, as it were, it had to justify its own existence."[3]

In the period following—in the age, that is, of the Church Fathers—the notion of the superiority of celibacy over marriage persisted as the dominant motif, while the denigration of marriage increased in intensity. Jerome, for example, outdid Tertullian in his antipathy to marriage,[4] while Augustine, who formulated the "goods of matrimony," maintained nevertheless the clear spiritual priority of celibacy and virginity. Marriage is a "remedy for concupiscence," wherein the venereal desire is channeled and rendered relatively harmless.[5] The original sin of sex (see on) is somewhat redeemed by the procreative ends of marriage; then marriage, by virtue of its unique mutual pledges, can be called a sacrament.[6]

Nothing illustrates this accommodating orientation to matrimony better than the Church's view on the question of digamy—remarriage after widowhood (I Cor. 7:15). Tertullian wrote three treatises on marriage, all of which, in substance, are "vigorous dissuasives against resuming the carnal ties from which the fortunate decease of a husband or wife has given release; and with each successive treatise the argument grows . . . until in the last . . . rejection of digamy is almost asserted as the distinguishing mark of the true Church."[7] As the spirit of asceticism grew within Christianity, second marriage fell increasingly into disfavor, so that much of patristic literature on sexual topics is devoted to a vindication of celibacy against marriage and of widowhood against digamy.[8] The patristic age is summed up by Dr. Bailey as follows:

They [the Church Fathers] were compelled by the Church's tenacious and reverential belief in the beneficent Creator-God of the Old

---

[2] Ibid., p. 5.

[3] John T. Noonan, Contraception: A History of Its Treatment By The Catholic Theologians and Canonists (Cambridge, Mass., 1965), p. 37.

[4] Bailey, op. cit., pp. 19–29.

[5] Ibid., pp. 22–25; Noonan, op. cit., pp. 126–29, 134–35.

[6] Ibid., pp. 92 ff. Sacramentum was roughly the Latin equivalent of Greek mysterion, applied to a variety of religious observances, rites, truths, etc. With Augustine it is the symbol of a sacred truth. Later, the term acquired a special meaning, that of the indissolubility of marriage.

[7] Ibid., p. 21.

[8] Ibid., pp. 20, 31–32.

Testament to confirm the essential goodness of all His works, *yet cultural and temperamental factors* [italics supplied] inhibited them from treating matrimony and sexuality in the positive spirit of Jewish naturalism. [9]

The medieval period—the age of the monks and the scholastics—saw little change, progress, or deepening of the concept of marriage. Legal questions preoccupied the minds of the thinkers of this period: What constitutes the "efficient cause" of the matrimonial bond? What act seals a marriage, and by what act can it be dissolved? [10] The towering figure of the age was, of course, Thomas Aquinas, who wrote extensively on the subject. Thoroughly permeated with Augustinianism, he carried forward that inherited body of doctrine in this matter without altering its essence. In his synthesis, "marriage has the purpose of and is essential to propagating the race. But the individual—and the married couple—are still free to choose continence that they may the better contemplate God." [11] The spirit of the age, moreover, was congenial to a neglect of deeper marriage philosophy; the courtly style of life had in any case separated marriage from whatever romance or human relatedness may have been associated with it. [12]

The Protestant Reformation did effect its changes with respect to marriage attitudes. Clerical celibacy was repudiated, but the underlying antipathetic orientation remained. Luther endorsed marriage in the Augustinian mood; it is a "medicine" and a "hospital for the sick"; [13] the only effective antidote against, or cure for, the incontinence which troubles every man. Appreciative of the moral honesty and social advantages offered by matrimony, Luther yet retains the sexual negativism of the Fathers and Schoolmen: "No matter what praise is given to marriage," he protests, "I will not concede to nature that it is no sin." [14]

Calvin's conception of marriage was much more affirmative. In his commentary to the verse "It is not good for man to be alone," he allowed that the social purpose is a primary one alongside the generative. Where Luther saw woman as a child-bearing means of sexual relief, Calvin saw her as a companion

[9] *Ibid.*, p. 42; see also William G. Cole, *Sex in Christianity and Psychoanalysis* (New York, 1966), Chs. 1 and 2.

[10] *Ibid.*, pp. 103–66.

[11] Elizabeth Draper, *Birth Control In The Modern World* (London, 1965), p. 161.

[12] Noonan, *op. cit.*, pp. 255–56. See Denis DeRougemont, *Love in The Western World* (New York, 1956), Book VI.

[13] *Hochzeitpredigt* on Heb. 13:4, *Werke* (E) III, 520.

[14] *Predigt vom ehelichen Leben, Werke* (E) XVI, 541. This and above, quoted by Bailey, *op. cit.*, p. 171.

and associate of man's whole life. [15] With the spread of the Reformation, biblical (Old Testament) patriarchs and their ideal of domesticity provided the model for the home life of the devout Protestant. [16] This brought in its train a higher conception of the purposes of wedlock. Three "causes for which matrimony was ordained" are listed in the Anglican Prayer Book of 1549 as "procreation, remedy, and mutual society." [17] Jeremy Taylor, John Cosin, and Thomas Comber, Anglican divines of the seventeenth century, assure us in their respective writings that the order is not one of priority; mutual society is, after all, listed first in Genesis. [18]

The appearance in 1923 of Martin Buber's small book, *I and Thou*, is regarded by Dr. Bailey as having had a far-reaching influence on modern thinking with respect to our subject. This "Copernican turning point" in the history of human thought "offered an interpretation of human confrontation which has, among other things, profoundly illuminated our understanding of the metaphysical aspects of sexual love and marriage." [19]

Successive Lambeth Conferences in the Anglican Church seem to describe the course of change in the Protestant position. The most progressive statement emanates from the Conference of 1958, wherein the relational aspect of marriage is exalted alongside the procreational. [20] Thereafter, "the dual purpose of marriage, the view of children as a blessing rather than as a duty, and the responsibility of parenthood in the full social setting and present-day context," as proclaimed at Lambeth, "was adopted by the conferences of other Churches, in Great Britain, on the Continent, and U.S.A." [21]

The new trend in modern Catholic thought began most notably in the work of Herbert Doms, instructor in Catholic Theology at the University of Breslau. In his significant book, translated into English as *The Meaning and End of Marriage* (1941), he developed theories differing radically from those of Augustine. [22] But the response of the Holy Office to the following question is indicative:

[15] *Commentarius In Genesim* to Gen. 2:18; see also Bailey, *op. cit.*, pp. 171–74.

[16] Bailey, p. 181.

[17] *Ibid.*, p. 197.

[18] *Ibid.*, pp. 198–99. See Note 43, below.

[19] *Ibid.*, p. 247; Cole, *op. cit.*, p. 26.

[20] *Ibid.*, pp. 257–59. For a full summary of text of the document on *The Family in Contemporary Society* from the 1958 Conference, see N. St. John-Stevas, *Birth Control and Public Policy* (Santa Barbara, 1960), pp. 33–36.

[21] Draper, *op. cit.*, p. 170.

[22] Noonan, *op. cit.*, pp. 496–97.

> Can the opinion of certain modern writers be admitted who either deny that the primary end of marriage is the generation and education of children or teach that the secondary ends are not essentially subordinate to the primary end, but are equally principal and independent?

The answer was "no." [23] Indeed, in 1952, Pope Pius XII "severely censured" those "who, be they priests or laymen . . . despite the Church's warnings and in contrast with her opinion, give marriage a preference in principle over virginity." [24] The trend had, however, begun in earnest and, in our own decade, has marched inexorably forward. In 1963, Louis Janssens of the faculty of the Catholic University of Louvain, Belgium, published an extraordinary monograph which, in effect, deplored the Augustinian contribution to Western theology. [25] He is but one of many who stand within the Catholic tradition alongside of its conservative exponents and call for a reappraisal of the Christian view of marriage. [26] The recent Vatican Council in its 1964 session heard leading theologians take a new turn, describing the "mutual complementation of the couple" as a value equal to procreation. [27] The new note is sounded, however cautiously, among clerical and lay scholars, even with respect to the matter of clerical celibacy. Marriage may indeed be a sacrament, says a Lutheran ecumenical theologian, but, owing to the inherited preference for the celibate state and the dominance of the "remedy for concupiscence" idea in the Church, marriage—at least "for those called to the service of the altar"—has been "the forbidden sacrament." [28]

[23] *Ibid.*, p. 499.

[24] Address to International Congress of Religious Orders in Rome; see *The New York Times*, Sept. 21, 1952.

[25] See D. D. Bromley, *Catholics and Birth Control* (New York, 1965), pp. 5–6; Louis Dupre, *Contraception and Catholics* (Baltimore, 1964), p. 17. Janssens had expressed controversial ideas much earlier; see Noonan, *op. cit.*, 465.

[26] See the above and Joseph E. Kerns, *The Theology of Marriage: The Historical Development of Christian Attitudes Toward Sex and Sanctity in Marriage* (New York, 1964), pp. 35–37, 49, 88, etc.; Michael Novak in *What Modern Catholics Think About Birth Control*, ed. W. Birmingham (New York, 1964), pp. 109–28. See also Noonan, *op. cit.*, pp. 508–14. Father James Kavanaugh's *A Modern Priest Looks at his Outdated Church* (New York, 1967), is an example of the more extreme statements of recent times. A three-volume work entitled *Two In One Flesh* (Westminster, Md., 1948) by the British priest E. C. Messenger, as well as the more popularly written *Peace of Soul* and *Three to Get Married* (New York, 1951) by Bishop Fulton Sheen, had sought to recast Catholic teaching on sex and marriage. Cole (*op. cit.*, pp. 154–55) pronounces such efforts a valiant but necessarily unsuccessful attempt at disengaging Augustinianism from the ongoing tradition which embodies it. See on, Ch. 5.

[27] Noonan, *op. cit.*, pp. 502–504.

[28] Jarislov Pelikan of Yale University, as reported by John Cogley in *The New York Times*, Dec. 16, 1966.

This radical avenue of thought elicited an encyclical from the present pope, Paul VI, defending clerical celibacy as a "brilliant jewel" and seeking to close discussion on the matter.[29] Only time will tell the effect of the emerging new orientation to marriage and its purposes upon the slightly less radical question of birth control.

Marriage in the Jewish Tradition

That marriage is a basic *mitzvah* in Judaism is affirmed by all the Codes of Jewish law.[30] The context of the citation by the Codes is primarily one of procreation, since such is the core of the legal imperative. The human benefits of companionship and fulfillment—while not properly the object of legislation—are exalted in Jewish tradition and even incorporated into the legal language of the Codes. With procreation as the thrust, but for all the reasons taken together, marriage per se is a requirement of the law, and even its deferral must be justified. Maimonides rules:

> If one is occupied with the study of Torah and fears that his efforts at supporting a wife will prevent his studying, then he may delay marriage [and continue his studies]. For, one engaged in the performance of a mitzvah is excused from another mitzvah.[31]

Indeed, in the Talmud's sympathetic observation, ". . . can one pursue the study of Torah with a millstone around his neck?"[32] Quite aside from study of Torah (see below), the "millstone" itself is a token of other reasons for postponement. Inferences from the Talmud suggest that one's sense of mitzvah could be augmented by the power of the (Jewish) court, which might compel a recalcitrant young man to marry. But personal circumstances confined this idea to the theoretical. For one thing, "the Torah teaches the proper procedure [in the sequence of the three verses, Deut. 20:5–7]: a man should first build a house, then plant a vineyard, and, after that, marry"[33]—which, adjusted to another economic system, counsels at least the ability to support a wife.[34]

---

[29] *Sacerdotalis Caelibatus*, June, 1967.

[30] *She'iltot*, No. 165 (see on p. 57); Maimonides, *Yad, Ishut* I , 1; *Tur, Shulhan Arukh, L'vush, Arokh HaShulhan—Even HaEzer*, I. See also *Tosefta Y'vamot*, Ch. 8.

[31] *Yad, loc. cit.*, 15, 2. But, say the Commentators to *Sh. Ar. E.H.* 1, 4, this is only after the fact, whereas no one should embark upon this course to begin with (*TaZ*, Par. 6 and *Nahlat Zvi*, Par. 7).

[32] *TB Kiddushin* 29b.

[33] *TB Sotah* 44a.

[34] See *Appei Zutrei*, Comm. to *E.H.* I, 3 (Isserles), where this is given as additional reason why the court ought not to coerce a man to do his duty in this regard, although Asheri and *Nimmukei*

For another, a man may defer marriage "until he finds one suitable to him";[35] else, in marrying a woman whom he will not love, he would come to violate the commandment "Love thy neighbor"![36]—as well as many other ethical imperatives.[37] Whatever the circumstances, the mitzvah of marriage imperiously awaits its fulfillment and delay must be adequately justified.

Why? "It is not good for man to be alone; I shall make him a helpmeet" is the stated reason for the creation of Eve in the second chapter of Genesis. That same chapter concludes with a pertinent etiological observation: "Therefore doth a man leave his father and mother and cleave unto his wife and they [shall] become as one flesh." No mention of procreation here; "increase and multiply" is pronounced in another context.[38] One might even assume that the "helpmeet" idea is primary in the purposes of creation woman, or of bisexuality, and hence also primary in the institution of marriage, with reproduction secondary. But, of course, this does not yet follow. Indeed the "helpmeet" of Genesis may even be understood in terms of procreation, just as R. Moses ben Nahman (Nahmanides, thirteenth century) sees it:

> "It is not good, etc." It is unseemly that man should be alone in the world and not procreate. All creatures were made male and female in order to perpetuate the species; even plantlife has seed within it. Or perhaps [as a Talmudic Sage suggests (*Brakhot* 61a)], man was created bisexual . . . but God saw that it would be good for the

---

Yosef (*Y'vamot* VI, 16) ruled that the court could when a man passed age twenty and refused to marry. Before *Appei Zutrei* (18th-cent. Italy), R. Solomon Luria (16th-cent. Poland) wrote, in *Yam Shel Sh'lomo*, *Y'vamot* VI, 40: Especially in these countries where there are bachelors who are not occupied with the study of Torah, nor are they above suspicion, it were indeed proper to coerce them to marry. Inasmuch, however, as "times are hard and large dowries are expected of them" they have a good reason (*amatla*) not to be so directed.

[35] *TB Bava Kamma* 80a. R. Judah Menz of Padua (d. 1509) writes, in *Resp. Mahari Mintz*, No. 10: Even *p'ru ur'vu* may be set aside until he "finds a woman who wants to marry him." R. Jonah Landsofer of Prague (d. 1712) in *Resp. Me'il Tz'dakah*, No. 33: "An unmarried man is not, after all, subject to coercion in this matter, for he can always claim, 'I have not yet found a woman acceptable in my sight or suitable to me.'" R. Raphael Hazzan of Saloniki (d. 1821) in *Hik'rei Lev* to *E.H.* 1: "He can always claim he'll fulfill the mitzvah later. He may say, 'I haven't yet found one suitable to me' or 'I can't afford it yet.'" R. Joseph Rosen of Rogatchev (d. 1936) in *Resp. Tzof'nat Pa'aneah*, No. 284: "The court can never coerce him because both he and she must be desirous." Most interesting is the Gloss by R. Jacob Castro of Egypt (d. 1610) in his *Erekh Lehem* to *E.H.* 1: "He *wants* to marry but is delaying until he finds a proper match, or for other such reason," which is to be contrasted with "'I don't want to marry' as is the custom of the *kutim*." Whatever group is meant by "*kutim*" (lit. Samaritans, but usually, where European censorship prevailed, a reference to Christians), this is a singular reference in our sources to the celibate customs of others or to "confirmed bachelorhood." See on for Ben Azzai and for the woman and marriage.

[36] *TB Kiddushin* 41a.

[37] *Avot d'Rabbi Nathan*, I, Chap. 26, 42a.

[38] See next chapter, Note 2.

helpmeet to be opposite him (*k'negdo*) and he would then be able to be separate from or joined to her as he wishes . . . "It is not good" because man cannot thus survive; only of creation that endures are we told that God "saw that it was good."[39]

A significant text in this connection serves as the opening paragraph of the third section of R. Jacob ben Asher's monumental Code of the fourteenth century, the *Tur*. The section devoted to marital laws (*Even HaEzer*) begins with a kind of preamble:

Blessed be God who desires the welfare of His creatures and who, knowing that it is not good for man to be alone, made him a helpmeet. *Furthermore* creation's purpose in man is that he reproduce himself, which is impossible without a helpmeet.[40]

The word "furthermore" [*v'od*] here is the subject of a discussion among the *Tur*'s commentaries. Why state a dual purpose? A man may say—one commentary interprets[41]—that he is prepared to forgo this "good" which God has arranged for him; he'll get along without her. Hence the *Tur*'s second reason, that of propagation, which is obligatory, and which is accomplished within marriage so that the children may be properly reared. Another explains:[42] a helpmeet in the form of, say, a personal valet or a friend could have been purchased for man with money; he needs a helpmeet with whom procreation is possible; hence both reasons are necessary of the Code's mention.[43] Similarly, in R. Mordecai Jaffe's *L'vush*, a Code contemporaneous with the *Shulhan Arukh*, we are told:

. . . Man's helpmeet is one with whom procreation may be accomplished, but she is of help and assistance in all his needs, not only procreation. . . . Therefore a man must marry . . .[44]

---

[39] *Perush HaRamban al HaTorah*, ed. Chavel (Jerusalem, 1962), I, 38 (to Gen. 2:18).

[40] *Tur Even HaEzer*, Par. 1.

[41] *BaH, ad. loc.*

[42] *D'rishah, ad. loc.*; and *Appei Zutrei* to *Shulhan Arukh*, E.H. 1, 1.

[43] John Cosin, Anglican divine of the 17th century, was certainly unaware of what his contemporaries, the authors of *BaH* and *D'rishah* (Joel Sirkes and Joshua Falk, both of whom died in the first half of that century in Poland) were writing on the Continent when he wrote similarly (*Notes on The Book of Common Prayer*, quoted by Bailey, p. 198) that even in Paradise mutual society was the chief cause for which matrimony was ordained, yet "society and help may be had without marriage . . . but procreation of children cannot lawfully be had without it."

[44] *L'vush (HaButz V'HaArgaman)*, 1, 1.

But let us rather begin from the Talmud, where the Mishnah (redacted by the second century) and *G'mara* (to fifth century) are the authoritative sources of all subsequent Jewish law. There we read:

> *Mishnah*: A man may not desist from the duty of procreation unless he already has children . . . *G'mara*: If he has children he may desist from procreation, but not from [further] marriage. This is in keeping with what R. Nahman said in the name of [R.] Samuel: even if a man has many children, he is not allowed to remain unmarried, as it is written "It is not good that man be alone." Some say [R. Nahman means] if he has no children he marries a woman who is capable of childbearing; if he does have children, he may marry a woman not capable of childbearing. [45]

In such a context, "It is not good that man be alone" cannot be said to refer to the procreative purpose. But then, perhaps "companionship" is not yet its point either. Perhaps the object of the marriage recommended here, though childless, is on the order of "allaying of concupiscence," or, at least, the avoidance of illicit sexual activity. Indeed, so it would seem from the Talmud's teaching elsewhere:

> He who reaches the age of twenty and has not married spends all his days in sin. "Sin," actually? Say better, "all his days in the thought of sin." [46]

It would seem that something on this order is implied by the interpretation given, in terms of the legal system, to the duty of marriage when procreation is not involved; that is, "that he not come to sin." [47] Indeed, so it would seem from the stigma attached to the unmarried: Said R. Huna to R. Hamnuna—the Talmud relates—"Don't appear before me again until you are married." "The School of R. Ishmael taught: Until a man is twenty, God sits and waits: 'when will he marry?' When he reaches twenty and has not married—'blast his bones!'" [48] It is among the duties of a father to his

[45] *TB Y'vamot* 61b.

[46] *TB Kiddushin* 29b.

[47] Maimonides, *Yad, Ishut*, 15, 16; *Nimmukei Yosef* to *Y'vamot*, Ch. VI (p. 224a), the latter cited by, e.g., *Beit Yosef* to *Tur E.H.*, end of Par. 1, and *Arokh HaShulhan, E.H.*, 1, 7.

[48] *Kiddushin, ibid.* This last phrase is usually taken as a goodhumored curse (the translation of the verb is, in any case, uncertain). *Maharsha* (*ad. loc.*), however, interprets: Since, as Talmud (*Niddah* 31a, and see Excursus, Ch. 7) says of the three partners in the creation of the embryo—God, father, and mother—the father contributes the portion which gives being and shape to the *bones*

children to see that they marry early.[49] R. Hisda took pride in having overcome temptation to sin by marrying at a young age.[50] This temptation, aside from the suspicion to which it exposes the unmarried man[51]—or woman[52]—is considered an obstacle to holiness. The City of Jerusalem issued an ordinance in the year 1749, effective four months hence, barring all unmarried men (ages twenty to sixty) from living within the precincts of that Holy City.[53]

Over and above its other objectives, marriage is the holier state. Bachelorhood is frowned upon from this standpoint, too—and that not only for Rabbis, as a kind of opposition to clerical celibacy; the rule applies equally to all men. The best known instance of "bachelorhood" in Jewish lore is that of (R. Simon) Ben Azzai, the Talmudic Sage who excused himself from fulfilling the duty of procreation which he did not hesitate to urge upon others. When his colleagues chided him for preaching better than he practiced, he responded: "What can I do? I am in love with [the study of] Torah. The world will be perpetuated through others."[54] His example (of permanent or temporary bachelorhood[55]) finds its way into the Codes, such as that of Maimonides, who writes:[56]

> One who is in love with the Torah and studies it and cleaves unto it always, as Ben Azzai did, commits no sin thereby. That is, pro-

of the embryo, then he who does not beget children just does not help in the creation of those bones! This would lend a procreational meaning to the passage. See *Drishah* to *Tur*, *E.H.* 1, Par. 6, for other interpretations (but cf. Ms. Munich: *"tippah nafsho"*).

[49] *Ibid.*, 30b. His sons are "in his power" to marry off. What about his daughters, who must be sought out by others? The duty of the father consists in his making them attractive. See also Note 52.

[50] *Ibid.*, 29b.

[51] *Mishnah* and *G'mara*, *Kiddushin* 82a.

[52] Maimonides (*Yad*, *loc. cit.*) rules: "Likewise, a woman should not remain unmarried, that she not be 'suspected,'" without a source for this ruling being offered by any of his annotators. Then, *RIAZ* (c. 1320, grandson of first *Tos'fot RiD*, R. Isaiah of Trani), writes (as recorded by *Shiltei HaGibborim* to Alfasi, *Y'vamot*, Ch. 6, and cited by *RaMA* to *E.H.* 1, 13): "A woman is not permitted to remain unmarried, because of 'suspicion' as the *Tosefta* plainly says." But, the *Tosefta* (*Y'vamot*, Ch. 8) reads: "A man is not permitted to remain unmarried but a woman *is*"! Azulai, in *Birkhei Yosef* to *E.H.* 1, 15, calls attention to this apparent error. But now S. Lieberman, in *Tosefet Rishonim*, *ad. loc.*, points out that the Vienna Ms. of the *Tosefta* does have the reading reported in the name of *RIAZ*—and the difficulty is resolved.

[53] *Sefer HaTakkanot*, Jerusalem, No. 53; quoted in J. D. Eisenstein, *Otzar Dinim Uminhagim*, p. 382.

[54] *TB Y'vamot* 63b. See also *Tosefta Y'vamot*, Ch. 5 and *Gen. Rabbah* 34, 20, for interesting textual variants.

[55] Ben Azzai may have been married briefly. See *TB Sotah* 4b, and *Tosafot* to *Y'vamot* 63b and to *K'tubot* 63a, *s.v. bratei*.

[56] *Yad*, *Ishut*, 15,3.

viding his sexual drive does not get the better of him;[57] if it does, he is required to marry even if he already has children, in order that he not come to thoughts of sin.

Other authorities grant Ben Azzai even less value as a precedent; his lone example, they urge, is just not to be followed.[58] The Talmud itself elsewhere expounds the biblical verse (Psalms 19:10) "The fear of the Lord is pure, enduring forever": When is fear of the Lord pure and enduring? "When one marries first and studies Torah afterwards. "[59] As far as normative Jewish practice is concerned, the precedent of Ben Azzai might as well never have existed. Traditional practice is best reflected by the representative conclusion on this matter by the late R. Israel Zalmonovitz of K'far Yavneh:

> We know only what we have seen among our saintly Rabbis and teachers. They marry . . . . at an early age and then occupy themselves with the study of Torah in holiness and in purity.[60]

Holiness, then, even in the negative sense of avoidance of sin or of the "thought of sin" takes its place alongside procreation as an element in the mitzvah of marriage. One codifier sees the "avoidance of sin" in a broader sense, as due to the husband's being "bounden to his household."[61] In any case, it must be noted that the "sin" here is not sex but illicit sex; i.e., outside of the sanctioned relationship. For, even on this negative side, matrimony is not a concessive justification for sexual activity which remains inherently sinful, nor is it a "remedy for the incontinent" nor a "veil" to cover original sin. The sin is not in the sex act—as will be seen in following chapters—but, like any other blessing, in its misuse. Marriage is, in fact, fancifully regarded as the cessation of "sin": "As soon as one marries," the Talmud tells us and the Codes reinforce it, "his sins are ended—as it is written (Prov. 18:22) 'Whoso findeth a wife findeth a good, and obtaineth favor of the Lord.'"[62]

---

[57] His ruling, up to here, is relayed in *Tur* and *Shulhan Arukh, E.H.* 1, 4.

[58] Al Fasi, whose Code precedes that of Maimonides and who equals him in authority, had omitted the instance of Ben Azzai. For this and other reasons, the author of the *Arokh HaShulhan* Code (*E.H.* 1, 14) declares Ben Azzai extraordinary and not to be emulated, since "even among the Talmudic Sages there was none like him." *Hiddushei Ritva* to *Y'vamot* 63b had made a similar observation, as did R. Yosef Karo himself in *Responsa*, No. 14. See also *Birkhei Yosef* and *Appei Zutrei* to *Sh. Ar.*, *ad. loc.*

[59] *TB Yoma* 72b. See also Aboab's *Menorat HaMaor*, ed. *Mosad Harav Kook*, p. 354.

[60] *Hai Nefesh*, I, 84.

[61] *Arokh HaShulhan, E.H.* 1, 1.

[62] *TB Y'vamot* 63b, *Tur, E.H.* 1,1 and *ReMA* to *Sh.Ar. E.H.* 1,1. The dictum is based on a wordplay: *mitpakkek*, "stopped-up, closed" and *va-yaphek*. "obtaineth [favor]."

Companionship and Fulfillment

Matrimony, the foregoing suggests, is ordained by law; first, for procreation; and second, for the holier state which comes with avoidance of sin. But then this is all that the law as *law* can require. "It is not good for man to be alone" is not a commandment, only an observation, and man would, after all, be privileged to forgo this "good" if he so chose, were it not for the obligatory categories referred to above.

Once done with the obligatory categories and stepping out, so to speak, of their role as juristic interpreters of the law's requirements, the Talmudic Sages assumed their role as edifying teachers and discoursed on marriage for its own sake. In obiter dicta of fetching beauty and deep insight, they hymned the praises of matrimony as a divine good for purposes of companionship and self-fulfillment. Some of these exalting sentiments follow.

Just "what kind of a helpmeet is a wife to a man?" is the question put in one such narrative. "She . . . enlightens his eyes and puts him on his feet" is the answer.[63] R. Yosei said of himself—the Talmud records elsewhere[64]— "Never have I called my wife 'my wife,' but always 'my home.'"[65] In keeping with this identification of "wife" with "home," a series of expositions on the value of marriage is offered in another passage:[66]

> R. Tanhum ben Hanilai said: Whoever is not married abides without joy, without blessing, without good. *Without joy*—as it is written (Deut. 14:26) "And thou shalt rejoice, thou and thy household." *Without blessing*—as it is written (Ezek. 44:30) "To cause blessing to rest in thy house." *Without good*—as it is written "It is not good that man be alone."

> In the West [Palestine] they say: *Without Torah*—as it is written (Job 6:13) "Have I no help [helpmeet]; is wisdom gone from me?" *Without a [protecting] wall*—as it is written (Jeremiah 31:22) "A woman encompasseth a man."[67] *Without peace*—as it is written (Job 5:24) "And thou shalt know that thy tent [household] is peace."

---

[63] *TB Y'vamot* 63a.

[64] *TB Shabbat* 118b.

[65] Cf. *Mishnah Yoma*, I, 1, *v'khipper b'ad beito—beito zo ishto.*

[66] *TB Y'vamot* 62b.

[67] *Tola'at Ya'akov* (See Note 78 below), a Prayer Book Commentary, pictures the wife as a buffer or sentinel, keeping disturbing elements away from her husband. The custom, incidentally, of the seven (or three) circuits made around the groom by the bride at a wedding is based on the quotation, as applied in the Talmudic passage here, of Jeremiah. See also *L'vush*, I, I.

The Midrashic parallel has this and more: "*Without life*—as it is written [here a proof text is cited which is significant for the scriptural basis of the outlook on marriage (Eccles. 9:9)] 'Enjoy life with the woman you love.'" [68]

Still another Midrash does the same for the wife: "a woman," we are told, "has no peace of mind except with a husband—as it is written [Ruth 3:1, in connection with finding a new husband] 'And Naomi said: my daughter, let me seek for you peace (*manoah*) wherein it shall be good for you.'" [69] More pointedly, the Talmud declares: A woman is a *golem* [a shapeless lump] and concludes a covenant [of marriage] only with him who transforms her into a [finished, useful] vessel, as it is written (Isaiah 54:5) "For thy Maker [God] is thy husband, etc. [70] [understood here with small "m"—meaning, thy husband is thy maker]." In legal contexts, too, the maxim or principle adduced to tip the scales and validate a questioned betrothal procedure is the melodic refrain: *Tav l'metav tan du mil'metav arm'lu*—"It is always to her advantage to be part of a tandem, married, rather than alone." [71] Or, in the Palestinian Talmud's counsel: her efforts towards marriage must be assisted, for, as Ecclesiastes (4:9) says, "Two are better than one." [72]

Rules of literal or figurative biblical exegesis aside, the rabbinic expositions relayed above tell us much about the biblical impact upon their view of marriage. Lessons in this vein were taught from biblical texts by works of philosophy and commentary after the classic period of the Talmud as well. In his systematic presentation of *Doctrines and Beliefs*, R. Saadia Gaon (d. 942) sees the marital state as the proper outlet for romance and mutual love, so that human happiness be advanced "... as Scripture says (Proverbs 5:19) [speaking of faithfulness to wife] 'Lovely hind, graceful doe ... in her love be thou ravished always.'" [73] R. Isaac Arama (d. 1493) saw in the example of Jacob and Rachel the proper appreciation of a woman for other than procreative ends. [74] And, to return to the Talmud, it is noteworthy that the Deuteronomic "draft deferment" (Deut. 24:5) according to which a man is to be excused

---

[68] *Gen. Rabbah*, 17, 2.

[69] *Ruth Rabbah*, 2, 15. Cf. Al-Nakawa's *Menorat HaMaor*, ed. Enelow, IV, 68.

[70] *TB Sanhedrin* 22b.

[71] *TB Y'vamot* 118b; *Kiddushin* 7a, 41a, etc.

[72] *TP Ta'anit* 4, 6.

[73] *Emunot V'Deot*, 10, 7. *Sha'ar HaMishgal* is treated separately from *Sha'ar HaHeshek*, the former *l'hakim bah zera*, i.e., procreation, as opposed to the latter, *l'yishuv ha-olam*. The latter refers to personal happiness, as pointed out by R. Norman Lamm, in an as yet unpublished lecture, *Morality and The Family*, originally scheduled as an address to the European Chief Rabbis Conference, May, 1967. On the passage from Prov., see *TB Eiruvin* 54b, and note its usage in the Codes as referring to love of Torah.

[74] *Akedat Yitzhak* (*Sha'ar* 60) to Gen. 30:1–2. Rachel says to Jacob: "Give me children, or else I am as dead." Jacob's anger, instead of the expected sympathy, was because she saw herself as a child-bearing instrumentality only.

from military service for the first year of his marriage, that he may "rejoice [with] his wife," also figures—as will be discussed (see on)—in the rabbinic system; *simhat ishto* is a factor in Talmud, Codes, and Responsa.

The husband finds not only his happiness and blessing in the marital state but his completeness as well. For, "a man without a wife is not called a man—as it is written 'Male and female created He them, and He called *their* name Man [Adam].'"[75] Similarly, the Zohar: "The Divine Presence rests only upon a married man, because an unmarried man is but half a man. The Divine Presence does not rest upon that which is imperfect."[76]

Nor did these sentiments remain literary aphorisms buried in the pages of the Talmud. They are cited and recited in the ethical treatises designed for popular or for scholarly use,[77] as well as Prayer Book commentaries in connection with the marriage ceremony.[78]

But the most eloquent testimony of the rabbinic affirmation of marriage—and of its intrinsic joys independent of the procreational ideal—is borne by the Seven Blessings of the Marriage Ceremony itself. One of these seven is a blessing over the wine, symbol of sources of pleasure which must be sanctified and enjoyed responsibly; one is an acknowledgement of the completeness of man when male and female become one; another is an expression of hope for the restoration of Mother Zion's dispersed children; and another marvels at the procreative potential of Man in a poetic image: "Blessed art Thou . . . who hast fashioned for Man out of his very self the fabric of perpetuity." But then follow the two remaining Blessings, both of which celebrate exuberantly (and exclusively?) the joys of companionship:

> O cause these loving companions greatly to rejoice, even as of old Thou didst gladden Thy creature in the Garden of Eden. Blessed art Thou, O Lord, who causest bridegroom and bride to rejoice.

> Blessed art Thou, O Lord our God, King of the universe, who hast created joy and gladness, bridegroom and bride, mirth and exultation, pleasure and delight, love, fellowship, peace, and companionship.

---

[75] *TB Y'vamot* 63a.

[76] *Zohar Hadash* 4, 50b.

[77] *ReMA* to *Sh. Ar.*, *E.H.* 1, 1; and, e.g., Al-Nekawa's *Menorat HaMaor*, ed. Enelow, IV, 36. Ch. 10 of this work (pp. 27–114, *Perek Nissuei Ishah*) contains a remarkable anthology of maxims in praise of the good wife and in description of the virtues and traits that make for marital happiness. See also Aboab's *Menorat HaMaor*, *Ner* III, *K'lal* VI. See Talmud, e. g., *Y'vamot* 63b; where quotations from, among others, Ecclesiastes and Ecclesiasticus are adduced on the joys of a good wife and the disaster of a bad one.

[78] See, e. g., R. Meier Ibn Gabbai's *Tola'at Ya'akov* (ed. Constantina, 1560), quoted also in *ShLaH*, *Otiyot* 101b.

Soon may there be heard again in the cities of Judah and in the streets of Jerusalem, the voice of joy and gladness, the voice of the bridegroom and the voice of the bride, the jubilant voice of bridegrooms from their marital canopies and of youths from their feasts of song. Blessed art Thou, O Lord, who causest the bridegroom to rejoice with the bride.

The text of these Blessings is given—exactly in the form and wording in use to this day—in the Talmud itself.[79] (The Talmudic era came to a close in the fifth century, roughly corresponding to the time of Augustine who died in 430.)

Speaking of Blessings, why has there not been one prescribed for the groom to recite, or to be recited for him, on the analogy of *birkhot ha-mitzvot?* That is, just as one pronounces a *b'rakhah* upon the performance of a mitzvah, such as lighting the Sabbath candles, why not offer here a blessing to "God, who hast sanctified us with His mitzvot and commanded us concerning procreation"? The answer is significant for our purposes. Because, says R. David Abudarham (d. 1340), who raises the question in discussing *b'rakhot* generally in his classic Liturgical Code, not all marriages have even the possibility of procreation:

> The Seven Blessings are recited even for one who marries a woman beyond her child–bearing years or a congenitally barren or sterile woman; even for a sterile man who marries. Without the mitzvah of procreation, the "mitzvah" of such marriages is not an obligatory one. Therefore, the *b'rakhah* for [obligatory] mitzvot was not prescribed for any marriage.[80]

When the Purposes Clash

Abudarham, however, merely means to separate marriage from procreation as two distinct considerations. He did assume that procreation—when the man is not sterile—would be accomplished in any case. But what, now, if the marriage itself makes this impossible? What if a conflict occurs among the stated purposes of marriage—if the duty of procreation clashes with the privilege of marital bliss? Such a conflict is implied in the following precept:

[79] *TB K'tubot* 8a.
[80] *Sefer Avudraham, Birkhot Erusin,* p. 98a.

> If a man married a woman and remained with her for ten years and she has not yet given birth, he is not allowed to neglect further the duty of procreation.[81]

What ought he to do, strictly speaking? Either divorce her or add a second wife, says Rashi. Indeed, the biblical precedent of Abraham is adduced here, where the text (Gen. 16:3) reports that Sarah, "after ten years," gave Hagar "to Abraham her husband for a wife" in order that a child be born. But the polygamy of the Patriarchs[82] was, despite its theoretical permissibility, not necessarily an available alternative, for a variety of reasons. The example of Abraham and Jacob, and even of Solomon and David, notwithstanding, the biblical ideal is one of monogamy: "I shall make him *a* helpmeet"; "he shall cleave unto his *wife*," and so on. The *Eshet Hayil* of Proverbs 31:10–31 — that paean of praise for the Woman of Valor, recited at the Sabbath Eve table — is certainly monogamous; monogamy is in fact assumed in all of Proverbs, Job, Song of Songs, and so forth, as it is in the Prophetic similes of marriage as symbolic of God's relation to Israel. It was, we are told, the difficulty of attaining the ideal of a happy home life that practically abrogated polygamy among the Jews after the Babylonian Exile:[83] "Monogamy was the result and not the cause of an idealized conception of family relations."[84]

In the Talmudic period, no instance of plural marriage among the more than two thousand Sages is recorded;[85] monogamy had become the custom as well as the ideal.[86] Polygamy disappeared entirely in the later Roman and Byzantine possessions, although, in countries under the rule of Islam, a second wife was the available solution to the problems of some. (The Church had

---

[81] *Mishnah and G'mara, TB Y'vamot* 64a; *Tosefta Y'vamot* Ch. 8; *Shulhan Arukh, E.H.* 154: 10 ff.; *TB K'tubot* 77a, etc.

[82] Augustine saw good purpose in the polygamy of the biblical patriarchs, signifying "the multitude that should thereafter be made subject to God" (*De bono conjugalis* 18, 21), whereas Calvin found it indefensible (*Commentarius in Genesim*, to Gen. 16:1.)

[83] M. Gudemann, *Das Judethum* (1902) pp. 7 ff., quoted in *Jewish Encyclopedia s.v.* Monogamy.

[84] Israel Abrahams, *Jewish Life In The Middle Ages* (New York and Philadelphia, 1958), p. 113.

[85] G.F. Moore, *Judaism* (Cambridge, 1927), II, 122.

[86] Bailey, *op. cit.*, p. 2; and, on p. 8: "Despite the exegetical quibbles of Shammai and Hillel, the rabbinical marriage ideal was one of permanent monogamy." In the Targum (4th-century Aramaic paraphrase) of the Book of Ruth (4:6), the kinsman says: "I cannot marry her because I am already married; I have no right to take an additional wife lest it lead to strife in my home." The law with respect to inheritance in Deut. 21:15, which begins "If a man take two wives, the one beloved, the other hated ... " suggests to R. Ishmael that the Torah teaches, in a bigamous marriage, one is going to be beloved, the other hated. In the words of *Midrash Tanhuma* (ed. S. Buber), *ad. loc.*, "two women in the home, strife in the home." Prohibition of polygamy was ascribed to the Bible itself by the Zadokites, a sectarian group living in Damascus during the first century BCE. They interpreted Lev. 18:18, against marrying "a woman and her sister, to be a rival unto her (*ishah el ahotah lo tikah, litz'ror*)," as meaning "one woman and another." See Louis Finkelstein, *Jewish Self-Government in the Middle Ages* (New York, 1924), p. 23. The Karaites, a sect arising

37

similar difficulties in enforcing monogamy on its Eastern communicants.[87]) With the growth of Eastern Jewish immigration into Western lands, the tendency toward freer practice of plural marriage was met with the anti-polygamy clause of the famous and durable *Takkanah*—the Ban—of R. Gershom of Mayence (d. 1028), "the Light of the Exile."[88] While his ordinance claimed authority only for the immediate vicinity of the Rhineland communities, it was accepted with little or no opposition far beyond that range.[89] Even in the Eastern lands, where the Ban held no sway, husbands would often make pledges or insert a clause in the marriage contract precluding the addition of a second wife.[90] This may be traced to the Talmud itself, to the sentiment of R. Ami of third-century Palestine, who holds that a man taking a second wife ought to release the first and pay her divorce settlement.[91]

in the 8th century that opposed the rabbinic interpretation of Scripture, went further and accounted for biblical instances to the contrary: The word *litz'ror* ("to be a rival"), they said, is the basis for the prohibition; one woman is made a rival or, more literally, is "vexed" by the addition of a second. Where vexation or neglect is likely, polygamy is forbidden, otherwise not. See Louis M. Epstein, *Marriage Laws in the Bible and Talmud* (Cambridge, Mass., 1942), pp. 13, 22–23. The reasoning is not unknown to the rabbinic law on the subject: see *TB Sanhedrin* 21a (*darish ta'ama dik'ra*) and *Sifrei* to Deut. 17:17, and Note 90 below.

[87] *Dictionary of Christian Antiquities*, p. 205, quoted by Abrahams, *op. cit.*, p. 118. Decrees against polygamy by church councils in the 5th and 9th centuries are cited by Ze'ev Falk, *Jewish Matrimonial Law in the Middle Ages* (London, 1966), pp. 22–24.

[88] Finkelstein, *op. cit.*, pp. 23 ff., 139 ff.; S.W. Baron, *A Social and Religious History of the Jews*, second ed. (Philadelphia, 1958), VI, 135–37, 393–94; Falk, *op. cit.*, pp. 1–34.

[89] The text of *Rabbenu Gershom Me'or HaGolah's* Ban on polygamy and other matters has not been preserved in its original or even in full quotation, but is partially cited in early rabbinic works, such as: The *Responsa of Meir of Rotenburg* (13th-century Germany), ed., Prague, p. 112d; in the 14th-century Code, *Kol Bo*, No. 116; in *Resp. Maharam Padua* of 16th-century Italy; and at the end of Nahmanides' *Responsa*. It is, of course, incorporated, as a Ban if not a law, in the Codes of East and West. On the date of expiration of the Ban, see *Responsa of R. Yosef Karo*, No. 14; Finkelstein, *op. cit.*, p. 29; Baron, *loc. cit.* Falk, *op. cit.*, pp. 13–19, elaborates the thesis that Gershom did not himself proclaim the Ban. Rather: the monogamic idea had become widely accepted; the tradition of the Rhineland communities was that an assembly of Rabbis of a previous generation had proclaimed a formal ban; Gershom was the most imposing authority of that generation.

[90] Conditional clauses in the *k'tubah* against bigamy are frequently mentioned in the Responsa of Maimonides (e.g., Nos. 181, 197). Falk, *op. cit.*, p. 12, Notes 3 and 4, points out that the insertion of this kind of clause "found its way into Moslem practice where it is called 'the Kairouan clause,' signifying that it originated in this city where many Rabbis lived." Such a clause is referred to in *Tur*, *E.H.*, 118 (towards the end), and the text of one is recorded in *Responsa of Simon Duran* (d. 1444), Vol. I, No. 94. R. Tam ibn Yahya of Turkey (d. 1542), in *Oholei Tam*, No. 84 (printed in *Tumat Y'sharim* of R. Benjamin Motol) cites R. Joseph Trani to the effect that local custom or the displeasure of one's wife—even without a pledge or clause in the *k'tubah*—should make it wrong for a man to take a second wife. See also *K'neset HaG'dolah* to *E.H.* 1, 16. The practice, however, was not legally or even quasi-legally banned and persisted in the Levantine countries. Today the State of Israel allows Oriental Jews to immigrate with their plural wives but prohibits polygamy to any citizen now within its borders.

[91] *TB Y'vamot* 65a. Hilai Gaon of eighth-century Babylonia makes divorce mandatory if the wife disapproves of the bigamy: *Otzar HaGeonim* to *Y'vamot*, *ad. loc.* (ed. Lewin, p. 154).

To be invoked here, that is, is the procedure ordinarily prescribed for a husband guilty of an injustice to his wife.

In Europe, again, universal monogamy was formalized by R. Gershom's Ban. Yet this Ban—and certainly voluntary pledges in the marriage contract — may have left the door open to exceptions.[92] The situation of childlessness, for example, would clearly seem to dictate an automatic waiver; in fact, an explicit statement to that effect is attributed to R. Gershom himself.[93] Such was the nature and desirability of monogamous marriage, however, that it won out even over the imperative of procreation. After long experience as rabbinic authority in Spain, the preeminent R. Solomon ben Adret (d. 1310) was moved to write:

> Already in olden times Rabbenu Gershom of blessed memory, the Light of the Exile, pronounced the Ban against anyone who would take a second wife while married . . . There were but two or three instances in these parts where men did so and, in each case, only because the first wife bore her husband no children. Even then, the husband did so only after taking great care to assuage his wife's feelings. And with all that, I haven't yet seen even one such marriage turn out happily.[94]

The ranking authorities in Germany of the twelfth century, R. Eliezer ben Nathan[95] and R. Eliezer ben Joel Halevi, had similarly opposed a bigamous solution to the problem of childlessness. The latter strongly condemned bigamy to the neglect of one's sick wife even for the sake of propagation. His Communal Council ruled: "Better that a (new) person should not be born than that this corruption ("kilkul") be perpetrated as a precedent for generations to come."[96] The judgment was relayed and seconded by R. Solomon Luria in sixteenth-century Poland.[97] Slightly earlier, in Padua, Italy, R. Judah Menz sided squarely with those who understood the Ban to embrace situations

---

[92] For bigamy in case of *iggun* or *moredet*, see Irving Agus, *T'shuvot Ba'alei Ha Tosafot*, pp. 130–31. Even before the affair of either Henry VIII or Phillipp of Hesse, Martin Luther approved of a bigamous solution to the problem of a friend whose marital life was wholly asexual owing to the illness of his wife (Cole, *op. cit.*, pp. 116–17).

[93] *Resp. Maharam Rotenburg*, No. 865. See also *Beit Yosef* to *Tur, E.H.* 1, end; and *Nimmukei Yosef, Y'vamot* VI, end; Isserles to *E.H.* 1, 10.

[94] *Responsa Rashba*, Vol. I, No. 1205. On the difference between this and Vol. III, No. 446, see *The Responsa of Solomon benAdret* by Isidore Epstein (London, 1927), p. 120, Note 63.

[95] His *Even HaEzer*, p. 121c.

[96] See V. Aptowitzer, *Mavo L'Sefer Ravyah*, p. 201.

[97] *Resp. Maharshal*, No. 65.

of barrenness;[98] he sought vigorously to scotch the rumor that his disciple, the renowned Rabbi of Constantinople, R. Elijah Mizrahi, had ruled otherwise.[99]

The added clause in the marriage contract against bigamy must also be said to include the eventuality of childlessness. R. Simon ben Zemah Duran (d. 1444) of Algiers decided: it was probably this very fear that a woman had in mind when she asked for the prenuptial pledge.[100] But another Eastern Responsum saw bigamy as preferable, at least, to contraception when the problem was not barrenness but pregnancy difficulties. R. Jacob Modiano of eighteenth-century Turkey discusses the dilemma of a man who had made a pledge to his wife not to marry a second woman; pregnancy makes her physically and mentally ill; what ought he to do? The reply first considers contraception; then rules that even R. Gershom had not intended his Ban in such a case and the man is to be released from his oath.[101] His conclusions are roundly challenged by his countryman, R. Joseph Crispin.[102]

With bigamy discountenanced, what remedy is left for childless couples, especially when the law of the land precludes plural marriage? Divorce against the wife's will is equally problematic; the selfsame Ban of R. Gershom forbids this as well, in further protection of the woman from ancient wrongs. Is childlessness, now, a reason to waive *this* clause of the Ban? Schools of thought take sides on this as well as the previous question, with R. Eliezer ben Nathan again the first to articulate a negative reply.[103] The end of the matter is epitomized by R. Jacob Tannenbaum of Hungary in a Responsum dated 1893:

> The Sages of previous generations have dealt at length with the matter and, it seems, could not find it in their hearts (*lo m'la'am libbam*) to permit, in actual practice, divorce against her will or the taking of a second wife because of childlessness.[104]

[98] *Resp. Mahari Mintz*, No. 10, citing also *Ravyah, Sefer HaT'rumah*, and *Agudah* for his point of view. But cf. *Pit'hei T'shuvah* to E.H. 154, para. 25, in the name of *Noda Biy'hudah*.

[99] Slightly later, R. Solomon ibn Hasson of Saloniki, in *Resp. Beit Sh'lomo, E.H.*, No. 6, reports that R. Elijah Mizrahi had written to him, affirming his concurrence with R. Judah Menz.

[100] *Resp. Tashbatz*, Vol. I, No. 94.

[101] *Resp. Rosh Mashbir*, No. 69. As opposed to the case of Ravyah, the wife was fine as long as not pregnant.

[102] *Resp. Big'dei Yom Tov, E.H.* No. 10.

[103] *Even HaEzer, loc. cit.* R. Joseph Karo in *Responsa*, No. 14, represents the opposite view.

[104] *Resp. Naharei Afars'mon, E.H.*, No. 18. See also Arukh *HaShulhan, E.H.* 154, 25; and *Resp. Tzitz Eliezer*, Vol. VII, No. 48, Ch. 1, where every mitigation of the ten-year time span is to be utilized.

He adds the ethical observation that since this has now become standard procedure, a woman enters marriage on the understanding that she is not subject to unilateral divorce due to barrenness—and for a husband to act otherwise would be a breach of that understanding. Indeed, R. Hayyim Yehudah Lev of Brody had earlier relayed the suggestion that such breach would be a violation of Lev. 25:17, "Ye shall not wrong one another." This is applied in the Talmud to, among others, one's own wife, who is "sensitive to hurt."[105]

That The Marriage Be Sustained

If unilateral divorce is unethical, should divorce by mutual consent be morally required? The answer would say much about the theory of marriage —whether procreation is indeed its sole or primary purpose, and whether the law must override the human situation of marital happiness. To begin with, a beautiful story wherein "true love" prevails in the end is relayed in two Midrashic sources—from the days when plural marriage was permitted even in practice.[106] A couple had been married for more than ten years without being blessed with offspring. Since the duty of procreation had yet to be fulfilled, they agreed to part. The Rabbi sought but failed to dissuade them, so bade them celebrate their separation, like their union, with a feast. During the merriment, the husband asked his wife to take with her her most desired object from his home, as a token of his continuing love. When the husband awoke from his inebriated state, he found himself in her father's house. *He* was, she said, the most precious treasure to her anywhere. They lived together "happily ever after."[107]

In a more legalistic context, the subject is dealt with in a classic Responsum of R. Isaac ben Sheshet (d. 1408), of Spain and Algiers. He counsels acceptance of the situation in which a childless man marries a barren woman—too young, too old, or sterile—for love or for money. The childless couple who have no desire to divorce are also to be left undisturbed. There is, he says, "nothing immoral or forbidden or even offensive to holiness" in such mar-

---

[105] *Resp. Sha'arei Deah*, No. 117. The Talmudic reference is *TB Bava M'tzia* 59a.

[106] *Shir Hashirim Rabbah* I, 4 and *Psikta d'Rav Kahana* XXII.

[107] Philo, of first-century Alexandria, writes similarly; he "forgives" the husband who continues, because of "familiarity," to live with a wife found to be sterile or barren: *De Specialibus Legibus*, Book III: 34, 36. Cf., also, *TB P'sahim* 113b.

riages, although procreation is not possible. [108] His ruling is incorporated in the Glosses of Isserles to the *Tur* and *Shulhan Arukh* Codes. [109] Again, R. Israel Lifschutz (Germany, c. 1770), in a Responsa work on the subject of divorce law, specifies that the court not interfere in a childless marriage to remind the husband of his duty *if* the couple is happy and peaceful. [110] To one whose conscience troubled him, R. Jonah Landsofer of Prague (d. 1712) went so far as to suggest that the man temporarily divorce his wife, marry another conditionally for as long as necessary to have children, then return to his first wife. For, the Talmud tells us, man's real happiness is "with the wife of his youth, as Scripture says (Prov. 5:18) '. . . and rejoice with the wife of thy youth'." Though she be barren, to return to her in love, he says, may even be called a mitzvah. [111] Another Responsum from about the same time advises a man who has a "fine, God-fearing" but barren wife that he may certainly remain with her; he may compensate, if need be, for not fulfilling the duty of procreation by engaging in more Torah study and by raising an orphan (which he had been doing) in his home. [112] And, a recent decision touching upon an aspect of infertility notes incidentally that the childless pair "live in peace and love, so that divorce is out of the question." [113]

A far greater number of Responsa of this kind deal more immediately with our subject, with the permissibility of contraception—as opposed to the imperative of divorce—when pregnancy would be harmful to the wife and yet both bigamy and procreation are ruled out. R. Moses Sofer had, to illustrate, considered proposing bigamy when conception would have been hazardous. Since R. Gershom's decree has been accepted, he says, only divorce and contraception are available alternatives. [114] Attitudes toward the former governed the treatment of the latter, with the result that even doubtfully acceptable birth control devices are justified in terms of the value of continuing the marriage and marital relations. The reasons for ruling contraception as preferable to abstinence—and even the point that marital sex is essential to the relationship—belong to a later chapter; for now, it is important to note

[108] *T'shuvot Rivash*, No. 15. See also *Avudraham*, Note 80, above. *Rivash's* phrase, here in quotes, is apparently based on the technical terms (*issur mitzvah, issur k'dushah*, etc.) of TB *Y'vamot* 20a.

[109] *RaMA* in *Darkhei Mosheh* to *Tur, E.H.* 1, 1, and to *Sh., Ar., Even HaEzer* 1, 3 : See *Biur HaGRA* thereto.

[110] *Or Yisrael*, No. 37, par. *s.v. v'hinneh.* (The author is not to be confused with his grandson of the same name, of *Tiferet Yisrael* fame.)

[111] *Resp. Me'il Tz'dakah*, No. 33. The Talmudic reference is TB *Y'vamot* 63b.

[112] *Resp. Big'dei K'hunah* (Fiorda, 1807), *E.H.*, No. 1, which see for a legal disquisition on the entire matter.

[113] *Resp. Netzer Matta'ai*, No. 18.

[114] *Resp. Hatam Sofer, E.H.*, No. 20.

the unanimous tendency on the part of Responsa writers to preserve the existing marital relationship despite the necessity for perennial contraception.

Actually, two or three formidable factors found in the Talmud itself are arrayed in Responsa literature for the purpose of justifying or legitimatizing continued marriage when the alternative of bigamy is unavailable and—despite the presumed primacy of procreation as the object of marriage—when barrenness has blighted the union or, worse, contraception is made necessary by medical considerations.

The first of these is the lovely concept of *sh'lom bayit* [the ideal of domestic peace]. This ideal is to be exalted above all others, including truth: "Great is [the cause of] peace," says the Talmud in the name of the School of R. Ishmael,[115] "for even God deviated" from strict truth in the interests of peace. Sarah had said (Gen. 18:12): "Can I, then, give birth, seeing that my husband is old?"—whereas God, in reporting this to Abraham, asked: "Why did Sarah laugh, saying 'How can I give birth, seeing that *I* am old?'" To preserve domestic peace between Abraham and Sarah, God had "modified" her statement so as not to offend Abraham. In the interests of marital peace, moreover, even the reverence due the Divine Name is to be momentarily set aside; thus, the biblical "Ordeal of Jealousy" (Numbers 5:11 ff.), by which the husband's suspicions against his wife are put to test, requires that verses containing these suspicions, together with the references to God included among them, be, in an awesome ritual, erased into the "bitter waters." From this biblical ordinance, and its exposition in no fewer than five instances in the Talmud,[116] our Responsa writers derive the lesson: since the Divine Name was permitted to be erased when the purpose of restoring confidence and peace between husband and wife was at issue, how much more so may such and such be done to preserve or restore that peace.

The second of such factors adduced by the Responsa is the pity of divorce. The biblical story to which this concept is attached is the famous one of King David's declining years when, as told in I Kings, Chapter 1, the young damsel Avishag the Shunnamite was brought to him to recall or retrieve his earlier warmth. She "became a companion to the king and ministered unto him." Why, however, did he not marry her? Because he had already reached the limit in the number of wives permitted to him; to divorce one of them would equally be an undesirable course of action. "R. Shaman bar Abba: Come and see how hard [on people] is divorce, for King David was permitted *yihud* (to be alone) [with Avishag without marrying her] but was not permitted

[115] *TB Y'vamot* 65b, and in *Perek Ha Shalom*, addendum to *Mas. Derekh Eretz Zuta*.

[116] *TB N'darim* 66b. See also *Hulin* 141a. In *Shabbat* 116a and *Sukkah* 53b, the peace spoken of is between God and Israel; in *Makkot* 11a, peace among all men.

to divorce [his wife in order to do so]."[117] There follows another series of touching maxims on the human tragedy of divorce and how it betokens the cessation of light and good and happiness.

An *agunah* is a woman who cannot remarry until the death of her missing husband is clearly established or her disputed divorce document is declared legal. The same word is applied to the wife who might be legally divorced for reasons of infertility or problems of pregnancy and then might find it difficult to remarry; figuratively, a married woman who would be forcibly separated from her husband is an *agunah*. The prevention of such a condition of *iggun*, or "anchorage" to nowhere, for the woman, is a third factor evoked in the Responsa to justify even questionable contraception rather than divorce or abstinence. The Talmud had set the precedent for seeking leniencies to prevent *iggun* where possible.[118]

Sometimes, in drawing his brief, the Rabbi will appeal to all the above factors: "Great is peace . . . ; for even the Divine Name was to be erased . . .; and cruel is divorce, and it would be shameful to separate the attached . . . ; and our Sages taught us to seek remedies for the prevention of *iggun*. . . ."[119] These considerations, offered as humane sentiment, have true legal force in that they contribute, alongside the heavier arguments, to the eventual ruling of the Responsum. The words of R. Aryeh Zunz of Plotzk, Poland, in the mid–nineteenth century, serve as one example:

> True, although this man has not fulfilled the duty of procreation and, strictly speaking, should divorce his wife so that he might do so—except that we are accustomed to overlook this, as Isserles has written—still separation is unacceptable . . . It seems to me that even though he has not fulfilled this duty, he need not divorce her because "great is peace", no, he need not separate from her, for the Sages would not have approved of such action nor would it be pleasing to his Maker to Whom peace is great.[120]

[117] *TB Sanhedrin* 22a.

[118] *TB Y'vamot* 88a; *Gittin* 3a.

[119] Phrases such as these are invoked by, among many other Responsa works: *Hemdat Sh'lomo* (Warsaw, c. 1836), No. 46; *Torat Hesed* (Lublin, 1890), No. 42:35; *Maharsham* (Warsaw, 1902) Intro. to Vol. III; *T shurat Shai* (Szeged, 1905), Second Series, No. 62; *Be'er Sh'muel* (Unsdorf, c. 1910), No. 66; *Hedvat Ya'akov* (Pietrekov, 1919) No. 37; *Havatzelet HaSharon* (Bilgoray, 1931), Vol. II, addendum to *E.H.* section; *Tzur Ya'ak'ov* (Provozna, 1932), No. 141, 35c. Also those mentioned below.

[120] *Resp. M'shivat Nefesh* (Warsaw, 1849 ed.—as distinct from a later edition by the same name, same author), No. 18.

No discussion of our subject is to be found among the many legal decisions of R. Isaac Elhanan (Spector), Chief Rabbi of Kovno in the nineteenth century. A lengthy Responsum by another rabbinic authority, [121] however—in which the latter proved, by close reasoning and mastery of related and unrelated source material, that a specific contraceptive is allowable in the case before him—was sent to R. Isaac Elhanan for comment. He wrote back (1895) [122] that, due to his failing eyes and health, he was not able to study the document but, because (a) there was precedent for such permission, and (b) at stake was the prevention of iggun, he accords his positive endorsement without reading the arguments. And the preface by R. Mosheh Feinstein of New York to his own comprehensive Responsum on our subject begins with:

> Who am I to enter the discussion [when great men have already ruled on it], but since iggun is at stake and the Sages require us to make a great effort to help [her], and preserving peace between husband and wife is so important that the Torah allows the Divine Name to be erased, I will therefore not be deterred by respect for these great men. [123]

So stating, he skillfully guides one through a labyrinthine maze of legal problems affecting contraception, only to demonstrate anew that these are ultimately subordinate to an overriding objective—that of preserving the existing marital relationship for its own sake. [124]

---

[121] R. Barukh Avraham Mirsky, recorded in his *Sefer Sh'mat'ta d'RaVA* (Jerusalem, 1949), Vol. II, *Y.D.*, No. 1.

[122] *Ibid.*, at end of Responsum.

[123] *Resp. Igg'rot Mosheh, Even HaEzer* (New York, 1961), No. 63.

[124] In another, brief Responsum (*ibid.*, No. 67) he deals with the question of one who contemplates marriage to a woman who, because of her physical condition, will have to practice contraception for a while. Can he, *to begin with*, enter upon such a marriage, especially since he, aged 40, has not yet fulfilled the duty of procreation? The Rabbi replies: strictly speaking, he ought to wait before marrying her until she is in a condition to conceive, or marry someone else. However, being that they are so attached to one another and, since she is in any case not well and may become sicker from the broken engagement or from fear that others, too, may not want to marry her, permission is possible in this special case. The Rabbi is here transferring from marriage to engagement the humane considerations set forth above. In doing so, he goes further than *Resp. L'vushei Mordkhai*, Vol. IV, No. 68, and *Maharsham*, Vol. I, No. 58, who had ruled otherwise in analogous situations, and now, too, *Resp. Tzitz Eliezer*, Vol. IX, No. 51, p. 214, who forbids it except with "the Pill."

3

The Mitzvah of Procreation

The duty of procreation has the popular distinction of being called the "first mitzvah" of the Torah.[1] Its primacy in the Jewish outlook does not derive, of course, from the pride of place enjoyed by *p'ru ur'vu* [be fruitful and multiply] at the outset of Scripture. Despite a common assumption to the contrary, the mitzvah is not based on the charge to Adam and Eve (Gen. 1:28), but according to most commentators, on that to the Sons of Noah after the Flood (Gen. 9:1 and 7) or to Jacob (Gen. 35:11). The earlier p'ru ur'vu is for "blessing only," analogous to the p'ru ur'vu said in connection with the fish and fowl (Gen. 1:22); the later one is for "commandment."[2] Says one modern commentator in explanation of the two separate utterances: both animals and man were "blessed" with fertility and with sexual instincts. But only man, uniquely aware of the consequences of his sexual indulgence,

[1] Even though proclaimed before the Sinai Revelation (and reaffirmed then in Deut. 5:27: *shuvu lakhem l'oholeikhem*) it is regarded as a commandment to Israel, according to the exegetical principle in *TB Sanhedrin* 59a, b; and as "permission" to other nations (see on). The first mitzvah addressed to Israel per se is in Exodus 12. See on, Note 71.

[2] *Rashi* (to *K'tubot* 5a and to Gen. 9:7) and *Tosafot* to *Y'vamot* 65b, *s.v. v'lo*. See also *Nahmanides* to Gen. 9:7 and, especially, *Maharsha* to *Sanhedrin* 59b, *s.v. vaharei*. This discussion is particularly pertinent in view of the observation made by a participant in the recent Vatican Council who, arguing for a liberalized policy on birth control, declared that "the world has changed somewhat in its population problems since Adam and Eve, alone in the Garden, were told to multiply." Cf. *Arokh HaShulhan*, E.H. 1, 2; and *P'shuto Shel Mikra*, I, 70.

might seek to avoid the attendant responsibilities of childbirth despite his sexual drive. Hence, the "commandment" of p'ru ur'vu was added in his case.[3]

Indeed, early compilations or catalogs of the commandments—such as that of Maimonides or of R. Moses of Coucy—which are arranged according to one structure or another, do not list procreation as the first.[4] But the widely used *Sefer HaHinnukh*, a fourteenth-century catalog and explication of commandments according to their biblical sequence, does rank procreation as first both in order and in importance. The author writes:

> The purpose of this commandment is that the world be populated; it is a great mitzvah for, through it, all other commandments— which were given to men and not to angels—may be fulfilled.[5]

The first-rank importance of the duty of procreation is set forth by the Talmud itself: "He who does not engage in procreation is as if he committed murder"; alternatively, "is as if he diminished the Divine image." Both of these expositions[6] are supported by the propinquity of p'ru ur'vu to the preceding verse (Gen. 9:6): "Whoso sheds the blood of man, by man shall his blood be shed, for in the image of God has He created man." Another scriptural verse (Gen. 17:7) is interpreted with telling force: "To be your God and [that] of your descendants after thee": If there are no "descendants after thee" upon whom will the Divine Presence rest? Upon sticks and stones?[7] And, "when a man is brought to judgment, he is asked: 'Did you deal honestly [in commerce]? Did you devote time regularly to the study of Torah? Did you undertake to fulfill the duty of procreation? Etc.'"[8]

---

[3] R. Meir Me'iri in *Torah Me'irah* (London, 1948) to Gen. 1 : 28 (I, 62). Another interesting comment comes from R. Isaac Abarbanel (d. 1508) in his Commentary, *ad. loc.* Man, created in the image of God, might seek to devote himself entirely to the intellectual and neglect the material or physical world. The Commandment instructs him that the preservation of the physical world is his duty, too.

[4] *Sefer HaMitzvot l'Rambam* (Positive Commandment, No. 212); *Sefer Mitzvot Gadol* (Positive No. 49); *Sefer Mitzvot Katan* (No. 284).

[5] *Sefer HaHinnukh*, No.1. This work is attributed more correctly to R. Aaron Halevy of Barcelona than to R. Aaron Halevy (*RaH*), colleague of *Rashba*. See Chaim Tchernowitz, *Tol'dot HaPoskim*, II, 96.

[6] TB *Y'vamot* 63b; *Gen. Rabbah* 34, 20.

[7] TB, *ibid.*, 64a.

[8] TB *Shabbat* 31a. No priorities can be determined from the sequence here. The passage is an exposition of the verse in Isaiah 33 : 6—*V'hayah emunat ittekha hosen*—where the third category is *hosen*, i.e., posterity.

Rabbinic Definition

The mitzvah of procreation is, in fact, three separate *mitzvot*—one biblical (Pentateuchal) and two rabbinic. The biblical command is defined, as to its minimal fulfillment, in the Mishnah:[9]

> The School of Shammai say [he has fulfilled his duty with] two sons. The School of Hillel say, a son and a daughter, as it is written (Gen. 1:27) "male and female created He them."[10]

Since the halakhah follows Hillel, the statutory obligation is discharged with the birth of one son and one daughter;[11] i.e., when the couple "replaces" itself.

In the Talmud itself, however, this definition becomes merely academic, for two additional categories of the mitzvah have yet to be fulfilled. One is known as *la-shevet*, from the exposition of the verse in Isaiah 45:18: "Not for void did He create the world, but for habitation (*la-shevet*) did He form it."[12] Man's duty is thus to go on contributing to the world's habitation. The second "rabbinic mitzvah" is known as *la-erev*, deriving from Ecclesiastes 11:6: "In the morning, sow thy seed, and in the evening (*la-erev*) do not withhold thy hand [from continuing to sow], for you know not which will succeed, this or that, or whether they shall both alike be good." "R. Joshua taught: if a man has married in his youth, let him also marry in his old age. If a man has had children in his youth, let him also have children in his old age, as it is written 'In the morning . . .'"[13] Infant mortality and the nature of progeny are unpredictable; it is best therefore to continue indefinitely. Both these rabbinic expositions have the force of law and are treated in the Responsa alongside

[9] *Y'vamot* VI, 6 (61b).

[10] *Tosefta* (*Y'vamot*, Ch. 8): R. Nathan relayed: The School of Shammai say—two sons and two daughters; The School of Hillel say—a son and a daughter. Alternatively: Shammai—a son and a daughter; Hillel—a son or a daughter.

[11] *TP* (*Y'vamot* VI, 6) reads: The School of Hillel say two sons, but even a son and a daughter. (Also *Tos'fot Had Mikamai* to *Y'vamot* 61b: two sons). But *Ritva* to *Y'vamot* VI, says two sons does not constitute fulfillment of the duty. *Resp. Avnei Nezer*, E.H., No. 1, cites the case of R. Joseph Trani, who had sons only and relied on Palestinian Talmud's version of Hillel. He also makes reference to Zohar (III, 148) where Moses (see *Y'vamot* 61b) is acknowledged to have fulfilled the duty though he had only two sons.

[12] *Mishnah, Eduyot* I, 13; *TB Y'vamot* 62a. This could be understood as minimizing: i.e., that even one child does contribute to *la-shevet* and hence is sufficient (See *Rava, ibid.*) or as maximizing; i.e., that if two children are born but do not survive, then *la-shevet* is still not fulfilled. It is, of course, taken in the latter sense in the *halakhah*.

[13] *Ibid.*, 62b.

the primary biblical one, removing, in effect, its Mishnaic delimitations.

It is, of course, tempting to discern in this post-Mishnaic extension a sociologic response—as is indeed conjectured by some writers[14]—to changed economic or social conditions, where increased fecundity became desirable. In one sense, however, these rabbinic mitzvot are not arbitrary extensions of the Mishnah's specifications at all; they are merely a guarantee of enforcement thereof. An esoteric concept is entertained in the Talmud, according to which procreation has the mystic value of providing bodies for the souls waiting to be born: "The Son of David [the Messiah] will not come until the souls in Guf [the region where they wait to be incarnated] have all been disposed of."[15] Unless this "unearthly" reason is to be assigned for the mitzvah of procreation,[16] the giving of birth by itself is not enough; one must give birth to viable children who, moreover, will themselves be able to beget offspring. P'ru ur'vu is for the purpose of and judged by la-shevet; without it the mitzvah is just not fulfilled. "If a man had children and they died . . . R. Yohanan said: He has not fulfilled the duty of propagation because la-shevet is required, which did not happen."[17] Furthermore, if his son is sterile[18] or his daughter barren,[19] he has not fulfilled his duty; whereas, on the other hand, "grandchildren are like children," so that if a man had only one son but his son had a daughter, his own duty is thus discharged.[20] Accordingly, since one may not know whether or not he has met the minimal requirements until his offspring are grown, his only guarantee is the fathering of more than that minimum.

---

[14] E.g., N. E. Himes, *Medical History of Contraception*, p. 69.

[15] *Ibid.* 62a; *Niddah* 13b. Noonan, *op. cit.*, p. 50, sees a "basic kinship" in this idea "with the medieval Christian theme of fecundity increasing the population of heaven." He locates the doctrine (p. 275) in the writings of Duns Scotus, according to whom procreation restores the "city of supernatural citizens," and in the words of St. Bernardine, who speaks of procreation "to fill paradise." The ideas may have some kinship but are not similar. Kinship should rather be sought in the following Talmudic story (*TB Sotah* 12a): Amram, the father of Moses, had originally decided not to have more children, since Pharaoh had decreed that all male children be cast into the Nile. Whereupon Miriam is said to have reproached him: you are more severe than Pharaoh, in that you will be preventing the birth of both male and female and depriving a male child of life in "this world and the next."

[16] *Ibid.*, 62a; *Niddah* 13b. An example of interpretive efforts at giving a rationalist cast to this concept is that of *Sefer HaMafteah* (1866) by M. A. Schatzkes (p. 117b): *Ha-n'shamot shebaguf* refers to *ha shof'tim mi-yisrael*—which is no help. The doctrine does find an echo in its literal sense in some Responsa (e.g., *Igg'rot Mosheh*, E.H., No. 62 in the case of births that will not survive infancy) and cf. *Arukh L'Ner* to *Y'vamot* 12b.

[17] *Y'vamot* 62a.

[18] *Ibid.*, 62b.

[19] *TP Y'vamot* VI, 9, and the Codes. *L'vush*, in codifying, explains that la-shevet has not been accomplished if sterile children are begotten.

[20] *Ibid.*, 62b and Codes.

In another sense, the rabbinic mitzvah of, at least, la-erev does represent an extension of the Mishnah. The dictum of R. Joshua (above) is, by the Talmud's admission, "not the same as" the Mishnah,[21] which is apparently satisfied with the minimum. Nonetheless, "the halakhah is in accordance with R. Joshua," [22] and the principle of ongoing procreational duty is thus established in Jewish law. Maimonides codifies:

> Although a man has fulfilled the mitzvah of p'ru ur'vu, he is commanded by the Rabbis [of the Talmud] not to desist from procreation while he yet has strength.[23]

An extreme opinion—recorded by *Tosafot* in another connection—has it that holding the line at the bare minimum of one son and one daughter could well lead to national dissolution.[24]

No real distinction is henceforth made in Codes and Responsa between the duty to fulfill the biblical or the rabbinic aspect of this mitzvah. Originally—to illustrate—marriage for one who had not yet fathered the minimum was to be undertaken even at the expense of the sale of a Torah Scroll—an expedient permitted only in order to finance either the study of Torah or marriage for minimal procreation.[25] That this be extended to include more than the minimum—that a Sefer Torah be sold to finance marriage for la-shevet and la-erev as well—is now sanctioned by the Codes.[26] As to the permissibility of contraception when necessary, the Responsa admit only a nominal distinction between the unfulfilled biblical or rabbinic mitzvah. The notion that "birth control" may be practiced on general principles now that two children are born was, accordingly, not at all to be assumed.[27] R. David Hoffman of Berlin (d. 1921), in the context of a case of pregnancy hazard, makes incidental reference to the practice—which he deplores—"among French [Jewish] women" who follow the *"zwei-kinder System."* [28] In 1955, R. Mordecai Breisch of Zurich, in a Responsum to a colleague in Montevideo,

---

[21] *Ibid.*
[22] *Ibid.*
[23] *Ishut,* 15, 16.
[24] *Tosafot* to *Bava Batra* 60b, *s.v. din hu.*
[25] *TB Megillah* 27a; *Sh. Ar., E.H.,* 1, 2.
[26] *Tur* (*E.H.,* 2) in the name of *Rosh; Sh. Ar., E.H.,* 1, 8; See *Beit Shmuel* to *E.H.* 1, Par. 2. This sanction may not be in keeping with *Sh'iltot* (Sec. *B'rakhah*) where only for *p'ru ur'vu* may a Torah Scroll be sold. The broadened sanction is, significantly, explained by *Biur HaGRA* (*E.H.* 1, Par. 19): "we follow R. Joshua rather than the *Mishnah.*"
[27] See on, Ch. 16.
[28] *Resp. M'lammed L'Ho'il,* Vol. III, No. 18 (*"Ba-avonoteinu ha-rabbim"*).

likewise refers to this "accursed fashion of France and elsewhere." [29] And the Catholic medical writer, H. Sutherland, reproduced in his book the following communication to him from R. Joseph H. Hertz of Britain: The moral obligation, if not the commandment, still rests upon the husband of propagating the race when he already has two children." [30] The Responsa, of course, speak of this moral obligation as a commandment, hardly less binding than that of the Mishnaic minimum.

Extralegal Considerations

It goes without saying that attitudes towards procreation were not shaped by law alone. Basic to the Jewish view of life is the imperative to have families of goodly size, let alone to be spared the blight of childlessness. Abraham protests to God (Gen. 15:2): "What canst Thou give me, seeing that I go childless?" and the anguish of the barren woman is a recurrent theme in the Bible. On the other hand, the most cherished blessing is fecundity, exemplified idyllically in the Psalmist's (Ps. 128) image of man whose "wife is as a fruitful vine" and whose "children are as olive plants around the table" and whose ultimate satisfaction is the sight of "children [born] to thy children." [31]

Nor can it be gainsaid that the historical circumstance of frequent massacres and forced conversions, with their decimation of Jewish communities, served to elicit compensatory tendencies. The people's will to replenish its depleted ranks gave an added dimension to its instinctive yearning for offspring. This point becomes especially significant when viewed against the antiprocreational stand, born of despair, taken by the first-century Gnostics, the fifth-century Manichees, or the twelfth-century Cathars, who taught (and lived accordingly) that procreation is to be avoided in an evil world. [32] Adoption of this attitude was unthinkable to the Jew. Unthinkable, that is, for more than a moment: The Talmud records that, when the Hadrianic (Roman) persecutions had imposed oppressive restrictions, whereby children could not be initiated into the Covenant of Abraham nor ever taught Torah, "it would have been in order to decree a ban on marriage" and not bring forth children to such a fate. [33] (The accompanying *Tosafot* naturally assumes this would-be

[29] *Resp. Helkat Yaakov*, Vol. II, No. 11.

[30] *Control of Life*, (1944), p. 188, quoted by I. Jakobovitz in *Journal of a Rabbi* (New York, 1966), p. 215.

[31] The blessedness of fecundity is expressed by the vision (*TB Sh'vuot* 30b) that in the days of the Messiah women will give birth every day.

[32] See Noonan, *op. cit., passim.*

[33] *TB Bava Batra* 60b.

ban to include only those who have already fulfilled their minimal duty of procreation! [34]) The thought itself was not meant to be taken seriously, R. Joseph Karo explains, but only as a sigh of lament.[35] It *could* not be taken seriously, a later codifier explains,[36] because of another, more representative teaching elsewhere in the Talmud: King Hezekiah, who prophetically saw that his offspring would be wicked, wanted to forbear from marriage and procreation. Isaiah reproved him, saying: "The secrets of God are none of your business. You have to perform your obligation, to do what is pleasing to God." [37]

Procreation, therefore, in the face of a precarious future, was essentially an act of faith. Despite a probable inclination to be equally trusting when medical considerations made pregnancy dangerous, another mitzvah, that of giving first consideration to avoiding such hazards, afforded a counterbalance, as we shall see. This may account, in part, for the fact that medical considerations—almost exclusively—are those reflected in the Responsa on contraceptive questions. Despite the most harrowing of economic and social hardships, motives for "family planning" based on individual comfort (of parents or of existing children), financial exigencies, and the like, were hardly ever entertained, at least by the non-permissive school described herein.[38] The fact, however, that contraceptive methods of questionable propriety were the only recourse generally available was a decisive factor even there, along with the awareness that minimal procreation was just not enough, in limiting both the questions and the answers to issues of *sakkanah* [physical danger]. We shall have much more to say on the subject in the following chapters.

The Responsa, moreover, addressing themselves to an individual's personal problem, would have no occasion to deal with the matter of "population explosion," nor was the Jewish community ever in a position to aggravate a problem such as this. Quite the contrary: the Jewish community is being reminded, in current writings,[39] that its problem is the reverse—to seek to replace its annihilated members. As to the Jewish ethical attitude to world affairs (see on, "Non-Jews and the Commandment"), recent "position papers" [40] interpret the Jewish concept of la-shevet as implying reasonable

---

[34] *Ibid., s.v. din. hu.*

[35] *Responsa,* No. 14 (*s.v. gam*).

[36] *Arokh HaShulhan, E.H.* 1, 1.

[37] *TB B'rakhot* 10a. To which, one might add the implied condemnation in *Pirkei Rabbi Eliezer,* Ch. 22, where the *hash-hatat zera* of the Generation of the Flood was said to be motivated by their desire to avoid begetting children who would ultimatly be destroyed in the Flood anyway. See also the comments of R. Elijah Mizrahi to Gen. 4:23 and the Midrash cited there; and see p. 240, Note 35, below, on *einam hagunim.*

[38] See Chs. 11 and 16.

[39] E.g., I. Jakobovitz, "The Cost of Jewish Survival," *Judaism: A Quarterly* (Fall, 1966).

[40] E.g., the statement prepared by Rabbi Ben Zion Bokser for the Law Committee of the Rabbinical Assembly, 1955.

or responsible habitation of the world and point to the halakhic concern for the welfare of existing children implicit in the law on contraception for nursing mothers. Some find contemporary applicability in an intriguing item in Talmud and Codes which bans marital relations "during a famine" [41] or other calamity; [42] the contention is that this bespeaks a desire to limit population because of food supply.[43] Actually, the context in both the Babylonian and Palestinian recensions of the Talmud (and Rashi's words) make it clear that we have here an admonition to avoid pleasurable indulgence out of sympathy for others in distress, rather than a call to population control.[44] The qualifications to the rule there and in the Codes (childless couples excluded,[45] or excluded from marital relations except when pregnancy is very likely)[46] also serve to make the purpose clear. But then again, this lesson of sympathy may have an even nobler application to the general problems of population and society. Despite the absence, then, of specific texts on population explosion, much can be deduced from the essence of Jewish teaching: procreation is a positive divine commandment, to be pursued in faith and trust; considerations of physical hazard and fundamental welfare of existing children are admissible, but never those of self-indulgence or convenience; and the method of contraception may not of itself violate conditions of propriety as will be set forth herein.

The Role of the Woman

A pertinent question of more than academic significance is whether the woman is included in those to whom the commandment of procreation, technically speaking, is addressed. The question, for our purposes, is answered in the negative. "Increase and multiply, fill the earth and subdue it" is inter-

---

[41] *TB T'a'anit* 11a: *Gen. Rabbah* 31, 17; *Sh. Ar., O.H.,* 240. 12; 574, 4.

[42] *TP Ta'anit* 1, 6; Isserles to *O.H.,* 240, 12.

[43] E.g., L. Wiesner, *"Kindersegen und Kinderlosigkeit in altrabbinischen Schrifttume,"* in *Monatsschrift,* 66 (1922), 38; Louis M. Epstein, *Sex Laws and Customs in Judaism* (1948), p. 145.

[44] I. Jakobovitz, *Journal of a Rabbi* (New York, 1966), p. 486, Note 376. For an interesting discussion of the entire matter, occasioned by the calamities of World War II, see *Resp. Beit Yisrael,* No. 152.

[45] *TB* and *TP, loc. cit.,* and Codes.

[46] *Matt'not K'hunah* to *Midrash, loc. cit.; Agudah,* commenting on *TP loc. cit.;* and *Magen Avraham,* to *O.H.* 574, 4. According to *Sh. Ar.* itself, and *ShLaH,* even couples with children are to abstain only when pregnancy is unlikely. *TaZ,* to *O.H., loc. cit.:* "this is a matter of extra piety *(middat hasidut),* not to be resorted to when the great mitzvah of procreation awaits primary fulfillment." See below, p. 248. The abstinence, incidentally, in the matter of Joshua *(TB Eiruvin* 63b) and Uriah *(Tosafot ad loc., s.v. kol z'man)* is obviously unrelated to population problems.

preted to apply to one whose business it is to subdue rather than to be subdued.[47] Among modern writers, Jakobovitz advances the homiletic suggestion that the command need not be addressed to woman because her instinct for childbirth is already strong enough; Eve was so called because she was the "mother of all living." [48] More prosaically, Preuss declares that if the commandment were put to the woman to fulfill, it might inspire a kind of well-motivated promiscuity.[49] It is in the nature of things, certainly in a patriarchal system, that the man, the more aggressive of the two, be responsible for the performance of the command.

This point's legal corollaries are many, given a society where polygyny (but not polyandry) is theoretically permitted. A childless woman would not be obliged to leave her present husband and seek a new one, and—more important for our purposes—she would be permitted to render herself sterile [50] if she had reason to, while the husband's duty of procreation could be fulfilled through another wife. The source of the latter ruling [51] goes even further: a woman is permitted to remain unmarried [52] or to marry a man known to be sterile; a man may not marry a sterile woman if she is his only wife. Conversely, a husband can sue for divorce if his wife is barren; his plea is automatic. A woman may not sue for divorce on grounds that her husband is sterile; not being "commanded" she has no *automatic* claim. However, if she pleads her own desire for children, independent of "command," her plea is accepted by the court and her husband is enjoined to divorce her with alimony rights.[53]

The "discrimination" in the law has obvious consequences for the rules of contraception, and the fact is well known that a woman may utilize certain devices while a man may not. These consequences, however, are a result of other legal differences between men and women—primarily biologically based differences—such as laws governing sterilization and *hash-hatat zera,* discussed further on. Nonetheless, the socially-based principle stated above is a factor in and of itself.

In this connection, we have seen that the duty of procreation is not limited to the technicalities of the biblical command alone. Perhaps, now, the woman should be regarded as subject at least to the extension thereof, to the rabbinic mitzvot of la-shevet and/or la-erev. Indeed this has been suggested and even

[47] *TB Y'vamot* 65b. See below, p. 240.

[48] Jakobovitz, *op. cit., p.* 216. See also *Arokh HaShulhan, E.H.* 1, 2, and 1, 4; and see below.

[49] Julius Preuss, *Biblisch-Talmudische Medizin,* p. 479. This idea may, in fact, be intended by the Midrash (*Gen. Rabbah* 8, 14): "that she not go seeking in the marketplace."

[50] *TB Y'vamot, loc. cit.,* and *Tosefta, Y'vamot,* Ch. 8; *Sefer HaHinnukh,* 291; and see on, Chapter 13, "An Oral Contraceptive."

[51] *Tosefta, ibid.*

[52] See previous chapter, Note 52.

[53] *Y'vamot, loc. cit.,* and Codes.

assumed by many Responsa,[54] some basing themselves on the authority of Tosafot,[55] where it does appear that women are included in the obligation of la-shevet.[56] If this is conceded, then the Talmudic leniencies on her behalf would be nullified. Further analysis, however, suggests that the woman is to be regarded as "involved in" la-shevet through her husband, but not "commanded" on her own.[57]

A far prettier definition of the role of woman in the legalities of procreation derives from the Talmudic Commentary of R. Nissim, a fourteenth-century primary authority, who was echoed in some more recent writings. The Talmud, in treating of betrothal by agent, whereby a man may send an object of value with an agent for the purposes of betrothing a woman, allows also that a woman may receive the object through an agent of her own. But, we are told there, "it is a greater mitzvah for her to receive the token of betrothal herself than through her agent."[58] This is because she then has a more active share in effecting the mitzvah of marriage. Taking this cue, R. Nissim writes:

> . . . even though she is not personally commanded concerning procreation, she performs a mitzvah in getting married because she thereby assists her husband in the fulfillment of his mitzvah of p'ru ur'vu.[59]

Of course, the circumstance that the Hebrew mitzvah means a "meritorious act" as well as a "commandment" serves as a bridge. R. Nissim's comment was taken up by Azulai (d. 1806) in his Bible Commentary in explanation of Leviticus 12:2: "When a woman conceives and gives birth. . ." The word tazria refers, he says, to the "woman's wonderful share in her husband's performance of the mitzvah of procreation, as R. Nissim suggests . . ."[60]

---

[54] *Atzei Arazim* Comm. to E.H. 5, Par. 9, refers to implication in Talmud (*Shabbat* 110b) that sterilization may be permissible to women because *p'ru ur'vu* does not apply. *Tosafot* to *Shabbat*, *ibid.*, *s.v. v'hatania*, had suggested *la-erev* applies: *Atzei Arazim* insists *la-shevet* at least does. Among the Responsa see, e.g., *Hatam Sofer*, E.H., No. 20. and others cited in Chapter 13; to which may be added *Sefer Hafla'ah* to *Kiddushin* 41a.

[55] To *Gittin* 41b., *s.v. lo tohu* and to *Bava Batra* 13a. See also *Tosafot* to *Hagigah* 2b, *s.v. lo tohu*.

[56] *Resp. Beit Yitzhak*, E.H., No. 91, concludes there are two points of view (*suggiyot halukot*) in the Talmud on the question: *Tosafot, loc. cit.*, maintain she is commanded *la-shevet*, while *Y'vamot* (Talmud and *Tosefta*, above), imply she is not.

[57] *Beit Mosheh* Comm. to E.H. 5, Par. 11; especially *Arokh HaShulhan*, E.H. 1, 4. See also *Pnei Y'hoshua* (Comm.) to *Tosafot, Gittin* 41b, *s.v. lo tohu*. Resp. *Mar'eh Y'hezkel*, No. 73, has an interesting reconciliation of the matter in terms of the woman's mitzvah taking effect only after she decides, without being obliged to, to marry.

[58] *TB Kiddushin* 41a.

[59] *Hiddushei RaN* to *Kiddushin, loc. cit.* See also *T'shuvot HaRaN*, No. 32.

[60] *Homat Anakh* to Lev. 12:2. See on, Ch. 7, "Excursus:—On 'Female Seed.'"

At least two Responsa writers since his time have—independently, it seems—made the same point: "the woman shares in the mitzvah, as R. Nissim suggests."[61]

Non-Jews and the Commandment

The universalistic sentiment of the Talmud that "the righteous among the nations of the world have a share in the World to Come"[62] expresses the Jewish religious attitude towards the rest of the world. Judaism need not be accepted by others for their "salvation"; only basic righteousness is required of them. The specifics are spelled out, in terms of the Jewish legal system, in a set of rules known as the "Seven Commandments of the Sons of Noah" or the "Noahide" or "Noachian" Laws. These are exegetically derived from various biblical verses relating to the non-Jew.[63] The Seven Commandments of *Bnai Noah* are: (1) The establishment of courts of justice; the prohibition (2) of blasphemy; (3) of idolatry;[64] (4) of incest; (5) of bloodshed; (6) of robbery; (7) of eating "flesh torn from a living animal."[65]

---

[61] *Resp. Im'rei Esh*, Y.D., No. 69; *Resp. Avnei Nezer*, E.H., No. 79. They are, however, interested primarily in deducing from this the prohibition against hash-hatat zera for women (see on). In a different context, *Arukh L'Ner* Comm. to *Y'vamot* 12b, suggests that the woman, too, should share in that Messianic concept, above, and help bring about the incarnation of souls. And, see Note 76, below.

[62] *Tosefta, Sanhedrin*, Ch. 13; *TB, ibid.*, 105a.

[63] *Tosefta, Avodah Zarah*, Ch. 9; *TB Sanhedrin* 56a. Maimonides writes (*Yad, Hilkhot M'lakhim*, 8, 11): He who observes these basic laws because they are commanded by God is among the righteous of the nations of the world. He who observes them because his own reason so dictates, is "not of their righteous but of their wise" men.

[64] "Joining something else" to God (e.g., Trinitarian concepts) is not called idolatry for this purpose. "The Descendants of Noah were not forbidden this (*l'shattef shem shamayim v'davar aher*): *Tosafot* to *Sanhedrin* 63b, *s.v. asur*. R. Joseph Caro (16th cent., in *Beit Yosef* to *Hoshen Mishpat*, 266) rules that Gentiles today are not the idolators of biblical times. Isserles (to *O.H.* 156) similarly: today's Gentiles are not idolators; their intention is to God above even though they add to Him "other things," which they are not forbidden to do. R. Jacob Emden (d. 1776) in *Resp. Sh'ilat Ya'avetz*, Vol. I, No. 41, specifies: if they acknowledge the One God as the Creator of all, even though they admit intermediaries (this is permitted to them) but not if they were to postulate more than one Absolute Power. This same R. Emden is the author of a daring "interfaith" statement (in his Commentary to *Seder Olam*, Hamburg, 1757, quoted in J.D. Eisenstein, *Otzar Dinim U'Minhagim*, p. 14), in which he charitably views Paul's objective as merely that of teaching the Gentiles the Seven Noahide Commandments and "joining," as above, which is not forbidden to them! And, R. Israel Lifschutz (d. 1860; *Tiferet Yisrael* to *Mishnah, Bava Kamma* 4, 4) distinguishes sharply between Gentiles of Bible days and Christians of his time, who "acknowledge the one God and honor Him and believe in (His) divinity, and call our Bible the 'Holy Scriptures' and observe, as required of them by the law of our Torah, the Seven Commandments of the Sons of Noah." See, now, the especially liberal views of R. Menahem HaMe'iri in Chapter 14 of Jacob Katz's *Exclusiveness and Tolerance*. (New York, 1962).

[65] *I.e.*, cruelty (*Sefer HaHinnukh*, No. 452).

Other positive and negative Commandments were deduced or refined from the above, and all subsequent discussion of the Gentile in Jewish law revolved around these Seven and their derivatives. Our question now is: Is procreation among them?

According to the text of the relevant passage in the Talmud, the answer is no.[66] But elsewhere, the Talmud had ruled that a convert to Judaism—ordinarily regarded "as a newborn babe"—who had begotten children before his conversion, is nevertheless said to have fulfilled thereby the mitzvah of procreation.[67] *Tosafot*, ever alert to such implied contradictions, calls our attention to this one: Evidently, then, the mitzvah of p'ru ur'vu is applicable to the non-Jew! Applicable, yes, Tosafot concludes, but mitzvah not.[68]

Meanwhile, another Tosafot is suggesting that Noahides *are* included in the mitzvah.[69] Reconciliation of the two is undertaken by the author of the foremost Commentary to Maimonides' great Code. That Code presents the Laws of the Sons of Noah in the section entitled "Laws of Kings"—meaning those provisions of the Torah which govern the Jewish King and his affairs of state in the Jewish Commonwealth. Maimonides outlines what is expected of the Gentile in such a commonwealth, or what is expected of him wherever he is.[70] Following the Talmud, his Code does not include procreation among these requisites; its Commentary, *Mishneh LaMelekh* of R. Judah Rozanes (Turkey, eighteenth century), explains. That second Tosafot—he tells us in a lengthy note covering many related issues—which held that the Sons of Noah are indeed included, refers to the Sons of Noah literally, meaning of that ancient period; not to Noah's descendants of today.[71]

The issue is joined, however, on another field with other contenders. A classic source in the matter is the authoritative *Sh'iltot*, a Code-like composition by eighth-century R. Ahai Gaon, who thus pre-dates even the Tosafot. Despite what the Talmud had implied, he declares:

> The House of Israel is obliged to marry and beget children and concern itself with the fulfillment of p'ru ur'vu, as it is written (Jeremiah 29:6) "Take ye wives and beget sons and daughters." And

---

[66] *TB Sanhedrin* 59b. Hence, hash-hatat zera is also not among them: *Tosafot, ad. loc., s.v. v'ha;* but see on.

[67] *TB Y'vamot* 62a and Codes.

[68] *Tosafot* to *Y'vamot, loc. cit., s.v. b'nai.*

[69] To *Hagigah* 2b, *s.v. lo tohu.*

[70] *Yad, Hilkhot M'lakhim,* Chs. 9 and 10. See below, p. 260.

[71] *Mishneh LaMelekh, ad. loc.,* Ch. 10, Note 7, Par. 20. Also, *Arukh L'Ner* to *Y'vamot, loc. cit.*

not only Israel but even Gentiles are bidden to procreate, as it is written (Gen. 9 : 7) "And ye, increase and multiply."[72]

Sh'iltot's standard Commentary (that of R. Naftali Berlin ["*N'tziv*"] of nineteenth-century Wolozhin) rallied to his defense by demonstrating how the Talmudic passage could be interpreted to yield the same idea,[73] although *Sh'iltot* is alone in his position.[74]

For our purposes, both for resolution of technical contradictions and for clarification of the matter generally, we can do no better than to read from the lucid yet comprehensive phrasing of the *Arokh HaShulhan*, a masterly restatement of the *Shulhan Arukh*, by R. Yehiel M. Epstein (d. 1908) of Navarrodok, Russia. Analyzing the words of *Sh'iltot* in their context and comparing them with that Code's language elsewhere,[75] he affirms:

> As to "habitation" of the world, all the human race is equal [in this responsibility]. Even though a mitzvah does not attach to each individual [among the Gentiles], [the obligation] rests on the generality of mankind to increase the world's population, in accordance with God's will as expressed to Adam and to Noah and his sons . . . With Israel the mitzvah was attached to each individual, just as the other mitzvot are; but Gentiles, who were not given the other commandments were not given this one [as a mitzvah] either—to individuals —but the blessing of God was on all humanity to increase and multiply and concern itself with the habitation of the world.[76]

In our own day, R. Menahem Kasher has offered an attractive formulation:[77] the instinct and desire (i.e., the blessing) for progeny are implanted within all people; Jews, Gentiles, women. The presence in the Torah of a commandment to this effect serves to raise an inborn instinct to the status of a holy obligation for the Jewish male.

As seen by Christianity itself, the commandment is, like all of the Torah, no longer binding. In support of its subordination of marriage to the higher

---

[72] *Sh'iltot d'Rav Ahai Gaon*, No. 165.

[73] *Ha'amek Sh'alah*, ad. loc.

[74] *Me'iri*, to *Y'vamot* 62, seems to join *Sh'iltot*. For further discussion, see *Maharsha* to *Hagigah* 2 and *Sanhedrin* 59; and *Sh'ilat Shalom* to *Sh'iltot*, ad. loc.

[75] In the section *Noah*, where the context treats of these commandments, *Sh'iltot* omits the words "even the Gentiles are bidden, etc." Only in the section quoted here, which is *V'zot Ha-B'rakhah*, in a context of "blessing," does he include them.

[76] *Arokh HaShulhan*, E.H. 1, Par. 5.

[77] *Torah Shlemah*, I, 167.

good of virginity, the early church argued that "God's original intention in creating male and female" had been "modified"; that "under the old covenant, marriage and coitus were necessary and, indeed, commanded. With the arrival of a new dispensation, however, carnal propagation ceased to be obligatory, and salvation became dependent, not upon generation, but upon regeneration."[78] Such was the expressed view of the Church Fathers; it was reiterated for our time by the eminent theologian Karl Barth: "Be fruitful and multiply" has "ceased to be an unconditional demand" since the birth of Christianity.[79]

[78] Bailey, *op. cit.*, pp. 42–43.
[79] *Church Dogmatics* III, 4, p. 268.

4

The Mitzvah of Marital Sex

The marital act of sexual relations partakes of personal and human components that are not the concern of law as law. The marriage contract, however, has a legal base in which at least the *fact* of marital intercourse plays an important role. Certainly in terms of the contraceptive question does the obligatory character of marital relations have legal consequences.

Onah: The Wife's Conjugal Rights

Once married, the mitzvah of *onah* [conjugal dues] rests upon the man. The word itself is found in Exodus 21:10, where the husband's obligations are specified as: *sh'er*, *k'sut* and *onah* [her "food, clothing and sexual rights"] — according, that is, to the accepted exegesis from among many in a passage in M'khilta (an early halakhic Midrash) and in both recensions of the Talmud.[1] The word *onah* being of uncertain etymology, these sources suggest it may either signify (deriving from *im t'anneh et b'notai* in Gen. 31:50) the pain of sexual relations denied;[2] or it may relate to the idea of regular recurrence

---

[1] *M'khilta* to Exodus 21, 10 (ed. Lauterbach [Philadelphia, 1949], III, 27–29); *TP K'tubot* V, 6 and, partially, in *TB K'tubot* 47b, 48a.

[2] See *Tosafot* to *K'tubot* 47b, *s.v. im*.

in the word's connotation of "time."[3] On the other hand, if onah does mean "[her] time" (or "its time" with reference to *sh'er* and *k'sut* respectively) then it may merely be a qualifying phrase and refer to the "regularity"of the previous, rather than constitute a third obligation; it may require the husband to supply her with clothes according to the "season," and not "fit for the summer when it is winter." On such a view, the duty of conjugal relations would be derived not from the biblical text but from logic: if the text is required to obligate him for food and clothing, which she could have secured outside of marriage, sex, for which marriage was contracted, is naturally his obligation.[4] But the first exegetical view is accepted (the Bible says "If these *three* . . .") and presupposed in the Mishnah and in the relevant Talmudic discussions,[5] as well as in the Codes,[6] where the details of the onah obligation are spelled out. The equation here, incidentally, of the woman's sexual rights with food and clothing as basic necessities of life has led a modern writer to say: "No more eloquent testimony to the importance of legitimate sex among the ancient Hebrews could be imagined."[7] Actually, Talmudic law goes further: a prenuptial agreement by the woman to forgo her claim to sexual rights is not to be recognized, while such an agreement against food and clothing may be.[8] The deprivation of sexual rights is *tza'ara d'gufa*, a personal hardship to the woman not subject to advance forfeiture;[9] the other rights are merely material goods.

The Marital Debt in Christian Writings

Again, the bearing of this factor on the contraceptive question is better understood by comparative reference to the Christian tradition, where the "marital debt" figures in theological writings. There it is known as the Pauline debt or concession, referring to I Cor. 7:3, where Paul writes: "Let the husband

---

[3] As found, perhaps, in *Hos.* 10:10. In rabbinic Hebrew there are many examples: *TB Y'vamot* 62b: *onah* (meaning half of a 24-hour period); *Mishnah, Niddah* I (7b): *shalosh onot*, etc. Interestingly, Rashbam interprets *onah* here as from *ma'on*, i.e., "shelter." This, too, could imply conjugal rights. Similarly, *ednah* in Gen. 18:12 can be related to *idan*, "time" (Daniel 7:12) as it is in *Gen. Rabbah* 48:20 (*see Matt'not K'hunah, ad. loc.*). Cf. *m'shammeshet b'iddim* (*Mishnah, Niddah* I, 1) and (Isaiah 64:5) *beged iddim;* but *Targum* to Lev. 12:2: *tazria-ta'adei* is probably not related.

[4] *M'khilta, TP* and *TB, loc. cit.*

[5] *Mishnah* and *G'mara TB K'tubot* 61b, 62a.

[6] E.g., *Tur* and *Sh. Ar., Even HaEzer* 76.

[7] Raphael Patai, *Family, Love And The Bible*, p. 149.

[8] *TB K'tubot* 56a; *Kiddushin* 19b; *Yad, Ishut* 12, 7.

[9] See the above and *Lehem Mishneh* to *Yad, Ishut*, 15, 1. See also *niha d'gufa, TB Y'vamot* 118b; and *lama nikhn'sah, K'tubot* 8b.

render to his wife what is due her and likewise the wife to her husband"; and in I Cor. 7:6, "But this I say by way of concession, not commandment." The implications are drawn by Augustine: "It would have been possible," he reasons, to attach no sin to intercourse for payment of the marital debt without procreative purpose, "had not Paul added . . . 'concession but not by commandment.' And now who will deny this to be a sin when admittedly those who do this have only a concession made on apostolic authority to excuse them?[10]—for demanding "the debt of the flesh" because of the "pleasure of lust."[11] The concession applies only to the initiating spouse; the other, in responding, was not sinning at all but fulfilling his or her marital duty. The "return of the debt" became an established purpose, second to procreation, of marital intercourse.[12] Albertus Magnus and Thomas Aquinas, in their respective commentaries to *The Sentences*—a corpus of lore compiled by Bishop Peter Lombard from the writings of the Church Fathers and Councils—carried the idea a little further and entertained the possibility that response to unexpressed intimations of desire might be regarded as "return" of the debt rather than as sinful initiation.[13]

Since, now, contraception is inadmissible for the Catholic couple except by mutually agreed-upon abstinence, what special circumstances would justify withholding of payment of the debt? Two Dominicans, Dominic Soto (fifteenth century) and Peter de Ledesma (sixteenth century), cautiously suggested that an abundance of offspring may justify such unilateral withholding;[14] the early seventeenth-century Jesuit Thomas Sanchez similarly held that intercourse might be legitimately refused for fear of danger or detriment to existing offspring.[15] This leniency was nonetheless omitted from the relevant writings of the Belgian Jesuit Leonard Lessius and the French St. Francis de Sales a half century later and rejected by the contemporary German Jesuit Paul Laymann.[16] In the eighteenth century, St. Alphonsus Liguori reaffirmed that, when the danger of incontinence was present, the Pauline duty prevailed in spite of exigencies.[17] The alternative of abstinence

---

[10] *Enchiridion* 78 : 21; quoted by Noonan, *op. cit.*, p. 130, who also cites Augustine's *Marriage and Concupiscence*, 1. 14: " . . . what does the Apostle concede by way of pardon, except this: that married persons, not containing themselves, demand the debt of the flesh from one another, not from a wish of progeny, but from the pleasure of lust." Cf. Elizabeth Draper, *Birth Control In The Modern World*, p. 161.

[11] See previous note.

[12] Noonan, *op. cit.*, p. 284.

[13] *Ibid.*, p. 285.

[14] *Ibid.*, p. 330, 332.

[15] *Ibid.*, p. 333.

[16] *Ibid.*, p. 334.

[17] *Ibid.*, p. 335.

was, of course, always available in such cases;[18] and the rhythm method, condemned by Augustine for its consciously nonprocreative character, was still tolerated only as a "lesser evil" to onanism in the first half of the twentieth century.[19]

The Husband's Mitzvah

While there are restrictions in Jewish law on the woman's privilege of denying marital relations to her husband—she is termed "rebellious" if she refuses sexual relations *or* housework without valid reason and can thereby forfeit her divorce settlement[20]—the burden and primary concern of the law is with her husband. The difference is illustrated by one of those unlikely but highly instructive Talmudic provisions: if a man took a vow to deny his wife the pleasure of marital intercourse, his vow is automatically null and void; he cannot vow against what the Torah requires of him. If, on the other hand, he vowed to deny *himself* that pleasure, his vow is valid[21] but, since she is after all involved as well, a time limit is imposed: two weeks according to the School of Shammai, one week according to the School of Hillel.[22]

It is, then, *his* obligation that is detailed in the Talmud and Codes. His conjugal debt falls due at specified intervals, which vary according to his occupation and ability.[23] If he wishes to change his occupation to one that, as it happens, would demand longer absences from home, he must secure his wife's permission, for the presumption of the Talmud[24]—and Codes[25]— is that "a woman prefers less income and the frivolity of [companionship with] her husband to greater income and separation from him." The law, moreover, goes beyond the law, so to speak, and adds a nice ethical dimension, one with interesting theological implications. The "curse of Eve" was that henceforth woman's "desire is unto thy husband, but he will rule over thee" (Gen. 3:16), which is said to account for woman's sexual modesty and her inhibition against overt initiation of sexual activity.[26] As a "curse," one might suppose that it must continue to be this way, but, as in other such mat-

---

[18] *Ibid.*, p. 336.

[19] *Ibid.*, p. 120, pp. 438–47. See Ch. 10 below, on intercourse during pregnancy.

[20] *Mishnah* and *G'mara*, TB *K'tubot* 63a and Codes.

[21] TB *N'darim* 81b.

[22] *Mishnah* and *G'mara*, TB *K'tubot* 61b, and Codes.

[23] *Ibid.* Yet, a larger fine for "rebelliousness" is imposed upon her than upon him because, says the Talmud, his sexual urge is more assertive. "Observe the brothel: who pays whom?"— TB *K'tubot* 64b.

[24] TB *K'tubot* 62b.

[25] Maimonides, *Yad, Ishut*, 14, 2; *Sh. Ar., E.H.*, 76, 5.

[26] TB *Eiruvin* 100b.

ters, the Jewish position has been: it is a curse but not a commandment.[27] And, as such, it is the husband's *duty* to spare her this curse; he is *obliged* to initiate such activity when she presumably desires it [28]—"even at times other than those of onah."[29] More, this applies even to an otherwise interdicted time: separation from one's wife for the twelve-hour half day before the normal separation of the menstrual period, known as *samukh l'vestah*, is a rabbinically added margin of pious carefulness, as it were.[30] If a man, now, were setting out on a journey at just that time, he can presume that her "desire is unto thy husband,"[31] and it is his duty to "visit" her even though it happens to be *samukh l'vestah*,[32] because this rabbinically added margin of safety "was not intended to set aside a mitzvah."[33] "Before setting out on a journey," or "when he notices her desire" by "her manner of dress or of action"—these and similar circumstances, as we shall see, add to his minimal obligation of onah. Indeed, the legalistic obligation itself is based on an "estimate" of her sexual needs; if these exceed the estimate, so does his duty.[34] Other significant provisions of the law—such as that forbidding the husband to force his attentions on his wife[35]—will be discussed anon. What it all adds up to is a concept of marital relations as the duty of the husband and the privilege of the wife. This is in contradistinction, for better or worse, to the Christian egalitarian view (I Cor. 7:4) and, for better, stands in neat contrast to the attitude deplored by modern writers, according to which sex is seen as the man's right and the woman's duty.[36]

The law does not recognize, it was stated above, a prenuptial agreement

---

[27] So the original Catholic position maintained with regard to the curse of childbirth pain. Anesthesia was opposed on grounds that the curse is the will of Providence (E. S. Cowles, *Religion and Medicine in the Church* [New York, 1925], p. 18). The Jewish view was that it may be a curse but it is not a commandment.

[28] TB Y'vamot 62b, Sh. Ar., O.H. 240, 1.

[29] TB P'sahim 72b.

[30] TB Sh'vuot 18b; see Note 32.

[31] Me'iri explains: Parting is sorrowful; it elicits tender feelings in her.

[32] TB Y'vamot, *op. cit.*; Sh. Ar., Y.D. 184, 10 and Isserles thereto. On *Rashba*, see *Maggid Mishneh* to *Yad, Issurei Biah* 4, 12. On Maimonides' omission of the law, see *Torat Hash'lamim* to YD., *loc. cit.* On *vestot d'rabbanan*, see SHaKH to Y.D. 184, 1.

[33] Ravad, *Ba'alei HaNefesh* (see Note 60, below), p. 140.

[34] Ravad, *ibid.*; *Tur, O.H.*, 240; *Yam Shel Sh'lomo, Y'vamot* VI, 30.

[35] *Eiruvin, loc. cit.*; Maimonides, *Yad, Deot*, 5, 4 and *Issurei Biah*, 21, 11; *Shulhan Arukh*, O.H., 240, 10 and E.H., 25, 2.

[36] In *McCalls* Magazine (Nov., 1966), W.H. Masters and V.E. Johnson, authors of *Human Sexual Response*, write (p. 173): "The concept, bolstered by ancient laws, that sex is a *husband's right and a wife's duty* [emphasis supplied] has made and continues to make for marriages in which sexuality is exploited and dishonored." The famous Dutch gynecologist, T.H. Van de Velde, found it necessary to insist that the woman, too, has a right to sexual pleasure.

on the part of the woman to waive permanently her sexual rights. She may, however, temporarily forgo these rights at any time at all. Not, Maimonides points out, if this thwarts another mitzvah which is not hers alone, namely if her husband has yet to discharge his duty of procreation! Her temporary waiver should await his fulfillment of the basic p'ru ur'vu.[37] In making this specification with regard to two overlapping responsibilities of the husband— onah and p'ru ur'vu—Maimonides has succeeded in reminding us of their essential independence one from the other.[38] Onah is a separate mitzvah and is concerned with the woman's other-than-procreative needs.

Nonprocreative Intercourse

Marital intercourse with even a conscious awareness of its nonprocreative character, it is already evident, required no added justification according to the Rabbis. In fact, the opposing voice of Philo, that first-century exponent of Jewish philosophy in Alexandria, only serves to set off this normative rabbinic view by contrast. Expounding the Decalogue commandment against adultery (Exodus 20), he condemned those who "mate with the barren woman," calling this, too, a figurative "destruction of seed."[39] His austere position, likely influenced by the Stoic preachment, did not go so far as to limit the purpose of the marital act to procreation alone, as he forgives the husband who continues, because of "familiarity," to live with a wife found to be sterile or barren. But he does seem to be in league with those Stoics who regarded marital intercourse during pregnancy as sinful because it is hardly procreative. (The views of the Stoics and especially of the Church Fathers on the matter of coitus during pregnancy are cited in Chapter 10, below, and their attitude towards coitus at any other time without procreational intent was briefly noted above.)

It might even appear that Philo's voice, although extreme, finds a suggestion of support in the words of one of the Talmudic Sages. In a singular point of view, R. Judah would define the biblical *zonah*, the harlot forbidden in marriage to a member of the priestly clan, as the woman known to be barren.[40] This idea is associated[41] with the biblical verse (Hoshea 4:10) "they shall commit harlotry and not increase." Intercourse, that is, which is not for

---

[37] *Yad, Ishut,* 15, 1; *Sh. Ar., E.H.* 76, 5.

[38] *Maggid Mishneh, a.l.:* "Our Master thus makes clear that onah and p'ru u'r'vu are two (mitzvot), mutually independent." Similarly, *Resp. Igg'rot Mosheh, E.H.,* No. 102.

[39] See above, Ch. 2, Note 107 and below, Ch. 6, Note 3.

[40] *Mishnah, Y'vamot* VI, 5 (61a,b).

[41] *TB, loc. cit.;* and *TP Y'vamot* VI, 5.

the sake of increase, is like that of a harlot. What is actually dismissed by R. Judah, however, is intercourse which can *never* be for the sake of increase; he would allow a *Kohen* to take a childbride who is not now but is yet to become childbearing.[42] The Palestinian Talmud continues the discussion by alluding to the Aggadah concerning the biblical Lamech, told fully in the Midrash and in Rashi's Bible Commentary:[43] According to this Aggadah, the sinful men of the Generation of the Flood took two wives, one for procreation and the other for sexual gratification. Very significantly for our purposes, the Palestinian Talmud argues that no legal deduction can be made from this narrative (which may actually be deploring the neglect of the fecund wife),[44] as the barren or older wife are permitted in marriage even to the *Kohen*. R. Judah's view is overruled and neither Talmud legislates against even Lamech's conduct. Another *Mishnah* which might seem to support Philo treats of the "Ordeal of Jealousy" (the "*Sotah*," Numbers 5:11 ff.). There the text questions by implication the propriety of having a wife who is barren.[45] Having another wife through whom the mitzvah of procreation can be discharged removes that question. This, after all, may even be the basis of Philo's stricture.

For, it is the consciously fruitless marriage, rather than specific acts of fruitless intercourse that so violates the very spirit of Judaism. Indeed, the biblical exclusion of one "maimed in his privy parts" (Deut. 23:2), and hence incapable of fathering children, is the basis for the following commentary by R. Samuel David Luzzatto in nineteenth-century Italy:

> The reason [behind this exclusion] is the ideal of procreation, for the woman whom the incapacitated man marries will not be able to give birth. Women of ancient Rome used to seek out sterile men so as not to conceive. Blessed be God who has sanctified us by Torah and Mitzvot and ordained that marriage be for perpetuation of the species and the enhancement of society, not for momentary pleasure alone. Our Rabbis also . . . made ordinances and rules to keep us far from immorality and to promote proper mating and domestic peace, to insure the welfare of parents and children and their love for one another. All this has prevailed in Israel throughout its Exile—until the "generation that was before us."[46]

[42] *Tosafot, ad. loc., s.v. kol.*

[43] *Gen. Rabbah* 23, 3; Rashi to Gen. 4:19 and also to Job 24:21. See Ch. 13 below for text.

[44] Preuss (p. 480) sees the Lamech story as a protest against the practice of maintaining concubines in addition to one's fruitful wife, who is then neglected.

[45] *Mishnah, Sotah,* IV, 3 (24b).

[46] *Perush SHaDaL al HaTorah,* ed. Schlesinger (Tel Aviv, 1965).

Of course, Luzzato's fine moral preachment here stands on not-so-fine exegetical grounds; it certainly cannot be taken as literal interpretation.[47] The woman, we have seen, is permitted to marry a sterile man; the sterile man is permitted to marry; and even the one "maimed in his privy parts" is allowed to marry under certain circumstances.[48] It was this latter provision, in fact, which had already served for Rabbenu Bahya (fourteenth century) as evidence that marriage (or coitus; he uses the words interchangeably) is not *only* for procreation, as others seemed to teach;[49] even marriage may be entered upon with no procreative possibility. We have, moreover, noted R. David Abudarham's acknowledgement of this legal fact, in that he gives the marriage of sterile persons as reason for the omission from all wedding ceremonies of a b'rakhah for the mitzvah of procreation.[50] The assumption is that that mitzvah is not identical with the imperative to marry.

That any specific act of intercourse in marriage may be entered upon, even when consciously nonprocreative, need hardly be demonstrated; it is presumed in both general and specific rabbinic preachment. The classic baraita of the Talmud on contraception for the "Three Women" (see on, Chapters 9 and 10) is, in the manner of or necessity for contraception, the subject of dispute between R. Meir and the other Sages, between Rashi and Rabbenu Tam on another level, and between the rigorists and permissivists among the later authorities to this very day. But one premise is crystal clear and beyond dispute: no moral objection is raised to the intercourse itself, although such intercourse is understood to be consciously or hopefully nonprocreative.

The principle is, in fact, so clearly established that it becomes a criterion for the relative permissibility of one kind of contraceptive device over another, as in the words of Rabbenu Tam:

> Such intercourse is in the natural manner, just like that with a child-bride or barren woman which was not forbidden on grounds of unfruitfulness.[51]

---

[47] The reason, as suggested by the authoritative *Sefer HaHinnukh*, No. 559, is to express the Torah's disapproval of the act of "making one's self a eunuch" to serve kings as a harem guard, etc.

[48] E.g., *giyyoret um'shuhreret*. See *TB Y'vamot* 76a; and *Sefer Hasidim*, No. 518.

[49] *Midrash Rabbenu Bahya al HaTorah*, to Deut. 23:2; see *ibid.*, to Lev. 27:2.

[50] See Ch. 2, Note 80.

[51] *Tosafot, Y'vamot* 12b. Cf. also *Mord'khai* to *Y'vamot*, Ch. I.

The issue becomes one of whether *hash-hatat zera* [improper emission of seed], subject of Chapter 6, is involved, not whether the act is nonprocreative. Philo's homily notwithstanding, this is the consistent rabbinic position. Even the moralists of the Middle Ages, in their tracts and books for the edification of the pious, cited the "Three Women" passage to demonstrate again that nonprocreative intercourse is not "improper emission of seed" and hence certainly acceptable.[52] The Zohar, too, made this clear;[53] and the mystic tradition even saw spiritual benefit in nonprocreative union.[54] For the halakhic tradition, the axiom was best formulated by *Nimmukei Yosef*, the early fifteenth-century Commentary to R. Isaac Al Fasi's Code:

> It follows from here and from all discussions elsewhere that *intercourse* with a woman incapable at all of child-bearing is permissible, and the prohibition of hash-hatat zera is not involved so long as the intercourse is in the manner of procreation; for the Rabbis have in every case permitted *marriage* with women too young or too old for childbearing. No prohibition is involved with a barren or sterile woman, except that the mitzvah of procreation is not thus being fulfilled.[55]

And so is it codified by Isserles in the *Shulhan Arukh*, in the very section in which hash-hatat zera is treated.[56] But, since the Talmud and Codes not only permit but enjoin marriage upon every man,[57] including those situations where childbearing is impossible,[58] the permissibility of consciously nonprocreative intercourse is taken for granted.[59] Marriage and marital relations

---

[52] E.g., Al-Nakawa's *Menorat HaMaor* (see Note 60, below), p. 64: "And relations with the Three Women, or the barren woman, are not *hash-hatat zera* as the *baraita* shows." *Sefer Hasidim*, No. 499, would condone this only after he, unknowingly, married such a one. See Ch. 2, Note 124.

[53] *Emor*, 90b. See R. Margoliot, in his *M'kor Hesed* to *Sefer Hasidim*, No. 176, p. 182.

[54] See *Sh'nei Luhot HaBrit, Sha'ar HaOtiyot*, p. 102b (*v'et ha-nefesh asher asu be-haran*) and see on, Chapter 6.

[55] To *Y'vamot*, Ch. V. The "*Rishonim*" in *Shittah M'kubbetzet* (see on) similarly express this axiom. See below, Note 100, for *Ritva* in connection with *onah*.

[56] To *Even HaEzer*, 23, 5.

[57] *Y'vamot* 61b; cf. Isserles to *E.H.* 1, 8 and *Beit Shmuel, ad. loc.*, and others cited in Ch. 2 above.

[58] Abudarham (Ch. 2, Note 80, above) calls this a mitzvah, too. But cf. *Maggid Mishneh* to *Ishut* 15, 7, in the name of R. Moses HaKohen. See Ch. 2.

[59] The question asked of *Rashba* as to whether a woman may take measures to end her sterility, although the measures themselves are disapproved of by her husband, presupposes that the continuation of a sterile relationship is not in question. The fact that Rashba's reply is part of the *Shulhan Arukh (Yoreh Deah* 234, 74) is additional proof to the author of *Resp. Pri HaSadeh*, Vol. I, No. 88, of this presupposition.

are both independent of procreation, achieving the many desiderata spoken of in Talmudic, Responsa, and Mystic literatures.

The pious man, however, seeks the proper *kavvanah*, or purposive intent, for his actions, and so another consideration is entailed here. Granted the legitimacy of marital relations independent of their possible fruitfulness, what motives, he would ask, are the more praiseworthy for engaging in such activity? A hierarchy of commendable motives (*kavvanot*) is accordingly charted in a popular guidebook on marital life written by R. Abraham ben David (*Ravad*) of Posquieres (twelfth century), a contemporary and official critic of Maimonides' Law Code. This unique little compendium of both legal and moral admonitions on our subject, called *Ba'alei HaNefesh* (that is, for those who "master their desires" with discipline), lists four purposive intentions of the marital act, as culled from the various Talmudic sources.[60] First is, of course, procreation; second is the conferral of those "benefits" which are said to accrue to the child and mother through intercourse during pregnancy (see Chapter 10); third is the performance of the mitzvah of onah which, he writes, "has nothing to do" with procreation but is a fulfillment of her yearning when she is, say, nursing, or when he is about to leave on a journey.[61] His fourth purpose is remarkable in making explicit the implicit partiality of the Talmud in favor of women in this matter. The husband's intention is a meritorious one if, says Ben David, he wants to avoid "thoughts of sin." This is good and praiseworthy, but not a mitzvah, because he is indulging himself when he could have exercised moderation, and because the pleasure of his wife did not require it! It is, in other words, a mitzvah to gratify *her* pleasure but not his own; moderation in sex, food, and drink should be *his* goal. Ben David reinforces the idea a few pages later on:

> Onah specified by the Sages is for the purpose of fulfilling the wife's desire, and he is not at liberty to do less without her consent . . . He should not be overzealous in conquering his own desire, lest this result in his neglect of the mitzvah . . . [62]

[60] *Ravad, Ba'alei HaNefesh, Sha'ar HaK'dushah*, (Jerusalem: Masorah ed., 1955) p. 131. The essence of this section of the book was incorporated in Israel Al-Nakawa's *M'norat HaMaor*, ed. Enelow, IV, 72 (end of 14th century), and in Isaac Aboab's later work (end of 15th) of the same name (*Ner* III, *Klal* VI, Part V; ed. Mosad Harav Kook, Jerusalem, 1961, p. 370), and in *Tur, O.H.* 240 and *E.H.* 25. Emden's *Siddur* (see next chapter) also includes it in the Friday Evening section. *Ravad's* book itself has been reprinted in many editions.

[61] See *Me'iri* in Note 31, above. Al-Nakawa (*op. cit.*, p. 73) adds: "or when he returns from a journey, for then she certainly has a desire unto him."

[62] *Ravad, op. cit.*, p. 139.

The institution of *syneisaktism* [spiritual marriage]—whereby a married couple live together but conduct themselves "as brother and sister" in the name of sexual asceticism—was a phenomenon of early Christianity[63] (and is not unknown even today, especially after the necessary procreation has been accomplished). If for no other reason than the fact onah is a mitzvah irrespective of procreative possibility, this institution or concept is unthinkable in Judaism. The question of contraceptive abstinence when necessary will be resumed later; here we see that even among the pious motives—not to speak of ordinarily legitimate sex—is the obligatory concern for the physical needs of one's wife.

The husband's needs do get a slightly better hearing in R. Isaac Aboab's paraphrase of Ben David's "four *kavvanot*."[64] He interpolates an additional facet into the fourth of these: the advantage to the husband in terms of physical release is to be included among the legitimate motives. Aboab, in this connection, relays the phrases of Maimonides to the effect that sexual expression for relief of physical pressures is both morally and physically salutary.[65] (An even earlier formulation of this idea, and a later, more expansive one, are discussed in the next chapter.) Having said this much, Aboab balances it with Maimonides' medical counsel in the opposite direction: overindulgence in sex is a common cause of physical debilitation and, like overeating, is morally and physically harmful. In this sense, say Maimonides and Aboab, Solomon advised (Proverbs 31:3) "Give not thy strength to women ... " Solomon's counsel had been relayed by R. Saadia Gaon (d. 942) in his philosophic work, where he nonetheless acknowledged that erotic expression is a means of deepening the bond between husband and wife.[66] Highly significant is the fact that while the *Tur* Code incorporated the words of Ben David and of Maimonides in full on this matter, the *Shulhan Arukh* Code did so only selectively,[67] omitting Ben David's opinion that the husband's desire to avoid sin is praiseworthy if not a positive mitzvah,[68] and omitting the beneficial physical effects for the husband acknowledged by Maimonides. What the *Shulhan Arukh* was then left with was only the latter's terrifying description of the results of sexual excess, and an austere, almost grudging, codification of marital relations in terms of duty. But despite the *Shulhan Arukh's* deliberate omission

Bailey, *op. cit.*, pp. 33–35.

Menorat HaMaor (see Note 60, above), pp. 372–73. Emden's paraphrase in his *Siddur* (*Mittot Kesef* 6, 6) follows Aboab in this; see next chapter.

Maimonides, *Yad, Deot*, 4, 19.

Emunot V'Deot, Part X, Chs. 6 and 7.

Tur and *Sh. Ar., O.H.*, 240; *Tur, E.H.* 25.

RaMA, ad. loc., restores this idea.

of other-than-spiritual benefits for the man as a decent motive—and its further omission of the word "passion" from Ben David's statement and the word "pleasure" from that of Maimonides, [69]—the duty to one's wife, including *her* pleasure, is still, the *Shulhan Arukh* records, a mitzvah to be performed with appropriate conscientiousness.

The lofty goals set for man notwithstanding, the average act of marital intercourse is not going to be occasioned by pious or altruistic motives. It is for that reason, says R. Jacob Emden (eighteenth century) in his Commentary to the *Tur* Code, [70] that no b'rakhah is recited before this act: most such acts are motivated not by mitzvah but by personal considerations. [71] And, if *his* intent is mitzvah, hers may not be; she may be merely accommodating him. Then, why not *birkat ha-nehenin* (the blessing for enjoyment of pleasures, such as food, if not the blessing for the performance of a mitzvah, such as lighting candles)? Because we are at least *bidden* to act from motives of mitzvah! Actually, as we shall see, even the pursuit of one's own pleasure is a legitimate motive.

The Quality of Onah

Be that as it may, the mitzvah of onah involves the "how" as well as the "when." With Ben David's laudable precept deduced from Talmudic teaching, of moderation for one's self but generosity to one's wife, the husband will not look upon his onah obligation as narrowly limited to the specifications of the law: in its *frequency*, as we have seen; as related to *procreational* intent or possibility, as we have also seen; nor, now, in its quality. The phrase used by Ben David in the above passage is *simhat ishto*, which may be translated "his wife's pleasure." The phrase, of course, is standard in the Talmud, alternating with *d'var mitzvah* and even with *simhat onah* to describe the marital debt. The obligation of the fact of marital sex is qualified by the content of *simhah* [joy] which must characterize it. Here again, the Bible, as understood by the Talmud, is the warrant for this idea: the Deuteronomic law, mentioned above, which affords a year's "draft deferment" to the newly married man, speaks in terms of this joy: "and he shall rejoice [with] his wife whom he has taken." *Simhat ishto* gives quality to the bare legal requirement of onah and

---

[69] See next chapter.

[70] *Mor U'k'tziah* to *O.H.*, 240.

[71] Aburdarham (Ch. 2, Note 80, above) had posed the question with regard to a *b'rakhah* for marriage; Emden now poses one with regard to the marital act. Emden suggests other answers to his question, seeking cumulative strength for their individual weaknesses. See next chapter. Cf., incidentally, *K'tubot* 5b, 6b: *mitkaven l'hana'at atzmo* in the matter of *liv'ol b'tulah b'shabbat*.

adds to its character and definition. "A man is required to give joy [*l'sammeah*] to his wife in the matter of mitzvah";[72] again, "even at times other than those of onah," and "even during pregnancy" when procreation is not involved, "if he notices that she desires it" [73] by her "manner of dress or of action." [74]

Since, moreover, the law of onah is cast in negative terms in the Bible (". . . her conjugal rights shall he not diminish"), the *simhah* content of that Deuteronomic law becomes a counterbalancing positive commandment in some of the Codes. Significantly, they take the nonprocreative period of pregnancy as an example. Thus, *Sefer Mitzvot Katan* of the thirteenth century, enumerates Positive Commandment No. 285:

> "To rejoice his wife"—as it is written (Deut. 24:5) "and he shall rejoice [with] his wife whom he has taken." The negative aspect is [in Exodus] "her onah shall he not diminish." And behold how great is this positive mitzvah . . . even when his wife is pregnant it is a mitzvah to cause her thus to be happy if he feels she is desirous . . .[75]

Sefer Harédim ["The Book of the Devout"] of the sixteenth century [76]—and its later, popular digests [77]—is similarly among the Codes that treat *simhat ishto* of Deuteronomy as a specific qualifying commandment for onah and refers, for an example, to the duty of marital relations during pregnancy as a mitzvah for him when desired by her.

The quality of onah—as much as can be the concern of the law—also involves the considerateness alluded to above, whereby the husband may not force his attentions upon his wife in time or in manner of coitus.[78] To these may be added the requirement of words of tenderness as prelude to the act; [79]

[72] *TB P'sahim* 72b; Cf. *Mas. Kallah.*

[73] Rashi, *ad. loc.*

[74] *Ravad, loc. cit.,* p. 136 and 140, probably based on *TB Eiruvin* 100b; *Tur, O.H.* 240 and *E.H.* 25.

[75] R. Isaac of Corbeil, *SMaK, im Amudei Golah,* ed. Ralbag (New York, 1959), p. 316. On the absence of reference to this verse in the Christian tradition, see following chapter.

[76] R. Eleazer Azkari, *Sefer Haredim,* Positive Biblical Commandments, Ch. 7, No. 7.

[77] See R. Abraham Danzig, *Mitzvat Mosheh (Kitzur Sefer Harédim),* Ch. 16:7. The other "marriage manuals," of course, refer to the mitzvah without attaching it to Deuteronomy. *Huppat Hatanim,* a marriage guide published in Venice in 1737, authored by R. Raphael Meldola, and republished often, is typical. It speaks of pregnancy and, like *Ravad,* adds the nursing period when, too, it is a mitzvah when she is desirous (ed. Jerusalem, n.d., p. 153). For Responsa, cf., e.g., *Igg'rot Mosheh, E.H.,* No. 102, p. 252: "The *onah* obligation applies in pregnancy, barrenness, etc."

[78] See above, Note 35.

[79] *TB B'rakhot* 62a and *Hagigah* 5b; *Yad, Deot* 5, 4; *Tur, O.H.* 240; *Ravad, op. cit.,* p. 134.

the exhortations against sexual relations with one's wife in a state of enmity,[80] because such is harlotry rather than conjugality;[81] against relations in a state of intoxication,[82] because no conscious love can be present;[83] when his mind has been made up to divorce her,[84] for similar reasons; while his mind is on another woman[85] for this is adultery.[86] And, Ben David adds in conclusion with regard to these exhortations:[87] "*Even if* the marital act is necessary for procreation, such as when she is not pregnant and needs to become so," he should not undertake the act under such immoral conditions.

Nothing demonstrates the essence of what has been said so far better than the following excerpt from a document on marriage written in the century following that of Ben David. It is the famous, oft-quoted and oft-reprinted *Iggeret HaKodesh* ["Epistle of Holiness"],[88] a "letter to a friend about marriage," by R. Moses ben Nahman (Nahmanides, d. 1270).[89] In

[80] *TB N'darim* 20b; *Tur* and *Sh. Ar.*, *O.H.* 240.

[81] Rashi, *ad. loc.* and Ravad, *op. cit.*, p. 135.

[82] Talmud and Codes, *loc. cit.* (and see *SMaK, loc. cit.*).

[83] *Ravad, op. cit.*, p. 136.

[84] Talmud and Codes, *loc. cit.*

[85] Talmud, *ibid.*: "A man should not drink from one cup while his eyes are on another . . . This need not even be mentioned, except for the case where both wives are his (and he may then think it acceptable)." The recommendation that no distracting sounds from the street be admitted is also explained in this manner.

[86] Rashi, *a.l.;* Aboab, *op. cit.*, p. 374: Because there must be a meeting of the minds. On all of the above, see also *Perush Avraham ben Natan HaYarhi L'Massekhet Kallah*, ed. Toledano, pp. 32 ff., and *Iggeret HaKodesh*, infra.

[87] *Ravad, op. cit.*, p. 136.

[88] Like Ravad's *kavvanot*, *Iggeret HaKodesh* was incorporated (wholly) in Al-Nakawa's *Menorat HaMaor, op. cit.*, pp. 87–112; and paraphrased in Aboab's work, *op. cit.*, pp. 379 ff.; and in Emden's *Siddur*, *loc. cit.* Also, it was quoted in full in *Reshit Hokhmah* of R.Elijah di Vidas, ed. Constantinople, pp. 219a ff.; in *Sefer HaMusar* of R. Judah Ibn Kalaaz, ed. Cracow, pp. 78a ff.; and in *Sh'vilei Emunah* of R.Meir Ibn Al-Dabi, ed. Amsterdam. pp. 34 ff.; and in *Huppat Hatanim* of R. Raphael Meldola (Venice, 1797; reprinted Jerusalem, n.d., pp. 138 ff.). The book itself was reprinted countless times, including the edition (Jerusalem: Masorah, 1955; bound with *Ba'alei HaNefesh*) used for reference here.

[89] *Iggeret HaKodesh* was always assumed to be the work of Nahmanides, and Al-Nekawa, di Vidas, and Meldola so attributed it. The modern editor of Al-Nekawa (H.G. Enelow, New York, 1934), as well as Louis Epstein, *Sex Laws and Customs in Judaism* (New York, 1935), also regard Nahmanides as the book's author. But, in 1944, Prof. Gershom Scholem, in an article in *Kiryat Sefer* (Hebrew University, XXI, 179 ff.) sought to prove that the book is actually the work of R.Joseph ibn Gikatilia (d. 1300), a younger contemporary of Nahmanides but a member of his Kabbalistic circle. Had *Iggeret HaKodesh* been reckoned by R. Jacob ben Asher, for example, as coming from Nahmanides, it would have been further honored by inclusion in the *Tur* Code like the work of Ravad was, Scholem contends. Yet, R. Charles Chavel, a foremost student of Nahmanides' works, lists *Iggeret HaKodesh* among them in the introduction to his *Perush Ha-Ramban al HaTorah* (Jerusalem, 1959), p. 14. In his more recent study, *Kit'vei HaRamban* (Jerusalem, 1964), Chavel also includes this work, but prefaces the analysis thereof by a lengthy note on the problem of its authorship (pp. 316–20). Omitting any reference to Scholem, he nevertheless concludes the work may come from a R. Azriel, also of Ramban's circle, and that it may at least be said to emanate from the school of Nahmanides.

its sixth chapter, entitled "On the Quality of the Act," the author has this to say:[90]

> . . . Therefore engage her first in conversation that puts her heart and mind at ease and gladdens her. Thus your mind and your intent will be in harmony with hers. Speak words which arouse her to passion, union, love, desire and *eros*[91]— and words which elicit attitudes of reverence for God, piety and modesty. Tell her of pious and good women who gave birth to fine and pure children . . . Speak with her words, some of love, some of erotic passion, some of piety and reverence . . .

> Never may you force her, for in such union the Divine Presence cannot abide. Your intent is then different from hers, and her mood not in accord with yours. Quarrel not with her, nor strike her, in connection with this act; as our Sages taught (T B *P' sahim* 49b) "Just as a lion tramples and devours and has no shame, so a boorish man strikes and copulates and has no shame." Rather win her over with words of graciousness and seductiveness . . . Hurry not to arouse passion until her mood is ready; begin in love; let her "semination" [92] take place first . . .

We will be returning to *Iggeret Hakodesh* in the next chapter. We have sought here to establish that familiarity with and application of the principles assuring the woman's sexual satisfaction is the husband's mitzvah.[93] That it can be said to apply to "technique" in the modern sense, is attested to by a recent Responsum of R. Mosheh Feinstein.[94] Asked by a prospective bridegroom whether the mitzvah of onah implies that he ought to study "medical

[90] Ed. Jerusalem, 1955 (bound with *Ba'alei HaNefesh*), p. 189.

[91] Heb. *agavim*.

[92] Orgasm? See Ch. 7, Note 31. But cf. Tristram Coffin in *The Sex Kick* (New York, 1966), p. 19: Female orgasm "first appeared in medical literature in the late 19th century."

[93] Against the narrower interpretation of such passages as being concerned with the woman's pleasure because this has a beneficial effect on her offspring, the provision in *Sefer Hasidim*, No. 509, makes two points. When pregnancy is likely, be especially concerned for her pleasure; when not, the man's pleasure is determinative but *only* if this accords fully with her desire. The verse "He who finds a wife finds good, etc." (Ch. 2, above), says the author, applies to the situation of sexual compatibility, when their "pleasures" coincide. But linking sexual pleasure to the concern with offspring is an admirable concept in its own right. We now know that sexual compatibility is a factor in fertility, which sounds very much like the words of R. Jonah Landsofer of Prague (d. 1712) who wrote (*Resp. Me'il Tz'dakah*, No. 33) that the "womb opens" to fertilization because of sexual pleasure or compatibility.

[94] *Resp. Igg'rot Mosheh, E.H.*, No. 102, p. 253.

books" on how intercourse ought properly to be performed in a manner "pleasing to his wife and conducive to domestic peace," the Rabbi answered in the affirmative. (He may not even have had to answer the question; what was uncertain to the questioner was whether he might read such books now, before marriage. To this the Rabbi replied—inadvertently capsulizing traditional Judaism's attitude to sex—that the books ought not to be read now because they may excite him to premarital sin; just a few days before the wedding, however, they should be read in order better to perform the mitzvah at the right time.)

The sexual satisfaction due one's wife will also be part of our next chapter; for our present purposes it is enough to advert to the role played by the marital act in the *sh'lom bayyit*, the domestic peace spoken of in a previous chapter. That the sexual component of marriage is essential to the very fabric of that state of affairs is attested to by the deeply poignant reflection of one Talmudic Sage on the cessation of sexual powers in his old age: he calls it the cessation of the instrumentality of domestic peace.[95] The same sentiment is part of the Midrashic understanding of Ecclesiastes' sad lament (12:5), of when "the caper-berry shall fail (*v'tafer ha-aviyonah*)": the caperberry signifies the sexual element: the instrument, says the Midrash, of peace in the home, of love between man and wife.[96]

The attitude to marital sex is uniformly affirmative and joyous, and characterized by a considerateness to the wife which makes for fundamental domestic peace. (A man "who respects his wife more than himself"—because "a slight to her is worse than a slight to him"—"can be sure his 'tent is at peace."[97]) Assuredly, this sh'lom bayyit, grounded in considerateness, then pervaded the totality of the marriage relationship—and into "old age" as well; in any case, the concept became a governing factor in the contraceptive question.

The Contraceptive Question

Enjoying as it does the high status of mitzvah and qualified as it is by life-affirming values such as simhah and sh'lom bayyit, just how powerful, now, is the imperative of onah when pregnancy must be avoided and these values stand to collide with the negative factors of contraception? Is onah of sufficient intrinsic importance that it may override whatever apprehensions are connected with the contraceptive methods available? The problem breaks

---

[95] *TB Shabbat* 152a; Rashi, *ad. loc.*
[96] *Kohelet Rabbah* 12, 5.
[97] *TB Y'vamot* 62b; Rashi, *ad. loc.*

down into several component questions: (a) Can an act otherwise considered a violation of the Torah be set aside in order that onah be fulfilled? (b) Assuming that it can do so only when contraception is required for health reasons, why not choose abstinence and avoid the legal or moral conflict? (We have, after all, seen that the wife can waive her sexual rights.) (c) Assuming we have solved the above questions in favor of contraception, can contracepted intercourse be deemed a fulfillment of onah in any case, or does onah require an unimpeded coital act?

The first of these questions can be answered forthwith in the negative. A violation of the Torah, such as onah during the mandatory separation of the menstrual period, is obviously inadmissible.[98] And, if hash-hatat zera (the "destruction" or "improper emission of seed," subject of Chapter 6) is involved in the particular method of contraception, and accordingly the method is to be considered a violation, then fulfillment of onah in this manner is a clear case of *mitzvah ha-ba'ah ba-averah* [a "mitzvah performed through a transgression"],[99] and, since the end does not justify the means in such a case, the onah would be consequently forbidden and only abstinence would be available. What saves us here, however, is the nature of hash-hatat zera which—without unduly anticipating the discussion in Chapter 6—may depend for its impropriety on the "destructiveness" or "waste" implied in that term. The *mokh*, or tampon (subject of Chapters 9 and 11) is a token of the various points of view on the propriety or impropriety of one or another contraceptive device or manner. So as not to anticipate *that* discussion, let us adduce here without comment the fact that two of the "*Rishonim*," those earlier authorities before the *Shulhan Arukh*, specifically mention onah as a mitigating factor in borderline interpretations of the propriety of *mokh*. R. Aaron Halevi (*RaH*, a disciple of *Rashba*) and R. Yomtov ben Abraham (*Ritva*), both of early fourteenth-century Spain, make this point.[100] A Talmudic precedent in another connection[101] led R. Jacob Emden (d. 1776) to generalize that "the prohibition of hash-hatat zera is annulled of itself for reasons of mitzvah"—and to append the words "*hiddush din*" ["a newly formulated point of law"][102] on the margin of his Responsum. His rule, subject to due qualification, illustrates this particu-

[98] *TB P'sahim* 72b; *Resp. Maharsham*, Vol. I, No. 58; *Resp. Neta Sorek*, No. 6.

[99] *TB Sukkah* 30a, in the case of ritual use of a stolen *lulav;* suggested in this connection by *Resp. Divrei Yissakhar*, No. 138.

[100] *RaH* and *Ritva* in *Shittah M'Kubbetzet* to *K'tubot* 39a. See *Resp. Havatzelet HaSharon*, Vol. II. First Addendum to *E.H.*, and *Resp. Igg'rot Mosheh, E.H.* 63, p. 154: "My eyes brightened when I saw confirmation of my view in *Ritva's* words, etc."

[101] *TB Y'vamot* 76a, in a test of normal sperm motility to certify one as not *krut shaf'khah* under Deut. 23 : 2. The test required extrusion of sperm, but indirectly caused. See Chapter 6.

[102] *Resp. Sh'eilat Ya'avetz*, No. 43. Emden, incidentally, composed a treatise on this and related subjects, called *Iggeret Bikkoret*.

lar trend, adopted with respect to onah[103] under one set of circumstances or another. Leaving to one side, for the moment, these special legal or personal circumstances, the key phrases in representative Responsa illustrate the power of onah to nullify *hash-hatah*. R. Abraham Sofer: "Because of the obligation of onah, no hash-hatat zera is involved."[104] R. Dov Graubart: "If there is mitzvah here, there is no *averah*, for no 'destruction' took place."[105] R. Zvi Meislich: "Since a great mitzvah [of *sh'lom bayyit*] is entailed, and divorce is cruel, we hold with Emden that the prohibition is annulled of itself by the mitzvah."[106] R. Shalom Schwadron: "Not that the physical hazard [concept was necessary to] set aside the prohibition; it was annulled of itself by the important *reason:* not to separate the couple."[107] R. Abraham Horowitz: "Divorce would avoid physical hazard, but since divorce is cruel, contraception was permitted because of onah."[108] And so on and on.

Why Not Abstinence?

Even those who ultimately accepted the principle that onah retroactively nullifies, so to speak, the factor of hash-hatat zera or renders it inadmissible in essence, had first to overcome their own objections. Obstacles of a theoretical nature still had to be eliminated. Why, for example, not presume that the wife can or should waive her marital rights at least temporarily? In that case, no physical hazard would obtain. (In Chapter 11, the factor of physical hazard will be explored; its implications for our subject are raised and resolved there. For the purposes of this chapter, we shall accept the hypothesis of R. Shalom Schwadron that we deal here with hash-hatat zera cancelled out by onah,

[103] *Resp. Sh'matt'ta D'RaVA*, for example, is enthusiastic in his endorsement of Emden's principle and adds: "Emden made a marginal note and a listing in the table of contents of this *hiddush din* so that we not overlook this important and correct generalization. And where is there greater reason of mitzvah than to bring peace between man and wife . . . and not to separate a wife from her husband."

[104] *Resp. Ktav Sofer*, E.H. No. 26.

[105] *Resp. Divrei Yissakhar, loc. cit.* He makes an analogy with the law (Maimonides, *Yad, Y'sodei Hatorah* 6, 7) of burning consecrated wood as an act of destruction (*ha-soref atzei hekdesh*) vs. using it for firewood.

[106] *Resp. Hedvat Ya'akov*, 2nd Recension, No. 37.

[107] *Resp. Maharsham*, Vol. III, Introductory, referring to *Resp. Zikhron Y'honatan. Sefer Ohel Avraham*, No. 99, had written that, because of physical danger, the prohibition was not just set aside but was never involved. *Maharsham* here and *Resp. Iggrot Mosheh, loc. cit.*, are saying that the prohibition was never involved, but that this retroactive nullification is the result of *simhat onah* rather than physical hazard (*sakkanah*).

[108] *Resp. Tzur Ya'akov*, No. 141. Similarly *Resp. Minhat HaKometz*, No. 94; *Resp. Hit'or'rut T'shuvah*, No. 3; and the others mentioned in the following notes; to which may now be added R. Isaac Halevy Herzog in *Heikhal Yitzhak*, E.H., Vol. II, No. 16 (1967).

not by physical hazard.[109]) With her waiver of marital rights, no mitzvah of onah exists, and we are back where we started from. This obstacle is removed by the weight of the following considerations:

(*a*) Contrary to what would appear from a reading of the sources, the woman is *not* allowed to waive her marital rights, even temporarily, for such reasons. So declares R. Hanokh Agus of Vilna[110] in a forthright statement recalling the legal datum, recorded above, that a woman's prenuptial agreement to forgo her conjugal rights is not recognized because, as opposed to food and clothing which are material goods, these rights are physical and personal. Voluntary waiver after marriage for a time is all right, but waiver due to pregnancy hazards is not voluntary, and the aforementioned legal principle applies! Other authorities, speaking less definitely, express the same sentiment in words which call into question the very propriety of abstinence. R. Samuel Rosenberg of Unsdorf (d. 1919)[111] writes: "Since abstinence for long periods is hard on body and soul, I find myself compelled to issue a lenient ruling in this case . . ." The Responsa mentioned above speak in the same vein.

(*b*) As intimated in this discussion, no "destruction" is involved when the act is part of the mitzvah. This idea is pressed further by consideration of the fact that the pregnancy and nursing periods are spoken of as times of relative danger (see Chapter 10). But "the Torah nowhere enjoins periodic abstinence during these periods," reasons R. Shraga Tannenbaum, also of Hungary,[112] and the concept of onah, therefore, must contemplate or embrace the kind of act which presumably is to be carried on with due attention to hazards. Even the celebrated "Three Women" passage (Chapter 10) suggests all alternatives but abstinence, in the specified situations.

(*c*) Most fundamental of all these considerations is the one that sees a double *hash-hatah*, or destruction, in abstinence. The *zera* [seed] is here precluded from fulfilling both of its functions, that of p'ru ur'vu as well as that of onah. Let the *mokh*, for argument's sake, be used in the case of illness so that at least the *zera* is performing one of its two functions, that of onah, now, and the other it can perform when her illness or pregnancy difficulty has been cured, says R. David Babad of Poland in the case before him.[113] If there is to be an act of "destructiveness" here, says R. Samuel Balkani,[114] "we have Talmudic precedent for an act which simultaneously destroys and builds and wherein

[109] See Note 107.
[110] *Sefer Marheshet*, Vol. II (1931), No. 9, 1 : 5.
[111] *Sefer Be'er Shmuel*, No. 66.
[112] *Resp. Neta Sorek*, No. 6.
[113] *Resp. Havatzelet HaSharon, loc. cit.* Similarly, *Resp. Damesek Eliezer*, No. 92.
[114] In *Sefer Ohel Avraham*, No. 91.

the constructiveness is the greater of the two. By abstinence he is certainly refraining from p'ru ur'vu; let him not refrain from onah, too."[115]

A paradigm, then, emerges from all the foregoing: There are two primary mitzvot: that of procreation and that of marital relations independent thereof. The *zera* can be said to be instrumental in both of these objectives. If pregnancy must be avoided, it does not follow that onah also must; quite the contrary, the "destruction" of one purpose because of medical necessity should not occasion the "destruction" of both. This is true, of course, only if we agree that contracepted intercourse is not a violation in itself but rather an alternative method of performing a "constructive" mitzvah. This means that the various contraceptive devices and the manner of their use must be examined against further concepts of propriety to determine whether they involve the kind of hash-hatat zera that can be deemed nullified retrospectively.

This striking and remarkable doctrine—that proper contraception saves one from "destroying" both mitzvot of marital relations—is not really as surprising as it may sound. It is implicit in the normative rabbinic attitude to the mitzvot involved and in a deeper understanding of the problem—a formidable one, indeed—of hash-hatat zera. The succeeding chapters will examine the respective weight accorded to the countervailing elements of our paradigm.

One small item must first be disposed of before closing this chapter. How much interference with the sex act, to prevent pregnancy, can be tolerated in terms of the requirements of onah? Do we not, by contraception, so change the character of the act as to deprive it of the claim to fulfillment of onah? For now, just one aspect of this question will be entertained: Is entrance of sperm into the uterus necessary for the sex act to be called such? If so, the above theoretical structure would necessarily collapse. The question is answered in our sources by analogy with forbidden sex acts, such as adultery and incest. There we see that the offender is liable under the law even if the intercourse were not completed; that is, took place without penetration.[116] Onah, nonetheless, is not fulfilled except by completed intercourse,[117] else the wife is then denied its attendant gratifications.[118] But, now, does

---

[115] "*Ha-shevah yeter al ha-kilkul.*" Similarly, *Resp. Pri HaSadeh*, Vol. I, No. 88: "*M'kalkel al m'nat l'takken lo havei m'kalkel.*"

[116] *TB Y'vamot* 53b, 54a: *ehad ha-m'areh v'ehad ha-gomer*. See also *Sefer Ha-Mitzvot* of R. Saadia Gaon, Neg. No. 92; Maimonides, *Commentary to the Mishnah, Sanhedrin*, Ch. 7; *Yad, Issurei Biah*, 1, 17; *Tur* and *Sh. Ar.*, *E.H.* 20, 1.

[117] *Resp. of Radbaz*, Vol. I, No. 118, and *Rashba* cited there; *Ezer Mikodesh* to E.H. 76, 1; *Sha'ar HaMelekh* to Maimonides, *Yad, Issurei Biah*, 3, 15.

[118] *Resp. Tzof'nat Pa'aneah (Dvinsk)* Vol. I, No. 12 ("*d'ein lah hana'at biah*").

completed intercourse necessarily include the passage of sperm into the uterus? Evidently not;[119] intercourse with the barren woman—defined in the Talmud as a "wombless" woman, as opposed to a merely sterile one[120] and used in the Responsa as precedent for permissive rulings with regard to hysterectomies[121]—is evidence for this assumption. And since pregnancy is a situation in which, as R. Shalom Schwadron imagined, "the uterus is naturally closed," [122] and since sexual relations are not only sanctioned but recommended or required during pregnancy, as we have amply seen, the point can be said to be proved conclusively. What remains to be analyzed is what does *not* constitute an adequate act of marital intercourse. Strange as it may seem, this requires a discussion first of the concept of the legitimacy of sexual pleasure and how that "pleasure" is a factor in the present question.

[119] *TP Y'vamot* VI, 1: "*biah g'murah*"; *TB Y'vamot* 55b: "*miruk ha-ever.*" For *hibbat biah*, (*TB K'tubot* 56a) see *Tosafot* to *Y'vamot* 65a, *s.v. ki.* Cf. *Resp. Damesek Eliezer*, E.H., No. 92.

[120] *TB Y'vamot* 42b, and *Rashi* thereto; *Nimmukei Yosef* thereto.

[121] See *Resp. Torat Hesed*, Vol. II, No. 43 : 34; *Resp. M'lamed L'ho'il*, No. 17; *Resp. Igg'rot Mosheh*, E.H., Nos. 3 and 66, *Resp. Tsur Ya'akov*, No. 17.

[122] *Resp. Maharsham*, I, No. 58. See also *Resp. Minhat HaKometz*, No. 94.

5

The Legitimacy
of Sexual Pleasure

The Ascetic Ideal

In order not to confuse the matter of sexual pleasure with the larger question of asceticism generally, it is well to distinguish at the outset between venereal indulgence on the one hand and the enjoyment of food, drink, and the worldly "pleasures" on the other. Asceticism and self-denial are features of Stoicism, of Christianity, and even more so of Hinduism; the religious life of Christianity to this very day is characterized by elements of monasticism, reclusion, and austerity. Such other-worldliness, again quite aside from sexual continence, is alien to Judaism.[1] Temperance and self-control are always recommended, and the medieval Jewish philosophers made a virtue of discipline and of the curbing of appetites, but all within the framework articulated by Maimonides:

> One might say: inasmuch as jealousy, passion, love of honor . . .
> [may] bring about a man's downfall, I will therefore remove myself
> to the other extreme. I will refrain from meat and wine or marriage

---

[1] See "That Men Should Not Enjoy Life." Ch. 11, *Where Judaism Differed*. A.H. Silver (New York, 1957), pp. 182–223.

or a pleasant home or attractive garments . . . This is an evil way and forbidden. He who follows these practices is a sinner! [2]

He gave hearty endorsement to the Talmudic observation: "Are not the prohibitions of the Torah sufficient for you, that you seek additional ones?" [3] Renunciation of the pleasures of this world is characteristically regarded as sinful ingratitude to its Creator. No lesser a Sage than Rav, founder of leading academies of Talmudic learning, is the authority for the declaration: "Man will have to render an account [to God] for all the good things which his eyes beheld but which he refused to enjoy." [4]

Of the "good things," however, sex seems to have a status of its own. Early Christianity had departed from Judaism not only in its attitude to all pleasures of this world but in giving special preeminence to sexual abstinence. To achieve spiritual perfection through renunciation of the world and the bodily appetites, every means was to be employed—fasting, solitude, prayer, mortification; "but always," our Anglican authority, D. S. Bailey, writes, "the decisive test, the critical discipline, was that of sexual continence. This cult of virginity followed inevitably from the ethical dualism implicit in St. Paul's comparison of the married with the single state to the advantage of the latter." [5] The Church Fathers, he continues, treat continence as "the first fruit of faith" and, significantly, regard it as "a new and distinctively Christian virtue." [6] The coital act was singled out for special contempt by Tertullian, Arnobius, and Jerome,[7] but it remained for Augustine to designate it as the vehicle of original sin. All of this is the more remarkable in view of the fact that in those instances when asceticism did invade the Jewish community, such as in moments of national calamity and spiritual stress, sexual abstemiousness was still not prescribed.[8] Prof. Gershom Scholem, in writing of the pietistic ascetics in medieval Germany (who foreshadowed the Lurianic Kabbalah of the post-Safed period and preceded the Hasidic revolution of the Baal Shem Tov [eighteenth century] with his emphasis on joyousness), has this to say:

[2] *Yad, Deot.* 3, 1.
[3] *Ibid.*, 3, 2; and *Sh'monah P'rakim,* Ch. 4 (based on *TP N'darim* Ch. 7).
[4] *TP Kiddushin* II, 65.
[5] D. S. Bailey, *Sexual Relations in Christian Thought,* pp. 19–20.
[6] *Ibid.*, p. 20, Note 1.
[7] *Ibid.*, p. 45.
[8] The attitude of the first-century Essene sect, said to have been a forerunner of Christian asceticism, was rejected by normative Judaism. For new evidence now from the Dead Sea Scrolls on this sect, see the article by Menahem Brayer in *Hebrew Medical Journal,* 38 (1965) (English, 302–295).

> There is, however, one important respect in which [medieval] Hasidism differs sharply from its Christian contemporaries: it does not enjoin sexual askesis [asceticism]; on the contrary, the greatest importance is assigned in the *Sefer Hasidim* to the establishment and maintenance of a reasonable marital life. Nowhere is penitence extended to sexual abstinence in marital relations. [9]

He sums up his reflections on Jewish spiritual history: "At no time was sexual asceticism accorded the dignity of a religious value, and the mystics make no exception." [10]

"Conceived In Sin"

Augustine (355–430), Bishop of Hippo in Africa, is the architect of a system of sexual thought which, together with the complementation of Aquinas in the thirteenth century, formed the twin pillars of the classic Church's attitudinal structure. Before the Fall of Man in the Garden of Eden, Augustine taught, sexual activity was wholly under control. It was obedient to the dictates of the will, never stirring in opposition to it or without its behest. But when pride and self-will led Adam and Eve into sin, a new experience befell them: "The eyes of both of them were opened and they knew they were naked" (Gen. 3:7). That is to say, they became conscious within themselves of a new and destructive impulse which he termed "concupiscence," or lust generated (as it were) by their act of rebellion, inordinate and independent of volition. Their awareness of nakedness was an awareness of the new disobedience of their genitals, no longer innocent or docile, no longer amenable to the will. Shame followed upon this demonstration of unruliness; they could not bear to look upon the manifest consequences of their sin; the *pudenda* had to be concealed lest they betray the truth of the Fall. [11]

The consequences of this sin are transmitted, Augustine taught, through the generative act from one generation to the next. Concupiscence continues to reveal itself in the unbidden motions—or absence of motions when bidden—of the genital organs; but, above all, concupiscence is displayed through the sexual impulses themselves, which are stronger than the other passions, less tractable, and can only be satisfied in an orgasm, which engulfs the rational

---

[9] G.C. Scholem. *Major Trends In Jewish Mysticism* (1941) (Schocken, 1965), p. 106.

[10] *Ibid.*, p. 235.

[11] Bailey, pp. 53–56.

faculties in violent sensual excitement. All of this led Augustine to a virtual equation of original sin with venereal concupiscence—so that every child can be said literally to have been conceived in the "sin" of its parents.[12] The link between this concept and the doctrines of Virgin Birth and Immaculate Conception is obvious.

A slight modification of the Augustinian theory was introduced by Gregory the Great (who reigned as Pope Gregory I from 590 to 604). In his view, the evil element in coitus is to be found not in the act itself nor in the concupiscence which impels it, but in the peculiar sensual pleasure [*voluptus carnis*] which accompanies it. The delectation incidental even to lawful intercourse is always sinful; how much more so when the couple's dominant motive is not procreational. For Gregory, coital evil lies not in the inordinate impulse of concupiscence but in the acquiescence of the will in the enjoyment thereof.[13] Gregory's view was, in turn, qualified by Aquinas some six centuries later when the medieval Scholastics revealed "in a slighter degree the same fundamental antipathy or indifference to carnal intercourse displayed in the literature of the early Church." They, too, "found the sexual act a source of theological embarrassment."[14] Aquinas located the seat of "coital evil" not in the act itself, nor in concupiscence, nor yet in venereal pleasure, but in what he regarded as the act's inevitable irrationality. As Augustine, influenced by Platonic dualism, had viewed with suspicion anything deflecting from contemplation of the Eternal, so Aquinas, equally inspired by Aristotle's doctrine of the golden mean, found an element of evil in whatever disturbed the exercise of the rational faculty.[15] In the final determination of the Scholastics, coital pleasure was not sinful as such, but it could not be pursued for its own sake without sin: within marriage the sin was always venial; outside of marriage, it was mortal.

The higher valuation of marriage advanced by the Protestant Reformation did not extend to its view of sexual activity. Luther regarded marriage as more natural and honest, but in his treatment of sex, he

> follows Augustine and Aquinas and ascribes our present experience of the venereal impulse to the Fall . . . We continue to bear the penalties accruing from the original transgression of Adam and Eve. Consequently coitus cannot now be performed entirely in the know-

[12] *Ibid.*, p. 55.
[13] *Ibid.*, p. 59.
[14] *Ibid.*, p. 133.
[15] *Ibid.*, pp. 135–36.

> l*e*dge and worship of God, but is accompanied by a sense of shame . . .
> somehow it is always unclean . . . [16]

Calvin, more affirmative about marriage, still "was somewhat uneasy—characteristically, on account of the pleasure concomitant with coitus. This pleasure, he held, must inevitably be attended by a certain element of evil due to the immoderate desire resulting from the corruption of human nature by the Fall";[17] yet when it is incidental to procreation, "the fault is covered over with the veil [of matrimony] so that it no longer appears in the sight of God."[18]

Original sin in this special connotation is, from the Jewish point of view, an unfortunate and untenable concept. It is the result of an orientation foreign to biblical and certainly to post-biblical Judaism. The departure and the contrast are best expressed or deplored by the Anglican Dr. Bailey:

> The Christian attitude to sexuality in all its aspects was profoundly affected by the ascendancy of Hellenistic dualism over Hebraic naturalism during the first great age of the Church. The Jewish conceptions of coitus, marriage, and children, positive and affirmative within their inevitable limits, were almost entirely over-laid by the Graeco-oriental tendency to regard the good life as one essentially of *ataraxia* or impassive detachment from all that might impede the rational exercise of contemplation, and to look upon sexuality as something not only emotionally disturbing, but also in some sense defiling and tainted with evil. It is futile to speculate how Christian thought might have developed, in this as in other realms of theology, had the early Church clung more closely to its Hebraic roots.[19]

These "Hebraic roots" teach no antipathy to sex, and the sin of Adam and Eve has no special connection with sexual activity. Since the only sex that is sinful in Judaism is the illegitimate variety, whatever rabbinic interpretations did see the sin of the first couple in sexual terms—they saw it in terms of several other kinds of sin—had to strain to find something improper about it: lack of modesty in that they indulged in the presence of "living things" (the serpent), for one example,[20] or indulging with unholy motives,

---

[16] *Ibid.*, pp. 170–71.
[17] *Ibid.*, pp. 171–72.
[18] Elizabeth Draper, *Birth Control In The Modern World*, p. 168. See also Note 103 below.
[19] Bailey, pp. 100–101.
[20] *Gen. Rabbah* 18, 10; cf. R. Jacob Emden, *Mor Uk'tziah* to O.H., 240.

for another.[21] Legitimate sexual activity simply cannot be called evil. Most certainly, whatever was the sin of Adam and Eve, it cannot be transmitted to their descendants. On the contrary: if male aggressiveness or female coyness is etiologically associated with the "curse of Eve" (Chapter 4, above), then, says the Talmud, it is the husband's mitzvah to spare her embarrassment and to initiate sexual activity.[22]

The striking example of divergence between the two religious traditions based upon the same Old Testament texts is afforded by another relevant passage. This one, in the Book of Psalms (51:7), serves as the principal textual support for the Christian teaching that original sin is both sexually defined and hereditarily transmitted: "Behold, I was brought forth in iniquity; in sin did my mother conceive me." Formidable as are the apparent implications of this verse, it strikes no roots or response in the entire Talmud; it is not the subject of elaboration there, in its literal meaning, at all. The single reference there is not connected with the sex act but, of all things, with the monthly cycle of conception.[23] It is one of the ironies of religious interpretation that the solitary Talmudic (see on for the Midrashic) discussion of this pregnant verse is a nonliteral, almost tongue-in-cheek application of it to the rhythm of conception—the Talmud's allusion, that is, to the "safe period" (see Chapter 13). The "iniquity" in the first half of the verse is understood as "near the time of iniquity"; that is, near the time when the menses begins and coitus would be forbidden; the "sin" in the second half refers to the "purging" of that sin of impurity [which the same root allows; cf. the next-but-one verse, Psalms 51:9: *t'hatt'eni b'ezov v'et'har*], that is, to the time after the menses and purification. According to one view in that Talmudic homily, then, conception takes place near the onset of the menses (near "iniquity"); according to the other, it takes place right after the purification (*from* that "sin"); that is, about sixteen days before the next period, as the Ogino-Knaus fertility determinations suggest. While this exegetical exercise may be disappointingly nonliteral, the failure of the Talmud to deduce the notion of sin in the marital act is highly significant.

How, then, is the biblical verse's literal meaning understood in the Jewish tradition, even outside of the Talmud? For this, the biblical context is important: David, it will be recalled, is offering a confessional prayer after having been rebuked by the Prophet Nathan for adultery and murder in the Bathsheba affair. Acknowledging his sin, he declares: "Behold, in iniquity

[21] *Iggeret HaKodesh* (Note 87, below). See also N. P. Williams, *The Ideas of the Fall and of Original Sin* (London, 1927), pp. 34, 45.

[22] TB *Eiruvin* 100b; See Chapter 4, Notes 26, 27.

[23] TB *Niddah* 31b. See Ch. 13.

was I brought forth . . . " What this meant to Jewish Bible interpreters is made manifest by the following examples, culled from exegetes, philosophers and Talmudists One selection for each century since Rashi is offered here: *Rashi* (d. 1105) of France, the Prince of Commentators, interprets: David is saying that the sex drive, which is the *cause* of so many sins, is *also* responsible for his coming into being.[24] R. *Abraham Ibn Ezra* (d. 1167) of Spain: the tendency to evil was, as it were, implanted in him at his very birth. R. *David Kimhi* (d.1235): the sex drive is inborn, but it can lead *either way*—in the direction of legitimate or illegitimate sexual activity. If it does lead to the latter, that's to be expected; sex offenses are more understandable than other kinds, for "this is natural, the other [kind of offense] is not natural."[25] R. *Menahem HaMe'iri* (d. 1306) of Perpignan:[26] David laments, "All my days, from my very birth, I have done nothing but evil." This David said by hyperbole, like (Isaiah 48:8) "A sinner from the womb calls unto Thee." And David continues "But Thou desirest truth"; meaning "But Thou didst not intend man to be this way. Thy intention was that he have sense and discernment."[26] R.*Isaac Arama* (d. 1493), philosopher of the Spanish Golden Age who wrote discourses after the example of Christian scholars: The tendency to sin (not necessarily sexual) is inborn, but that's *no excuse*. "I should have overcome it."[27] R. *Moses Alsheik* (sixteenth century), pupil of R. Joseph Karo: David is referring to the sin of illegitimate sex of his earlier ancestors who *were* guilty of it, namely the daughter of Lot whose union with her inebriated father gave birth to Moab, from whence came Ruth; and Boaz, whose union with Ruth was not strictly proper.[28] R. *David Altschul* (seventeenth century) of Galicia: "The act by which I was born *resembles* the act of which I am guilty. . . . "[29] And so on.

To the Rabbis, then, David's compelling metaphor of sin accompanying his very conception was never taken as expressive of the sinfulness of conception, nor certainly of the inherited or inexorable character of sin. Indeed, the "Impulse to Evil," the *Yetzer HaRa*, spoken of in some of the biblical commentaries above, is, as it were, inborn, but it is termed "evil" only by virtue of what it can lead to, and it is always subject to man's control and mastery.

---

[24] Rashi, Ibn Ezra, and *M'tzudat David* flank the text in *Mikraot G'dolot*, "the Rabbinical Bible."

[25] *Perush RaDaK al K'tuvim*. Found in *Mikdash M'at*, to Psalms, *ad. loc.*

[26] *Perush L'Sefer T'hillim L'Rabbi Menahem HaMeiri*, ed. J. Cohen (1936).

[27] *Akedat Yitzhak, Sha'ar* 63 (to Lev. 16; discussing Yom Kippur service. His point is that the Day does not automatically afford atonement without the accompanying confession of remorse over wrongdoing).

[28] *Rom'mot El, Perush Alsheikh L'Sefer T'hillim, ad. loc.*

[29] *M'tzudat David*. See Note 24, above.

When it does not lead to immorality, this same impulse can, in and of itself, be called "very good," for the Rabbis taught: Were it not for the Impulse to Evil, no man would build a house, take a wife, beget a child, or engage in business—as Solomon said (Eccles. 4:4) "I saw that all labor and skillful work come from a man's rivalry with his neighbor."[30]

The *Yetzer HaRa*, this "Impulse to Evil," is the libido driving man to many goals, both good and bad. Sex is the essence of man's drive, of his life-force. It is the strongest and most basic, and it can therefore lead to great evil—or great good. Evidence that legitimate sex is not to be equated with *Yetzer HaRa* is the fact that its name is based on Gen. 8:21: "The impulse of man is evil from his youth"[31]—and the great Flood obviously did not serve as punishment for legitimate sex but for "violence" or corruption. If legitimate sexual conduct were encompassed in the sins of the Generation of the Flood, Noah and his wife would not have been called righteous and would not have been spared! The "Impulse to Evil" leads either way, as the Rabbis also taught: "Serve God with both Impulses [to good and to evil],"[32] for both can lead to holiness. And, as they taught in another context, "*Yetzer*, the child and the woman are three things which a man should thrust aside with his left hand and draw near with his right";[33]—that is, disciplined control is the key.

A three-tiered "summary" of this element in the Jewish sex ethic may be discerned in the *Tur* Code, where its author relays the relevant statements of Maimonides. In a chapter of the *Tur* on marital relations (*Even HaEzer*, 25), R. Jacob ben Asher begins his legal formulation by affirming: (1) the unrivalled power of sex; (2) the unqualified legitimacy of sexual activity in marriage; and (3) the pious approach of reserve and decency. He says:

> Maimonides has written: no prohibition in all the Torah is as difficult for man to stay away from as that of forbidden sexual relationships.... Therefore let a man avoid situations that tempt or excite, and turn his mind to Torah and wisdom—for temptation comes only to the heart devoid of wisdom ...[34]

---

[30] *Gen. Rabbah*, 9, 9; Cf. Zohar, Gen. 137b.

[31] See *TB Kiddushin* 30b.

[32] *Mishnah, B'rakhot* IX, 5 (54a; cf. 61a).

[33] *TB Sotah* 47a (See Rashi).

[34] *Yad, Issurei Biah*, 22, 18–21. By "difficult to stay away from" is meant difficult on his emotions, although he does succeed in self-control. Maimonides quotes in this connection the Talmudic narrative (*TB Yoma* 75a) that Israel, at first, balked when Moses taught them to desist from the immorality they had known in Egypt—(*bokheh l'mishp'hotav-al iskei mishp'hotav*).

But a man's own wife is permitted to him and, with her, he is allowed to do as he pleases. He may cohabit with her whenever he pleases, kiss her wherever he pleases, and cohabit naturally or unnaturally . . . [35]

Still, the way of piety is not to be frivolous about this but to approach it with holiness, and not deviate from the natural[36] . . . Nor should one indulge overmuch and find himself always with his wife, for that is lacking [in decency] and boorish.[37]

The *Tur* proceeds then to delineate the requirements of onah, in fact as in quality (described in our previous chapter). The *Tur* has another primary treatment of marital sex elsewhere in his Code, this one among the laws of daily conduct. There (*Orah Hayyim*), the chapter number is 240, which gives R. Jacob Emden the opportunity for a word play, of significance to our present discussion.[38] Sex in its proper circumstances—"there is nothing better than that," says Emden. "In wrong circumstances, there is nothing worse. A handy token of this is the number of the pertinent section in [*Tur* and *Shulhan Arukh*] *Orah Hayyim*, which by chance is 240 [*RaM*, in Hebrew characters] meaning that sex, when proper, is *RaM* [exalted], when improper it is just the reverse, *MaR* [bitter]."

Modern Christian writers miss this distinction entirely and seem not to be aware that they view the "Old Testament," for example, through the lens of early Christian interpretation. Father Kerns, for one, accordingly sees an antisexual teaching in the story of Adam and Eve and is then admittedly perplexed as how to reconcile this with the Bible's general acceptance of licit sex.[39] Likewise, Professor Noonan, unaccountably, writes:

The Old Testament also contains a strain which qualifies its positive acceptance of sexuality: Woman embodies an attraction which may cause disaster. Eve and Delilah are temptresses to sin. Bathsheba is the occasion of David's fall, Tamar of Amnon's (II Kings 13).[40]

---

[35] *Ibid.*, 21, 9. See on, Ch. 8.

[36] *Ibid.*

[37] *Ibid.*, 21, 11.

[38] *Siddur Beit Ya'akov, Mittot Kesef* 7, 3:17. (Lemberg ed., p. 160). See on, Note 100. In a similar vein. R.Israel Ba'al Shem Tov taught that human love should inspire one religiously, for the source of such love (*hesed*) reflects the divine attribute of *hesed*. Even incestuous love is called *hesed* (Lev. 20:17), for it is the corruption of that supernal divine love.

[39] Joseph E. Kerns, S.J., *The Theology of Marriage* (1964), pp. 9–12.

[40] Noonan, *Contraception* . . . , p. 33.

Woman is indeed a temptress—but the temptation cast by neither Eve nor Delilah was to sexual sin. In the other two cases, the sin *was* sexual but illicit: with Bathsheba it was adultery-cum-murder; with Tamar it was the rape of a half-sister! The distinction between licit and illicit sex in the Jewish view is real and obvious; it is blurred only by the habit of reading these texts in the light of an unconscious but persistent Augustinianism.[41]

Pleasure as Motive

Pope Gregory I defined original sin—we noted above—in terms of the pleasure accompanying the conjugal act. But Gregory did more than modify this particular concept; he "out-Augustined Augustine" and became the most extreme voice in the matter of coital pleasure. Not only is pleasure an unlawful purpose in intercourse, he wrote in his *Pastoral Rule*, but, if any pleasure is "mixed" with it, the married have "transgressed the law of marriage;"[42] they have "befouled" their intercourse thereby. He expressed himself similarly in his celebrated letter to the Archbishop of Canterbury.[43] In the context of such a doctrine, Professor Noonan writes, the very idea of contraception:

> . . . would have appeared as a monstrous denial of the single excuse for coitus . . . . Enhanced in authority by Gregory's personal prestige and increasing in importance as the papacy increased in authority in the Middle Ages, this doctrine assured the absolute condemnation of contraception by the entire ecclesiastical organization.[44]

Gregory's doctrine was dourly set forth in the medieval period by Huguccio (twelfth century), chief of the commentators to Gratian's *Decretum* (a compilation of canonical authority completed in Bologna in 1140 and treated as part of the basic law of the Church until 1917).[45] Coitus, he wrote,

---

[41] Even the idea (Noonan, *ibid.*) that "ritual continence may be a way of gaining divine favor" (as in Exodus 19 : 15: "Prepare yourselves for three days [for the Sinai theophany]; come not near a woman") is better understood in terms of the ritual immersion that the Bible prescribes following seminal or menstrual flow and the like. See *TB Shabbat* 66a. R. Joshua Ibn Shu'aib, *Drashot, Tazria* p. 48d, explains, moreover, that it is the semen rather than the sperm that makes the ritual immersion necessary. (See on, Chapter 6, Note 46). Cf. Note 98, below.

[42] Noonan, *op. cit.*, p. 150.

[43] *Ibid.*, p. 151.

[44] *Ibid.*, p. 152.

[45] *Ibid.*, pp. 172–74.

"can never be without sin, for it always occurs and is exercised with . . . a certain pleasure."[46] Huguccio's position was "far from unique among the orthodox"; its "theological popularity in the late twelfth century can scarcely be doubted." Most strikingly, it was repeated by a "star pupil" of his who became the most energetic of medieval popes—Innocent III—who rhetorically asked: "Who does not know that conjugal intercourse is never committed without itching of the flesh, and heat and foul concupiscence . . . ?"[47]

The aforesaid relates, it should be noted, to the sin of pleasure in coitus and not yet to the sin of undertaking coitus with pleasure as its primary object. "Pleasure as the purpose of intercourse was firmly branded sin" by even the milder theologians from the twelfth through the fifteenth centuries,[48] as well as by the Dominicans Cajetan and Soto and the authoritative Counter-Reformation "Roman Catechism" of the sixteenth.[49] The suggestion that intercourse for pleasure be permitted was called "brutish" by the Louvain theologians of the seventeenth century; the Holy Office confirmed their censure of the proposition that "a marital act exercised for pleasure alone lacks entirely any fault and any defect."[50]

More temperate views were not entirely lacking. Denis the Carthusian (fifteenth century) wrote, in a work designed for the devout English laity (among whom was Thomas More) that "the married can mutually love each other because of the mutual pleasure they have in the marital act."[51] Martin Le Maistre (d. 1481) of the University of Paris, building upon the idea that coitus is lawful to avoid adultery, proceeds to say ". . . conjugal intercourse to avoid the sadness coming from the absence of venereal pleasure is not culpable" and has its procreative benefits too, since it, in turn, keeps the couple healthy and "the healthy are more fit for generation."[52] Similarly John Major (sixteenth-century Paris and Glasgow: " . . . whatever men say, it is difficult to prove that a man sins in knowing his own wife for the sake of having pleasure."[53] That a moderate seeking of pleasure was a proper end, if other ends were not wilfully excluded, was then endorsed by leading theologians at the turn of this century.[54] And yet:

[46] *Ibid.*, p. 197.
[47] *Ibid.*
[48] *Ibid.*, p. 250.
[49] *Ibid.*, p. 321.
[50] *Ibid.*, pp. 326–27.
[51] *Ibid.*, p. 305.
[52] *Ibid.*, p. 308.
[53] *Ibid.*, p. 311.
[54] *Ibid.*, pp. 492–93; Dorothy Bromley, *Catholics and Birth Control*, p. 18.

> . . . even into the nineteenth and twentieth centuries the minds of seminarians were shaped by moral textbooks that sounded as if they had been composed by a disgruntled St. Jerome. . . . In a moral textbook widely in use throughout Jesuit houses of study in Europe in this century, the author Fr. Noldin, describes the sex act as "a thing filthy in itself." In an equally influential work of Genicot-Salsmans, we find the definition of marriage as that which gives people the "right to perform indecent acts."[55]

Approaching the question without cultural prejudice, the unadorned biological layer of the sex act does seem to exhaust itself in its procreational objective, with the pleasurable sensations a kind of accompanying inducement. The physiologic facts led Maimonides to conclude:

> The purpose of intercourse is to perpetuate the species, not for the pleasure of the act *alone*. This pleasurable aspect was implanted in living beings in order to stimulate them to the first purpose [of coitus] which is to inseminate. Clear evidence of this fact is that passion subsides and pleasure ceases after semination . . . for if pleasure were the purpose, that pleasure would continue for as long as one wished . . .[56]

Although his context is one in which he moralizes about deviations from normal intercourse and asks the pious not to take advantage of whatever leniency there may be in the law in such cases, and although he proceeds to make due provision for the needs and the pleasure of both husband and wife, his statement is nevertheless illuminating. As it stands, it is better than that of Emden in this particular regard, to whom sexual pleasure is a "mighty inducement" to compensate for the natural inhibition against indulging in something so physical.[57] A century later, Arthur Schopenhauer gave thorough and eloquent expression to the idea that sex is nature's trick to insure the survival of the species; that not only pleasure but specific sexual attraction and romantic notions are all a grand illusion; that we are dupes of a cunning and irresistible natural force which seeks the preservation of the species and—explaining why certain bodily types of women are more attractive

---

[55] Daniel Sullivan, "A History of Catholic Thinking on Contraception" in *What Modern Catholics Think About Birth Control*, ed. W. Birmingham (Signet, 1964), p. 57.

[56] *Commentary to the Mishnah, Sanhedrin*, Ch. VII.

[57] R. Jacob Emden, *Mor U'k'tziah*, Comm. to O.H., 240. See also *Arokh HaShulhan, E.H.*, 23, 1.

to certain men—this same instinct seeks the possible enhancement of the stock of the species.[58] Onto this bare biological base, Schopenhauer continues, we have imposed cultural forms for the enhancement of society: sanctions, for example, against rape, which blind nature may demand but which society can never tolerate.[59] This same blind nature could also lead to gross overpopulation, says another savant, the Irish cultural historian, W.E.H. Lecky, writing at the turn of this century. Were it not for the "birth control" of late marriages or other such checks on the powerful sexual drives of humanity, this force, he declares, could lead us down the road of population havoc and ruin.[60]

To return to the psychosocial layer superimposed upon the biological, unashamed acceptance of the former seems to have been a problem. This layer, of personal delectation or of the warmth of human relational satisfaction for its own sake, troubled the moralists, Christians especially, and Jews to some extent. The ethic of purposefulness demanded that the act of a pious man be directed to a goal beyond himself, as it were; while the ordinary Jew was allowed permissible pleasures for his own sake, the pious one sought assurance that his pleasure was also a mitzvah, for his wife's sake or for the greater glory of God. If, as Maimonides had observed, the objective of intercourse is not pleasure alone, then it follows that the pious man's motive ought not to be pleasure alone either—as we noted in the previous chapter's discussion of kavvanot, of motives.[61] Of course this leaves more than procreation: R. Isaac Aboab's moral treatise formulates the broader pious motive: "One should not intend his own pleasure alone—but his wife's as well."[62] The "Book of the Pious" (the Sefer Hasidim of the early thirteenth century) would endorse this and much more. Concern with the wife's pleasure should be the rule especially during her fertile days, in keeping with the prevalent assumption that her pleasure in coitus has salutary effect on the child conceived then.[63] On other than fertile days the husband can consider his own pleasure first, as long, that is, as his actions are not in disharmony with her wishes.

---

[58] Arthur Schopenhauer, "Metaphysics of The Love of The Sexes," in Vol. III of his *The World as Will and Reality.*

[59] A disquisition on the different dimensions of *persona* and *bios* in sex relations is offered by Helmut Thielicke, *The Ethics of Sex* (New York, 1964), es. pp. 22–25.

[60] W.E.H. Lecky, *History of European Morals*, II, 71.

[61] See Chapter 4, pp. 69–71.

[62] *M'norat HaMaor, Ner* III, *Klal* VI, Part V, Ch. 3. (Ed. *Mosad HaRav Kook*, p. 390).

[63] *Sefer Hasidim*, No. 509; *Iggeret Hakodesh* (See Chapter 4, Note 89), pp. 189–90, and the two books called *M'norat HaMaor* in the sections based thereon; etc. As to the woman's *kavvanah*, as opposed to the man's, in its effect on the child, see the above and *Perush Avraham Min Hahar* to *N'darim* 20 and Azulai in *Bir'khei Yosef* to *O.H.* 240.

Here the *Sefer Hasidim* gives wistful but affirmative expression to the ideal of sexual compatibility. Interpreting the verse in Proverbs 18:22, "Whoso findeth a wife findeth a good, and obtaineth favor of the Lord,"[64] the author of this widely accepted compendium says:

> All these [sexual] matters must take her wishes and his into consideration (*l'fi da'at ishto ul'fi da'ato*). If a man finds a wife whose wishes happen to coincide with his own in these matters (*she'- tih'yeh kir'tzono*)—then he has "obtained favor of the Lord" and [the verse in Eccles. 9:7 applies:] "God hath favored thy deeds."[65]

Both the pious and the ordinary, then, would qualify for Herman Wouk's felicitous observation concerning the Jewish sexual outlook:

> What in other cultures has been a deed of shame, or of comedy, or of orgy, or of physical necessity, or of high romance, has been in Judaism one of the main things God wants men to do. If it also turns out to be the keenest pleasure in life, that is no surprise to a people eternally sure God is good.[66]

Some, evidently, were not able to trust themselves with the sheer enjoyment of pleasure; R. Abraham ben David has a word of "reassurance" for them in his *Ba'alei HaNefesh*, discussed in our previous chapter.[67] They may be uneasy with the pleasure of coitus; when this uneasiness is occasioned by piety, he says, it can *also* be an acceptable way of worshipping God. The focus of his remarks is a passage in the Talmud itself, subject of diverse interpretations. A certain man is described there as going about his marital relations "as if he were coerced by a demon (*k'ilu k'fa'o shed*)."[68] To the commentators, this phrase suggests an act carried out hurriedly because of fear of or possession by a demon.[69] Although the whole idea is overruled in the Talmud in favor of the principle that "a man may do with his wife as he

[64] See Chapter 2 above, Note 62.

[65] *Sefer Hasidim, loc. cit.*, end. A gross kind of sexual incompatibility is acknowledged by the Talmud (*TB K'tubot* 63b) where a woman who denies her husband sexual privileges because "he is repulsive to me (*ma'is alai*)" is absolved from granting them. Maimonides (*Yad, Ishut*, 14, 8) says this means he must give her a divorce with settlement. *Maggid Mishneh* thereto justifies Maimonides' position but reports the dissenting views of other authorities who fear this may embolden a woman "who has set her eyes on another," to upset her marriage in this way.

[66] Herman Wouk, *This Is My God* (Dell Paperback ed., 1964), p. 125.

[67] See pp. 69–71.

[68] *TB N'darim* 20b.

[69] See Rashi and *RaN. ad. loc.* and *Ravad*, next Note.

pleases," Ben David feels it necessary to deal with the concept, to explain it—and to condone it. Conjugal relations should take place in the "middle of the night," when no voices of people going about in the streets may be heard The purpose, he explains, is so that thoughts of another woman not intrude. Similarly, those who hurry through the act also do so to avoid the intrusion of strange thoughts. Even though it is better not to hurry, "in order that one's wife derive greater pleasure," those who are "not sure of themselves and do hurry," provided "their wives are in accord with this"— they also *mean well*, for "all hearts [that] seek God" and "all deeds done for God's sake are good."[70]

Wellbeing As a Motive

Another strand is interwoven with the others in the tapestry of sexual pleasure. The austere Maimonides counseled minimal indulgence in sex, just as he had advised "not to eat except what one needs for one's health."[71] But while depicting in vivid terms the horrible results of sexual overindulgence, he acknowledges the beneficial effects of its moderate expression—in terms of physical release.[72] An older contemporary, the Bible exegete R. Abraham Ibn Ezra, preceded Maimonides in this regard. In his Commentary to Lev. 18 : 20 (which we shall consider separately forthwith), he makes reference to three objectives of intercourse: (1) procreation; (2) relief of physical tension;[73] and (3) satisfaction of lust analogous to animal lust. His formulation is accepted by Nahmanides, Bahya, Ibn Seneh, and other scholars in their respective Bible Commentaries.[74]

No statement of the health value of sexual intercourse, however, is more expansive and well-nigh lyrical than the one offered by R. Jacob Emden (d. 1776). It is to be found, of all places, in his Prayer Book-Compendium as part of a comprehensive presentation of the subject of conjugal sex:[75]

---

[70] *Ba'alei HaNefesh* (see Chap. 4, Note 60), p. 135.

[71] *Yad, Deot*, 3, 2.

[72] *Yad, ibid.*, and 4, 19.

[73] The versions vary between *l'hakel mi-le'ut ha-guf* (to "relieve the fulness of the body") and *l'hakel mi-lehut haguf* (" . . . the moistures of the body.") Our editions of *Perush Ibn Ezra* in *Mikraot G'dolot* read *mi-le'ut*, as does the Amsterdam edition (1722) of *Margaliot Tovah* containing Ibn Ezra's text with three super-commentaries (see on). But in the Mantoba (1559) edition of Ibn Seneh's *M'kor Hayyim*, one of these three, the quotation from Ibn Ezra reads *mi-lehat;* all quotations of it in Ramban, Bahya, and *Moshav Z'kenim* (see on) read *mi-lehut*.

[74] See above Note, and Notes 82, 83 below. Nahmanides' comment to Lev. 18:19 can be better understood in terms of his citation of Ibn Ezra in 18:20. (See ed. Chavel, pp. 104–105). Also, cf. *Drashot al Hatorah* of R. Joshua Ibn Shu'aib, *Tazria*, p. 48d: "mitzvah of sex for onah, procreation, or health."

[75] *Siddur Beit Ya'akov* (See on, Note 100), Ch. VII, *Hulia* I.

When sperm is "surplus," nature prepares to discharge it, like other surpluses to be discharged. If, therefore, when the reproductive organs are ready to expel it but it gathers up inside, this is harmful and intercourse is necessary. Moreover, for one overcome by depression or insanity, intercourse is beneficial, for it dissipates melancholy, calms bad temper, and gladdens the soul. Also, a healthy man . . . . who becomes sexually aroused involuntarily and feels a heaviness in his loins, yet does not cohabit . . . his sperm gathers . . . and creates bad vapors which may affect the heart, brain, and stomach, damaging his health and causing possibly fatal illnesses. [76] So it happened with some who were accustomed to sexual release and then refrained for a long time; they died suddenly [!] Therefore, coitus is good for such a one; it cleanses the body of its fulness, lightens heavyheadedness and brightens his eyes . . . [The evils of overindulgence are repeated here] . . . but in moderation, coitus is good and beneficial in the ways stated . . . [77] Just as proper and disciplined eating preserves life and sustains strength and health, so proper sexual expression is a source of pleasure and benefit to body and soul. As despicable eating habits, in quality or quantity, destroy body and soul, so improper sex habits destroy body and soul. [78]

This unique manifesto is as suspect as it is remarkable. Its tone is much too uninhibitedly self-serving for Emden, who didn't mind quoting it in full from whatever was his source although it does not quite tally with his own outlook. To him, as we have seen in the previous chapter, the motive ought to be the mitzvah; the b'rakhah for mitzvot is, however, not prescribed for the sexual act because this motive may more realistically be said to be absent, as a rule. [79] Emden's own formulation would have been balanced with still more moralistic reserve, such as the Talmud's observation that the "appetite grows with the eating," so to speak. Man's sexual hunger is intensified by his indulgence, and is quieted by nonindulgence, says the Talmud. [80] And

---

[76] "A certain degree of direct sexual satisfaction appears to be absolutely necessary for by far the greater number of natures and frustration of this variable individual need is avenged by manifestations which, on account of their injurious effect on functional activity . . . we must regard as illness"—Sigmund Freud, *Collected Papers*, II, 83, quoted by David Bakan, *Sigmund Freud and the Jewish Mystical Tradition* (Schocken ed., 1965), pp. 291–92.

[77] *Siddur*, etc., *loc. cit.*, Pars. 1–2.

[78] *Ibid.*, *Hulia* III, Pars. 3, 17.

[79] Ch. 4 above, Note 70.

[80] *Sanhedrin* 107a, "*masbi'o ra'ev, mar'ivo save'a.*" Cf. Rashi to parallel passage, *Sukkah* 52b.

the curbing of appetites is always a moral imperative. Yet if Emden did not author the piece, he endorses it enough to quote it in its entirety, and the purpose of physical and mental relief is thus to be accepted on a par at least with other pious motives for conjugal love.

We return now to consider the exegesis of that Leviticus verse (18 : 20) which occasioned the listing by Ibn Ezra of three coital objectives. That passage reads in the English versions "Thou shalt not lie carnally with thy neighbor's wife, to defile thyself with her." "Carnally" in this rendering is on the order of a euphemism, for the Hebrew uses the word zera (*lo titen sh'khovt'kha l'zora*), and a more literal translation would be closer to "Thou shalt not lie seminally with thy neighbor's wife." [81] Now, what does the stress on "seminal" mean? It is to teach, Ibn Ezra suggests, that adulterous intercourse *even* for the "seminal" purpose of fulfilling, hypothetically, the duty of procreation, is equally forbidden! If a man were to claim his adultery was for the sake of achieving even so laudatory a goal, he is instructed by this verse that he still "defiles himself" therewith. [82] Nahmanides suggests an alternative exegesis on the same basis: not *even* seminally, but *because* it is seminal; that is, one of the chief evils of adultery is the consequent confusion of paternity, which may even lead a child of unknown paternity to marry a consanguineous relative. Whether seminally or not, however, he "defiles himself" by an adulterous union. A third variation is that of fourteenth-century R. Samuel Zarza (Ibn Seneh), who writes: "*even* seminally, meaning *even* if a man intends procreation" — which, since it confuses paternity, becomes the *worst* of possible motives — "in either case, he 'defiles himself.' "[83] Adultery is bad independently of procreational involvement; the relationship is a defiling one.

With multiple objectives of legitimate as well as of illegitimate sexual interaction, the very idea of higher "motives" is seen to be essentially irrelevant. [84] Love and physical needs are imperious, and one can easily deceive himself as to motives; procreation is not even in one's power to bring about.

---

[81] Even *shikhvat* may mean "effusion," says R. David Hoffman in *Sefer Vayikra*, II, 292.

[82] A book recently published for the first time — *Moshav Z'kenim al HaTorah*, ed. Sasson (London 1959) — records biblical exegeses of the *Ba'alei HaTosafot*. There, to Lev. *ad. loc.* we read: "*R. Eleazar of Worms* asked: 'Since he did not intend procreation but his own pleasure, is he guiltless? . . . even if his intent was procreation, such as if his wife were barren and he reasoned: "I will go to my neighbor's wife, perhaps I will be able to beget a child"; the Torah instructs him that this, too, is forbidden.' "

[83] *M'kor Hayyim* (ed. Mantoba, 1559); also in *Margaliot Tovah* (see Note 73) to Lev., *ad. loc.*

[84] When Judah was moved to cohabit with Tamar (Gen. 38 : 13–30), thinking her a prostitute, he was actually being impelled to do so by "the angel appointed over [matters of] passion — (*mal'akh ha-m'muneh al ha-ta'avah*)" because the procreational outcome was desired from on high, says the Midrash, *Gen. Rabbah* 85 : 9.

The higher motives, when actually present, may indeed sanctify, but the act justifies itself on its own terms, even though there is an attendant physical pleasure which resembles the satisfaction derived from less legitimately fulfilled desire. The exposition of a Midrash on the Psalms passage above bears this out. "No man," says that Midrash, "even if he be the most pious, can act without the semblance of sin." David is thus said to claim that his own parents were not free of the same passion which later led him to sin:

> "Did father Jesse really intend to bring me into the world? Why, he had only his own pleasure in mind. You know this is so, because as soon as they satisfied their desires, he turned his face to one side and she turned her face to the other side. It was You who then led each drop [of semen] to its proper place." This is what David meant in saying [elsewhere, Psalm 27:10: *ki avi v'imi azavuni*, etc.] "For, though my father and my mother have forsaken me, God has gathered me in."[85]

Lest one be guilty of the heresy that even legitimate sexual activity is somehow sinful when it lacks procreative intent, a standard commentary elucidates the above Midrash. The commentary, printed together with the text in the larger editions, is the work of R. Ze'ev Wolf Einhorn of nineteenth-century Lithuania:

> The act of both the father and the mother has an aspect which —from the standpoint of higher spiritual understanding—*resembles* sin. David, now, would not impugn his parents' honor; therefore the Midrash explains [his meaning in saying "Behold in iniquity," etc.]: Even the most pious can only beget children in the way which embraces eroticism and passion—*which they share in common with those who sin*—except for the difference in intention. But even if the intention of the righteous is only to fulfil the mitzvah of procreation, yet, since ultimately conception is not up to them, all they really have is the act of passion and pleasure.[86]

It is not even unlikely that the aforementioned heresy made inroads into the creed of Judaism and subtly left its mark on the minds of some of its spokesmen. No less monumental an authority than Maimonides was

---

[85] *Lev. Rabbah* 14, 10; *Yalkut to Psalms,* 765.
[86] *Perush Maharzu* to *Lev. Rabbah, ibid.*

accused of such heretical deviation by the author of a popular work, assumed to be none other than his successor and admirer, Nahmanides (d. 1270).[87] It seems that Maimonides had betrayed a discernible Greek influence in his attitude to the spiritual versus the physical pleasures. In his *Guide for the Perplexed*, he expounded a philosophy wherein the pursuit of spiritual and intellectual fulfillment is the high road of human endeavor; the indulgence in sexual pleasures is not only less worthy but partakes of the sense of touch, which, as Aristotle had taught, is the lowliest of the five senses.[88]

Nahmanides challenges him reverently but boldly in his *Iggeret Ha-Kodesh*, the "Epistle of Holiness," written to a friend on the subject of marriage.[89] "Know," he says, "that sexual intercourse is *holy and pure* when carried on properly, in the proper time and with the proper intentions." He continues:

> No one should claim that it is ugly or unseemly. God forbid! For intercourse is called "knowing" (Gen 4 : 1) and not in vain is it called thus . . . . Understand that if marital intercourse did not partake of great holiness, it would not be called "knowing." The matter is not as our Rabbi and Guide—of blessed memory—supposed, in his Guide For The Perplexed, where he endorses Aristotle's teaching that the sense of touch is unworthy. God forbid. That Greek scoundrel[90] is wrong and his error proceeds from his view of the universe. Had he believed that one God created the world he would not have slipped into such error. But we who have the Torah and believe that God created all in his wisdom [do not believe that he] created anything inherently ugly or unseemly. If we were to say that intercourse is repulsive then we blaspheme God who made the genitals . . . Hands can write a Sefer Torah and are then honorable and exalted; hands, too, can perform evil deeds and then they are ugly. So the genitals . . . Whatever ugliness there is comes from how a man uses them. All organs of the body are neutral; the use made of them determines whether they are holy or unholy . . .

[87] See Chapter 4, Note 89.

[88] *Guide For The Perplexed*, Part II, Sec. 36. The Aristotelian idea can be found in his *Nichomachean Ethics*, Part III, 10 (Loeb Classics, pp. 176 ff.). Other medieval Jewish philosophers carried forward the notion that the sense of touch (*hush ha-mishush*) is the lowliest. See especially Bahya's *Kad HaKemah s.v. z'nut*.

[89] *Iggeret HaKodesh* (see Chapter 4, Note 88), p. 175.

[90] "*Ha-y'vani ha-b'liya'al.*" In some editions (e.g. Al-Nakawa [see above Note]) the reading is *ha-y'vani ha-tameh*.

> Therefore marital intercourse, under proper circumstances, is an exalted matter . . . Now you can understand what our Rabbis meant when they declared [91] that when a husband unites with his wife in holiness, the Divine Presence abides with them.

The latter teaching with respect to the Divine Presence, incidentally, contrasts markedly with that expressed even among the moderate spokesmen of medieval Christianity. Earlier in that same century, Pope Innocent III declared that "the sexual act was itself so shameful as to be inherently wicked." "Robert (Cardinal) of Courcon, Hugh of Pisa, Gauthier of Montagne, and others held similar views. Peter Lombard and Gratien, neither of them among the extremists, nevertheless warned their listeners that *the Holy Spirit absented himself from the room of married folk performing the act even for generation alone.*" [92]

There is yet another point of illuminating contrast between the message of this brief document from the School of Nahmanides and that of his non-Jewish contemporaries. The latter so regarded the act of coitus that they advised abstinence therefrom during special feast days and the holy season; in keeping with the idea that the Holy Spirit cannot be present and that the act is anything but holy, they recommended abstinence on Thursdays in memory of the capture of Jesus; on Fridays in memory of his death; on Saturdays in honor of the Virgin Mary; on Sundays in honor of the Resurrection; and on Mondays in commemoration of the departed souls. [93] In our "Epistle of Holiness," on the contrary, the author explains why the pious Jew prefers Friday night for marital love:

> Understand, therefore, that the pious have not selected the weekdays, on which physical activity predominates, for their marital relations. They prefer the Sabbath which is spiritual, holy unto the Lord. [94]

The holy person performs an act of holiness at a time of holiness. Aboab's paraphrase of Nahmanides adds the phrase here: *n'shamah y'teirah*, the "extra

[91] *TB Sotah* 17a; *Mas Kallah*, beg.

[92] Daniel Sullivan, "A History of Catholic Thinking on Contraception" (see Note 55 above), p. 54. (Italics supplied.) On the other hand, Calvin (*Institutes of the Christian Religion*, IV, XIX, 34) wondered how Rome could claim that marriage is a sacrament, graced by the Holy Spirit, while the Holy Spirit is said to be absent from the marital act.

[93] Bailey, *op. cit.*, pp. 133–34. He comments (*ibid.*, Note 3): "Doubtless it was supposed that a few free Tuesdays or Wednesdays would occur during the lifetime of a married couple!" He cites other such prohibitions, too, that, e.g., required the married to abstain for 40 days before Easter, Pentecost, and Christmas. Cf. also Sullivan, *op. cit.*

[94] *Iggeret HaKodesh*, *ibid.*, p. 179.

soul" that the Sabbath confers on one; the time of extra spirituality is most appropriate.[95] To the fourteenth-century moralist-preacher, R. Joshua Ibn Shu'aib, the logic is cogent: "Would Sabbath be selected for an act unworthy in any way?"[96] If the religious calendar is to displace marital sex, only a day on which all physical indulgences are denied, such as Yom Kippur, has such power, but not a day on which only holiness is to prevail.[97]

By far the most vivid and colorful execution of the association of marital relations with Friday night is to be found in the aforementioned Prayer Book-Compendium of R. Jacob Emden. The idea itself is Talmudic;[98] the time-honored custom of reciting the Song of Songs on Friday evening reflects it; the Zohar interprets it;[99] the treatises on morals and customs assume it; but it was Emden's *Siddur* that carried it to new heights. While the laws of marital sex are arranged in the *Tur* and *Shulhan Arukh* Codes in the volume

---

[95] *M'norat HaMaor, Ner* III, *K'lal* VI, Part VI, Ch. 1.

[96] *D'rashot al HaTorah* (ed. Cracow, 1778) p. 48d.

[97] The *Ba'al HaTurim* Comm. (to Deut. 24 : 5) offers delightful "proof" of this principle. To suggestions that marital relations ought to be avoided on days such as Rosh HaShanah, when one's thoughts ought to be concentrated on the solemnity of the day, he counters: The *gematria* (numerical value of the letters) of *v'simmah* ("and he shall rejoice with his wife") adds up to 364 —meaning that such rejoicing may take place on any day of the calendar but Yom Kippur! Of course, *Tishah B'Av* and the *Shivah* week of mourning are included by the Rabbis in this prohibition—again for reasons of mourning rather than of holiness. Two legal details bear this out further: (1) Only a token part of the seventh day of *Shivah* is actually to be observed, on the principle of *mik'tzat hayom k'khulo* and "not to mourn overmuch." According to *Tosafot* and *Rosh* (to *Moed Katan* 21b), this means a brief observance on the morning of the last day, which is our present custom. Nahmanides, however, in *Torat HaAdam* (ed. Venice, 1595, p. 70b, c) requires only a token observance on the night before, since that's when the seventh day begins. A Responsum by *RaDBaZ* (cited in *Pit'hei T'shuvah* to Y.D., 395, 1) mediates between the two by applying the latter view to matters of mitzvah, i.e., Torah study and marital relations, which may resume on the eve of the seventh day; other matters must wait until after morning. (See my article on *Lag BaOmer, Sefirah and Mourning Observances*, in *Proceedings* of the Rabbinical Assembly, 1962, p. 215, Note 23.) (2) The Talmudic admonition to refrain from sex relations during famine or other calamity (see above, Ch. 3, Notes 41–42) is understood as a gesture of sympathy only because of the pleasure involved; when conception is, however, likely and procreation has not yet been fulfilled, this gesture need not be observed (see *ibid.*, Notes 44–46).

[98] See *TB K'tubot* 62b, attaching to Psalms 1:3, "*piryo yitten b'itto v'alehu lo yibbol*," referring the latter half of the clause to the physical relaxation of the Sabbath. See also *TB Bava Kamma* 82a, reference to garlic on Fridays in connection with Friday evening onah, and Maimonides' Mishnah Commentary to *N'darim* VIII (63b). See also *Ba'er Hetev* to *Sh. Ar, Even Ha-Ezer* 76, 5: (*v'sham'ru*) *b'nei yisrael et ha-shabbat, rashei tevot: biah.* (In *Elyah Rabbah* to *O.H.* 240, this *rashei tevot* is attributed to 16th-century *Resp. Binyamin Z'ev.*) Cf. also *Yam Shel Sh'lomo, Baba Kamma* 7 : 43 : 5. Rashi to *K'tubot, ad. loc.* simply explains that Sabbath is the "time of pleasure, rest and physical wellbeing."

[99]   ... Friday evening, from which all the six days of the week derive their blessing ... Those aware of this mystery of the union of the Holy One with the [congregation of Israel] on Sabbath might consider, therefore, this time the most appropriate one for their own marital union.

Zohar, Exodus (*B'shallah*), 63b; and see Zohar, *Yitro* 89a and Zohar, Gen. 50a and 112b.

on daily conduct (i.e. *Orah Hayyim*, the"way of daily life"), immediately following the section on (weekday) Evening Prayers, and while most Prayer Books (of those that come with lengthy introductory or supplementary lore of a legal or inspirational character) expatiate on marital laws in the section on the Marriage Ceremony, Emden presents his material in the Friday Evening Section.[100] His style is magnificent and highly original: The entire Sabbath Section is comprised of Seven "Chambers." The first is the *Prozdor* [Corridor]: the prelude of *Erev Shabbat*, just before the Sabbath. Then comes the *Traklin* [Ante-Chamber] which is the Friday Evening Prayers, and so on. After the Meal (in the Golden Couch Chamber)[101] comes *Mittot HaKesef* [the Silver Bed Chamber] of Emden's Sabbath Palace which is, of course, the point at which—before proceeding to the other "Chambers" through Saturday evening—he lists the laws, customs, and philosophy of conjugal love. Among much else, he offers the manifesto, relayed above, on the salutary physical and mental effects of such love; then, in neatly rhymed couplets, he discourses to this effect:

> The wise men of the other nations claim that there is disgrace in the sense of touch. This is not the view of our Torah and of its Sages . . . To us the sexual act is worthy, good, and beneficial even to the soul. No other human activity compares with it; when performed with pure and clean intention it is certainly holy. There is nothing impure or defective about it, rather much exaltation . . . Because of its great sanctity it requires privacy and much modesty . . . This precious and awesome and elevated act requires decency and discretion . . . Even the physical ills I mentioned result only from overindulgence. But benefit and health accrue to the body, too, when the act is performed in proper measure as to frequency and quality.[102]

These texts and attitudes speak for themselves. It should not be necessary to add to them a single expository word to demonstrate that a "Judeo-

---

[100] *Siddur Beit Ya'akov, Hanhagat Leil Shabbat*, (ed. Lemberg), pp. 135–61.

[101] He calls the Dining Room the "Golden Couch Chamber" (*Mittot HaZahav*), with reference to the ancient couches on which one would luxuriously recline while eating. The use of the word couch, however, leads him to make interesting observations, based on the Talmudic ones, of the identity of food and sex symbols. See *TB Yoma* 75a.

[102] Since his presentation in the *Siddur* is composed essentially of block quotations from others, and since I have already cited selections from his *Siddur* elsewhere, I have chosen to cite here his views in his own words as found in his Commentary to the *Tur* Code—*Mor Uk'tziah —Orah Hayyim*, 240.

Christian sexual ethic" is at the very least an untenable assumption, [103] a fallacy in concept.

Sexual Pleasure and the Contraceptive Question

While the author of "Epistle of Holiness" was writing in Spain, another great Rabbi was composing a Talmudic Commentary in Trani, Italy, to be known as *Tos'fot RiD*, the *Tosafot* of R. Isaiah Da Trani (d. 1270). This Commentary will be introduced in Chapter 8;[104] at this point his contribution to our subject of pleasure is in order. Not that he is the first to put into a legal context the straightforward assertion that the pursuit of pleasure is a legitimate reason for *contracepted* intercourse; R. Isaac of a century earlier, had, in the standard Talmudic *Tosafot*, acknowledged the claim of pleasure or desire even in special circumstances.[105] Da Trani makes the matter eminently clear:

> If one's intent is to avoid pregnancy so as not to mar his wife's beauty or so as to avoid [always] the fulfillment of the mitzvah of procreation, then [the contracepted coitus mentioned there] is forbidden. But if his intent is to spare her physical hazard or to pursue his own pleasure, then this is permitted.[106]

But it was left for another estimable Rabbi, an authority of sixteenth-century Poland, to formulate the "pleasure principle" in terms of (*a*) the definition of the integrity of the sex act and (*b*) the criterion for an acceptable contraceptive device. This definition-and-criterion emerges from R. Solomon Luria's discussion of the Talmudic passage (subject of Chapter 11) concern-

[103] It must be taken as indicative of the essential difference toward the Bible (Old Testament) between the two traditions that in addition to the interpretation of Adam, of "Conceived in Sin," etc., the pro-sexual verses, such as the Deuteronomic provision for "rejoicing [with] one's wife" (Chs. 3 and 4 above), find no reflection at all either in biblical exegesis or matrimonial writings of the Church. The single exception that I have found is its mention by Calvin (*In Quattor Relig. Lib. Mos., Opera* I, p. 515) who, however, sees it as indication that God allows husband and wife to enjoy themselves if such is incidental to procreation and the building of society—this then is the "veil" covering the unholiness of sex. The implication, according to William G. Cole, in *Sex in Christianity and Psychoanalysis* (ed. Galaxy, New York, p. 125), is that this "seemed very generous of God, yet the Reformer was not altogether sure that he approved." Calvin's general attitude, incidentally, is demonstrated by his comment (*Commentarius in Genesium*) to Gen. 29 : 11, where he tells us that the phrase "and Jacob kissed Rachel" was a "redactional slip" by Moses, since the two were not yet married! See De Vaux in Anchor Bible (to Gen., *ad loc.*).

[104] See Chapter 8, Note 101.

[105] See Ch. 8, pp. 156–57.

[106] *Tos'fot RiD* to *Y'vamot* 12b.

ing the contraceptive *mokh*. [107] After analyzing the matter from the standpoint of Talmudic and post-Talmudic sources, he considers this device in terms of whether or not it interferes with normal intercourse. But what, now, is normal intercourse? Since the possibility of procreation is being precluded—of necessity, let us say—what remains? What remains is that *mutual pleasure* must still be present in the coital act. How do we know this is so? Because the Talmud describes the coital act as the heterosexual relationship in which *guf neheneh min ha-guf* ["one body derives pleasure from another"]. [108] Luria proceeded to claim that mokh did not interfere with mutual pleasure, and hence was an acceptable device; others disagreed, as we shall see. [109] What interests us here, however, is that now the criterion for the device's acceptability is none other than pleasure. If procreation must be avoided, then the contraceptive device must be one which will least spoil the essence of a normal sex act by least interfering with its natural gratifications. Having granted the desirability of pleasure for the wife and husband, whether incidental or consciously intended, it must follow that this pleasure not be unduly compromised if (necessarily contracepted) *onah* is to be properly fulfilled.

We have now reached a climactic point in our exposition of the factors involved in the Jewish attitude toward birth control and its comparative relationship to the Christian view. Once we grant that procreation is not the only purpose of coitus (and accept the restrictions on how this may be prevented, as discussed in Chapters 6 and 8) and once we raise the pleasure principle to the level of a minimal criterion of normal, if contracepted, intercourse, the lines between the two religious traditions *with respect to contraception* are sharply drawn. The entire structure of concern with natural law that is of importance to the Church is now seen to be irrelevant in Jewish law. The *nature* of the sex act is its pleasurable yield as well as its procreative possibility. The sex act retains its "integrity," as long as the pleasure which belongs to it still obtains. Other authorities will add to this criterion a stricter interpretation of

[107] *Yam Shel Sh'lomo* to *Y'vamot*, Ch. 6 : 4. See on, Chapter 11, pp. 210 ff.

[108] The source of this phrase is interesting, too. In a Talmudic exegesis (*TB M'gillah* 13a; see Rashi) of a verse in the biblical book of Esther (2:16), the detail of exactly when Esther was received by the King—"And Esther was received by King Ahasuerus in his palace in the tenth month, the month of Tevet"—is explained as being significant for the following reason: Tevet, a cold winter month, is the time when the mutual pleasure of warm bodily contact in intercourse is that much greater. Her being with the King at that time was providential, in order that she seem more pleasing to him.

[109] Later authorities—of those who had access to Luria's Commentary—will agree or disagree about the mokh and about his interpretation of the relevant literary material.

the normal manner of coitus, but the criterion itself is un-challenged.[110]

It remains for now to examine a sample Responsum where this criterion is earnestly applied. A unique example comes from the intensely pious milieu of nineteenth-century Hungary, yet must certainly raise eyebrows when translated into our present culture. R. Hayyim Sofer (d. 1868; a disciple of the famous R. Moses [*Hatam*] Sofer, but not one of his family) adjudges the mokh against the aforementioned criterion:

> The matter is clear to me, with the help of Him Who endows man with knowledge, that there are two senses in which mokh must be understood:
>
> (1) If the mokh obstructs the entire area of the vaginal canal, with the result that the membrum is insulated and accordingly prevented from impinging upon the vaginal walls — then the husband is guilty of hash-hatat zera, for such intercourse is not in the proper manner as implied by Gen. 2:24: "and he shall cleave to his wife, and they shall be as one flesh," i.e., that there be contact between him and her and the bodies derive pleasure from such contact. Furthermore, the movement of life, which is the sperm, adds to the pleasure of bodies which have become as one. But with a "curtain" of mokh separating his flesh from hers, this is not "the way of a man with a maid" (Proverbs 30 : 19) and, in so doing, he casts his seed on a mokh as if on "wood and stones." Intercourse is not permitted except where the excitation derives from the unimpeded conjunction of genital organs and the sperm runs its course in the vaginal canal.
>
> (2) The second kind of mokh is placed at the entrance to the uterus [i.e., a diaphragm]. This leaves the rest of the canal free for un-impeded contact and for the release of sperm in full physical pleasure and in the "flaming ardor of passion" (Song of Songs 8 : 6), except that the sperm does not actually enter the uterus. Conception is prevented, but the natural gratifications of the sex act are not di-minished and the act is therefore clearly permissible.[111]

R. Sofer continues along these lines, expounding further the remark-able principle that the more interference with the pleasure the less acceptable the contraceptive device, and vice versa.

[110] See *Resp. Damesek Eliezer*, No. 92, quoted below in Chapter 11, Note 80. Also, *Resp. Minhat HaKometz*, No. 94, who expatiates on Luria's criterion.

[111] *Resp. Mahaneh Hayyim* (Pressburg, 1862), No. 53.

Part 3

THE NEGATIVE FACTORS

6

Improper Emission
of Generative Seed

Fundamental to the rabbinic legal position on contraception is the problem of *hotza'at zera l'vattalah* [improper emission of seed], known more commonly as *hash-hatat zera.*[1] The latter phrase may be translated "destruction of seed," but the verb (*shi-het, hish-hit*) means "to corrupt" as well as "to destroy." Hence, "abuse" of the generative process or improper seminal emission, rather than "waste of nature", is intended by both Hebrew phrases. At least in its blatant form of masturbation or self-pollution, this is an offense most unequivocally condemned in Talmudic and extra-Talmudic literature. So that its severity as a problem in connection with our subject may be appreciated at the outset, only the following need be noted: if a choice were to be made between so radical a procedure as sterilization, on the one hand, and the use of a device which may be said to thwart the normal course of seminal emission on the other, the former would entail far fewer legal difficulties. The touchstone for the acceptability of a birth control measure is the extent to which it runs afoul of the formidable prohibition of hash-hatat zera.

---

[1] A plausible distinction between the two phrases is offered in *Resp. Hinnukh Beit Yitzhak, E.H.*, No. 7, but they are otherwise used interchangeably.

Sources: Bible and Talmud

In tracing the prohibition to its sources, the Rabbis saw it implied in various scriptural verses, although no explicit text—the "act of Onan" will be discussed separately—could be claimed for it. The sin is indeed great; but the Rabbis did not allow themselves to blur the distinction between a biblically and rabbinically forbidden act. A law may be formulated by the Talmudic Rabbis and be called biblical [*d'oraita*] if it follows accepted norms of biblical interpretation or, conversely, it may be found in Scripture but lack the force of a biblical command; its enforcement is then called rabbinic [*d'rabbanan*]. While the query as to which category hash-hatat zera falls under may hardly be more than academic, the discussion is important for an understanding of the subject itself.[2]

(1) In assessing the sin's severity and/or source of prohibition, the Rabbis expounded, for one example, the Decalogue's commandment against adultery (Exod. 20 : 13). Since adultery is forbidden by other biblical texts (e.g., Lev. 18 : 20), the prohibition in the Ten Commandments was given another, wider application, to immorality generally.[3] Accordingly, the evil of self-pollution [*niuf b'yad*][4] is said to be encompassed by this broad injunction against sexual offenses.[5] But such exegesis is not to be taken literally, others point out; the biblical derivation is a mere "peg" [*asmakhta*] on which to attach the prohibition.[6] After all, we are reminded, the Talmudic legal principle restricts the literal applicability of that command to the case of violation of the married woman; extensions thereto are homiletic only.[7] No less an authority than Maimonides summarizes his discussion of the moral —as opposed to the merely legal—sex offenses by stating that hash-hatat

---

[2] *Resp. Beit Yitzhak*, No. 91, believes the question to be more than academic, as it determines the position of Rashi *vs.* Rabbenu Tam in the *Baraita*. See also *Resp. Maharash Engel*, Vol. VI, No. 18 on *s'feko l'humra. Resp. Heikhal Yitzhak* (Herzog), Vol. II (1967), No. 16, concludes that the practical rulings of the respondents imply that "*ein kan issur Torah.*"

[3] Philo and—for an example in the church—Alexander of Hales in his *Summa Theologica* also gave such wider interpretations to this commandment.

[4] *Mekhilta* to Exodus, quoted in *TB Niddah* 13a; *Sefer Mitzvot Katan*, Neg. 292; *Or Ha-Shanim* 4, Neg. 119; *Marheshet*, Vol. II, No. 9, Par. 2:3.

[5] See Maimonides, *Mishnah Commentary, Sanhedrin* Ch. 7:4; and Perla's Commentary to Saadia's *Sefer Mitzvot*, Neg. 92.

[6] E.g., *Resp. Pnei Y'hoshua E.H.*, Vol. II, No. 44; *Arukh L'Ner* to Niddah 13; *Resp. Hava-tzelet HaSharon*, Vol. II, Addendum to *E.H.; Resp. Dovev Meisharim*, Vol. I. No. 20.

[7] *Ezer Mikodesh*, Comm. to *E.H.* 23, Par. 2, "*ein ni'uf ela b'eshet ish,*" quoted by Rashi to Exod. 20:13.

zera is not punishable [by the court] because it is not an explicit negative commandment.[8]

(2) Other authorities infer the condemnation, if not the prohibition, from the Bible's description of the Generation destroyed by the Flood; the same verb root is used there (Gen. 6 : 12) as in hash-hatat zera: "For all flesh has corrupted itself upon the land" [hish-hit kol basar et darko al ha-aretz], which literally reads "destroyed its way on the ground."[9] The Zohar (see on) sees this sin as the "last straw" in a series of evil deeds committed by that Generation; they had corrupted themselves in many ways, but this sin made their liquidation inevitable.[10] Theoretical problems stand in the way of this exegesis, too.[11] Indeed, one Responsa writer, in connection with this and other exegetical attempts, notes that hash-hatat zera is not included in the authoritative lists of (613) mitzvot (positive and negative commandments) of the Torah.[12]

(3) Of course, the most obvious biblical background for the sin of improper emission of seed would be the narrative of "the act of [Er and] Onan" in Gen. 38 (treated separately, Ch. 8).[13] While the word "onanism" has entered the dictionary through the church's interpretation of this scriptural passage, it plays a far less decisive role in Jewish exegesis (see on). It is indeed the basis for the strongly worded teaching of R. Yohanan: "Whoever emits semen in vain is deserving of death; as it is written: '[What Onan did] displeased the Lord, and He slew him.'"[14] The Zohar will have more to say on this; some writers of ethical tracts combine this exegesis with that of the Flood narrative—since again the same verb root [shi-het] is used in connec-

---

[8] "Ein lokin mi-d'rashah"—Mai., Mishnah Comm., loc. cit.; Emden, in Mitpahat S'farim (see on, Note 65) also points out that the inclusion of another meaning such as this into the biblical negative command can only have rabbinic legal status.

[9] Sanhedrin 108b, Rosh HaShanah 12a; Rashi to Niddah 13a, 43a and Shabbat 41a, all s.v. k'ilu; Ramban in Hiddushei Rashba to Niddah, Ch. 2; Hiddushei Ran and Hiddushei Ritva also to Niddah, Ch. 2. Also, L'vush, 23, 1.; Magen Avraham to Sh. Ar., O.H. 3, Par. 14.

[10] Zohar, Gen. p. 56b, 57a. Cf. also Azulai in Petah Einayim to Niddah, Ch. 2.

[11] This would be "punishment" without previous "warning," says Mishneh L'Melekh (Note 23 below). Arukh L'Ner, loc. cit., agrees, then offers: lo tohu b'ra'ah, lashevet y'tzarah—if not la-shevet, then back to tohu.

[12] Resp. Minhat Y'hiel, Vol. II, No. 22. He nevertheless ascribes biblical status to it, under No. 4 below. Also, he apparently overlooked the fact that Sefer Mitzvot Katan (Note 2 above) does list it as Negative No. 292, although derived from lo tin'af.

[13] Maggid Mishneh to Yad, Issurei Biah 21; Pri M'gadim (Eshel Avraham) to Sh. Ar., O.H. 3, Par. 14; Ben Yohai (see Note 66).

[14] TB Niddah 13a. The sin is "onanism," not contraception as supposed by, e.g., Noonan, Contraception . . . , p. 10.

tion with Onan—to strengthen their case against the practice.[15] But, since the nature of Onan's sin, as we shall see, is complicated by the context (levirate law, corrupt intent, etc.), and since the "emission of semen," there, is only an element of that larger context, biblical-law status could not yet be granted to the prohibition itself.[16] Other situations are just not analogous. Hence, the Talmudic language here that the guilty one "is deserving of death" is homiletic only and certainly cannot, we are reminded in an early Responsum, be taken literally; the Rabbis used the same hyperbole elsewhere.[17] A work written by R. Moses Trani (d. 1580), whose express purpose it was to determine which of the commandments are biblical and which rabbinic, remains in doubt about the status of hash-hatat zera even after discussing the Onan passage.[18] So that while the adultery injunction was termed a mere "peg," the Onan narrative is called a *remez*, a "hint" or intimation of a prohibition.[19] An eighteenth-century moralist, perhaps finding it strange that what is taken as so severe a sin is not explicitly proscribed by Scripture, advances the curious notion that the absence of explicit reference is *because* of the severity:

> Since this evil is so great and since many do yield to the temptation, the Torah therefore did not forbid it explicitly in keeping with [the Talmudic principle] "better that they sin unwittingly rather than knowingly." But yet the Torah let us know through a narrative, such as that of Er and Onan, that the practice is evil.[20]

(4) Another possible scriptural basis for the sin of hash-hatat zera has its share of support and objection, but it opens the door to more serious theoretical problems. According to this exegesis, the sin is actually implied in the commandment to "be fruitful and multiply."[21] Since "destruction of

[15] *Sha'arei T'shuvah l'Rabbenu Yonah*, No. 113; Bahya, *Commentary to the Bible*, Gen. 38.

[16] Maimonides omits the dictum of R. Yohanan from his treatment of the subject in his Law Code (*Issurei Biah*, 21). So does *Shulhan Arukh, E.H.* 23. *Resp. Shmat'ta D'RaVA*, Vol. II, p. 16 suggests that the reason for this omission is that, according to these authorities, Onan is still a "Noahide." (See Nahmanides to Lev. 24:10.) See also *Resp. Dovev Meisharim, loc. cit.*

[17] *Resp. Pnei Y'hoshua, loc. cit.* The question submitted to him concerned the medical necessity of emitting semen to save the man's life from disease. See on, Note 128.

[18] *Kiryat Sefer*, to *Yad, Issurei Biah*, 21. (He repeats "*efshar*" twice. *Resp. Minhat Y'hiel, loc., cit.*, says of him *harei she-gam hu mistappek bazeh.*)

[19] Emden (Note 65 below: *lo nizkar batorah b'ferush, rak b'remez*); *Resp. M'shivat Nefesh*, No. 18, states explicitly that the Onan narrative is only a *remez;* and *Resp. Torat Hesed*, Vol. II, No. 43:2, holds that such is the view of Nahmanides and of *Mishneh L'Melekh* (Note 23 below).

[20] R. Pinhas Elias in *Sefer HaB'rit*, Part I, Ch. 16:3.

[21] *Tosafot, Sanhedrin* 59b, *s.v. v'ha; Mishnat R. Eliezer*, Ch. 18, p. 338; also, Yemenite Midrash Fragment. (See Al-Nakawa's *Menorat HaManor*, ed. Enelow, IV, 63.)

seed" is the obverse of p'ru ur'vu, the practice would constructively constitute a violation or a negation of the biblical command of fruitfulness.[22] The implications of this line of reasoning, however, make it unsatisfactory,[23] if not unacceptable,[24] to others; most important: if this sin is implied in "be fruitful," then one who has already fulfilled or cannot fulfill the positive commandment of procreation should be allowed to engage in "destruction of seed."[25] This cannot be, say the earlier commentators.[26] "Heaven forbid that this should be so," says R. Jacob Ettlinger of nineteenth-century Altona, "for then the sterile or impotent or one who has fulfilled p'ru ur'vu would be permitted this vice!" "Rather," says he, "the prohibition is independent of the commandment of fruitfulness." Whence, then, the prohibition, according to R. Ettlinger? There is, he concludes, "no explicit biblical source" at all for "this great sin" except perhaps *bal tash-hit*, the general prohibition (Deut. 20 : 19) against destructiveness. Or, more probably, he suggests, there is nontextual biblical warrant [*halakhah l'mosheh mi-sinai*] for it; it is "a law transmitted directly to Moses" without being written.[27]

(5) Still another attempt at locating a scriptural base for the sin is all but entirely overlooked, perhaps because it is not found in Talmudic literature. The Bible Commentary of Abraham Ibn Ezra (d. 1167) cites an unidentified R. Aaron HaKohen, according to whom the injunction of Leviticus (18 : 6) against incest (*ish ish el kol sh'er b'saro*) — literally, immorality "with one's own flesh" — includes hash-hatat zera.[28] Ibn Ezra relays his words without prejudice, but the Responsa writer who calls our attention thereto discounts this interpretation. First, the meaning of the verse is plain, as Ibn Ezra himself expounded it. Second,

---

[22] Suggesting, on this basis, after *Tosafot, loc., cit.*, that the sin is biblical rather than rabbinic, are: R. Hayyim Pallagi in his *Tokhahat Hayyim*, Vol. II, Ch. 12, p. 156 (to which he calls attention in *Resp. Hayyim V'Shalom*, Vol. II, No. 18); *Resp. Minhat Y'hiel, loc. cit.*

[23] The matter is discussed at length in *Mishneh L'Melekh* commentary to Maimonides' *Yad, Hil'khot M'lakhim* 10:7. This commentary itself is the subject of further discussion: *Resp. Im'rei Esh*, Y.D. No. 69, understands *Mishneh L'Melekh* to hold that Nahmanides (see on) accepts the biblical basis but surmounts the problem (see Notes 16 and 25); but *Resp. Torat Hesed, ibid.*, 43:3, draws the lines with *Tosafot* on one side (biblical authority) and Nahmanides on the other (rabbinic).

[24] *Resp. M'shivat Nefesh, loc. cit.; Resp. Pnei Y'hoshua, loc. cit.;* and see Notes 26, 27.

[25] This conclusion is indeed assumed in the question of the sin's applicability to women, who are technically not answerable to p'ru ur'vu. See above, Ch. 3, and below, this Chapter.

[26] So *Tos'fei HaRosh* to *Niddah* 13a; *Ramban* in *Hiddushei RaN* to *Niddah*, Ch. 2.

[27] *Resp. Binyan Tziyyon*, No. 137; see also his *Arukh L'Ner* to *Niddah* 13b.

[28] *Perush Avraham Ibn Ezra*, Lev. 18:6.

We, after all, rely on Maimonides, from whose pure lips the clear utterance has gone forth, that [this sin] is not an explicit biblical negative . . . and not as R. Aaron HaKohen [would have it].[29]

(6) Other scriptural sources remain to be mentioned but, although derived by the Talmud, they are not based on the Pentateuch itself and are therefore not called *d'oraita;* they lack the imperative force of a Pentateuchal command: "Ye that inflame yourselves among the terebinths . . . that slay the children"—Isaiah's (57 : 5) denunciation of idolatrous child sacrifice—yields, by Midrashic exegesis, the message that self-pollution slays unborn children.[30] Isaiah's condemnatory words elsewhere (in 1 : 15), "Your hands are full of blood," are likewise taken to suggest the idea of murder.[31] That phrase became part of the legal language of the Codes, further to underscore the gravity of hash-hatat zera.[32]

With or without literal biblical sanctions, the sin, in the rabbinic view, is serious enough. He who destroys his generative seed commits murder (see on), acts like a beast which takes no heed what it does,[33] cannot receive the *Sh'khinah* [Presence of God],[34] stands "under the ban,"[35] and is guilty of autoerotic indecency.[36]

Sources: The Mystic Tradition

But it was the Mystic tradition in Judaism, chiefly through its principal textbook, the Zohar, which crystallized and reinforced the sense of horror at hash-hatat zera and exerted profound influence on the populace and legal authorities alike. The very language of the Zohar—its awesome phrase that declared the vice to be "a sin more serious than all the sins of the Torah"

---

[29] *Resp. Shevet M'nasheh,* No. 102. This Respondent is also alone in citing another overlooked reference, the *Piskei Tosafot* to *Z'vahim,* No. 54, where *m'na'afim b'yad* is listed in a lesser category, as opposed to *gufei averah,* for which *big'dei k'hunah m'khapp'rim.* The *Tosafot* itself on which it is based is probably from the *Tos'fot Sens* collection, since it does not appear in our Talmud editions, where *Tos'fot Tukh* are printed.

[30] "*Ha-nehamim be-eilim shoh'tei y'ladim*": *al tikrei shoh-tei* (slay) *ela soh'tei* (press out)— *TB Niddah* 13a, and *Kallah Rabbati,* Ch. 2; *Sha'arei T'shuvah L'Rabbenu Yonah,* No. 113.

[31] R. Elazar in *TB Niddah* 13b.

[32] E.g., Maimonides, *Yad, Issurei Biah* 21, 18; *Shulhan Arukh, E.H.,* 23, 2.

[33] *TB Massekhet Kallah; Kallah Rabbati,* Ch. 2; *Midrash HaGadol* to Gen. p. 645.

[34] *TB Niddah* 13b, and Zohar, below.

[35] *Niddah, ibid.* This, to the author of *Resp. Pnei Y'hoshua,* above, proves that the source is not biblical, else a special rabbinic ban (akin to excommunication) would not be necessary.

[36] *Ibid.; Kallah; Kallah Rabbati, loc. cit.*

—was incorporated into the authoritative Law Code[37] and was not to be ignored.[38] Hence, the situation whereby, in so many Responsa on the subject of birth control, when the Rabbi was about to be permissive, he hesitated, with words to this effect: "I should like to allow this contraceptive measure but, since the Zohar and the Talmud speak in such grave terms about the evil of hash-hatat zera, I cannot permit it; unless, etc."

The story of the Flood is one occasion for the Zohar to express itself on this subject, but its primary opportunity for expatiating on the enormity of the sin comes in its interpretation of the story of Er and Onan. After pointing up the importance of marriage as fulfillment of the divine intent for man and chastising him who would avoid this fulfillment, the Zohar roundly excoriates one who would cast his seed on the ground. This is the sin whereby "one pollutes himself more so than through any other sin in this world or the next."[39] And, in interpreting a later verse in Genesis, that of the approach of Jacob's death, the Zohar describes the welcome in the next world awaiting him who "destroys his seed." For, such a man is guilty not only of murder but of the murder of his own children and therefore stands condemned as a criminal more reprehensible than any other.[40]

Much of later mystic literature on the subject is a creative reaction to a disputed point in the above-quoted Zohar passage. The Zohar affirmed that even penitence will not avail him who is guilty of the sin of hash-hatat zera. Although elsewhere[41] the Zohar does allow that "complete" penitence, coupled with immersion in Torah study, will help in such a case, the declaration here that repentance is not enough contradicts the hallowed Jewish doctrine that "Nothing stands in the way of sincere penitence."[42] The contradiction gave the classic medieval Kabbalists an opportunity to explain. The sin involved here is different from all others, a chain of these mystic

---

[37] *Shulhan Arukh*, E.H. 23. See also *Beit Yosef* to *Tur*, O.H. 3 and E.H. 23 and his *Bedek HaBayit* to *Tur*, E.H. 25.

[38] But "more serious than" is an untenable legal judgment. See *Beit Shmuel* on the incident reported by *Sefer Hasidim*, No. 176, where a choice had to be made, as cited also in *Helkat M'hokek* to E.H. 23. See also *Atzei Arazim, ad loc.*, Par. 1. *Resp. Maharsham*, Vol. I, No. 48 quotes *Noam M'gadim, Vayiggash*, who rejects Zohar's "hierarchy" of sins on the basis of *Kiddushin* 13a, "*Kashin [arayot] yoter mi-dor ha-mabul.*"

[39] Zohar, *Vayeshev*, p. 188a.

[40] *Ibid.*, *Vay'hi*, p. 219b. Cf. the words of Calvin, Ch. 8, below.

[41] Zohar, *Ruth*, 12; See *Resp. Maharsham* Vol. I, No. 58. Also Zohar, *Vayak-hel;* see *Sh'nei Luhot HaB'rit* (Note 43, below).

[42] The rule is cited in Maimonides' Code, *Hilkhot T'shuvah*, Ch. 3:14. Its Talmudic source is *TP Peah* 1:1.

writers tell us, in that penitence is not so easy.[43] For, penitence requires a compensating good deed with that same part of the body that had sinned. He who sinned with the hands, by stealing, ought to make good by giving charity; he who slandered, by saying a kind word. But destruction of seed involves more than one organ: The seed begins to form in the brain, travels through the spinal cord and, when released, represents the whole person. Effective repentance, therefore, requires a compensating act of much more than the usual; it requires an extraordinary effort of the whole person.[44]

That human generative seed represents the whole person was less important to some than that it "begins forming in the brain," the source of "thought and wisdom."[45] R. Joshua Ibn Shu'aib, an early fourteenth-century preacher, was not speaking as a mystic when he wrote:

> This drop [of sperm] comes from a holy place, the abode of the soul, the brain . . . Therefore we are forbidden to destroy seed, because to do so is verily to commit an act of destruction, of stunting.[46]

And, just as energetic penitence corrects the abuse of the "whole person," so the "mental" offense can be offset by immersion in Torah study, as the above writers provide. One treatise on an aspect of Torah law conveys this idea in its Preface: the rigorous study of the contents of this book, says the author, is a good specific against the sin of improper emission which offends against the brain![47] Nor should the significant fact be overlooked that the practice is often referred to as *pogem ba-b'rit* or *pogem biv'rit kodesh*, sinning against the Covenant of circumcision.[48] Perhaps, too, the linguistic fact that offspring are called "seed" in biblical and rabbinic Hebrew ("Thou and thy seed after thee," "we are the seed of Abraham"[49]) helped to heighten the awareness of the sanctity or fatefulness of seminal emission and deepened

[43] R. Moses Cordovero in *Eilima Rabbata;* R. Elijah de Vidas in *Reshit Hokhmah, Sha'ar Hak'dushah*, Ch. 17; R. Abraham Halevi Hurwitz in *Emek B'rakhah*, sec. *shabbat shuvah;* and especially R. Isaiah Hurvitz in *Sh'nei Luhot HaB'rit, Otiyot*, pp. 88 ff. Also *Resp. Beit Ya'akov* (17th cent.), No. 122; *Tokhahat Hayyim, loc. cit.*

[44] See also *Appei Zutrei*, Comm. to *E.H.* 23, Par. 6.

[45] R. Mosheh Prager, *Zera Kodesh* (1796), p. 20.

[46] *D'rashot al HaTorah*, p. 48d. He goes on to make a distinction between sperm and semen. The reason why ritual immersion is required after seminal discharge (Lev. 15:16–18) is because, although sperm has potential life, the remaining "husk" of the semen contaminates the body like other discharges.

[47] R. Abraham Bornstein, *Eg'lei Tal* (1905), Preface. He goes on to quote the Zohar on *ba'avodah kashah—zo kushia; b'homer—kal vahomer; uvil'venim—libbun halakhah*, etc. in further exposition of the idea that vigorous mental activity is an antidote or preventive.

[48] Cf. works cited in Notes 43, 45.

[49] See *Areshet Sefatenu*, II, 273–76 for many references in Bible, Talmud, and liturgy.

the moral sensitivity to impropriety or abuse.[50] Significant, also, is the fact that one looks in vain for any reference in all this literature to the familiar notion that impotence or insanity are consequences of self-pollution. It is seen here as a primarily spiritual misdemeanor.[51]

Even an involuntary (e.g., nocturnal) emission of seed is a serious matter from this standpoint. The Talmud had cautioned against lewd "thoughts during the day" which might lead to seminal "emission during the night."[52] Actions or situations, too, which could bring about such emission are to be carefully avoided.[53] But lewd thoughts or excitational situations aside, the emission itself is regarded in the Talmud as a natural function, of acknowledged necessity, and even a "good sign" in time of illness.[54] But the mystic tradition viewed the involuntary occurrence far more gravely than did the Talmud. Ancient legends persisted, according to which demons or evil spirits were created from the sperm of, say, Adam during his long separation from Eve.[55] Such demons, as in the incubus and succubus notions of world literature,[56] are "impregnated" by one's sperm emitted during sleep and give birth to more demons and spirits.[57] Myths of this sort pervaded the folk literature, as is reflected in fictional accounts—such as those of I.B. Singer—describing this dark demimonde.[58] They added a harsh vivid-

---

[50] On the other hand, the Mishnah (*Avot* 3, 1), in seeking to teach a moral lesson, says "Remember three things, so that you come not to sin [for lack of humility]: where you came from, etc. [You came from] a putrefying drop, etc." In other instances, too, the Talmud refers to the prefoetal child as the "drop" [*tippah*].

[51] Personal exile ["*ger yihyeh zar'akha*"], poverty, etc. are held out as punishment in the classic works. A small tract was published at the beginning of this century (Jerusalem, 1909) called *HaZera L'Minehu* (by H.L. Zuta) addressed to young men. In the tradition of the weightier works before it, but with a decidedly naturalistic bent, the tract preaches the sanctity of seed as the potential of life and pleads that it therefore be spared abuse.

[52] *TB K'tubot* 46a, *Avodah Zarah* 20b.

[53] *TB Niddah* 13a ("*ohez b'amah*," etc.). (On the spelling *b'amah* instead of *b'ammah*, see Glosses of Emden to *Niddah, ad. loc.*)

[54] *TB B'rakhot* 57b. Also, surprisingly, as a sign of grace: "He who experiences an involuntary emission on Yom Kippur—[may regard it as a sign that] his sins are [to be] forgiven"!—*TB Yoma* 88a (end). And its inevitability is realistically assumed: "Is, then, everyone like Father Jacob . . . [of whom it is said that he] had not previously experienced seminal emission [before the conception of Reuben, 'the first-fruit of my vigor,' Gen. 49:3]) ?"—*TB Y'vamot* 76a.

[55] *Gen. Rabbah* 20, 28; 24, 6. *TB Eiruvin* 18b; Rashi to Samuel 7, 14 ("*nig'ei b'nei adam*").

[56] See, e.g., W. E. H. Lecky, *History of the Rise and Influence of the Spirit of Rationalism in Europe* (New York 1884), I, 48–49.

[57] Zohar, Gen., 19b; 54b. Cf. *Resp. Maharam Lublin*, No. 116, cited by *Ba'er Hetev* to *E.H.* 6, Par. 13.

[58] The narrator in *Gimpel the Fool* declaims: "I was not born. My father sinned as did Onan, and from his seed I was created—half-spirit, half-demon." As for nonfiction, see also *Appei Zutrei*, Comm. to *E.H.* 23. Alternatively: an ancient legend recorded in *Midrash Talpiyyot* (ed. Izmir 1736, *s.v. anaf yosef*, p. 144) has it that the Ten Martyrs met their deaths as a result of Joseph's improperly emitted semen. See also *Likkutei Torah* of *ARI*, to Noah; Azulai, in *Petah Einayim* to *Niddah* Ch. 2; *Resp. T'shurat Shai*, 2nd Recension, No. 62.

ness to the more rarefied concept that exposed semen somehow contaminates the environment and offends against the holiness that should obtain.[59]

The foregoing notions, together with the more normative consciousness that eroticism and sexual passion, inadequately mastered, were involved in the emission, gave rise to the intense anxiety felt among the pious with regard to involuntary seminal discharge. Full-length books were composed, in fact, that prescribed "*tikkunim*," spiritual exercises and procedures in prevention of, or for purification from, such "occurrences."[60] An extract from this literature, from a seventeenth-century treatise on how to "correct" the spiritual damage of hash-hatat zera, found its way into the "*Kitzur Shulhan Arukh*," the household manual of selections from the Code of Jewish Law.[61] The founder of the Hasidic Movement, R. Israel Baal Shem Tov (d. 1760), sought to relieve the people's anxiety in this matter or to cast it, as it were, in a more high-minded perspective. Many *mitzvot* abound, he taught, by which a man may increase holiness; he ought not trouble himself with anxieties over the involuntary reflexes of the body:

> Let not a man concern himself—if he brought about a seminal emission unwillingly—about the emission itself, but about the impure thought that caused it.[62]

Other Hasidic teachers, however, reminded their followers that neither the effect nor the cause should be viewed with an easy conscience.[63]

The mystic tradition seems to have far outdistanced the Talmudic in its horror of hash-hatat zera—and R. Jacob Emden said so. The Zohar had made its appearance for the first time in the thirteenth century, representing itself as the work of the second-century Tanna, R. Simon ben Yohai.[64] Emden wrote an exhaustive critique of this work, advancing numerous arguments to disprove its antiquity and authority, either on intrinsic grounds

---

[59] *Ibid.*, and Zohar, Gen., 56b.

[60] Such "*Tikkunim*" are found in *Sh'nei Luhot HaB'rit, loc. cit.*; in *Mishnat Hasidim* (in the name of ARI), Sec. *T'shuvah*, Ch. 9 : 11; *Ginzei Hayyim*, Sec. *Kuntres T'shuvah*, 13; *Taharat Yom Tov*, by Yom Tov Deutsch; *Zera Kodesh* of R. Mosheh Prager; *Appei Zutrei, loc. cit.*, and *Tokhahat Hayyim, loc. cit.*

[61] *Y'sod Yosef* of R. Yosef Darshan (1679), cited in *Kitzur Shulhan Arukh* 151, 6.

[62] *Shiv'hei HaBesht*, 57; *Or Torah* of R. Ber of Mezrich, Sec. *Re'eh*, both quoted by A. J. Heschel in "R. Nahman of Kossov, A Friend of the Baal Shem Tov," *Wolfson Jubilee Volume* (Jerusalem: American Academy for Jewish Research, 1965), Hebrew Section, p. 139.

[63] R. Nahman of Bratslav: and R. Eliezer Hurvitz in *Noam M'gadim* to *M'tzora* 71a; cited by Heschel in footnote to *ibid.*

[64] For an account of the story of Zohar's authorship, see Meyer Waxman, *A History of Jewish Literature* (sec. ed.; New York, 1943) II, 392–402; and above, Ch. 1.

or because it is inconsistent with the Talmud. Among these points of argument is his contention that hash-hatat zera, "which is mentioned in the Torah only by *remez*," while grave, is not painted in such terrifying hues in the Talmud as it is in the Zohar. He refers to the matter of repentance, discussed above, and concludes, "Therefore I say one ought certainly not pay attention to these exaggerations."[65]

A lesser known figure, R. Moses Konitz, took upon himself the task of responding to each of Emden's charges, in a book called *Ben Yohai*. His response to this point adds the specious proof that "none of the wise men of Israel opened his mouth to protest" when the author of the *Shulhan Arukh* cited the Zohar to the effect that this sin is "more serious than all the sins of the Torah." That's because, he says, they know that the Zohar and Talmud concur.[66] On the other hand, R. David Pipano of Sophia, at the beginning of our century, quotes Emden at length in his Commentary to the *Shulhan Arukh* and endorses him fully in his quarrel with the Zohar.[67]

Nature of the Offense: "Murder" or "Immorality"?

The Zohar and its literary descendants did much more than add shrillness to the condemnation; as we have seen, they sharpened the perspective as well: at least two separate aspects of the sin are discernible in the above passage. One is "homicide" [*ihu katil b'nohi*, "he kills his own children"], and the other is "self-defilement" [*d'ista'ev bei bar nash*, "through which a man defiles himself"]. The first has a parallel in the history of the church's doctrine on contraception, expressed in the *Decretals*, the collection of authoritative decrees begun under Pope Gregory IX in 1230 and serving as official church law until 1915. Concerning the participant in contraceptive acts, the precept reads, "let him be held a homicide."[68] A seventeenth-century Jesuit moralist even attributes the idea to Jewish teaching: In his *Commentary* to the Onan text in Genesis, Cornelius à Lapide writes, "This sin is compared by the Hebrews to homicide."[69] A Responsum later in that century by

[65] *Mitpahat S'farim*, I, 20.

[66] *Ben Yohai* (ed. Vienna, 1815), Reply No. 19.

[67] *Av'nei HaEfod* (Sophia, 1912), Comm. to *E.H.* 23 ("*hetev harah lo*"). So also, *Resp. Tzitz Eliezer*, Vol. IX, No. 51.

[68] Noonan, *op. cit.*, p. 178. See also *ibid.*, pp. 360–65, where contraception as homicide was the reigning doctrine in the 16th and 17th centuries. But J. Fletcher, in *Morals and Medicine* (Beacon, 1960), p. 89, regards the "killing little unborn babies" argument as more a popular form of objection than a technical one by moralists. He may be speaking of recent years.

[69] Noonan, *op. cit.*, p. 364, who concludes: "Talmudic tradition was thus invoked to support the canon law." The argument of homicide declined among moralists, Noonan says (p. 365), in the 18th century. While many earlier authorities had discussed contraception under "Thou Shalt Not Kill," Alphonsus Liguori (d. 1787) charted a new course.

R. Yair Bachrach momentarily entertains a related idea, in seeking to interpret hash-hatat zera: "From every drop, [living] holy seed could have been
born."[70] On the other hand, R. Jacob Emden, despite his reservations
about the Zohar and his fight against the abuses of "practical Kabbalah,"
writes: more important than the homicide interpretation is the fact that
this sin "adds to the forces of uncleanness in the world."[71] We learn this,
he says, "from the Kabbalists, whose teachings we need turn to in this matter."
Figuratively, the two facets were later termed that of the sixth and seventh
commandments, "murder" and "adultery,"[72] two of the three cardinal
sins which are to be avoided even at risk of martyrdom. But we had been
reminded concerning such characterizations that they not be taken literally,
for the Talmud calls slander "murder" as well (i.e., character "assassination")
also by hyperbole.[73]

Of the two sides of the coin, accordingly, the "self-defilement" aspect
is far more pronounced, almost to the exclusion of the other. The "murder"
side did have its day in court, but it usually served the cause of leniency.
Thus, when no viable foetus could in any case have been born from a relationship, this fact became relevant to the question of contraception.

In the matter, for example, of chronic miscarriages, where contraception
was requested in order to be spared this futile pain, many authorities reason
that since no viable child would in any case be born, one might permit an
otherwise forbidden contraceptive.[74] (An argument of the "*Rishonim*" versus
Rashi, discussed in Chapter 11, turns on this point of nonviable seed [*zera
she-eino molid*].) The question arose, too, in cases of impotence, where the
marital relations took the unintended form of coitus interruptus. Could the
relations legitimately continue under such circumstances? Some Respondents
added to the fact of unintended "onanism" (discussed below, Chapter 8),
their consideration that virile sperm was not anyway being destroyed, and
ruled permissively.[75]

The most poignant instance in this category comes from the Responsa
of the Kovno Ghetto during a relatively tolerable phase of Nazi occupation
(called *Responsa "Out of the Depths"*).[76] The concentration camp overseers
had forbidden pregnancy on penalty of death. The Rabbi, to whom the

[70] *Resp. Havvot Ya'ir*, No. 31.

[71] *Resp. Sh'elat Ya'avetz*, No. 43.

[72] *Resp. Tzofnat Pa'ane'ah*, No. 30, and elsewhere.

[73] *Resp. Pnei Y'hoshua, loc. cit.*

[74] *Ohel Avraham*, No. 90 and elsewhere; *Resp. Z'kan Aharon*, Vol. I, No. 83, p. 82.

[75] *Resp. Im'rei Esh*, Y. D. No. 69; *Resp. P'ri HaSadeh*, Vol. I, No. 77. See also *Resp. Minhat
Pittim*, No. 25 and *Resp. Alehu Ra'anan*, No. 21. See Ch. 8.

[76] *Resp. Mima'amakim*, Vol. I, No. 18.

problem was addressed, permitted contraception which, even if not other-wise permissible, would be justified on the grounds that no viable child—or mother!—could "survive" a noncontracepted relationship.

A slightly different turn was taken by the "homicide" aspect of our question in the eighteenth century, after spermatozoa were first seen through the microscope by Anthony van Leeuwenhoek of Holland (1677). Conclud-ing that each sperm cell is a rudimentary embryo, one of his disciples had sent a drawing to the Royal Society of London. The drawing depicted, he said, what he had seen through his microscope—a tiny but complete human figure, a "homunculus." [77] In Jewish sources, this new development is reflected matter-of-factly by our prolific R. Jacob Emden in his treatise on certain anatomic questions. [78] But a note of polemical triumph is discern-ible in the words, some years later, of *Sefer Ha'Brit*, where the author writes:

> Now it has been seen through the viewing instrument that magnifies, which is called a microscope, that a drop of man's sperm, while yet in its original temperature, contains small creatures in man's image and likeness. They live and move to and fro within the sperm. Now you can understand how right the Sages [of the Talmud] were and how all their words are true and just, even in matters hard to know or imagine. You will also understand why the Zohar found this evil to be so severe, . . . and why repentance is so difficult, etc. How strange the Talmudic idea that hash-hatat zera is "like murder" seemed to the "philosophizers" among us before the microscope was invented. They thought that destroying seed is like destroying wood which has not yet been made into a chair, not knowing that seed is potentially the "chair" itself, the end product in miniature. [79]

The writer of a later Responsum was not impressed:

> This [kind of argument] is not supported by reason or nature. A child is born from the seed of father and mother together. [80]

More comprehensive in scope is the compactly written Responsum of R. Joseph Hayyim ben Eliyahu of late nineteenth-century Turkey, on

---

[77] See Laurence Sterne's *Tristram Shandy, passim.*

[78] *Iggeret Bikkoret* ([1736)]; Zhitomir, 1867), p. 25b. This did not affect his Responsa published 1739, referred to in Notes 71 above and 134 below.

[79] *Sefer HaB'rit* (1797), Part I, Ch. 16:3;, Jerusalem ed., 1960, pp. 151–52.

[80] *Resp. Shevet M'nasheh* (Berlin, 1896), No. 102.

whether one with a physical impediment to impregnation could therefore indulge in hash-hatat zera.[81] The Rabbi sought to seal the homicide versus pollution argument from both sides. The "microscope will show," he wrote, the miniature form of a man in the sperm; to cast this [albeit imperfect] man to the ground is like willfully killing a doomed [and therefore not viable] man, which, too, is forbidden.[82] Hence, "murder" is indeed involved. But, he continues, there is more: if murder alone were involved, then intercourse with sterile, barren, or pregnant wives would have been forbidden on grounds of fruitlessness. The prohibition, one must conclude, is independent, for the biblical narrative of the Generation of the Flood relates that "all flesh had corrupted itself." Now, among that "all flesh" were surely many who were impotent or sterile, yet they too presumably were punished! Evidently, the sin is not murder but something else. Of that something else, the author offers a neat and original definition:

> Hash-hatat zera is not incurred because the seed goes to waste, but because it is cast where it should not have been cast according to the Creator's decree [which is] in the female of his species . . . even if she is barren.

The definition is original in formulation, that is, for Jewish sources,[83] but it has a striking parallel in Catholic teaching. The section on contraception in the work of the leading moral theologian of the early sixteenth century (Cardinal Cajetan, d. 1534) was entitled, "The Sin of Matrimony in Regard to the Vessel," which he defines as "semination outside the natural vessel."[84] And, a century earlier, the celebrated academician, Martin LeMaistre (d. 1481) had written, in connection with such improper emission, in his *Moral Questions:* Suppose the seed were "not fit for generation." The evil of autoeroticism, he answered, remains.[85]

The autoerotic factor is a discernible element in the complex of hash-hatat zera, alongside the other interwoven strands.[86] Even when isolated one from the other for separate consideration, the strands remain elusive of definitive characterization. From the standpoint of Jewish tradition they, taken together, constitute a moral offense which, analyze it as one will,

---

[81] *Resp. Rav P'alim*, Vol. III (1898), *E.H.*, No. 2.

[82] "*Ha-horeg et ha-t'refah*," *TB Sanhedrin* 78a; Mai., *Hilkhot Rotzeah* 2, 7.

[83] Cf. *Resp. Yaskil Avdi*, Vol. II, No. 6 ("*hishbiah ha-ta'anah*").

[84] *Summula Peccatorum*, cited by Noonan, *op. cit.* pp. 312, 366.

[85] *Moral Questions*, II, fol. 54r, cited by Noonan, p. 368.

[86] See Maimonides, *Yad, Sh'ar Avot HaTum'ot*, 5, 4.

remains repugnant in itself. On the other hand, heterosexual relations, even when admittedly nonprocreative, are not at all subject to the strictures of hash-hatat zera, for, though a child cannot be conceived, no "murder" is said to take place, nor is a contribution made to the forces of evil;[87] on the contrary, the mystics tell us, something is contributed to the forces of good.[88] One mystically oriented author of Responsa addressed himself, with rhetorical challenge, to those who would speak of contraception in terms of constructive homicide: "In the case of relations with a sterile woman, which you permit, where did your apprehensions [of murder] run away to?"[89] In fact, if strict logic were to be pursued, abstinence from sexual relations or postponed marriage or celibacy could also be considered "murder." Just as the Talmud declares that he who *destroys* his seed is "as if he shed blood," we are also told there that "he who does *not engage* in procreation is as if he shed blood,"[90] although no act of destruction took place. The latter is passive, says the late Chief Rabbi Isaac Herzog in a volume of Responsa just published (1967), while the former "contaminates the soul."[91]

Hash-hatat Zera and the Woman

Additional light is shed upon the matter of definition when the status of the woman in this legal system is considered. The applicability to her of the positive command of procreation was explored (above, Ch. 3). Yet, the question remains: is she included in those to whom the negative of hash-hatat zera applies?

No, answers Rabbenu Tam and, in his famous ruling in *Tosafot*,[92] permits the woman to employ an otherwise objectionable contraceptive device. Since she is not answerable to p'ru ur'vu, neither is she included in the prohibition of hash-hatat zera.

But whereas Rabbenu Tam assumes her destruction of her husband's seed, the other Commentators to the relevant Talmudic passage apparently have in mind the question of her "destruction" of *her own* seed.[93] Indeed, the existence of "female seed" is presupposed by some authorities, as it was

[87] *Zohar, Emor*, 90a; *Ya'vetz, ARI*, and *T'shurat Shai*, all *loc. cit.*

[88] See *Sh'nei Luhot HaB'rit, Sha'ar HaOtiyot*, p. 102b. See also Glosses of Ovadiah Hadayah to *Simhat Kohen*, p. 82, and the latter's *Resp. Yaskil Avdi, loc. cit.;* and see Ch. 4.

[89] R. S. Y. Tabak, in *Resp. T'shurat Shai, loc. cit.* He goes on to interpret even the "homicide" idea in terms of "uncleanness."

[90] *TB Y'vamot* 63b. See *Y'feh Toar* to Gen. Rabbah, 34, 20.

[91] *Resp. Heikhal Yitzhak*, Vol. II, No: 16.

[92] To *Y'vamot* 12b (and to *K'tuvot* 39a, both) *s.v. shalosh.*

[93] *Ramban, RaN*, and *Ritva*, as well as *Azulai*, in their respective *Hiddushim* to *Niddah*, Ch. 2.

by ancient and medieval medical writers; an excursus on the subject follows this chapter. The question of hash-hatat zera in her case refers, on this assumption, to some kind of impropriety in connection with her own "seed," not —contra Rabbenu Tam—to the destruction or frustration of the effectiveness of her husband's seed.[94]

The element, then, of possible autoeroticism is present here, quite aside from that of contraception. The passage in the Talmud which sets off the discussion is one which makes a distinction between men and women with regard to manual examination of the genital area. Women, for whom it is important to be aware of the exact time of the onset of ritual impurity of menses, are encouraged in such examination; while the opposite is true of men, to whom it can only be autoerotic.[95] One of three inferences is possible from this Talmudic ruling: either that the examination in her case does not involve possible hash-hatat zera because "seed" is not improperly emitted thereby;[96] that female semination does occur but it matters not because the prohibition does not apply to women, just as the command of p'ru ur'vu does not;[97] or, that the prohibition may apply to them even though the commandment does not.[98]

The two sides of the coin of hash-hatat zera, "pollution" and "contraception," are once again apparent. In Nahmanides' analysis,[99] a woman may indeed be permitted sterilization,[100] which is a function of p'ru ur'vu, while being forbidden hash-hatat zera, which is a function of erotic stimulation. The two are distinct factors; just as they are, he tells us, in the case of men. The distinction is made even sharper by Asheri,[101] who writes:

> Hash-hatat zera is involved only when one improperly emits seed, whether man or woman. But after it has been emitted, *hash-hatah* is not applicable—[to measures taken to frustrate its procreative power].[102]

[94] *Ramban, Ritva,* and *Rosh,* in *Shittah M'kubbetzet* to *K'tubot* 39a.

[95] *Mishnah* and *G'mara,* TB *Niddah* 13a.

[96] Because *nashim mazriot bifnim v'ish mazria mibahutz: Marginal Tosafot* and *Tos'fei HaRosh,* both to *Niddah* 13a.

[97] Because *lav b'not issur hargashah: Tosafot* to *Y'vamot, ibid.,* and R. Tam according to *Ramban* in *Hiddushei Rashba* and in *Hiddushei RaN, Niddah,* Ch. 2.

[98] *Ri,* in *Tosafot* to *K'tubot, ad loc., Ramban* in *Hiddushim, loc. cit.; Ritva* in *Hiddushim* to *Y'vamot* 12b. See also *Ma'adanei Yomtov* to *Rosh* on *Niddah,* Ch. 2, Par. 2.

[99] *Hiddushei Ramban,* cited both in *Hiddushei Rashba* and *Hiddushei RaN* to *Niddah,* Ch. 2. See also *Mishneh L'Melekh, M'lakhim* 10, 7, and *Resp. Imrei Esh, Y.D.* No. 69.

[100] See below, Ch. 13.

[101] *Tos'fot HaRosh* to *Y'vamot* 12b.

[102] See also *Resp. Torat Hesed,* Vol. II, 44:22.

The nineteenth-century author of an extensive Responsum also discerns two types of hash-hatat zera: one, the bringing forth of seed improperly, for man or woman, as a result of autoerotic stimulation; and, two, the actual destruction of the sperm's potency after emission.[103] In our own century, the famous *Hazon Ish*, R. Isaiah Karelitz, has affirmed the distinction between improper seminal stimulation by either sex and subsequent frustration of reproductive ends.[104]

With this distinction in mind, we are the better prepared to determine which aspect of the two, if either, is a violation for the woman. The erotic factor, while different in the two sexes, does play its part. This is evident from what is probably Talmudic literature's single source reference to female homosexuality. The Talmud calls this activity "delinquent," and the Codes forbid it on moral grounds.[105] The offense is of a lesser category but nonetheless serves the Responsa as support for the view that an autoerotic hash-hatat zera is forbidden to the woman.[106] Nahmanides, for his own part, having separated the interlocking factors, declares women to be included in the prohibition on these grounds, for even though p'ru ur'vu does not apply to them, the act itself is immoral.[107]

What about her destruction of *his* seed, now, after its due and proper insemination? This leaves us only with p'ru ur'vu, as was conceded by R. Hanokh Agus of Vilna in a recent Responsum:

> Hash-hatat zera is a prohibition entirely independent of p'ru ur'vu . . . It is determined by the manner of the seed's emission from the body. After it has been discharged and has entered the womb—then what the woman is or is not permitted to do depends upon the separate question of her duty of p'ru ur'vu.[108]

And, since p'ru ur'vu is generally taken as not binding upon her, is there any violation that her destruction of seed—after the sex act has been unimpeded—would incur? True, the rabbinic injunction of *la-shevet*, of contributing on

[103] R. Hayyim Sofer, in *Resp. Mahaneh Hayyim* (1868), No. 53.

[104] *Even HaEzer* 36:2, 3. See next Chapter.

[105] *TB Yvamot* 76a; see *Rashi, ad loc.*, and *Tosafot s.v. ha-m'sol'lot; Yad, Issurei Biah*, 21, 8; *Tur, Sh. Ar.* and especially *L'vush* to E.H. 20, 2.

[106] *Resp. Torat Hesed*, E.H., Vol. II, No. 49 : 19. He believes *hashhatat zera shelah* is worse than *zera ba'alah* and maintains that such is the view of *Rashba* and even of the *Shulhan Arukh* because of the latter's stricter view in previous note, above, compared with its more lenient ruling in Note 120 below.

[107] *Hiddushim, loc. cit.; Shittah M'kubbetzet, loc. cit.*

[108] *Sefer Marheshet* (1931), Vol. II, No. 9:2:3.

general principles to propagation, would still apply.[109] Or, in the words of another nineteenth-century Responsum, if she "destroys [his] seed" she betrays her charge as a wife.[110]

But our concern here is with whether hash-hatat zera is a *violation* for the woman, regardless of her husband's wishes or her own. Evidence from Talmudic law on this point is considered by the Responsa. They discuss, for example, the divorce provision with respect to the matter of vows— that imposing wrongful vows on a wife can be grounds for divorce. One such is obscurely worded in the Mishnah: "He had her vow that she would 'fill and empty. . . .' " [111] This may either mean (1) "fill and empty" pitchers of water —a nonsense task which a man has his wife undertake in order to demean her[112] —and she is entitled on that account to divorce and settlement; or, it may be (2) a euphemism for postcoital contraception,[113] in which case her right not to be required to do so is indicative. He may not require this of her for one of two reasons: (*a*) either on general principles, because she does not want to be deprived of children, or (*b*) because a technical violation of hash-hatat zera [of his seed] does obtain even though p'ru ur'vu does not.[114] The Codes, by the way, list both of the above versions of the meaning of the vow; [115] with regard to the two possible reasons for her entitlement to divorce on the latter version (2), the authorities and Responsa have taken sides.[116] They conclude, in the main, that a prohibition of postcoital contraception is not derivable from the fact that such a vow is out of order.[117]

[109] See Chapter 3, pp. 48, 54–56, and Chapter 13, pp. 241–42.

[110] *Resp. Hinnukh Beit Yitzhak*, E.H., No. 7. See also *Avnei Nezer*, etc., as quoted above, Ch. 3, p. 55–56.

[111] *Mishnah, K'tubot* VII, 5 (71b).

[112] *Ibid.*, 72a.

[113] *Ibid.*, Rashi. In *TP K'tubot* VII, 5: "There [in Babylonia] they interpret 'like the act of Er' [see *Korban HaEdah* and *Pnai Mosheh*]. But here [in Palestine] we interpret it in terms of demeaning or futile tasks."

[114] R. Isaac bar Sheshet, in *Shittah M'kubetzet* to *K'tubot*, 71.

[115] Maimonides, *Yad, Ishut* 14, 5 ("they are both true"— *Maggid Mishneh, ad loc.*); *Tur*, E.H. 76; and *RaMA* to *Sh. Ar.*, E.H. 76, 12.

[116] Rashi is silent here as to why he may not so require her. However, an earlier recension of Rashi's Talmud Commentary (*Mahadura Kamma*) is cited by *Shittah M'Kubetzet, loc. cit.*, which does offer a reason, but the one in terms of her wishes (*a*), rather than violation (*b*).

[117] *Beit Meir*, E.H., 23, concludes that a prohibition is derivable, as does *Resp. R. Akiva Eger*, No. 71. *Resp. Shoel U'Meshiv, loc. cit.*, inclines towards that conclusion. *Resp. Binyan Tziyyon*, No. 137, argues that since Rashi omitted the first reason (*a*) from the final recension of his Commentary (*Mahadura Batra*), the violation reason (*b*) is implicitly accepted by him. On the other hand, *Resp. Imrei Esh*, Y.D., No. 68, holds that it is the fact of the vow rather than its contents that is discountenanced by the Talmud. Similarly, in *Ohel Avraham*, the author of No. 90 sees the vow as an attempt to demean her; the author of No. 91 challenges him, points to *Yad* (above, Note 115) where this is listed separately from "*kalon*" vow; while No. 94 rejects this challenge and No. 99

Laws of ritual immersion and of bathing likewise relate to the question of hash-hatat zera and the woman. A Mishnah requires the kind of cleansing (as part of the purification process for special purposes), which would even destroy recently implanted seed.[118] A subsidiary provision would allow any woman to deliberately cleanse herself in this manner in order to begin the counting of "clean" days immediately.[119] This law is part of the *Shulhan Arukh*;[120] but how allow her to "destroy" seed for no reason? The seed that is thus removed, is the answer suggested, would not impregnate; although "three days" is generally assigned for the seed to be "absorbed," the seed that does impregnate usually is absorbed immediately.[121] For reasons such as this—and that the cleansing is too external—R. Akiva Eger, who holds the strict view that a woman is forbidden destruction of her husband's seed, finds no contradiction between his view and the provision of the *Shulhan Arukh*.[122] Others do find the latter to be proof that no violation obtains in the woman's case; furthermore, in an allusion to the "rhythm method" (see Chapter 13), the *Maharil*, a classic source of law and custom, specifies that such cleansing not be done even within three days if these coincide with the period of high fertility.[123] Through an authoritative annotator to the *Shulhan Arukh*, namely the *Magen Avraham*, *Maharil*'s provision also became part of that much more widely accepted standard Code.[124] This is generally taken to be an offer of "good advice" to her for the protection of the reproductive possibility, not at all evidence of a possible violation on her part.[125]

---

says that if *Beit Meir* is right, Rabbenu Tam's position could never be maintained. *Resp. Avnei Nezer*, E.H., No. 81, and *Resp. Zikhron Y'honatan*, E.H., No. 3, argue that the existence of two reasons for the objectionability of the vow makes it impossible to conclude that prohibition is to be inferred. Similarly, *Resp. Beit Av*, Vol. VII, No. 12:2; and *Resp. Helkat Ya'akov*, Vol. II, No. 12, find no prohibition to be inferrable. See Ch. 11.

[118] *Mishnah, Mikvaot*, 8, 4. See especially *Perush HaRosh* thereto. The special purposes are, e.g., the eating of consecrated foods such as *t'rumah* (*asukah b'tohorot*). See Maimonides, *Yad, Sh'ar Avot HaTum'ot* 5, 8.

[119] *Rosh* to *Niddah*, Ch. 4, beg. R. Akiva Eger, *Resp.* No. 71, calls *Rosh* "*mara d'hai dina*." This law actually derives from *Sefer HaT'rumah* (*Hilkhot Niddah*, No. 95), by the Tosafist R. Barukh of Worms. See also *Rashba, Torat HaBayit, Beit Zera, Sha'ar* 5.

[120] *Yoreh Deah*, 196, 13.

[121] R. Yonathan Eibeschutz, *Sefer K'reti Uf'leti, Hilkhot Niddah* 184, 17. The author of *Sidrei Taharah* raises objections to this answer.

[122] *Resp. R. Akiva Eger*, No. 72. See Ch. 8, p. 164, and Ch. 11, pp. 216 ff.

[123] *Sefer Maharil, Hil'khot Erev Yom Kippur*, p. 44a. *Sefer Maharil* is a compilation of the Rhineland communities' laws and customs on the authority of R. Jacob HaLevi Moellin (d. 1427) of Mainz. See S. Steiman, *Custom and Survival* (New York, 1963), and cf. p. 52 there.

[124] *Magen Avraham* to *Sh. Ar., O.H.* 606, 4. R. Akiva Eiger (*Resp.* No. 71); *Hatam Sofer*, Y.D. No. 172; and others who take issue with *Magen Avraham* were not aware, says *Resp. Torat Hesed*, Vol. II, 43 : 21, that the law derives from *Maharil*. See Ch. 13, Note 80 and Ch. 11, p. 217. Also see *B'er HaGolah* to *Sh. Ar. Y.D., loc. cit.*, on the "custom of women."

[125] See Chapter 11, p. 223.

According to the preponderance of legal analysis and opinion (here and in Chapter 11), hash-hatat zera, then, is not forbidden to the woman in terms of a violation as such—after, that is, semination took place properly. Whatever inhibition does obtain is because ultimately reproduction is affected. She can be said to have almost as much choice, according to this view, in determining whether the process should continue at that point as she might have had before the coition took place.

The Broader Definition

Another dimension of hash-hatat zera remains to be considered. Part of one of its synonymous phrases is the word *l'vattalah* [in vain], which does suggest that the impropriety of the emission is judged by whether or not seed is "brought forth in vain." Many practical and theoretical questions are determined on the strength of this phrase. Procuring the husband's seed for the purposes of artificial insemination, for example, would be declared proper if this is now its only way of effecting procreation; hence, it is not "brought forth in vain." [126] Extrusion of sperm for medical reasons (to save one's life or health) would also not be "in vain"; [127] nor would it for sterility tests. [128] Still, the manner of its procurement is restricted to one which is relatively indirect. The Talmudic precedent on this point deals with a test of normal sperm motility to certify one as not *k'rut shaf'khah* under Deut. 23:2. [129]

It is important to note parenthetically that Catholic authorities are virtually unanimous in prohibiting the procural of semen in any manner that resembles "onanism" for either fertility tests or artificial insemination. [130] As to medical exigencies, Thomas Sanchez (d. 1610), a preeminent Jesuit authority, defended the soundness of the proposition that such procural may not be resorted to even to save a life, on the grounds that "the administration of the seed" must be denied in all cases to man in order to prevent the

---

[126] *Resp. Z'kan Aharon*, Vol. II. *E.H.* No. 97; *Resp. Emek Halakhah*, No. 68, and many others. Some dispute this reasoning; e.g., *Resp. Divrei Malkiel*, Vol. III, No. 107; *Resp. T'shuvah Sh'lemah*, Vol. II, No. 4. The factor of indirectness is important; see Note 128.

[127] The classic Responsum on this is that of *Resp. P'nei Y'hoshua, E.H.*, Vol. II, No. 44. See above Note 17.

[128] On all three of the above categories, see *Otzar HaPoskim*, I, 111, and IV, 168–79 for important qualifications. The description here does not touch upon the wide divergence of opinion and legislation in these matters.

[129] *TB Y'vamot* 76a. See *Arukh L'Ner* thereto on why the possibility of this test is omitted from Codes. See *S'dei Hemed, K'lalim* 7, 20 on the indirect factor.

[130] J. Fletcher, *Morals and Medicine*, pp. 110–16.

risk of abuse.[131] A disciple, Paul Laymann, reaffirmed the position when queried about related matters: "For a similar reason, the doctors of divinity commonly say that in no case is it lawful to procure emission of seed or pollution."[132]

To return to the Talmudic precedent, it was R. Jacob Emden, again, who invoked its example for the contraceptive question. He supported his argument in favor of a contraceptive device, when necessary, on the grounds that the mitzvah of marital relations renders the act no longer "in vain," generalizing from the Talmudic case that "the prohibition of hash-hatat zera is annulled of itself for reasons of mitzvah."[133] He boldly calls his legal finding a "*hiddush din*" [a newly formulated point of law] and appends those words to the margin of his Responsum and to the book's Table of Contents. Actually, the concept preceded him; that onah may cancel hash-hatah was suggested by earlier authorities.[134] More important, he was followed by many others (listed in Chapter 4 above) in applying the principle to specific cases of contraception.[135]

In our listing of rulings on this point in Chapter 4, another facet was shown forth. The mitzvah of onah, it was said there, is a qualitative one as well, and too much interference with its natural properties could be said to vitiate the performance of the mitzvah. To elaborate, just as marriage has two essential functions, the procreational and the relational, so the marital act has these two essential functions. If the first cannot be pursued because of hazard to mother or child, then the second ought to. As was also intimated in that chapter, abstinence would be a negation of both purposes—a double hash-hatah, as it were. Carrying this a bit further, use of a contraceptive device that interferes with the satisfactions of the sexual relationship can be declared a double hash-hatah, or, in the opinion of many, *only* when both purposes are negated is there a "destruction of seed" or a "bringing forth of semen in vain." The seed itself, as has been asserted, is the instrument of the sex act. To deprive it of both of its functions is to destroy it. The principle had been articulated by R. Solomon Luria, to whom the criterion for the "integrity of the sex act" is the mutual pleasure inherent in a heterosexual relationship [*guf neheneh min ha-guf*]. To him, the contraceptive device in question did not violate hash-hatat zera because the attendant gratifications were said to remain intact. The best statement on the subject comes from

---

[131] *The Holy Sacrament of Matrimony*, 9. 17. 15, quoted by Noonan, *op. cit.*, pp. 368–69.
[132] *Moral Theology*, 5, 10, 3, 1, by *ibid*, p. 370.
[133] *Resp. Sh'elat Ya'avetz*, No. 43.
[134] RaH and Ritva in *Shittah M'kubbetzet* to *K'tubot* 39.
[135] See Chapter 4, pp. 76 ff.

R. Hayyim Sofer—quoted above in our discussion of sexual pleasure—who would have differed with Luria and insisted on even less interference with the course of the seed itself.[136] Against the background of our present chapter, his words bear a second reading:

> The matter is clear to me, with the help of Him Who endows man with knowledge, that there are two senses in which mokh must be understood:
>
> (1) If the mokh obstructs the entire area of the vaginal canal, with the result that the membrum is insulated and accordingly prevented from impinging upon the vaginal walls—then the husband is guilty of hash-hatat zera, for such intercourse is not in the proper manner as implied by (Gen. 2 : 24) "and he shall cleave to his wife, and they shall be as one flesh," i.e., that there be contact between him and her and the bodies derive pleasure from such contact. Furthermore, the movement of life, which is the sperm, adds to the pleasure of bodies which have become as one. But with a "curtain" of mokh separating his flesh from hers, this is not "the way of a man with a maid" (Prov. 30 : 19) and, in so doing, he casts his seed on a mokh as if on "wood and stones." Intercourse is not permitted except where the excitation derives from the unimpeded conjunction of genital organs and the sperm runs its course in the vaginal canal.
>
> (2) The second kind of mokh is placed at the entrance to the uterus [i.e., a diaphragm]. This leaves the rest of the canal free for unimpeded contact and for the release of sperm in full physical pleasure and in the "flaming ardor of passion" (Song of Songs 8 : 6) except that the sperm does not actually enter the uterus. Conception is prevented, but the natural gratifications of the sex act are not diminished and the act is therefore clearly permissible.

Others have expressed similar views, though less lyrical, on the integrity of the sex act in terms of the sperm's discharge and the attendant satisfactions in terms of the wife's privilege of onah.[137] The implications of this line of reasoning are far-reaching. R. Mosheh Feinstein, without reference to the above document, has developed a similar thesis, at least theoretically,

[136] See Chapter 5, pp. 103–05.
[137] See, e.g., *Hit'or'rut T'shuvah*, No. 3; *Resp. Minhat HaKometz*, No. 94; *Resp. Alehu Ra'anan*, No. 21.

on *l'vattalah*—which we shall encounter in a later chapter—that would acknowledge the dual purpose of zera and regard as "in vain" or as "destruction" a situation wherein the seed is deprived of both functions.[138] Other Respondents have, in their analysis of the matter, contributed to such a thesis, which yields a new definition of hash-hatat zera. Heterosexuality is the key to that definition, as we shall see, and the violation will be one which offends against its proper framework.

As an abuse of the sacred or potent generative faculties, then, hash-hatat zera is a fundamental aspect of the larger question of contraception. An offense of uncertain scriptural derivation and even elusive of characterization as to its nature, it is the starting point of virtually every rabbinic Responsum on the subject of birth control. One after another, these hundreds of Responsa will analyze the factors involved and determine whether the violation, in one sense or another, has been incurred. The specific contraceptive method will be weighed against the circumstances, precedent rulings and analyses will be painstakingly explored and logically arrayed, and the decision will be rendered with erudition and humaneness. Some methods will be adjudged acceptable per se; some only by virtue of the mitzvah to avoid the hazards of a dangerous pregnancy. And, according to the narrower definition of hash-hatat zera, this will be a case of setting aside an acknowledged prohibition in deference to the commandment to safeguard against hazard. According to the broader definition, the discharge of sperm has a purpose other than its procreative one, namely to afford the inherent gratifications of the sex act. Where pregnancy must be avoided, hash-hatat zera will then come to mean the "destruction" of both of its purposes; if it serves for neither procreation nor the integrity of the sex act, it is only then said to be improperly emitted, and the contraceptive method would be judged accordingly. Of the narrower and broader definitions, the latter is considered less frequently in the Responsa—but not because it is at all inconsistent with the concerns of the other Responsa. Both underlie the conscious rationale of the authorities in adjudging questions as to the methods or circumstances of artificial contraception—when, that is, the mitzvah of procreation must be set aside.

[138] See Chapter 8, pp. 152–53 and pp. 163–65.

7

Excursus—On "Female Seed"

References to "female seed" are to be found in the Talmudic Commentaries and in the Responsa cited above. What kind of "seed" are they talking about, and what role, if any, does it play in the reproductive process?

In colorful Midrashic passages, the Rabbis express their sense of marvel at the wondrous phenomenon of childbirth.[1] The miracle of reproduction, the gestation, sustenance, and growth of the embryo, the process of birth itself—these are imaginatively described and philosophically interpreted. One such passage that bears on our subject is recorded in the Talmud and reads as follows:[2]

> There are three partners in man . . . his father supplies the semen of the white substance out of which are formed the child's bones, sinews, nails, brain, and the white in his eye. His mother supplies the semen of the red substance [so, ed. Soncino; Heb. *mazra'at odem*] out of which is formed his skin, flesh, hair and black of his eye. God gives him the soul and breath, beauty of features, eye-

---

[1] Such as *Lev. Rabbah* to *Tazria;* similarly *Midrash Aggadah, Midrash HaGadol,* and *Tanhuma,* to *Tazria.* Also, *Yalkut Shimoni* to Job, 905. A small Apocryphal Midrash, devoted entirely to the theme, is called *Sefer Y'tzirat HaV'lad,* published by Jellinek in his *Beit HaMidrash.*

[2] *Niddah* 31a. See also *She'iltot, Yitro,* 56.

sight, hearing, speech, understanding, and discernment.[3] When his time comes to depart this world, God takes his share and leaves the shares of his mother and father with them.

Another Midrashic image, not reflected in the Talmud, declares:

> Job said "Hast Thou not poured me out like milk and curdled me like cheese, . . ." (Job 10:10–12). A mother's womb is full of standing blood, which flows therefrom in menstruation. But, at God's will, a drop of whiteness enters and falls into its midst and behold a child is formed. This is likened unto a bowl of milk: when a drop of rennet falls into it, it congeals and stands; if not it continues as liquid.[4]

Early Embryological Theories

These two passages reflect a point of issue in the ongoing debate among the learned men of yore. Since knowledge of the existence and function of the female ovum had to wait for modern times (see on), the issues before them were: What is the nature of the woman's contribution to the substance of the embryo? Is it a kind of female "seed," or perhaps menstrual blood? And how does her contribution compare in "importance" to the man's?

Of the several embryological theories current in the ancient Graeco-Roman world, that of Aristotle had taught that the embryo is created by the blood of woman, which is its matter, and the seed of the man, which gives it form.[5] In the more popular version of the theory, the "matter" and "form" elements became less important, and the general idea that a foetus is formed from female blood and male seed prevailed. So Jerome and Augustine —and the Talmudic commentators. (The Talmud itself does not go beyond *mazra'at odem;* above.) Many Stoics, on the other hand, believed the male seed to provide both form and "pneuma," and the female, pneuma alone. A third view held the female to be a mere repository of the male seed, a kind of field or soil which nurtures rather than contributes substance to the seed implanted within it. This is probably the view of Soranos and Tertullian

---

[3] Cf. the interpretation in *Lev. Rabbah* 14, 5 of Psalms 27: 10 ("For my father and my mother have forsaken me, but God has gathered me in"): The parents do their share in impregnation, then the seed (or seeds) are left for God to gather in.

[4] *Lev. Rabbah* 14, 9; *Yalkut* to Job, 10, 10.

[5] *Generation of Animals,* 1, 20, 729a; 2. 3, 737a.

and is reflected in the many agricultural metaphors for reproduction found in the writings of Philo and others.[6]

But the woman has seed, too, say the ancients. The first-century Roman physician, Galen, wrote a work called *De Semine* ["Seed"], of which Book 2, Chapter I is devoted to the "female seed."[7] He describes the female testes (apparently the ovaries) and says "they emit seed into the vulva." Coitus would not be possible without "female seed," he says; moreover, "female seed, colder and wetter than male seed, helps the latter pass to the uterus." Early-medieval medical texts also locate and describe the function of female seed: Cophonis (twelfth century) and Ricardi (thirteenth century) speak of female testes ejecting seed, coarser and wetter than male sperm, joining with the latter in the uterus to form the foetus.[8]

In Jewish texts, explicit reference to female sperm is found only in the works of Maimonides, in both legal and medical commentation on the Mishnah. The Mishnah, for the purpose of making legal distinctions between blood to be regarded as menstrual and otherwise, had offered a schematic diagram of the anatomy involved:

> The Sages referred to [the anatomy of] a woman by metaphor: [she has] a chamber, an ante-chamber and an upper chamber.[9]

Maimonides takes advantage of the opportunity afforded him by this passage to elaborate—in his Mishnah Commentary[10] and in his Law Code[11]—on the basis (he tells us)[12] of his own surgical experience. Between the "chamber" and the "antechamber" are the "woman's two ovaries as well as the ducts, where her sperm (*shikhvat zera*) ripens." The word used (*beitzim*) can mean either "ovaries" or "testes." According to him, then, a woman has both ovaries and seed; he says nothing, however, about their role, or the role of menstrual blood, in the formation of the foetus.

[6] Noonan, *op. cit.*, p. 89.

[7] Galen, *Opera*, tranlated by J.D. Feliciano (Venice, 1560). Although Galen wrote in the first century, his views still held sway at least as late as the 16th, for some 22 Latin translations of his work were published then: Noonan, *op. cit.*, p. 337.

[8] G.W. Corner, *Anatomical Texts of the Earlier Middle Ages* (Carnegie Institute of Washington, 1927), p. 53 (Cophonis); p. 65 (Second Salernitan Demonstration); p. 86 (Nicolai); and p. 104 (Ricardi).

[9] *Mishnah, Niddah* II, 5 (17b).

[10] To *Niddah, ad loc.*

[11] *Issurei Biah*, 5, 4. See Preuss, *op. cit.*, pp. 133–34.

[12] *Ibid.* See *Me'iri* to *Niddah* 17b, and M. M. Kasher, in *Noam*, Vol. 8 (5725), 325–31 on the privilege of nonacceptance of Maimonides' medical interpretations in this chapter of his by later halakhic authorities with more advanced information.

The Meaning of "Tazria"

A long succession of Jewish Bible Commentators do, however, discuss this question and related ones. The occasion is the interpretation of a key phrase in Leviticus (12 : 2), *ishah ki tazria v'yal'dah*. If *tazria* is to be understood in its apparent sense, grammatically the causative (and transitive) verb form of the root *zera*, then the phrase would be translated "When a woman seminates and gives birth."[13] But the Aramaic Targum, the earliest translation of the Bible dating from Talmudic times, renders: "When a woman conceives [is made to carry] and gives birth," without reference to semination of any kind.[14] R. Saadia Gaon (d. 942) translates similarly.[15]

The questions that might bother the Bible student familiar with contemporary culture, however, are aired by the twelfth-century Bible scholar, R. Abraham Ibn Ezra, who writes:[16]

> The view of the Greek savants is that woman has (the) seed and the male seed causes it to jell but the whole child comes from the woman's blood. Actually, [however], *tazria* means "she gives forth seed," for she is like the earth.[17]

Each of the points referred to obscurely by Ibn Ezra is explicated more fully by the later Commentators. R. Moses ben Nahman (Nahmanides), the illustrious Sage of thirteenth-century Spain, suggests that the foetus is formed of her uteral blood[18] which is *called* "seed"; that her ovaries either emit no seed or that the seed from there has no function in the reproductive process. He tells us:[19]

---

[13] Cf., on the other hand, Num. 5 : 28: *v'nikk'ta v'nizr'ah zera*, which is properly intransitive and passive. Another subject of discussion in the Commentaries to *tazria*, by the way, is *ishah mazra-'at t'hillah*, the notion that when her "semination" precedes his, a male child is conceived.

[14] In standard editions of the Hebrew Pentateuch, Lev. 12:2.

[15] *Perush RaSaG al HaTorah*, ed. J. Kapah (Jerusalem: *Mosad Harav Kook*, 1963), *ad loc.*

[16] His Bible Commentary, Lev., *ibid.*

[17] "Unlike Galen," Ibn Ezra holds that male and female contributions interact equally — *Ohel Yosef* Comm. to Ibn Ezra, by R. Y'hudah Krinzky.

[18] The distinction between menstrual and uteral blood is very important for Ramban, if not for others. In his Comment to Lev. 18:19, he asserts that menstrual blood is "fatal" to the conceptus, hence the separation of *niddah*. So also, Ibn Shu'aib, *Drashot, Tazria*, 50c. But to the Talmud (*Niddah* 31b; see Rashi) the distinction is not necessary. Since there are halakhic authorities who would permit artificial insemination during the *niddah* period, this is evidently not a concern.

[19] His Bible Commentary, *ibid.* See ed. Chavel, *Perush HaRamban al HaTorah, Mosad HaRav Kook* (Jerusalem, 1965), II, 64–65.

When the Sages spoke of the woman "emitting her semen" [*Niddah* 31a, above] they did not mean that the foetus is formed from her seed.[20] For, although she has "eggs" [ovaries] like the eggs [testicles] of the man, either she creates no seed there or that seed . . . has nothing to do with the foetus.[21] By "her seed" they meant the blood of the uterus which unites with the male sperm. For, in their view, the child is created from the woman's blood and from the man's "white," and both are called "seed." As they say [*Niddah*, above]: Man has three partners [in his formation], etc.; the father contributes (*mazria loven*) the "white" [from which come the lighter parts of the body] and the mother (*mazra'at odem*) the "red" [from which the darker parts], etc., and God gives the soul, etc., . . . And this is the view of the physicians too.

"Female sperm," then, is deprived by Nahmanides of relevant function or even of existence, although in his Commentary to an earlier verse he seems to give us a choice. On Gen. 2:18 ("it is not good for Man to be alone"), he writes:

It is unseemly that Man should be alone and not procreate. For all creatures of two sexes were made so that they could procreate, and even plants and trees have their seed within them. Humans, too, may originally have been bisexual, as the Talmud records [*B'rakhot* 61a], but were then made separate [sexual] with the reproductive faculty (*koah ha-molid*) given to the female; or—*in view of the well-known controversy about the reproductive process*—one could say that *seed* was given to the female.

"Blood of the womb" is the operative substance. This is what the woman "seminates" and this is what shares—equally, it would seem—with the husband's sperm in the formation of the embryo. But Ibn Ezra, now, had

---

[20] "*Lo she-yé-aseh ha'v'lad mi-zera ha-ishah.*" Two variants may be listed: *Moshav Z'kenim* (a recently published work), ed. Sasson (London, 1959), of Bible comments by *Ba'alei ha-Tosafot*: *Lo she-t'he mattelet zera;* and *Tur* (see next note) *Lo shé-t'he ma'alat zera.*

[21] The author of the *Tur* Code also wrote a Bible Commentary but contented himself with relating the exact words of Nahmanides when he had no reason to dissent. His Commentary to this verse preserves a variant:

. . . They did not mean that she gives forth seed (*she-t'hé ma'alat zera*). For, although she does not have "ovaries" like those of a man by which she might create seed . . .

See his *Perush al Hatorah (Me Rabbenu Ya'akov ben K'vod etc. Rabbenu HaRosh)*, ed. Shurkin (New York, 1956).

made reference to the Greek idea that the *whole* foetus comes from the woman's blood, that the male has no substantive role to play in the reproductive process. Nahmanides turns to this question as he continues his Commentary to *tazria*:

> But, to the Greek philosophers, the entire body of the foetus comes from the mother's blood; the father gives nothing but the form (*hyle*) to the matter . . .[22] Accordingly, tazria here would mean "she nurtures seed," as the Targum renders: "she carries seed."[23]

R. Joshua Ibn Shu'aib, an early fourteenth-century preacher, to whose recorded homilies we are indebted for the transmission of much classic exegesis, offers the following:

> Many views have been written in connection with this [embryological] question. Some have maintained that the foetus is formed from female blood, and the male has no share except to give it form by his seed . . . Others have written that the foetus comes from both of them, from the male seed and the female blood. This is the view of the greatest of physicians—and also that of *our Rabbis who must have heard it from them* [emphasis supplied] . . . and there are other views but there is no need to transcribe them here.[24]

The phrase in italics is especially interesting in view of an incidental reference bearing on our subject in a Responsum of R. Isaac bar Sheshet (d. 1408). Discussing the creditability of Greek and Arabic science as opposed to the Talmudic, he writes:

> As another example, the Talmud gives equal share to the father and mother in the formation of the foetus . . . but *they* believe that

[22] A slip of the pen is said to have occurred here. Nahmanides meant to use the Greek *hyle* for "matter" rather than for "form," as he does correctly in his Commentary to Gen. 1:1 (ed. Chavel, p. 12). Aboab's supercommentary (see Note 27, below) explains the apparent slip. Also, Prof. G. Scholem, in *Kiryat Sefer*, XXI (1944), 179ff. points to this error as further proof that Ramban is not the author of *Iggeret HaKodesh*. However, *Moshav Z'kenim* (see Note 20, above) preserves a reading of Ramban's comment here in which the word *hyle* is not found altogether.

[23] In *Iggeret HaKodesh* (See Ch. 4, above, Note 88), Ch. 3, his partiality to the simile of the "Greek philosophers" is evident. In that epistle "to a friend" on the subject of marital relations, the author declares:
> The "seed" of woman is like matter and . . . the seed of man is like the form created by an artisan upon that matter, which is what tazria really means . . .

[24] *Drashot al HaTorah*, p. 49ab.

all is from the mother and that the function of the father's seed is merely to jell and congeal hers, as rennet does to milk.[25]

Regardless of the respective contribution of man and woman, the problem of her "seed" remains. Nahmanides, as we have seen, effectively read it out of existence. The word tazria merely refers to the woman's return of the deposited seed, as his later supercommentaries explain. Rabbenu Bahya ben Asher (d. 1340), a Bible Commentator of a century later who leaned heavily on Nahmanides, thus clarifies the latter's (and hence also Ibn Ezra's) explanation of tazria as "nurtures": The woman "gives [back] the male seed deposited with her, just as the earth gives forth the seed deposited within it. Her own so-called 'seed' is actually menstrual blood; she has no 'female sperm.' "[26] Still another supercommentary on Nahmanides, that of R. Isaac Aboab (d. 1492), makes essentially the same point.[27]

Discussion of the role of her "seed" continues, nevertheless, beyond that time. A scholar who bridged more than one contemporary intellectual discipline was R. Levi ben Gershon (d. 1344), a philosopher who wrote Commentaries both on Aristotelian works and on the Bible. (Since Aristotle was known to the medieval world through Arabic interpreters such as Averroes, it was on the latter's Commentary to De Animalibus that Levi ben Gershon's supercommentary was written. His views on our subject are to be found there as well as on the passage in Leviticus.) While Averroes claims that the foetus is formed by the menstrual blood and that the woman's seed has no share in the process, Gersonides argues, following Galen, that her seed does have a helpful role: it prepares the feminine substance to be acted upon by the male seed, and that's what tazria means.[28] Another rabbinic authority who immersed himself in a study of the physiology of the time was R. Simon ben Tsemah Duran (d. 1444), whose philosophic magnum opus, called Magen Avot, makes extensive analyses of biology, zoology, and physiology.[29] There,[30] he affirms the Aristotelian ideas that the foetus comes from menstrual blood and male sperm, that woman has seed but that it has no share in the reproductive process, although he cites Galen to the contrary. What, then, does tazria mean? It refers to the woman's orgasm. This, he says, is

[25] Resp. Rivash, No. 447.

[26] Midrash Rabbenu Bahya al Hamishah Hum'shei Torah (New York, 1945).

[27] Hamishah Hum'shei Torah. Ramban Im Perush R. Yitzhak Abohav al Perusho. (Venice ed., 1548).

[28] Ralbag—Perush al HaTorah Derekh Beur (Venice ed. 1547); Photo. ed. (New York, 1948).

[29] Magen Avot (Livorno, 1785), which book serves as an "Introduction" to his better-known work by the same name, a Commentary to (Pirkei) Avot—Magen Avot (Livorno, 1763).

[30] Ibid., pp. 40a, 40b, 41a.

for pleasure alone, to make marital relations and childbirth more attractive,[31] although orgasm may or may not accompany conception: we find that women often conceive without orgasm. Only the blood of the womb, therefore, joins with the male sperm to form the foetus, the male being the active cause and the female the substantive.[32] And, he says, the Talmud's reference to woman's semination refers to this menstrual blood (does it not say *mazra'at odem* ["emits the red substance"]?) and not to whatever seed Galen was talking about.

On the basis of the Talmud alone, then, later Commentators conclude that the female "semination" referred to there involves the blood of the womb. So says R. Yom Tov Heller in seventeenth-century Cracow;[33] so concludes the eighteenth-century author of *Sefer HaB'rit*,[34] who elaborates in keeping with his "scientific" orientation: "Her seed is not white but red, made up of the distillation or refinement of the blood that gathers in the womb at the time of coitus."[35] And so declares the twentieth-century Sage of B'nei B'rak, the *Hazon Ish*, adding that the secretion is erotically stimulated.[36]

The concept of "female seed," on the other hand, associated with Galen and with Maimonides, finds its place among Catholic theological writers up to the eighteenth century:[37] to them it was certainly not blood of the womb but some form of seminal emission suggested by Galen and his successors.[38] (A twentieth-century theologian assumes that what the earlier church writers had in mind was a discharge from the Bartholin glands.[39]) Being associated with orgasm and made analogous to male ejaculation, the process of feminine "semination," largely unspecified, figured in their discussions of marital relations.

But this entire notion is a medically, rather than a theologically, created one. Rabbinic Bible Commentators, accordingly, who were outside of the

---

[31] *Ibid.*, p. 40b (and, in brief, to [*Pirkei*] *Avot*, III, 1). A century later, the Dominican Cardinal Cajetan made the same point (see Note 37, below).

[32] In his Commentary to *Avot, loc. cit.*, he asks why only *tippah s'ruhah* and not *zera ha'em* is mentioned. To teach, he says, that even the more important of the two formative substances is only *tippah s'ruhah*.

[33] *Ma'adanei Yomtov* to *Rosh, Niddah*, Ch. 2., Par. 2.

[34] Vol. I, 17 (Jerusalem, 1960) p. 156.

[35] Cf. *Kar'nei Or*, a Commentary to Ibn Ezra by R. Judah Krinzky: "Female blood accumulates in *the form of* seed at the climax of intercourse."

[36] To *Even HaEzer*, 36, 3 ("*al y'dei himmud*") probably by analogy with *dam himmud* of *Niddah* 66a, etc.

[37] Cardinal Cajetan, *On the Summa Theologica*, 2; Thomas Sanchez, *The Holy Sacrament of Matrimony*, 9, 19; St. Alphonsum Liguori, *Moral Theology*, 6, 9.

[38] See Notes 7, 8, above.

[39] B. Merkelbach, *Quaestiones de castitate et luxuria*. Quoted by Noonan, *op. cit.*, p. 337, Note 49.

intellectual sphere of Galen or Aristotle, did not, in explaining tazria, feel called upon to reckon with the notion of female seed—or even of the respective contributions of the man and woman to the embryo. As the Targum in Talmudic times (and Saadia) had translated tazria simply as "conceive," so did R. Samuel ben Meir in the twelfth century [*tazria-tit'abber*].[40] Don Isaac Abravanel of the fifteenth century also interprets simply, if not so precisely, "woman's seed is her children," like the earth gives forth its produce.[41] Azulai, in the eighteenth century, suggests that tazria refers to woman's wonderful share, whatever it may be, in the man's mitzvah of procreation.[42] And Malbim, in the nineteenth century, refers tazria to the readiness of the woman's reproductive organs to receive and "absorb" the male sperm.[43] (Others cite the technical exegesis found in *Tosafot* for this "superfluous" word.[44])

The Ovum

Strange to relate, it was not until 1827 that the female ovum was identified in the microscope and the fact established that the ovaries secrete ova instead of seed.[45] True, in 1672 de Graaf discovered small lumps on the surface of the ovary, later called Graafian follicles, which contained some kind of generative particle. He reasoned that the particle, which made its way from the ovary to the womb and had become itself the beginning of the embryo, must be like a hen's egg and not at all like male semen.[46] But not until Carl Ernest von Baer actually saw the human ovum in 1827, and others advanced his findings with further discoveries until the end of the nineteenth century, was the process—whereby the embryo is formed through the fertilization of egg cells by male sperm cells—clearly understood.[47] In fact, the examination of sperm cells through crude microscopes by Leeuwenhoek in 1677

[40] *Perush Rashbam al HaTorah* to Lev., *ad loc.*

[41] *Abarvanel al HaTorah*, to Lev., *ad loc.*

[42] Hayyim Yosef David Azulai, *Homat Anakh*, to Lev., *ad loc.* See above, Chapter 3.

[43] Meir Leib ben Yehiel Michael, *HaTorah V'HaMitzvah*, to Lev., *ad loc.* Also in the (late) 19th century, S.R. Hirsch and David Hoffman in their commentaries to the passage, refer to *mazria* in Gen. 1, 11. The word has a connotation of "sprouting," and its use in Lev. reminds man that he is, after all, part of nature and governed by laws of nature, etc.

[44] N. Tz. Y. Berlin, *Ha'amek Davar*, to Lev., *ad loc.*, (but see his *Ha'amek Sh'alah* to *Sh'iltot, Yitro*, 56); and Barukh Epstein, *Torah T'mimah*, to Lev., *ad loc.*, citing *Tosafot* to *Niddah* 18a, *s.v. shalyah*.

[45] F. H. Garrison, *Introduction to the History of Medicine* (Philadelphia, 1914), p. 400.

[46] D. C. Darlington, *The Facts of Life* (New York, 1952), p. 72; R. H. Shyrock, *The Development of Modern Medicine*, p. 273.

[47] Garrison, op. cit., p. 390; Shyrock, *op. cit.*, p. 273.

combined, with the findings of de Graaf in 1672, to create two opposing groups of theorists for the next two hundred years. The "ovulists" located the generative (and hereditary) core of life in the ovum, while the "spermatists" insisted it is to be found in the male semen. [48]

Two Jewish sources reflect this intellectual ferment and, although the ovum principle was still only a theory, assumed its validity. Already in much earlier times, the Bible Commentators referred to above, notably Nahmanides, Bahya, and Duran, [49] used the hen's egg as a simile for human reproduction; they distinguished between the egg rolling in the ground and one which was "fertilized" by the rooster, from which a chick could be hatched. [50] But during the interim period of 1672–1827, a work by R. Jacob Emden tells us:

> Modern researchers do not postulate a need for female seed in reproduction, for it contains nothing of the substance of the foetus . . . since they have discovered through the microscope and many experiments that man [!] and other creatures are formed by an egg lodged in the ovary [literally, a cluster of eggs] in the woman, which constitutes the substance of the foetus . . . The sperm . . . meets the first egg closest to the uterus and ready to be affected by it; the egg absorbs the warm vapor of the sperm, in which is the spirit of life with a finite form . . . acting "like leaven in the dough," it has the power of growth and formation and takes sustenance from the egg, which, when invested with life and movement, leaves the ovaries and enters a more spacious area. [51]

Either R. Jacob Emden, whose book was published in 1736, anticipated later discoveries too eagerly or the current medical-history textbooks date the relevant determinations a bit late.

The other of the two works from rabbinic authors in this interim period likewise reflects the new science and seems to anticipate the given date of 1827 by several years. In his *Sefer HaB'rit* (1797), R. Pinhas Eliahu gives the "spermatists" and "ovulists" equal space: [52]

---

[48] Darlington, *op. cit.*, pp. 34, 70.

[49] Nahmanides and Bahya, *loc. cit.*; Duran, *op. cit.*, pp. 37a, 37b, 38a, etc. Duran also speaks of eggs inside and outside the body (now known as oviparous and viviparous).

[50] This has its roots in the Talmud: *TB Beitzah* 6a (*bei'a d'safna me'ar'a*, etc.)

[51] *Iggeret Bikkoret* (ed. Zhitomir. 1867), p. 25b (50).

[52] Vol. I, 17. (Ed. *Orah*, Jerusalem, 1960), p. 156.

When the woman receives the sperm, her ovaries ["cluster of eggs"] undergo a change. One of the eggs, after about three days, travels through a duct, which is called in their language "Fallopian tube," near the uterus. This is what the Talmud meant in saying that sperm is absorbed "up to three days"[53] . . . From the husk of that egg the placenta is formed . . . but in the formation of the egg is a kind of moisture, known as lymph . . . the foetus abides in the placenta like the chick in its egg—and this is what the Talmud meant in saying that a foetus in the womb is "like a nut in a cup of water." [54] Some experts have written that all man's features are *in potentia* in the egg . . . but others write that in the male sperm is the form of a miniature man.[55] What wonders! . . . and they say one or two of these sperm enters the female ovum and absorbs the moisture there and, in this way, grows and expands. Only God knows the truth in this matter!

In keeping with one of the stated purposes of this author in writing his book—namely the reconciliation of Talmudic observations with the science of his day—we are told the following as well:[56]

Man was not formed from the entire drop, just from the refined essence of it, say our Sages[57] . . . how so? . . . the woman has tiny eggs . . . like those of a hen . . . and the thick of the semen is cast away while the refined essence combines with the ova, etc.

In the same spirit, one might submit that the ancient notion that blood of the womb comprises the feminine contribution to the formation of the embryo adumbrates an insight into reality as modern science knows it. The ovum, according to today's knowledge, imbeds itself into the previously prepared uterine lining and feeds itself heavily there upon the mother's blood vessels.[58]

We are now in a far better position to understand a legal query of our

---

[53] Cf. *TB B'rakhot* 60a ("*sh'loshah yamim lik'litah*") and *Maharil* and *Magen Avraham*, Ch. 6, Notes 121, 123–24. Cf. *Resp. R. Akiva Eger*, No. 72 (1834): "The essence of the sperm enters in a narrow place, into a thin duct, and there it ripens and is absorbed within three days."

[54] *TB Niddah*, 31a.

[55] See Ch. 6, Note 79. The quotation here, with its deference to both points of view, may be among the changes for the second edition. See his Introduction, *op. cit.*, p. 13.

[56] *Op. cit.*, p. 155.

[57] *Niddah, ibid.* And see *Ibn Shu'aib*, Ch. 6, Note 46.

[58] Irving C. Fischer, "Human Reproduction," in *The Encyclopedia of Sexual Behavior*, ed. A. Ellis and A. Abarbanel (New York, 1961), II, 903.

previous chapter: whether or how hash-hatat zera applies to the woman. Nahmanides, we have seen here, is among those who question the existence of female sperm; the woman's zera is a (red) secretion of the uterus, not (a white) one from the ovaries. Even if this "seed" is involved in the formation of the embryo, its "destruction," as Nahmanides had ruled in his capacity as Talmudic rather than biblical commentator, would be forbidden on grounds of autoeroticism rather than contraception;[59] just as she, not answerable to p'ru ur'vu, may render herself sterile. The same reasoning would apply to destruction, as it were, of an ovum instead of "seed" or uteral blood: if the autoerotic factor is to be discounted, then the only remaining question is whether she may destroy her husband's seed after its proper insemination. There she must reckon, not with a technical violation, but with the fact that her contraceptive act would thwart a potential embryo. The common assumption, in fact, that where contraception is indicated the woman may take active measures while the man may not, is not at all affected by the discovery of the ovum. The legal distinction between the sexes in the use of birth control devices derives, contrary to that assumption as pointed out earlier,[60] less from the social duty of procreation and more from the biological differences: sterilization is permitted, the sex act has already been properly completed, and so on. This distinction remains the same even when the secretion of her "seed" is irrelevant to conception and the principle of fertilization of egg cells becomes operative instead.

A recent Responsum, by way of illustration, assimilates the newer understanding of the physiologic process and makes use of it in a legal context. Affirming the essential difference between the Talmudic tampon and the principle of diaphragm, he represents the latter as a device which "seals off the entrance to the uterus, where the woman's ova are found. One of these ova would ordinarily receive the sperm and expand, and conception would thus have taken place."[61]

[59] Chapter 6, p. 124.
[60] Chapter 3, p. 54.
[61] *Resp. Minhat HaKometz* (1934), No. 94.

8

The "Act of Er and Onan"

When a ministerial committee joined forces with the Planned Parenthood League in Poughkeepsie, N.Y., in 1952, the Dean of Catholic clergy for Dutchess County denounced the non-Catholic ministers who supported the League, saying: "This is a point on which Catholic, Protestant, and Jews should all be agreed, since it is the Bible which expressly forbids birth control." [1] He was, says the author of the report, referring to the biblical narrative (Gen. 38 : 7–10) concerning Judah; his two sons, Er and Onan; and his daughter-in-law, Tamar:

> Er, Judah's first-born, was wicked in the sight of the Lord, and the Lord slew him. And Judah said unto Onan: "Go unto thy brother's wife and perform the levirate duty and raise up offspring for thy brother." Now Onan knew that the offspring would not be his; and it came to pass, when he went in unto his brother's wife, that he would spill [it] on the ground, lest he should give seed for his brother. And the thing which he did was evil in the sight of the Lord; and He slew him also.

1 As quoted in *The Time Has Come; A Catholic Doctor's Proposal to End the Battle Over Birth Control,* by John Rock, p. 82.

Onan in the Church

This pivotal narrative, referred to in the Talmud (see on) as "the act of Er and Onan," played a crucial role in the history of the Church's doctrine on contraception and gave rise to the modern term "onanism." (Er is mentioned with Onan in Christian writings only infrequently.[2]) Both historical and moral considerations account for Onan's far greater prominence in the Church's position on contraception than in that of the Jewish tradition. The first important use of the passage was made in order to counter heterodox sectarians: the strange fourth-century Gnostics, in opposing all procreation in this world, practiced intercourse without seminal intromission; some repudiated marriage. Against both these ideas, Epiphanius, head of a monastery in Palestine and later bishop in Cyprus, invoked the story of "that immense and frightful crime" of Onan.[3] But it was Jerome's translation of the Pentateuch in the year 400, because of the considerable popularity it enjoyed, which gave far greater impetus to the homiletic use of the passage. Where the text reads "the thing which he [Onan] did was evil in the sight of the Lord," Jerome paraphrases: *rem detestabilem fecerat* [Onan "did a detestable thing."].[4]

More notably still, the influential Augustine (d. 430) applies our passage specifically to ordinary contraception in marriage, an application which was to have far-reaching effect. In his *Adulterous Marriages*,[5] he declares it lawless and shameful to lie with one's wife where the conception of offspring is avoided: "This is what Onan, son of Judah, did, and God slew him for it." In the ninth century, the Second Diocesan Statute of Theodulphus, Bishop of Orleans, dated about 813, reads: "It is called uncleanness or the detestable

[2] Augustine (*Against Faustus*, 22. 84) comments that Er is etymologically the symbol of active evil [*er-ra*]. This idea, by the way, is to be found in *Midrash Lekah Tov*, to Gen., *ad loc.*: *er, hu l'hipukh ra;* and see *Zohar*, Gen. 186b. Also, a Frankish penitential of the eighth century speaks of the sin of the "sons of Judah," as does 13th-century Albertus Magnus, according to Noonan, pp. 162, 234. See also Denis the Carthusian, below. Otherwise, Er is virtually ignored.

[3] Noonan, *Contraception . . .* , pp. 97, 98.

[4] *Ibid.*, p. 102. But Noonan errs in attributing to Jerome an emphasis "on an act" which is absent from the text and which is "most important of all" of Jerome's contribution. Noonan confuses the text "appeared evil before the Lord"—which refers to Er—with that of Onan, where we are told "the thing which he *did* was evil." The emphasis on an act is in the text itself. And Jerome's use of the word "detestable" is no worse than the adjectives of Epiphanius above, or of Zeno of Verona, who had used "detestable" in connection with Er and Onan. A reviewer of Noonan's book (Magdalen Goffin, in the *New York Review of Books* [July 7, 1966], p. 4) was, accordingly, led to compound the error and write: "To suit his argument, St. Jerome tampered with that perennial standby, the Onan text."

[5] 2.12. Noonan, p. 137.

sin not to lie naturally with a woman, whence it is read that Onan son of Judah was struck by God when, having entered into his wife, he poured out his seed on the earth." [6]

Lesser authorities added the influence of their written or spoken judgments as well. In the twelfth century, Peter Cantor equated the Sodomites with Onan. [7] If a husband does not want more children than he can feed, says Peter de Palude, Dominican archbishop of the fifteenth century, let him practice *amplexus reservatus*, a kind of intercourse without semination, rather than the method of Onan. [8] In that same century, Martin Le Maistre of the University of Paris appealed to the story of Onan to point up the sinfulness of using "mode or time or place to prevent the generation of offspring." [9] Another contemporary, Denis the Carthusian (d. 1471), a monk in the Netherlands and author of a short catechism of moral life for the married, wrote, in his Commentary on Genesis, that Er "abused the vessel of his wife by pouring out seed outside of it" and that Onan, too, "knew his wife uselessly and unnaturally." Still another contemporary, the Franciscan Cherubino, in his *Rule of Married Life* written for the laity, refers to Onan in order to instruct them against coitus interruptus. In the sixteenth century Thomas de Vio, known as Cardinal Cajetan (d. 1534), general of the Dominican order and advisor to four popes, listed Onan's sin under "The Sin of Matrimony in Regard to the Vessel" in his *Little Summa of Sins*. He calls such emission of seed outside the woman's vessel "manifestly a great crime."

For a moment, the question of Onan's intent figures in the teaching: In the late sixteenth century, the Capuchin preacher St. Laurence of Brindisi wrote, in his *Explication on Genesis*, that Onan was punished for intercourse "to satisfy lust alone so that generation is not desired" which is a mortal sin. But this relatively liberal interpretation was rejected by seventeenth-century Francis de Sales who, in his *Introduction to the Devout Life*, criticized "heretics" who blamed Onan for his intention rather than his act. [10]

The practice of coitus interruptus was denounced as the sin of Onan by two influential Jesuits of that (sixteenth) century—Leonard Lessius in his *Justice and the Law* and the Louvain exegete Cornelius à Lapide in his *Commentary on the Pentateuch*. The latter, we have seen, makes reference to the Hebrews: Onan's act "destroyed the foetus and the conceptus in the seed;

[6] *Ibid.*, p. 161.
[7] *Ibid.*, p. 226.
[8] *Ibid.*, p. 298.
[9] This, and the following three examples, *ibid.*, p. 359.
[10] *Ibid.*, p. 360.

hence this sin is compared by the Hebrews to homicide." [11] In the nineteenth century, the term "onanism" came into wide use, with a corresponding tendency to dwell on the sin of Onan. The American Francis P. Kenrick, Bishop of Philadelphia, and three French churchmen, John Gury, Bishops Thomas Gousset and John Bouvier, in their respective treatises, based their opposition to coitus interruptus on Onan; but the last of these three admitted doubts about the interpretation of Onan's act and motive, although the "authority of a great multitude of doctors" constrained him to hold that the punishment was for the contraceptive act. [12]

Indeed, a wider variety of interpretations of the nature of Onan's sin characterized twentieth-century biblical exegesis. The levirate element in the narrative (see on) was taken into account and the sin viewed in a broader perspective. In 1962, the various exegetical positions taken by Christian (Protestant and Catholic) Bible commentaries in recent times were collated in an article by Father A.M. DuBarle, [13] who summarized their views of Onan's sin and subsumed them under separate headings: (1) the contraceptive method; (2) lack of family affection; (3) levirate violation; (4) egotism and the contraceptive act; (5) acceptance of an obligation of the law, and then evading the duty imposed by it. Without necessarily rejecting these possibilities, Pope Pius XI, in his all-important encyclical on marital conduct, *Casti Connubii*, December 31, 1930, had affirmed:

> It is, therefore, not remarkable that Holy Writ itself testifies that the Divine Majesty pursued this wicked crime with detestation and punished it with death, as St. Augustine recalls. [14]

Bernard Häring in 1954 and Francis Hürth in 1955, two leading contemporary theologians, reasserted that Onan's sin was his contraceptive act, [15] while Cardinal Suenens, later of the Ecumenical Council Steering Committee, wrote in 1961:

[11] *Ibid.*, p. 364: "Talmudic tradition was thus invoked to support the canon law."

[12] *Ibid.*, p. 405.

[13] "La Bible et les pères ont-ils parlé de la contraception?" in *La Vie Spirituelle, XV, Supplement* (1962), 575–76. See Noonan, pp. 34–35, and *What Modern Catholics Think About Birth Control*, p. 40.

[14] Noonan, *op. cit.*, p. 528: "It seems unlikely that *Casti Connubii* intended to resolve definitively a point of exegesis where there was respectable exegetical authority on both sides. The interpretation given by Pius XI was by quotation of Augustine, not by independent papal determination."

[15] *Ibid.*, p. 527.

> She [the church] will never say that the use of contraceptives is licit. Onanism was condemned in no uncertain terms in *Casti Connubii* which recalled all the Church's traditional teaching on the subject. [16]

The exegetical uncertainty raised by DuBarle, however, blunted the presentation by the American Jesuits, John C. Ford and Gerald Kelly, in their 1963 book, *Marriage Questions*. [17] The teaching derivable from the Onan story, they write, "is not so clearly established that one can assert that there is certainly a divine revelation on this point." On the other hand, levirate violation cannot explain the passage, says a colleague of theirs in another work of the same time: "Since death was not a punishment established for the violation of the levirate law . . . it was rather because of his contraceptive act." [18] (This pertinent observation about the levirate law is discussed below, pp. 150–51).

While the Protestant tradition has not been active in deriving strict legal or even moral implications from the story of Onan, the rigorist teachings of Calvin are, of course, an exception. [19] To practice coitus interruptus, Calvin writes, is "doubly monstrous." "It is to extinguish the hope of the race and to kill before he is born the son who was hoped for." Onan, he continues, both defrauded his late brother of his right and "no less cruelly than foully" committed this crime (of contraception). [20] Another significant Protestant voice is that of the seventeenth-century Anglican bishop and author, Jeremy Taylor. He censured Onan who, he wrote, "did separate his act from its proper end." [21]

Onan In The Jewish Tradition

Determination of the nature of Er-and-Onan's act is the first of a few textual problems connected therewith. To begin with, the wording of the

---

[16] Leon Josef Cardinal Suenens, *Love and Control: The Contemporary Problem*, trans. G. J. Robinson (Newman Press, 1961), p. 103.

[17] John C. Ford, S. J. and Gerald Kelly, S. J., *Contemporary Moral Theology; Vol II: Marriage Questions* (Newman Press, 1963), pp. 271–72.

[18] Joseph S. Duhamel, *The Catholic Church and Birth Control* (Paulist Press, 1963), p. 21. See also Henry Davis, *Moral and Pastoral Theology* (New York, 1943), II, 207.

[19] For two other examples of Calvin's interpretations of Old Testament passages, see above, Ch. 5, Note 103.

[20] *Commentarius in Genesium, ad loc.*

[21] *The Rule and Exercise of Holy Living*, II, 3, found in his *Works* (10 vols.; London, 1847–56), III, p. 64; quoted by Bailey, p. 208.

biblical text seems to describe a classic example of coitus interruptus. In Jewish exegetical literature outside the Talmud—the Midrash primarily[22]—this is indeed said to have been the contraceptive method of both Er and Onan.[23] But in the Talmud itself the act of Er and Onan is seen instead as that of unnatural intercourse.[24] The Midrashic exegesis of interrupted coitus ("threshing inside and winnowing outside") is cited by Rashi in his popular Bible Commentary, making that tradition the better known of the two. Reasons for the two traditions and attempted reconciliation of the Midrashic and Talmudic ones are to be found in the relevant literature.[25]

Whichever their method, the "evil" of both Er and Onan[26] involved a contraceptive act, although the Bible does not specify Er's evil nor his possible motive. Onan sought to frustrate the levirate law, but what could Er's purpose have been? It was, the Talmud suggests, to avoid marring Tamar's beauty with a pregnancy.[27] Only one of our sources[28] fills in some background: Judah's daughter-in-law was so called because she was as stately as a palm tree ("*Tamar*"); the daughter of Shem son of Noah, she was (known to be) exceedingly attractive; Er married her but took means to avoid pregnancy and preserve her storied beauty. This presumed motive for Er's practice of contraception was relayed by many Bible Commentators; one of them, however, the twelfth-century French exegete R. Joseph B'khor Shor adds to it an alternative suggestion: "Er didn't want the trouble of raising children, for there *are* such people who care only about their own convenience."[29]

In apocryphal literature, Er and Onan are encountered again, in *The*

---

[22] *Midrash Gen. Rabbah* 85, 5, and 6; *Midrash Lekah Tov, ad loc.; Midrash Sekhel Tov, ad loc.; Mishnat R. Eliezer*, Ch. 18. Possibly also *Targum* and Abraham Ibn Ezra's Bible Commentary, *ad loc*. Also *Zohar, Gen.*, p. 186b for Er and 188a for Onan; *RaLBaG's* Bible Commentary, *ad loc.*

[23] Or, of Er alone: *Midrash HaGadol* on the passage; *TP K'tubot*, VII, 5.

[24] *TB Y'vamot* 34b; see on, *shello k'darkah;* cf. Pseudo-Rashi to I Chron. 2 : 3.

[25] See *Hiddushei Ritva; Maharsha; Mahadura Batra;* and *R'shash*—all to *Y'vamot, ad loc.* —and Ibn Ezra to Gen., *loc. cit.* See also *Pardes Yosef* to Gen., *ad loc.,* for an interesting reconciliation. The Bible Commentary called *Hazz'kuni* (or *Hizz'kuni*, of 13th-century R. Hizkiah ben Manoah), a distillation of earlier exegesis, relays a third interpretation, a curious rendering of "seed" and "ground" in agricultural terms. The contraceptive method would then be unspecified. And, according to Max Weber (*Ancient Judaism*, p. 190), not contraception is condemned here but idolatry, on the theory that Lev. 20 : 2 against sacrificing children to Moloch (*asher yitten mi-zar'o la-molekh*) referred literally to seed. This, he says, determined the "rejection of Onan's sin."

[26] "*Vayamet gam oto,*" *TB Y'vamot, ibid.; Kallah Rabbati*, Ch. 2; *Mishnat R. Eliezer, loc. cit.;* Bahya's *Commentary to the Bible, ad loc.;* though according to Avraham ben HaRambam's *Commentary, ad loc.,* only Onan was guilty of contraception.

[27] *Y'vamot, loc. cit.*

[28] *Midrash HaGadol, loc. cit.*

[29] *Perush Rabbenu Yosef B'khor Shor.* He was a pupil of Rabbenu Tam.

Testament of the Twelve Patriarchs, dating from the first pre-Christian century. There[30] a different motive for both (and a different method for Er, i.e., abstinence) is assigned, namely the opposition of Judah's wife to foreigners: Tamar was from Aram rather than from Canaan, and Er and Onan were ordered by their mother to avoid having children with her. The political situation that led the author to attribute such sentiments to her is open to conjecture. In any case, this apocryphal narrative had no bearing whatever on Jewish legal or literary discussion of our subject.

But even Onan's motive in the biblical narrative requires further explication, especially as the matter is somewhat complicated by the levirate law in the context, and by the question of the consequent gravity of Onan's sin. According to the levirate provision (Deut. 25), a man was required to marry his deceased brother's childless widow in order to maintain the brother's "name" and family line.[31] Now, if this law had indeed been ordained "before Sinai"[32]—or, if not ordained then as a mitzvah, had been an accepted practice instituted by Judah[33] which, since socially so beneficial an institution, was subsequently made part of Torah legislation[34]—then we have solved only part of the problem. The matter of Onan's punishment must still be resolved. For, according to Deut. 25:9, the punishment for neglect of this duty is not death but public disgrace. Does this mean, then, that the contraceptive act itself was the offense incurring the death penalty?[35] But the overall context suggests that the levirate dereliction is the burden of the narrative and of Onan's sin.

Among modern writers, it may be stated parenthetically, the prevalent view is that Onan was punished for an ethical offense or combination of offenses, which, taken together, warranted condign punishment. The late Professor Gandz, for example, described Onan's sin as deception of a poor widow who had married him for offspring and was denied it.[36] On the

[30] In "*The Testament of Judah*," Par. 10.

[31] Of course, polygamy was presupposed. In Talmudic times, the ceremony of release (*halitzah*) from levirate obligation, as provided by the Torah, was recommended as standard procedure instead.

[32] So, *Shir HaShirim Rabbah* 81, 16; *Lev. Rabbah*, Ch. 2; *Midrash Mishlei* 31, 29; and see *Tosafot Y'shanim* to *Y'vamot*, beg.

[33] *Gen. Rabbah*, 85, 6; *Seder Eliyahu Rabbah*, Ch. 6; *Lekah Tov, ad loc.*

[34] *Midrash HaGadol*, to Gen.; Maimonides' *Guide to the Perplexed*, Part III, Ch. 49. So also *Me'iri* and *Ritva*, both to *Y'vamot* 5b; and Nahmanides, *Comm. to the Bible*, Gen.; Ibn Ezra, *Comm. to the Bible*, Deut., *ad loc.*

[35] As implied by R. Yohanan in *Niddah* 13a; by *Sha'arei T'shuvah* and *Zohar*, etc. cited above, Ch. 6. See also C. F. DeVine, "The Sin of Onan, Gen. 38:8-10," in *Catholic Biblical Quarterly*, IV (1942), 323.

[36] Solomon Gandz, in N. E. Himes, *Medical History of Contraception*, p. 73.

other hand, the death penalty question is "resolved," so to speak, in another vein entirely by a contemporary author. He claims that the Bible here relates the *natural* effect of so unhealthy a practice as coitus interruptus; "we do not have to assume childishly that a thunderbolt descended from heaven and struck Onan dead"; he suffered a heart attack from the nervous strain of such a practice! [37]

Clarifying light can be shed on the question of Onan's sin and its implications if we bear in mind an important point generally overlooked. A brother's wife, even after his demise, is a relative forbidden in marriage by the Torah on penalty of death [*karet*] though not by the human court (Lev. 18:16). Only the levirate situation can alter this circumstance and remove the relationship from the category of the "consanguineous" and incestuous. If Onan, now, engages in marital relations with a sister-in-law—which relations were especially made permissible only so that he raise offspring in the name of his deceased brother (*v'hakem zera l'ahikha*)—but, in doing so, frustrates this very aspect of procreative purpose, then all he is left with is a forbidden relationship, forbidden on penalty of death! [38] "Noahides," the people of the generations before Sinai, were, from the Talmudic point of view, also commanded concerning such incestuous unions. [39]

Our point is best borne out by consideration of a passage in the Palestinian Talmud where important distinctions are drawn between a levirate sister-in-law [*y'vamah*] and an ordinary wife. [40] The latter may be chosen "for beauty, for money, for other qualities," but a *y'vamah* for the levirate mitzvah only. R. Yosei ben Halafta is described in that passage as having taken actual measures to reduce the sexual pleasure of marital relations with his *y'vamah*. After all, the purpose in such a case is levirate mitzvah; the sexual pleasure of onah [41] pertains only to an ordinary marriage. [42] Similarly, on another level, R. Meir, whose legal position "takes the rare few into account (*hayish l'mi'uta*)," maintains that minors should not fulfill the levirate law at all for fear (a fear very relevant to our point) that subsequently "the boy may be found to be impotent or the girl barren, and they will remain with a forbidden union (*v-nimtz'u pog'in b'ervah*). [43]

[37] Nathan Drazin, *Marriage Made in Heaven* (New York, 1958), p. 59.

[38] This, in answer to the question of death penalty posed by Father Duhamel, above, Note 18.

[39] *Sanhedrin* 57b; and see *Akedat Yitzhak* to Gen. 38.

[40] *TP Y'vamot*, beg. (with partial parallels in *Gen. Rabbah* 85, 6, and *TB Shabbat* 118b).

[41] See *P'nai Mosheh* to *TP, loc. cit.*

[42] Or perhaps even to marriage with a y'vamah after the initial levirate acquisition. See *Tosafot* to *Shabbat* 118b, *s.v. aima*.

[43] *TB Y'vamot* 61b and elsewhere.

Clearly, the levirate marriage is special, a case *sui generis;* one can hardly, therefore, deduce from Onan's act much instruction for conduct in ordinary marriages.[44] Onan's sin, as well as his penalty, must be seen in terms of the special circumstances of that situation. As was demonstrated earlier (Chapter 6, pp. 111–14), the disinclination of the Rabbis to derive a clear biblical prohibition of hash-hatat zera from the story of Onan, reflects the fact that these special circumstances allowed for no more than a *remez*, an "intimation" of the evil of this method of contraception considered in isolation. Moreover, Onan's unworthy intent, we shall see, plays its part as well, which fact further sets his case apart from the ordinary marital or contraceptive situations.

Coitus Interruptus

While the above may explain the reluctance of Talmudic tradition to derive from the Onan narrative much more than a remez against hash-hatat zera or against contraception for motives other than Onan's,[45] one would yet expect the text to serve as condemnation of the method itself even where contraception is indicated. Neither is this exegesis taken for granted, however, although the method is ultimately unanimously outlawed. For, despite the Onan story, the practice of coitus interruptus had actually been recommended in the Talmud, by R. Eliezer, in the case of a lactating mother (as discussed in Chapter 10, pp. 187 ff.). In order to prevent a second pregnancy, which would diminish the mother's milk for the existing infant, R. Eliezer would have the husband preclude conception in this manner. The other Sages did not concur in the recommendation.[46]

Parenthetically, R. Eliezer's surprising recommendation here of a practice generally taken to be objectionable, is explained by R. Mosheh Feinstein in a manner similar to that set forth in Chapter 6, above. He writes: since this is the same R. Eliezer in whose name the Talmud quotes a dictum warning against even *unintentional* improper emission of seed, his endorsement of coitus interruptus for reasons of the health of the child is all the more instructive. It means that, to him at least, seed is not said to be "uselessly" [*l'vattalah,* "in vain"] destroyed if a proper purpose is served thereby, and if this is the only manner in which that purpose can now be served. Onah

---

[44] The very phrase used by *Pnai Mosheh, loc. cit.,* namely, that R. Yosei ben Halafta sought to decrease his pleasure (*ha-kol k'dei l'ma-et hana'ato*) is used by 19th-century *Mahaneh Hayyim,* No. 53, coincidentally, to describe the contraceptive method that is not allowable because it reduces (*m'ma-et hana-ato*) the proper sexual gratifications of onah.

[45] On this reluctance, see Ch. 6, pp. 111–14.

[46] *Y'vamot* 34b; and *Tosefta Niddah,* Ch. 2, according to the *Gloss* of Eliyahu of Vilna.

(marital relations) is that purpose; since normal intercourse would cause a hazard to health, the emission of seed for onah, where there is no alternative, is not *l'vattalah;* where there is an alternative, it *is*, even according to him.[47] To the other Sages and to the Law, it is *l'vattalah* in either case; coitus interruptus is forbidden.

Maimonides unequivocally disallows the practice:

> It is forbidden to destroy [improperly emit] seed. Therefore, a man may not practice coitus interruptus, etc.[48]

The other law codes follow suit without deviation.[49]

A unique feature characterizes the Responsa in this area of our subject. They are, by and large, not concerned with questions of contraception, that is, with whether coitus interruptus may be practiced as a contraceptive measure.[50] Their concern is, rather, with unfortunate physical conditions whereby the sexual relations take this form unintentionally. May the marital relations in such cases, is the question asked, legitimately be continued?

A classic Responsum comes from one of the pillars of Jewish legal authority—Asheri, known as "*Rosh*," of fourteenth-century Germany and Spain. Lenient on other related matters, he takes a strict stand on the issue before us:

> With regard to your question concerning the woman whose canal is obstructed, with the result that semination can never be internal, and you inquire since her husband's intent is to have normal rather than interrupted intercourse, should it not be permitted. It would seem to me that it is forbidden, since semination takes place outside *always* [without a chance of completed normal intercourse]. The verse "and he would cast his seed on the ground" [*v'shi'het*, a verbal form indicating ongoing activity] is applicable to him and it is forbidden.[51]

Although the *Tur* Code, composed by Asheri's own son, did not include this severe ruling—perhaps the most severe legal interpretation of the Onan

---

[47] *Resp. Igg'rot Mosheh, E.H.,* No. 63, p. 154.

[48] *Yad, Issurei Biah,* 21, 18.

[49] *SMaG, Neg.* 126; *Tur, Shulhan Arukh,* and *L'vush, Even HaEzer,* 23, 1; *Rabbenu Y'ruham, Part II, N'tiv* 23.

[50] One exception is *Resp. M'lammed L'Ho'il,* Vol. III, No. 18.

[51] *T'shuvot HaRosh, Klal* 33, No. 3.

passage—the author of the *Shulhan Arukh* Code did.[52] Two nineteenth-century Responsa, addressing themselves to similar queries, build upon it. R. Abraham Sofer regrets the ruling, because it can lead to separating a wife from her husband; if medical care can even possibly have cured her then she is permitted to him on that possibility alone.[53] R. Eliezer Deutsch[54] qualifies and elucidates Asheri's ruling along similar lines: in the case considered by Asheri, the act of coitus interruptus was unintentional *and* unavoidable; hence the word "always." Where, however, such as in the case before *him*, internal semination is sometimes possible, then his intent for completed intercourse can be said to be realistic and such intercourse may be carried on.[55]

By far, the best effort at delimiting the applicability of Asheri's verdict to the rare case described by him, comes from R. Isaac Glueck (Responsum dated 1870), whose own case was one of a relatively temporary obstruction.[56] He draws many fine distinctions and proves his thesis by citing *Tosafot*, where, in turn, a Responsum of an early authority (R. Yitzhak ben Avraham) is discussed.[57] There the case is a divorce suit on grounds of nonconsummation, but the husband's counterclaim attributes this to a physical obstruction on her part. The reply of that early Responsum (and *Tosafot*) is that the couple continue as is, for one could expect a let-up in the impediment before long. Proof, says R. Glueck, that when the obstruction is not permanent, etc., Asheri's Responsum does not apply. If it had been intended to, Asheri would not have been so precise in his descriptions and, moreover, he would have himself cited the authority of *Tosafot* and registered his disagreement. Nor did the *Shulhan Arukh* codify the case of *Tosafot* in the section of hash-hatat zera as it did Asheri's.[58] As long as the possibility exists of normal relations, then, unintended coitus interruptus as part of an ordinary heterosexual act is not blameworthy.[59] Indeed, as two Responsa from our

[52] *Even HaEzer*, 23, 5; also in his *Beit Yosef* to the *Tur*.

[53] *Resp. K'tav Sofer* ([1859], Presburg 1889), *E.H.*, No. 26.

[54] *Resp. Pri HaSadeh* (Hungary, 1896), Vol. I, No. 77.

[55] Two more contemporaneous Respondents (R. Meir Auerbach, *Resp. Imrei Binah*, No. 8 [1869], and R. Judah Assad, *Resp. Y'hudah Ya'aleh*, Y. D., No. 238 [1873]) maintain that Asheri takes sides against *Arukh* (see on, Note 108) on permissibility of unavoidable (*psik reishei*) unintentional act; but since *Sh.Ar.* codifies Asheri, etc.

[56] *Resp. Hinnukh Beit Yitzhak* (Paks, 1890), *E.H.*, No. 7.

[57] *Tosafot*, Y'vamot 65b, *s.v. ki*.

[58] The author adduces further proof from the act of defloration, where the rupture of the hymen is *hekhsher mitzvah* for more complete coition to follow.

[59] R. Mordecai Silberer invited several authorities of his day to submit their ideas on a case before him similar to that of Asheri. Their answers, which make points like those set forth above, are included in his book, *T'shuvah L'Marei Dakhya* (Vienna, 1875).

own century independently explain, there was just no concept of "wife" in Asheri's case; hence no "intent" at all can ever render the act heterosexual, nor can the mitzvah of onah be said to appertain to such a forlorn situation.[60]

Other Responsa in this area dealt with questions of impotence where, again, the coition was accordingly incomplete. The principles of intent and of the adequacy of even infrequent completion were invoked here, too.[61] In one case, the author, R. Hanokh Padwa, writing from London to a colleague in Jerusalem, sought compassionately to have the questioner reassured, for such "anxieties will only break his spirit and adversely affect" his marital relations.[62]

We turn now to another facet of the "act of Er and Onan," deferring for a later moment important further discussion of the role of intent in connection therewith.

Unnatural Intercourse

While the intentional practice of coitus interruptus was legally banned, unnatural intercourse, which is indeed said to be the "act of Er and Onan" according to the Sages of the Talmud, was found by them to be permitted. This difference in law, incidentally, shows once again that the narrative of Onan could not serve as a firm basis for legal judgments in other situations where the circumstances differed.

In the matter of unnatural coitus [*biah shello k'darkah*], which generic phrase embraces many deviations,[63] we can discern an interesting case history of legal-moral polar tension. Here we have an example of an act which, while sanctioned by the law, was a source of embarrassment to the many moralists who could not bring themselves to accept so liberal a ruling even in theory.

The generalized license is given in the Talmud—after overruling a

---

[60] R. David Menahem Mannes Babad, *Resp. Havatzelet HaSharon*, Vol. II (1931), First Addendum to *Even HaEzer* ("*ein lo ishut bah . . .* [einah] *ishto shehittirah lo hatorah*"); and the aforementioned *Resp. Igg'rot Mosheh*, E.H., No. 63 (1935), p. 160 ("*ein lah nak'vut*").

[61] *Resp. Im'rei Esh*, Y.D., No. 69; *Resp. P'ri HaSadeh*, loc. cit.; *Resp. Y'hudah Ya'aleh*, loc. cit. See also *Resp. Minhat Y'hiel*, Vol. II, No. 22: 11, where he adduces proof, similar to that of R. Glueck above, from *Maharsham* (Vol. III, No. 161) where an impotent man was allowed to remarry only if he notified her beforehand about his condition. Again, he says, hash-hatat zera was evidently not at issue.

[62] *Resp. Heshev HaEfod*, No. 60.

[63] Usually at least three types of variation are implied: (1) *hi l'ma'alah*, the dorsal position; (2) *panim k'neged oref* or *derekh m'kom hatashmish me'ahorayim*—"retro"; (3) *pi hatabd'at*, i.e., *shello bim'kom zera*—"a tergo"; (and sometimes including *derekh evarim*. See *D'rishah* to *Tur*, E.H. 25, 3, and sources quoted below).

dissenting view—for a "man to do with his wife what he will." [64] The narrative there illustrates: when a wife reported "I prepared the table for him but he overturned it," she was told by R. Judah that the Torah permits such conduct. The husband-wife relationship presupposes this sort of freedom. In another Talmudic passage, where the context deals with the subject of the Noahide Laws, the conclusion is likewise clear that so-called unnatural coitus is permitted. [65]

The history of the law after the Talmud, however, strikes a kind of "yes-but" stance. Maimonides, first of all, in his *Mishnah Commentary*, acknowledges that the law of the Talmud permits "unnatural" intercourse, but he reminds us of the Talmudic authority who sought to decree it improper. Despite the law, therefore, the pious ought anyway to keep far from such immoral conduct. [66] (Most legal codes that permitted the practice similarly added a cautionary moral note. [67]) In relaying the law in his Code, he adds a proviso that unnatural relations are permitted, but without semination. [68] The latter is understood by his Commentators to be a logical application of the general prohibition of hash-hatat zera. [69] His contemporary, R. Abraham ben David, in his manual of marital regulations, is restrictive in another way; he sees full legal sanction in this matter as limited to the milder forms of unnatural intercourse. [70]

Independently of both Maimonides and Ben David, on the other hand, *Tosafot*, that Talmudic commentary which seeks to reconcile cross-Talmudic inconsistencies, confronts in its own way the problem posed by the leniency of the Sages in law against what they themselves seem to condemn in Er and Onan. [71] Two solutions are offered by R. Isaac in *Tosafot*, known as *Ri*, his first coinciding with that of Maimonides: (1) No semination (*b'lo hotza'at zera*) is contemplated in the law's leniency. The permitted practice is therefore unlike even the act of Onan; or (2) Semination is indeed allowed, but only when the *intent* of the ordinary husband is unlike that of Onan, in which case the act is permissible "once in a while," but not as a habitual practice.

---

[64] *TB N'darim* 20b.

[65] *TB Sanhedrin* 58b.

[66] To *Sanhedrin*, Ch. VII.

[67] E.g., Asheri, according to *Beit Yosef* to *Tur, E.H.*, 25; *Kol Bo*, Par. 76 (ed. Fiorda, 1782), p. 66a, and see on.

[68] *Yad, Issurei Biah*, 21, 9. So also *Hiddushei RaN* and *Hiddushei Rabbenu Yonah*, both to *Sanhedrin* 58b.

[69] In addition to Commentators in *Yad*, see R. Mosheh Trani, *Kiryat Sefer* to *Yad, ad loc.*, where *hotza'at zera* may be *d'oraita*, while *k'revat evarim* is *patur*, hence the proviso.

[70] *Ravad, Ba'alei HaNefesh, Sha'ar HaK'dushah* (Jerusalem, 1955), p. 137.

[71] *Tosafot* to *Y'vamot* 34b, *s.v. v'lo;* and, similarly, *Tosafot* to *Sanhedrin* 58b, *s.v. mi ika.*

This famous "second answer" of *Ri* effectively reaffirms the broader permissiveness of the law in this connection and becomes the focus of subsequent discussion. Endorsement of it is assumed for the major Codifiers,[72] although it presupposes a more liberal interpretation of the basic factor involved, that of hash-hatat zera. The implication is spelled out and confirmed by R. Joshua Falk (seventeenth century) in his Commentary to the *Tur* Code: this, too, being contemplated as part of legitimate coitus, must be deemed proper emission of seed.[73] Independently, R. Naftali Zvi Yehudah Berlin in the nineteenth century,[74] and R. Mosheh Feinstein in the twentieth,[75] offered similar expositions of the permissive ruling: such coitus, though irregular, still appertains to acceptable conjugal relations and hash-hatat zera is just not applicable. Scandalous as this may seem at first glance, the act is proper to heterosexual expression—as affirmed once again in a recently published Talmudic Commentary of the nineteenth-century Rabbi of Pinsk.[76]

It is noteworthy that *"mit'avveh,"* referring to the husband's heterosexual "desire," qualifies as acceptable intent in *Ri's* view. This, too, awaits our later discussion of the role of intent.[77] But what could *Ri's* "once in a while" mean? Such stipulation is most untypical of any legal system, certainly of the Talmud. And, when *Ri* speaks of "intent" *and* "once in a while," what does he mean? Does acceptable intent make it proper all the time; conversely, would "once in a while" be permitted even without the proper "intent"?[78] Perhaps *Ri's* unique stipulation was occasioned by the verb form (*v'shi-het*) in the Onan example (as in Asheri's Responsum, above), which to him suggested that Onan was guilty of an ongoing sin, for total birth prevention rather than contraception "once in a while." The act may be proper to the marital relationship but not more so than the procreative function.

Regardless of how the above points of casuistry were dealt with, *Ri's* ruling was generally accepted—until a reaction set in. The Zohar (see Chapters

[72] Asheri reportedly ruled favorably on the matter, but his statement is strangely missing from our editions of *Rosh*. Nevertheless, his son Jacob rules permissively in *Tur, E.H.* 25 and *O.H.* 240 as does *Beit Yosef* thereto in Asheri's name. Luria, in *Yam Shel Sh'lomo to Y'vamot*, Ch. 3, Par. 18; *Hagahot HaBaH* to *Y'vamot* 34b; and *Div'rei Hamudot* to *Niddah*, Ch. 2, Par. 10, all report Rosh's permissive ruling, referring to *Y'vamot*, Ch. 3, Par. 6 as the spot where his missing comment was to be found. See below, Notes 85–91, 93, 99, 101, 104, for later lenient rulings.

[73] *Drishah* to *Tur, E.H.* 23, 1. And see *Tos'fot RiD*, Note 99 below.

[74] *Resp. Meshiv Davar, Y.D.*, No. 88.

[75] *Resp. Igg'rot Mosheh, E.H.* No. 63, p. 156.

[76] R. Elazar Mosheh Hurwitz, in *K'vutzei M'far'shei HaShas, Y'vamot*, p. 45 (n.d.).

[77] Below, pp. 163–65. On *shello k'darkah* generally, see also *Shir HaShirim Rabbah* to *gan na'ul* and *gal na'ul*, to *Song* 4:12.

[78] *Meshiv Davar* and *Igg'rot Mosheh, ibid.*, and *Erekh Shai* to *Sh. Ar., E.H.* 25.

1 and 6) appeared in the thirteenth or early fourteenth century and exerted its restrictive influence in terms of greater austerity and deeper horror of the evil of hash-hatat zera. This influence is particularly evident, of course, among the mystically oriented authorities. R. Joseph Karo, author of the standard *Shulhan Arukh* Code, himself a mystic who did seek to confine his Code to normative law alone, betrays its influence nevertheless. We have seen (above pp. 114–15) that he incorporated, in the matter at hand, the attitude of the Zohar into the text of the *Shulhan Arukh*. But especially notable is the difference between his earlier Commentary to the *Tur* Code and his words in a later Review thereof. He had previously cited *Ri's* "second answer" in the name of Asheri without further comment; now he was moved to add:

> Had *Ri* seen what the Zohar says about the gravity of hash-hatat zera, namely that it is the most severe of sins, he never would have written what he did write.[79]

But the high-water mark in the moralistic rejection of leniency in this matter comes in the pages of a small yet influential work called *Sefer Harédim* [The Book of the Devout]. Written by one R. Elazar Azkari,[80] a member of that circle of mystics who came together in Safed and which included the author of the *Shulhan Arukh*, the book combines theology, codification, and a treatise on repentance. It is in the latter section that the author expatiates on our subject.[81] He begins by citing a Zohar passage on the evil of Er and Onan's act and by specifying unnatural intercourse as an example thereof. He continues by pointing to the "error" of those who believe this permissible by Talmudic law. Ingeniously he demonstrates at length that the relevant Talmudic passages are to be otherwise understood. He concludes most interestingly with the following peroration and narrative:

> Hence there is no sanction at all for unnatural intercourse. And woe unto him who is lenient, for the author of the Zohar has written that there is no remedy for this sin except great and constant repentance. The following happened right here in Safed in the year

[79] *Bedek HaBayit* to *Beit Yosef*, E.H. 25. The author of *N'tivot HaShalom*, *N'tiv* 11, 1, refers to the "difference of opinion" between Zohar and Talmud on this matter, recommends, as does *Pnai Mosheh* to *Sh. Ar.*, E.H. 25, Par. 2, that we follow the former, "now that we know." (Zohar passages that bear more specifically on the matter at hand are: Exodus 259a, 263b, etc.).

[80] Or Azikri, according to the correction offered by G. Scholem, in *Major Trends in Jewish Mysticism*, Ch. 7, Note 14.

[81] *Sefer Harédim*, Part III, Ch. 2. The book was composed 1588, published in 1601, a year after its author's death.

1548 in the presence of R. Joseph Karo, R. Isaac Masoud, R. Abraham Shalom, my teacher R. Joseph Sagis, and several others: a wife appeared before them and reported that her husband had been indulging in such a practice. The Rabbis thereupon excommunicated him and wanted to "burn him with fire." In the end they "ran him out" of Palestine. May God protect the remnant of Israel from sin and guilt.

The influence of *Sefer Harédim* in this matter can best be gauged by the endorsement it enjoys in the much larger, more popular *Sh'nei Luhot HaB'rit* of the next century.[82] This is the great moralistic treatise of R. Isaiah Hurvitz (d. 1628), where the wide range of Jewish practice and teaching shine forth in full mystic splendor. The author of this "*Sh'LaH*" quotes verbatim the entire lengthy passage from *Sefer Harédim;* then, a few pages later, he charges his readers as follows:

Study, therefore, to observe and fulfill the laws of marital relationship—the laws enumerated in the *Tur* Code to *Orah Hayyim* 240 and *Even HaEzer* 25. Omit nothing from what is written there. A man should know by heart every word there—except in the matter of unnatural intercourse. In that connection I have cited above the words of *Sefer Harédim;* "to *him* you must hearken."[83]

Other treatises, similarly oriented,[84] followed the *Sh'LaH's* lead. But the nonmystic rabbinic authorities continued to affirm the law as they saw it. One early eighteenth-century Commentary to the *Shulhan Arukh* took the trouble to refute *Sefer Harédim's* reasoning point by point before restoring the Talmud's ruling;[85] the others merely restated the law in its permissive form. R. Solomon Luria, a contemporary of the authors of *Shulhan Arukh* and *Harédim*, reaffiirmed the Talmud's maximal leniency;[86] another, R. Mosheh Isserles, was among many who codified the permissive ruling

[82] *Sh'nei Luhot HaB'rit*, I, *Sha'ar HaOtiot* (Amsterdam ed.) 100, a, b.

[83] *Ibid.*, p. 102b. The *Shulhan Arukh* was not yet popular enough to warrant mention.

[84] Such as, e.g., *Yosef Ometz*, Par. 193. This book, by Joseph Yospe Hahn, *Dayyan* of Frankfurt am Main, lists the practices accepted by that community, much like *Maharil* had done. It was first published there in 1723.

[85] Elijah Shapiro of Prague in *Eliyah Rabbah* to *Orah Hayyim* (actually written as a Commentary to *L'vush*), 240, Par. 10. See also *Yad Aharon*, II, No. 9, 1.

[86] *Yam Shel Sh'lomo* to *Y'vamot*, Ch. 3, Par. 18. His conclusion is "*b'khol inyan sharei.*" His entire comment is found also in *Hagahot HaBaH* to *Y'vamot*, Ch. 3, Par. 6. See Note 72, above.

alongside the nonpermissive.[87] R. Mordecai Jaffe, a younger contemporary of the above four Codifiers, disposes easily of a case where unnatural coitus was medically necessary. The kind he speaks of is a milder form but one which presumes nonprocreative semination. Yet he lists it in juxtaposition with Asheri's disapproving Responsum (above) in the matter of medically necessitated interrupted coitus to the clear advantage of the former.[88] Discussing this case, R. Yomtov Lippman Heller of seventeenth-century Poland notes that the Talmud's original ruling comprehends even the most extreme definition of "unnatural"; and milder variations (such as that referred to here and that of Ben David above) are called "unnatural" only "by homonym or metaphor."[89] These milder forms, he continues, are stigmatized (in *Massekhet Kallah*) as "brazen" [*derekh azzut*], which does not yet place them in the class of hash-hatat zera if that were involved. In the eighteenth century, the Rabbi of Eisenstadt refers in his Responsa to a marginal gloss on his antique edition of the *Shulhan Arukh* (published in Venice in 1594), which warns against the more extreme forms.[90] He dismisses the gloss as a superimposed pious comment, inconsistent with the Talmud's ruling but written, most likely, to raise the moral level in its author's own locale. And in the early nineteenth century the author of a popular Commentary to the *Shulhan Arukh* states likewise that *Ri's* ruling was maximal;[91] it was more permissive than would appear from the writings of later authorities.[92] But, he added, "in these times" it is "good to be strict" about such things. The formal permissibility served R. Menaham Shneirson of Lubavitch (d. 1866) as added evidence that precoital contraception (with mokh; see Chapter 11, p. 224) is certainly permissible when necessary. If the Talmud and *Ri* allow *shello k'darkah* as theoretically proper to the marital relation, then a contracepted relationship may certainly be sanctioned.[93]

---

[87] *RaMA* to *Sh. Arukh, E.H.* 25, 2 ("*v'yesh mekilim*"). So also *Rabbenu Y'ruham, N'tiv* 23; *Agudah,* Par. 336. See Notes 90–93, 97–99 below.

[88] *L'vush, E.H.* 23, 5.

[89] *Div'rei Hamudot* to *Rosh, Niddah,* Ch. 2, Par. 10 ("*b'derekh shittuf ha-shem o b'derekh hash'alah*"). His understanding of the Talmud is based on Rosh (above, Note 72); *Resp. M'lammed L'Ho'il* (see on) does not assume this means he endorsed it.

[90] *Resp. Panim M'irot,* Vol. II, No. 158.

[91] *Y'shuot Ya'akov* to *E.H.* 25.

[92] Many writers, such as Lauterbach, omitting all of the sources quoted in the notes preceding (and following) this one, err in their conclusions about the extent of the law. It must also be said that even R. David Hoffman (*Resp. M'lamed L'ho'il,* Vol. III, No. 18) had no access to the permissive rulings, for he said there were none.

[93] *Resp. Tzemah Tzedek (Hahadashot), E.H.,* No. 89. The author of *Igg'rot Mosheh, loc. cit.,* writes (p. 157) that he was delighted to hear that this Responsum agrees with what he himself had theoretically concluded.

One more element is involved in the matter at hand. Ben David, we have seen, restricted the Talmud's sanction to the milder forms. Actually, he retreats even further: this too, would be disallowed if the process were painful to the wife.[94] Textual support is not lacking in biblical narratives for the suggestion, by linguistic usage, that "pain" [*innui*] is involved in the practice.[95] Ben David, whose objections may thus be more ethical than moral, forbids even the least of these practices if they cause discomfort or are not acceptable to the wife; her approval, he argues, must be presumed even in (Talmud and) *Tosafot's* permission, above. At about the same time (late twelfth, or early thirteenth century) in another land, the author of *Sefer Hasidim* [The Book of the Pious][96] similarly requires that the wife's comfort and approval be consulted.[97] And, in the same spirit, a Responsum of the nineteenth century reasons that the "unnatural" form would be less "painful" in cases where pregnancy is a physical hazard; the husband's resort to this practice as a contraceptive method, sparing her thereby the greater danger, would be a favor to her rather than "pain" and, on those grounds, once again ethical rather than moral, it should be permitted.[98]

The attitude of the law, one may thus conclude, is eminently more favorable to "unnatural" than to "interrupted" intercourse when such is indicated, despite the association of both practices with the "act of Er and Onan." This difference demonstrates what our discussion has sought to make clear, that the text did not serve as the authority for the condemnation of a contraceptive act outside the special context of the Onan situation. But the most decisive statement exemplifying this point comes from still another source, the words of the estimable R. Isaiah da Trani, in his Talmudic Commentary called *Tos'fot RiD*. He writes:[99]

---

[94] *Ba'alei HaNefesh, loc. cit.,* p. 138.

[95] Shechem's rape of Dinah (Gen. 34 : 2) reads *vayishkav otah vay'annehah,* which latter word suggests the *innui* of unnatural intercourse. (Cf. Laban's *im t'anneh et b'notai* [Gen. 31 : 50], as per *Rashi, Bible Comm., ad loc.,* and see his Comm. to *TB Yoma* 77b). See also *TB Kiddushin* 22b; Rashi to *Sanhedrin* 58b, and our *Tosafot* to *Y'vamot* 34b. Also *M'kor Hesed* to *Sefer Hasidim,* No. 509, Note 12.

[96] *Sefer Hasidim,* No. 509, ed. *Mosad HaRav Kook,* p. 340.

[97] Cf. R. Abraham ben Nathan HaYarhi, *Pérush Massekhet Kallah Rabbati,* ed. Toledano (1906), p. 37. Other works make passing reference to the requirement that the woman's comfort be considered: e.g., Horovitz in *Rosenheim Festschrift; Resp. Igg'rot Mosheh, loc. cit.,* p. 156.

[98] *Resp. Y'hudah Ya'aleh, Y.D.,* No. 222; although comparative legal reasoning causes him to prefer other contraceptive recommendations. In No. 238 he hazards the suggestion that even unavoidable coitus interruptus may be condonable if "it is all right with her." See Note 55 above.

[99] *Tos'fot RiD* to *Y'vamot,* 12b.

And if you ask how the Sages permitted [unnatural intercourse, which involved] emission of seed like the act of Er and Onan, the answer is: What is the act of Er and Onan which is forbidden by the Torah? Wherever his *intent* is to avoid pregnancy so as not to mar her beauty and/or so as not to fulfill the mitzvah of procreation. But if his intent is to spare her physical hazard, then it is permitted. So also if he does so for his own pleasure but not to avoid pregnancy [for the above reasons]; as implied in *N'darim* 20b.[100] Er and Onan, whose intent was to avoid pregnancy, sinned; but he whose intent is for pleasure, does not sin. For "a man may do with his wife what he will" and it is not called destruction of seed. If it were, then he would not have been permitted to have relations with the minor, the pregnant, or the sterile woman.

This remarkable ruling was written in thirteenth-century Italy, but published for the first time in twentieth-century Palestine.[101] The discovery of this ancient document, from a period contemporary with the *Tosafot* on the margins of the Talmud, does not represent a new departure. Many voices in the intervening centuries arrived at a similar understanding of the principle underlying the standpoint of Talmud and *Tosafot*.[102] The principle is made explicit by *Tos'fot RiD*, whose formulation offers, as it were, a statement in miniature of the liberal Jewish view of marital sex and of birth control: (1) It affirms the legitimacy of pleasure as a function or objective of marital relations and even of contraception; (2) it defines proper grounds for contraception by placing the avoidance of physical hazard in opposition to less worthy motives—cosmetic ones, or total birth prevention ("to mar her beauty and/or so as not to fulfill the mitzvah of procreation"); and (3) it declares a heterosexual act, though other-than-procreative even in manner, to be proper to the conjugal relationship and not hash-hatat zera. Equally important, it makes two theoretical points: (1) it removes this deviation from the sphere of the moral or immoral, making it immoral only if the intent is contraception for the wrong reasons; and (2) it thus reaffirms the special character of "the act of Er and Onan."

Publication of *Tos'fot RiD* being a relatively recent occurrence, its vital

[100] See Note 64, above.

[101] Jerusalem, 1931. The edition bears a prefatory letter by then Chief Rabbi A.I. Kook welcoming the publication "for the first time" of this early text. R. Menahem Kasher, in his *Torah Sh'lemah* to Gen. 38, Note 44, refers to "*Tos'fot RiD*, published from MS. in Jerusalem in 1931." He calls it "something new" and relays the text in full as it appears here.

[102] See Notes 73–76, above.

implications are reflected only in the Responsa of R. Mosheh Feinstein, who carries forward its concept of intent.[103] To this may now be added the Responsa, just published this year (1967), of the late Chief Rabbi of Israel, Isaac Halevy Herzog (d. 1959).[104] His discovery of *Tos'fot RiD* and his conclusions therefrom must be noted. He writes:

> . . . It follows from here that he whose intent is not to avoid procreation but to prevent her illness—even if not a case of real danger—this is then no longer "the act of Er and Onan" . . .[105]

And, more important is his endorsement of *Tos'fot RiD* even against other authorities:

> *Tos'fot RiD,* now, was not seen by the great Later Authorities who dealt with the subject. We have a principle that "where the Later did not see the words of the Earlier Authorities [we follow the Earlier even where the Later differ, on the assumption that their own access to the Earlier would have led them to concur]" [106] and *RiD* is an ancient master and a strong foundation for the lenient view [on contraception].

The Factor of Intent

The matter of intent, introduced often in this context, requires a word of general explication, as it plays a part on more than one level of our subject. The relevant principle of theoretic law is that of *davar she-eino mitkavven,* i.e., the performance of one act while having intended another, with or without its companion principle of *p'sik reishei,* the unavoidability of that unintended effect—and this, in turn, with or without the subsidiary qualification of *niha lei,* the advantage or "wantedness" of that unintended, unavoidable effect. An example of this total principle was afforded above in the instance

---

[103] In *Resp. Igg'rot Mosheh, E.H.,* No. 63 (pp. 156–57), written 1935 and published 1961, the author incorporates *RiD's* concept into his own exposition of intent (see above, pp. 152–53, and below). In *ibid.* No. 64, p. 164 (1958) he responds to a questioner's reference to it and, in doing so, reaffirms his own position on the general subject of intent. Incidentally, the publisher of the 1931 edition notes in his preface that what *RiD* says on our subject effectively disputes what *Resp. Or Gadol* (No. 31, dated 1891, published 1924) had to say. Outside of the Responsa, there is the reference by Kasher (above, Note 101) with its lenient conclusions appropriately drawn.

[104] *Heikhal Yitzhak, E.H.,* Vol. II (Jerusalem, 1967). Vol. I was published earlier.

[105] *Ibid.,* No. 16. The Responsum itself was written in 1940.

[106] The words in brackets are left to be filled in by the reader. I have inserted here the language, in paraphrase, of *Resp. Mararik* No. 94, cited by Isserles (as 96) to *Hoshen Mishpat,* 25, 2 (end). Cf. p. 15, Note 17 and p. 222, Note 138.

of Asheri's Responsum, that of unintended, undesired, but unavoidable coitus interruptus. The Talmudic sources of the rule of unintended effect[107] actually deal with Sabbath prohibitions where "creative" (i.e., deliberate, purposive) work (*m'lekhet mahshevet*) is the forbidden activity and, by implication, intent is a basic factor. In the classic example, if one's intended act (e.g. to move a chair) brings in its train an unintended, forbidden act (making a groove in the floor), that act is still permissible on the Sabbath.[108] Query, now, whether this principle is to be restricted to Sabbath laws only. A book called *Ohel Avraham* contains the back-and-forth correspondence of several nineteenth-century Rabbis; the question of unintentional contraceptive effect and whether this principle of intent applies only to Sabbath laws, are among those discussed there at length.[109] Actually, the question of applicability of this canon outside the sphere of Sabbath laws was itself debated by earlier sources, and the classic instance of that question concerns us here directly: One of the first Codelike post-Talmudic treatises, the eighth-century *Sh'iltot* of R. Ahai Gaon,[110] suggests that the drinking of a potion for medicinal reasons, which has an unintended side effect of sterilization, would still be forbidden (to males; see Chapter 13) since the principle covers Sabbath laws alone. Against this suggestion, *Tosafot*[111] cites evidence that the rule is applicable generally. On other contraceptive questions, then, the Responsa do apply the principle. R. Akiva Eger for example could understand permitting a postcoital douche for cleansing purposes, even when it has the unintended effect of destroying seed.[112] Other authorities similarly assume the rule's applicability and draw their respective conclusions.[113]

All of this has an interesting analogy in Catholic thought, where the principle of double effect is known: An evil means might never be justified by a good end, this principle claims, but, if the evil were not a means but the inevitable consequence of a good act, the act might be performed and the evil tolerated, for the subjective intention is directed to the good end; the bad effect is "beyond his intention."[114] Noonan traces the rule in Cathol-

[107] *TB Beitzah* 23b, *Shabbat* 29b, and elsewhere.

[108] See *RaSH* (R. Shimshon) to *Mas. Kil'ayim*, 9:2. *Tosafot* to *Yoma* 34b, 35a records views of *Rabbenu Tam* vs. *Arukh* (*s.v. savar*) in classic difference of opinion on permissibility *ab initio* of unavoidable, unintentional act. This is a fourth facet.

[109] Nos. 90–102.

[110] To *Emor*, Par. 105.

[111] To *Shabbat* 110b, *s.v. talmud lomar*. See also, at some length, *Atzei Arazim* Comm. to *E.H.*, 5, Par. 21.

[112] *Responsa*, No. 72.

[113] *Resp. Imrei Esh*, Y.D. 69; *Resp. Y'hudah Ya'aleh*, Y.D. 222; *Pri HaSadeh, loc. cit.; Resp. Hedvat Ya'akov*, Vol. II, No. 37.

[114] See Joseph Fletcher, *Morals and Medicine*, pp. 112–13.

icism either to sixteenth-century Navarrus or to Aquinas.[115] The application by Aquinas of this principle in connection with abortion also has its rabbinic parallels (see on). The word "prophylactic" (literally, "prevention"), reflects the rule in operation, where the condom is permitted primarily for the prevention of disease. Catholic sanction of "the pill" for other than contraceptive purposes is another example: the Pill is licit to regulate an irregular menstrual cycle; the unintended contraceptive effect is then tolerated.

Having said all this about intent, we may find it to be totally irrelevant to contraception in Jewish law, which is complicated by a unique consideration. That consideration is the Talmudic prohibition even of *unintentional* seminal emission and the Talmudic and Zoharic safeguards enjoined to prevent it. If even prurient thoughts are to be avoided and other situations which may even tend to induce an emission outside the marital act are disallowed,[116] then even the best of intentions would be insufficient here and the entire principle of *davar she-eino mitkavven* would have to be declared impertinent. What we have said in a previous chapter, however, has prepared us for this problem. Since hash-hatat zera is *hash-hatah*, that is, abuse or corruption, only if not part of the marital act, then no improper emission intended or otherwise is involved here. In the words of R. Mosheh Feinstein, the act would not be *l'vattalah* or *hash-hatah* and this would be so "intrinsically and not as a prohibition which was set aside."[117] In other words, hash-hatat zera would not be allowable merely because another act was intended and this resulted unavoidably. It would be allowable—indeed it would not be said to obtain—if the emission *were* intended, but intended for and as part of the heterosexual act. Not intent, but heterosexual context is the governing concept once again.

[115] Noonan, *op. cit.*, p. 455, footnote.

[116] *TB Avodah Zarah* 20b; *Niddah* 13a, b; See also in connection with the present application, *Hazon Ish, E.H.*, 36, 2; and see Ch. 6.

[117] *Resp. Igg'rot Mosheh, loc. cit.*, pp. 63–64 ("*b'etzem, v'lo mi-ta'am dihui issurin*").

Part 4

THE CLASSIC TALMUDIC PASSAGE

9

A Device Called "Mokh"

The Baraita of The "Three Women"

Whatever interpretation or application the "act of Er and Onan" may find in rabbinic law, the bulk of the voluminous literature of birth control legislation in the Responsa bases itself not upon that biblical text but upon another pivotal Talmudic one. This is the *baraita* (literally "outside," referring to a text which is not part of the official Mishnah but does derive from Mishnaic times and, therefore, although "outside" that canon, still partakes of comparable authority in the Talmud) of *shalosh nashim*, the *baraita* of the "Three Women." This passage appears, with minor variations, no fewer than five times in the Talmud[1] and once more in the *Tosefta*.[2] It reads as follows:

> R. Bebai recited before R. Nahman: Three [categories of] women must [or may; see on] use a *mokh* in marital intercourse: a minor, a pregnant woman, and a nursing mother. The minor, because [otherwise] she might become pregnant and die. A pregnant woman, because [otherwise] she might cause her foetus to become a *sandal*.

[1] *TB Y'vamot* 12b and 100b, *K'tubot* 39a, *Niddah* 45a, *N'darim* 35b.
[2] *Niddah*, Ch. II, with emendation of R. Elijah Gaon.

A nursing woman, because [otherwise] she might have to wean her child prematurely, and he would die. And what is a minor? From the age of eleven years and a day until the age of twelve years and a day. One who is under or over this age carries on her marital intercourse in the usual manner—so says *R. Meir*. But the [other] *Sages* say: The one as well as the other carries on her marital intercourse in the usual manner, and mercy be vouchsafed from Heaven, for [Scripture says, (Psalms 116 : 6)], "The Lord preserveth the simple." [3]

The "Three Women" themselves are the subject of the following chapter, where the three categories are considered individually; the multifarious levels of debate on the meaning and legal implications of this *baraita* are examined in the chapter following that one. All of this must be preceded by a look at the nature and status in Talmudic law of the *mokh* itself.

Mokh in the Talmud

The word mokh probably derives from the root *makhokh* [to crush, soften] and appears to be a generic term for a tuft of wool [4] or cotton. In the Mishnah in a different context, [5] the word is used in three senses: an absorbent to remove moisture in the ear, an insertion in the shoe for comfort, and a tampon for feminine hygiene. Accordingly, mokh can be understood as one of two possible birth control devices: following that interpretation of the baraita which assumes a use of this mokh before (i.e. during) coitus, its translation would approximate tampon; if its use is presumed afterwards, then mokh is a postcoital absorbent.

Mokh figures—outside, that is, of the central baraita—in about three other Talmudic discussions. As to the Talmud's legal attitude to the device, it will be seen that in each of the three cases, permissibility is not the issue; the legal attitude is therefore an indifferent one.

(1) The first concerns itself with the matter of *hav-hanah*, determining cases of doubtful paternity. Talmudic law requires a waiting period of three months before a widow or divorcee may remarry. Thus paternity can be established: if she were to marry after less than three months and give birth seven, eight, or nine months later, the child could either be the premature conceptus of the second husband or the full-term conceptus of the first. In

---

[3] According to the text in *TB Y'vamot* 12b.

[4] Preuss, p. 479.

[5] *Mishnah, Shabbat*, VI, 5 (64b).

the case, now, of women marrying for the first time but whose previous chastity is reasonably suspect, it is proposed that a similar waiting period be instituted.[6] The slave-girl, the captive woman, and the proselyte, says R. Judah in this Talmudic discussion, should wait three months after manumission from slavery, redemption from captivity, or conversion from paganism before marrying. R. Yosei, however, holds that no such waiting period is necessary. Why not? Because, a later Talmudic Rabbi explains, he (R. Yosei) believes, "a woman playing the harlot (*ishah m'zannah*) can be presumed to have taken contraceptive precautions with a mokh." Contraceptive precautions? What about such a woman who has no expectations of being freed or proselytized, or better still, what about R. Yosei's similar waiver of the waiting period, against the view of R. Judah, for the seduced or raped as well? Can they, too, be presumed to have taken precautions? Yes, they can be presumed, it is further explained, to have taken postcoital contraceptive measures. In either case, the other authorities make no such presumptions and require the waiting period. This Talmudic passage, of course, yields no proscription against the use of mokh during coitus or afterwards; it makes legally indifferent reference to it.[7]

(2) Another Talmudic discussion in which mokh incidentally figures is the one enjoining against the remarriage of a widow or divorcee while

[6] *TB Y'vamot* 35a; *K'tubot* 37a.

[7] Noonan (pp. 11, 51) discusses this passage as representative of the Talmudic attitude to birth control. In doing so, he makes several errors. First, he takes the "woman playing the harlot" as a fourth category, rather than as a generalized description of the following three, creating a new Talmudic ruling for a harlot. Then, he can't determine if these three categories will, "*like the harlot*," take precoital or postcoital precautions, as if Rabbi Yosei's legal presumption were a recommendation, and a double one at that! Third, he assumes the purpose of the contraception is that "she can be sure her child is born after she has been received," when clearly the child will be anyway: the time of the conception is the question at issue. But his most serious error is caused, understandably, by dependence on a partially misleading English translation in the Soncino edition of the Talmud. He says (p. 51):

> A dictum, not assigned to any rabbi and not attached to any clear context, proclaims "Let, however, a preventive measure be made in respect of a proselyte and an emancipated slave." It is not clear why the emancipated slave should use contraceptives, unless the view is that she will engage in illicit intercourse and her illegitimate children should be prevented. No judgment is given on the behavior of the harlot who expels seed after coitus; but approval seems implicit.

The phrase in the original text, here translated "let, however, a preventive measure be made," (*ligzor*) is not a proclamation nor does it refer to contraception at all; the "preventive measure" is addressed to the Rabbis themselves and not to the harlot; "let a three-month waiting period be required before marriage" is what it means. The Talmud is not legislating for the harlot (illegitimate children, moreover, are born only from adulterous or incestuous unions); this entire Talmudic passage, insofar as it deals with contraception at all, is descriptive rather than prescriptive or permissive. Its concern is the status of the conceptus.

she is either pregnant or nursing her child.[8] R. Meir would penalize him who marries a woman in such condition; he must divorce her and may never take her back. But the (other) Sages require him to divorce her only temporarily until the period of pregnancy or lactation is past. In discussing the reasoning behind all this,[9] the hazard to the child brought on by a possible superfoetation (see on, Chapter 10) is considered, only to be argued: if there is such danger, why may a man have marital relations with his own wife during her pregnancy? Just as it is permitted there so it should be permitted here—either with the precaution of mokh according to R. Meir who, in our baraita, requires it in such cases, or without such precaution according to the Sages who do not feel it necessary. The Talmud proceeds, in responding, to make a distinction between the situation when the child born or about to be born is the son of the present husband on the one hand or the son of a previous husband on the other.[10] As to the mokh itself, it is, once again, treated here with an attitude of legal indifference, and its legality is irrelevant to the issue being decided.

(3) The third instance of a reference to mokh outside our baraita is also an incidental one, except that here the context is more revealing as to the nature of the mokh and hence more frequently cited in subsequent legal discussions. Detection of the onset of the menstrual period is the occasion for this reference. The first Mishnah in the tractate *Niddah* speaks of regular and irregular menses and of the requirements of periodic examination. The question here is whether, in cases of irregularity, the period of impurity begins with the actual discovery of menstrual blood; or should it perhaps be said to begin earlier, retroactively rendering impure whatever consecrated foods, or the like, she may have handled prior to the discovery. Shammai maintains no such retroactive time period need be assumed (*dayyan sha'atan*); but Hillel declares her period of impurity retroactive to the last examination. In the Talmudic discussion[11] (which became known as "*reish Niddah*," that discussion at the "beginning" of the tractate *Niddah*), the hypothetical case of a woman using a mokh for contraceptive purposes is considered in this connection. Shall we say the mokh may have absorbed menstrual blood and thus prevented its earlier detection? In such a case, Shammai would have agreed, says the Talmudic discussant Abayei, that the impurity may have begun earlier than the time of its detection.

It is difficult to avoid either of two conclusions from this latter passage:

[8] *TB Y'vamot* 36b, *K'tubot* 60a.
[9] *Ibid.*, 42a, b.
[10] See on, Chapter 10, Notes 54, 71.
[11] *TB Niddah* 3a, b.

(a) mokh is assumed, without prejudice and without reference to special categories of women, to be used almost as a matter of course, and (b) the mokh spoken of here is clearly one remaining in place during and before coitus (*kodem tashmish, bish'at tashmish*) rather than one used as an absorbent afterwards (*ahar tashmish*). Of these two conclusions, both liberal from the standpoint of the baraita and its interpretation, Rashi draws the second but not the first. Mokh is used precoitally, but it cannot be considered generally permissible. This passage must be said to reflect the practice of the three categories of women specifically granted sanction by the baraita of the Three Women, he says, not of women in general. Since the second of these conclusions—that mokh is precoital—is practically undeniable, many later authorities have seconded Rashi's disinclination to accept the first conclusion, for what would result would be an implied sanction for women in general to use mokh even during coitus, a legal conclusion acceptable only to the most lenient school of thought. Accordingly, authorities such as "*Ri*" (R. Isaac), in *Tosafot*, [12] as well as Asheri, [13] will cite the passage in *reish Niddah* to substantiate Rashi's understanding of mokh in the baraita as a precoital instrument, contra Rabbenu Tam there. [14] But *reish Niddah* will be denied its implication of general permissibility, as in Rashi's qualification above, or as in variations thereof. One Responsa writer, for example, holds that *reish Niddah* is simply exceptional. It must refer to "delinquent" women [*nashim p'rutzot*] who are using the mokh illicitly; hence no legal attitude is derivable therefrom. [15] Another applies it to women "similar" to the Three ["*k'ein shalosh*"]; to say "the same" would have Rashi here taking sides there between R. Meir and the Sages in the baraita. [16] Indeed, in terms of the practical birth control question, *Arokh HaShulhan*, a modern-day Code, makes this Talmudic passage the basis for his generalization on the side of Rashi; women "similar" to the Three ("*kayotze bazeh*") may use even precoital mokh [*kodem tashmish*], "as implied specifically in *reish Niddah*." [17]

Apart from Rashi, other "early" [*Rishonim*] Talmudic Commentators

[12] To *K'tubot* 39a, *s.v. shalosh.*

[13] In *Shittah M'kubbetzet* to *K'tubot* 39a; and in *Tos'fot HaRosh* to *K'tubot, ad loc.*

[14] As quoted in *Tosafot* to *Y'vamot* 12b, *s.v. shalosh.* But according to R. Tam in his *Sefer HaYashar*, he, too, may be said to assume that *kodem tashmish* is all right for women in general, based on *reish Niddah*. See on, *Resp. Torat Hesed, Resp. Divrei Yissakhar,* Ch. 11, below.

[15] *Resp. Zikharon Y'honatan, E.H.,* No. 2. R. Akiva Eger, *Resp.* No. 71, suggests it speaks of *eilonit.*

[16] *Resp. Div'rei Malkiel, E.H.,* Vol. I, No. 70. *Resp. Damesek Eliezer, E.H.,* No. 92, does refer the passage to the three women. See also *Resp. S'ridei Esh,* quoted in Chapter 11, below.

[17] *Arokh HaShulhan, E.H.,* 23, 6.

who interpret *reish Niddah* see it as a reference to women in general,[18] al-though we have no word from them on the baraita itself. Some "later" [*Aharonim*] authorities, notably R. Solomon Luria,[19] will utilize *reish Niddah* to demonstrate that our baraita can yield only the most lenient of possible conclusions, as we shall see.[20] That this third Talmudic mention of mokh ought not to be enlisted on behalf of a prohibition thereof is asserted by the *Hazon Ish*. He observes that to apply the passage in *reish Niddah* to the Three Women where physical hazard is involved, or else to "delinquent" women, is to give it a forced interpretation, "for [the fact of] such special circum-stances would have been articulated by the Talmud."[21]

In neither of these three instances where mokh figures in Talmudic exchanges is the permissibility of its use at issue. The last of the three lent itself more than the first two to arguments that the Talmud has no objection to its use. Still, clear proof even from here—or from a reference in *Tosafot*[22] —could not be claimed incontestably. The baraita itself is susceptible to a whole spectrum of interpretations and hence the body of literature described below in Chapter 11. Ordinarily, the larger context of a baraita in the Tal-mudic give and take reveals more of its meaning when that meaning is other-wise unclear. The baraita of the Three Women, however, in each of its sev-eral instances, is brought by the Talmud to prove something entirely un-related to contraception, so that an attitude towards the contraceptive act itself cannot be discerned therefrom. Moreover, the point at issue between R. Meir and the Sages may also be something other than contraception;

---

[18] *Ramban* and *Ran* in their respective *Hiddushim* to *Niddah*, Ch. 1 (*Resp. Zikhron Y'honatan*, above, claims *Ramban* for his point of view). See Ch. 11, Notes 77, 78. Rashi's interpretation is challenged by *RaSaSH* to *Niddah* 3.

[19] *Yam Shel Sh'lomo*, *Y'vamot*, 6, 4.

[20] Ch. 11, pp. 210 ff.

[21] *Hazon Ish*, E.H. 37, 2.

[22] *Tosafot* to *M'gillah* 13b, *s.v. v'tovelet*, presumes the use of mokh, for reasons other than medical hazard, by Esther. This, taken together with the reference to mokh in *Esther Rabbah*, Ch. VI [and *Yalkut* 1056] becomes evidence for its permissibility in her marriage to Mordecai, according to R. Aryeh Leib, the 18th-century author of *Turei Even*, *M'gillah, ad loc.*, if not to *Maharsha, ad loc.*, or to *Resp. Binyan Tziyyon*, No. 137. *Resp. Hatam Sofer*, Y.D., No. 172, sees this *Tosafot's* presumption as evidence for *ahar tashmish* only; his son, in *Resp. K'tav Sofer*, E.H., No. 26, while wondering why his father "troubled himself" with details of this question, accepts it as evidence, as do *Resp. Yad Eliyahu*, No. 70; *Hedvat Ya'akov* II, No. 37; *Maharsham* I, No. 58; *Imrei Esh*, Y.D., No. 68. *Resp. Damesek Eliezer*, E.H., No. 92, says *Tosafot* speaks only for the view of R. Meir who happens to be the author of the exegesis on *l'kahah lo l'vat*. *Resp. Igg'rot Mosheh*, E.H., No. 63, pp. 161–62, takes the reference in *Tosafot* as clear proof for the lenient position (*r'ayah g'dolah l'heter bish'at tashmish*), as had *Resp. Torat Hesed*, II, No. 44. *Resp. Minhat HaKometz* No. 94, had pointed out that the evidence here is for even far less serious a cause than physical hazard—*shello yitma zar'o bein hagoyyim*, and *Resp. Heikhal Yitzhak* (Herzog), Vol. II, No. 16, sees this as *r'ayah alimta* that the author of *Turei Even* would permit mokh.

they may well be differing on the extent or reality of the physical hazard of noncontracepted coitus in these circumstances. A convincing case could be made (see Chapter 11) on the basis of R. Hai Gaon, Maimonides, and others, that this is indeed the meaning of the baraita.[23] On the other hand, the point at issue may be: under what circumstances may considerations of hash-hatat zera be set aside? It is, of course, the latter sense in which the baraita was understood by the majority of Commentators and Responsa writers of recent times, and hence its crucial relevance to our subject. Almost without exception, the Respondents began their treatment of the contraceptive question with an analysis of our baraita to determine whether or not it implied permission in the case before them.[24] We will be better able to appreciate their deliberations if we pause to examine the three categories of that baraita.

[23] That such is the meaning of the baraita is the contention of the present writer, as argued in his (Hebrew) thesis submitted under the title, *The Baraita of the Three Women: Its Interpretation in The Literature of The Early and Later Authorities* (June, 1966), to the faculty of the Jewish Theological Seminary of America.

[24] The author of *Resp. Rosh Mashbir* (actually the author's son wrote this particular Responsum) in Vol. II, No. 69, first discusses the question of contraception without reference to our baraita. When reminded of its relevance, he reproached himself: "How come I overlooked (*eikh lo hirgashti ani hahedyot*, etc.) a baraita so familiar to every beginning pupil?"

10

The "Three Women" of the Baraita

We might have expected a Talmudic ruling on contraception for the commonplace of a woman suffering from illness or threatened by a physical hazard in pregnancy. Yet the ruling in such circumstances must instead be inferred from three other examples, where the danger is speculative or debatable. Each of the three is the object of much legal and sociological interest.

The Child Bride

The first of the Three Women required by R. Meir to practice contraception is the child bride, that is, a wife in her twelfth year. The very inclusion of this category is puzzling. To begin with, marriage to so young a bride would seem to be morally questionable; in fact, the Talmud implies as much in an Aggadic passage where such an act is listed among those that "delay the Messiah."[1] And yet, a minor bride is legally marriageable.

Exactly what the Aggadah means to condemn is the subject of discussion: not that a man actively commits a sin in marrying a minor not yet fruitful; but he is, says Rashi, guilty of effective neglect of the duty of procreation, and thus is at least temporarily derelict. Maimonides takes a stricter view on marriage to a minor, apparently forbidding it outright. In the section on

---

[1] *Niddah* 13a. See above p. 49 for discussion of *m'akk'vim ha-mashiah*.

Laws of Matrimony in his great Code, he disallows marriage to the barren, older, or minor bride unless one has or has had another wife for procreation.[2] In Laws of Forbidden Sexual Union, however, he seems to single out the minor bride,[3] without the "unless" clause—and does so in the same breath, so to speak, as he records the prohibition of hash-hatat zera. He thus gives the impression that an actual transgression is incurred, which leaves later authorities the task of squaring his words with the Talmud's clear sanction of marriage to a minor. Some indeed conclude that he sees here, as opposed to Rashi, a violation of hash-hatat zera;[4] but since the intercourse is, after all, legitimate, others reject this conclusion and instead offer various reconciling explanations.[5]

Noteworthy among these explanations is the more moralistic suggestion of a recent Responsum: there is an unseemly lewdness in taking a child bride even when one has another fecund wife, hence Maimonides' stricture.[6] This would not be so with a barren woman closer to his own age—an interesting distinction between lewdness and (proper) companionship, although both are nonprocreative. That great age discrepancies or excessive youth in marriage smacks of lewdness is found elsewhere in the Law. The biblical verse (Lev. 19:29) "Profane not thy daughter to make her a harlot" was applied to him who "gives his daughter in marriage to an old man."[7] This, Rashi explains, would lead to her infidelity. But the marriage of a child bride to one of her own generation was, on the contrary, a safeguard of morality, and the institution is of biblical derivation. The *patria potestas* gave power to the father to arrange the marriage or betrothal of his minor daughter. The mother or siblings could do so for a fatherless daughter, and she, upon reaching her majority, could dissolve the marriage, if she wished, through

[2] *Yad, Hilkhot Ishut*, 15:7.

[3] *Ibid., Issurei Biah* 21:18 (and 21:26). His language is relayed verbatim in, e.g., *Kol Bo*, No. 76.

[4] *Radbaz* (*Responsa*, Vol. III, No. 596); and *BaH* (to *Even HaEzer* 23).

[5] *Mishneh L'Melekh* to *Issurei Biah* 21:26; *Birkhei Yosef* (to *E.H.* 23); and *Hit'-or'rut T'shuvah*, No. 3—each in its own way—explain Rambam's straightforward negative and his juxtaposition thereof with hash-hatat zera (see *Yad Aharon, E.H.*, Vol. I to *Beit Yosef, E.H.* 23) as no more than a stronger expression of the Talmud's general disapproval, i.e., *m'akk'vin ha-mashiah*, but not that an active violation is incurred especially when one fulfills p'ru ur'vu otherwise. *Atzei Arazim* (to *E.H.* 23) sees the temptation to spare a wife in her late minority the difficulties of dangerous pregnancy, hence this is merely another case of entering with foreknowledge into a situation where a questionable contraceptive will become necessary (see Ch. 2, Note 124). It is, says *Resp. Beit HaYotzer, E.H.* No. 3, only this *k'tannah* in her twelfth year that Rambam has reference to. *Maharsham* Vol. I, No. 48, similarly makes distinction between legitimacy of mokh before and after the fact (*k'var l'kahah*) on the basis of *Sefer Hasidim*, No. 499, as does *Helkat M'hokek* in explaining Isserles to *E.H.* 23, 5.

[6] *Resp. Damesek Eliezer* (*E.H.*, No. 92).

[7] *TB Sanhedrin* 76a. For qualification of the rule, see *Hagahot V'Hiddushim* of Emden, *ad loc.*

mi'un [refusal] rather than formal divorce.[8] Whatever explication, then, is given to the words of Maimonides, the law remains that one is permitted to marry a minor, whether or not he has or has had another wife.[9] R. Menahem HaMe'iri of Perpignan, just a century after Maimonides, sums up the moral-legal problem in one sentence: Marriage to a minor bespeaks lewd intentions; where, however, one's intentions are good, he may certainly marry her (for the Sages did provide for such marriages).[10]

The Sages themselves, on the other hand, invoked an ethico-social consideration to *delimit* the father's power: "A man is forbidden to betroth his daughter while she is a minor, until she is grown and says 'I wish to marry so and so.' "[11] Historical circumstances, however, dictated otherwise, and a Rabbi in thirteenth-century France finds himself in the position of justifying the contrary practice, which he does in the following plaintive manner:

> As to our custom now of betrothing our daughters even while they are still minor, this is due to the fact that [the persecutions of] Exile overcome us every day. And if one can afford now to give his daughter a dowry, he fears that tomorrow he may not be able to, and his daughter will remain forever unmarried.[12]

Similarly, a fourteenth-century Code quotes R. Peretz of Corbeil, France:

> The Talmudic admonition against child marriages applied only to the period when many Jewish families were settled in the same town. Now, however [after the Crusades], when our numbers are reduced and our people scattered, we are in the habit of marrying girls under the age of twelve, lest the proper opportunity be forever lost.[13]

And, from sixteenth-century Poland, R. Mordecai Yaffe, in his comprehensive Code, the *L'vush*, offers both reasons:

---

[8] The uncomfortable conclusion of Rashi in his Commentary to Gen. 21:9—probably based on *Seder Olam*, Ch. 1; *Mas. Soferim* 21, 9—that Rebecca was a mere 3 years old when Isaac married her, is not necessary of acceptance. *Tosafot* to *Y'vamot* 61b, *s.v. v'khen*, gives an alternate calculation and sets her age accordingly at 14.

[9] The extralegal nature of Rambam's disallowal of marriage to minors is made clear by *TaZ* (to *E.H., ibid.: mi-tzad humra v'lo min ha-din*). But see *Tosefta Y'vamot*, Ch. 8.

[10] *Beit HaB'hirah* to *Niddah* 13b. See also his more general statement in commenting on *Sanhedrin* 76a.

[11] *Kiddushin* 41a, and, cf. 82b.

[12] Quoted by *Tosafot, ibid.*, 41a, *s.v. asur*. See also Isserles to *E.H.* 37, 8.

[13] *Kol Bo*, No. 76 (Fiorda, 1782), p. 64a.

> Some say that our present custom of betrothing minor daughters
> despite the Talmudic disapproval is due to the fact that we are in
> Exile and do not always have enough for a dowry; therefore we
> marry them while we are still able. Also, we are few in number
> and do not always find a proper match; our practice is to marry
> them early when a proper match presents itself.[14]

An unspoken fear of sexual violation by invaders may be involved here,
which, after all, is akin to the reason given by the Talmud for the original
institution of betrothal of minor daughters.[15] Other sociological factors were
likewise present.[16] But the institution was clearly not limited to ancient times.
A Responsum of eighteenth-century R. Jacob Emden deals with the question, frowning on the practice.[17] And, late in that same century, a Rabbi
in the Eastern communities bemoans the fact in his Commentary to the
Shulhan Arukh:

> We have seen that this leniency has spread, especially in the cities
> of Turkey, where girls marry around the age of nine, and no one
> protests. No transgression seems to be incurred except that pro-
> creation in such cases is delayed for so many years. One should
> avoid such practice, especially if he has no other wife.[18]

Nor, of course, was it limited to the Jews (or Indians and Moslems).[19] During
the age of chivalry (examples are found in the eleventh to fourteenth centuries),

[14] *L'vush (HaButz V'HaArgaman)* 37, 8 (Berdichev, 1819), p. 186.

[15] The evils of child marriage in India, focus of the *Mother India* controversy and reforms
in 1927, may have been the result of a custom beginning with the Moslem invasions of that country.
The Moslems would not violate a married woman. Cf. D. and V. Mace, *Marriage East and West*
(Dolphin ed.), pp. 194–95.

[16] Leopold Löw, in *Lebensalter*, p. 167 and Note 140, cites the bizarre case in *Zot Torat
HaK'naot*, p. 14b (a polemic against the *Besht Hasidim*) in which a local epidemic of child marriages is reported to have taken place in the late 17th century among the followers of the Pseudo-
Messiah Shabbetai Zvi. The young marriages were arranged, in that unfortunate milieu of
frenetic Messianic dreams, in order to bring forth the souls from the primeval *Guf* for new bodies
on earth and thus hasten the birth of the Redeemer. Löw (p. 168) also cites the case of the
Galician Jews in the next century who were alarmed by rumors of an impending government
decree (*die Theresianische Judenordnung*) of 1775, which would require government approval
of marriages and limit this approval. Parents rushed to marry their minor children while they
still could. *Resp. Noda Biy'hudah*, First Series, *E.H.* Nos. 63–64, deal with the legal question of dissolving these marriages when the scare (*ha-ra'ash ha-gadol*) had passed.

[17] *Resp. She'elat Ya'avetz*, No. 14.

[18] Jacob Pardo, in *Appei Zutrei*, Commentary to *Even HaEzer*, 23 (publ. 1798).

[19] See Note 15, above.

child marriages were common in England and Europe. The Church struggled unsuccessfully to raise the age limit to twelve years.[20]

Granted now the legal validity and, at times, the social necessity of child marriages, we come to the problem of our present subject: the physical hazards of pregnancy at so tender an age, seeing that R. Meir and the Sages take sides in our baraita on the seriousness of this danger.[21] According to the Talmud, pregnancy is dangerous to both mother and foetus during her twelfth year. Before that, pregnancy does not occur; after that, it is not hazardous.[22] The Palestinian Talmud[23] interprets this much less rigidly: it is not the age of twelve that makes the difference but the onset of puberty, whenever it may be. R. Meir accordingly requires the use of a contraceptive during the transitional period in order to avoid any danger to the young bride;[24] the Sages do not require it. According to the author of a modern work on Talmudic medicine,[25] "the Rabbis" looked with apprehension upon the practice, so prevalent then in the Orient, of union with minor brides; since they could not halt the practice, they "bade" [empfahlen] those involved to use the contraceptive.[26] Actually, the Talmud tells us only that R. Meir would have so legislated.

The Pregnant Wife

The second of the Three Women of our classical Talmudic passage is the pregnant wife. In her case, too, a special set of factors describes her moral and physical situation.

The morality of intercourse during pregnancy is not an issue in Jewish sources (see above, Chapter 4), but has something of a history within the Church. In between the two, the Essenes, that sect living on the margin of Jewish life in the early Christian era, were a kind of halfway station between

[20] R. H. Bainton, "Christianity and Sex", ed. Doniger, Sex and Religion Today, p. 44; D. and V. Mace, op. cit., p. 202.

[21] Lauterbach (see Bibliography) suggests that their dispute concerns the minor bride only. We know, however, from Y'vamot 37a, 42b, and elsewere, that they differ on the pregnant and nursing mother as well. Sefer Y'tzirat HaVlad in Beit HaMidrash, ed. Jellinek, Vol. I, p. 156, based on the version in Likkutei HaPardes L'Rashi, cites the dispute on the minor bride alone.

[22] Rabbah Bar Livai, Y'vamot 12b. See also Niddah 45a.

[23] TP Pesahim, VIII, 1. See also Tosafot, Y'vamot 12b, s.v. ahar.

[24] Duran in Magen Avot (see above, Ch. 7, Note 29), p. 45a, takes pride in this Talmudic caution. No other literature of antiquity, he says, took this fear into consideration.

[25] Preuss, Julius, Biblisch-Talmudische Medizin, p. 441.

[26] Duran, loc. cit., also writes "they" (plural) required a contraceptive (am'ru she-t'shammesh b'mokh).

the two traditions. Of the Essenes who were not actually celibate, Josephus writes: "They do not approach those with child, showing that they marry not for self-indulgence, but for the procreation of children."[27]

The Stoic distrust of pleasure and its emphasis on procreative purpose had a perceptible influence on early Christian teaching in this matter. Seneca, a first-century philosopher of Stoicism, gave voice to an attitude that found its place in later Christian doctrine: "Nothing is fouler than to love a wife like an adulteress," he wrote.[28] One ought to act with his wife as a husband, not a lover, and ought "at least to imitate the beasts" who do not mate when pregnant, he taught. Origen in the second century and Jerome in the fourth adopted Seneca's teaching,[29] adding mention of risk to the foetus. Clement of Alexandria wrote that it is "wicked to trouble nature" with "demanding lust" when the matrix is occupied with a foetus. Ambrose, too, counseled imitation of the beasts who, "once they know the womb is filled . . . no longer indulge in intercourse or the wantonness of love."[30] In the ninth century, a Penitential prescribes a forty-day penance for intercourse during the last three months of pregnancy. Coitus during pregnancy was "lechery and shame" in the Canterbury Tales,representing the mores of the thirteenth century, and the injunction to "imitate the beasts" was heard in that century by Archbishop William Peraldus and in the fifteenth century by St. Bernardine.[31]

Danger to the foetus as rationale becomes more pronounced from the thirteenth century and on: The *Decretum* of Gratian, a twelfth-century monk, and the *Sentences* of his contemporary Peter Lombard, were influential texts for the next six hundred years of doctrine.[32] In both, Seneca's precept is restated, combining an emphasis on procreative purpose with an implication of risk to the embryo. Then, Alexander of Hales, in 1240, taught that mortal sin is incurred "if there is a strong presumption" of danger to the embryo. At about the same time, St. Albert quoted the eleventh-century Arabic sage Ibn Sina, known as Avicenna to the Western world and author of the widely

[27] *The Jewish War*, Loeb Classical Library, 2, 120. 160. See now more evidence from the Dead Sea Scrolls, as interpreted in M. Brayer's article in *Hebrew Medical Journal*, Vol. 38 (1965).

[28] Seneca, *Fragments*, ed. Haase, No. 84; quoted by Noonan, *op. cit.*, p. 47.

[29] For Origen and Jerome, see Noonan, *op. cit.*, pp. 48, 85; for Ambrose, p. 85; for Clement, p. 77.

[30] Preuss, *op. cit.*, p. 445, on the other hand, traces the fear of a second pregnancy to an analogy with lower animals whose uteri have "two horns" and *can* conceive while pregnant!

[31] Noonan, p. 165 (but cf. Notes 56, 60, below); and p. 248.

[32] *Ibid.*, p. 173.

accepted *Canons of Medicine*, as teaching that coitus could cause abortion in that "delight" might make the matrix open and the embryo fall out. The danger, Albert said, was particularly acute in the first four months. Aquinas followed Albert on the matter; after Aquinas there is mortal sin "if" there is, or "by reason of," danger of abortion.[33]

The Catholic position on intercourse in pregnancy has other implications. In 1873, Auguste Lecomte, a theologian at Louvain, published a work, taking into account the new knowledge of the "safe period" and asking that confessors suggest this method as preferable to "onanism." His book was violently attacked by an anonymous priest, accusing him of "defending intercourse in marriage not to generate children but only to have pleasure ... a horrible crime against nature." Intercourse might lawfully be had during pregnancy to quiet concupiscence, he wrote, but choosing the sterile period is "avoiding generation by human design."[34] On the other hand, this very argument was used by John Rock, a Catholic gynecologist who played a major role in developing the contraceptive pill. Since ovulation is naturally inhibited by secretions of progesterone during pregnancy, he reasoned, nature evidently prevents a new pregnancy which might endanger the existing foetus. Why could not man follow this pattern and similarly inhibit ovulation by synthetic hormone preparations, which accomplish the same end, when a new pregnancy might endanger (the education of) existing offspring?[35]

The morality of coitus during pregnancy, it has been observed, is not brought into question in the Jewish tradition; in fact, it is actually recommended for several reasons. Its legitimacy is even taken as a criterion for permitting a contraceptive device by R. Shalom Schwadron of Berzon (d. 1908),[36] much like Rabbénu Tam had made the barren or minor wife a criterion. He ruled that a pessary (actually, according to his description, a diaphragm) is permissible because "this rubber pessary covers the mouth of the uterus so as to prevent the entrance of sperm. The intercourse is therefore normal, as with a pregnant woman, the mouth of whose uterus is naturally closed."

What, however, is the physical hazard feared by the Talmud? The pregnant woman must (or may) use a contraceptive device "for fear that [otherwise] she might cause her foetus to become a *sandal*." This is explained[37] as

---

[33] *Ibid.*, p. 284 n. See on, Peter de Ledesma.

[34] Noonan, *op. cit.*, pp. 440–41.

[35] John Rock, *The Time Has Come*, pp. 169, 174.

[36] *Resp. Maharsham*, I, No. 58. See Ch. 12, below.

[37] Rashi to *Y'vamot* 12b and to *Niddah* 45a (and 25b); Maimonides, *Mishnah Commentary* to *Niddah*, Chapter 3; *Meiri, ad loc.*

a "flat fish" in colloquial terms, as a *foetus compressus* or *foetus papyraceus*, that is, a foetus aborted because it is compressed or flattened, in more technical terminology.[38] But this presupposes the possibility of a second conception during pregnancy, i.e., superfoetation, which, although assumed by Aristotle[39] and Pliny,[40] is denied by the Talmud[41] where we are told: "A woman cannot conceive while already pregnant." The Palestinian Talmud also seems to deny the possibility of superfoetation.[42] How, then, explain the Talmud's fear? A second *viable* conception cannot take place, says *Tosafot*;[43] our fear here is that a nonviable foetus will be conceived. Rabbénu Tam rejects even this;[44] to him the need for contraception is to prevent the sperm, not a new foetus, from doing damage.[45] An early Commentator suggests that "something" is created by the sperm which adversely affects the foetus.[46] The development of the foetus is "disturbed" by entrance of new sperm, which could fertilize and create a superfoetation, says fifteenth-century R. Simon Duran in another valiant attempt to explain the hazard.[47]

Superfoetation is indeed assumed to be possible, if not likely, in the following two instances, both intrinsically interesting and relevant to our baraita. The first is from a descendant of the above Duran, writing towards the end of the sixteenth century. Tangential to a discussion of the laws of menstrual purity, he cites a case from "medical history" emanating from Rome:

> . . . And this is what, by the way, the baraita [of the Three Women] means by *shemma* [lest], i.e., the minor bride *lest* she conceive and

[38] Preuss, *op. cit.*, p. 486.

[39] *De generat*, IV, 87, 88.

[40] *Natural History*, VII, 11.

[41] *Niddah* 27a.

[42] *TP Niddah*, Ch. III and *TP Y'vamot*, Ch. IV; and see *Tosafot, Sotah* 42b. Jakobovitz, in *Jewish Medical Ethics* (p. 325, Note 132) says the Palestinian Talmud accepted the possibility. But Azulai in his Commentary (*Birkhei Yosef*) to *Even HaEzer* 4, Par. 8, had demonstrated that the meaning of the Palestinian Talmud's relevant statements is, in effect, the same as that of the Babylonian, i.e., that a second pregnancy, at least of a viable foetus, cannot take place. Independently, David Frankel, who, like Azulai, lived in the 18th century, actually suggested (in his Commentary *Korban HaEdah* to *TP Y'vamot*, IV) that the text there be emended to read, as in *TB*, "a woman *cannot* conceive while pregnant."

[43] *Y'vamot* 12b, *s.v. shemma*.

[44] *Tosafot, loc. cit. Shitta M'kubetzet* to *K'tubot* 39 places *Rosh* with *R. Tam* and *Ritva* with *Rashi. Hiddushei Rashba* and *Hiddushei Ran* to *Niddah* 26 side with *Rashi*. Azulai, *op. cit.*, cites a third view: she can conceive a *sandal* while pregnant. See also *Nimmukei Yosef* to *Y'vamot*, Ch. 1 and *Pahad Yitzhak s.v. m'ubberet*.

[45] See *Torat Hesed*, II, 44:15–17 where this point is used in service of an unconventional view of R. Tam and *ahar tashmish*. (See Ch. 11 below, Note 15.)

[46] R. Menahem HaMe'iri in *Beit HaB'hirah* to *Y'vamot* 12b.

[47] *Magen Avot, loc. cit.*

die; the pregnant woman *lest* her foetus become a *sandal;* the nursing mother, *lest*, etc. The word "lest" shows that all women are not alike in this matter. There are some whose retentive power [of the embryo] is very strong, and there are those who are weak congenitally or otherwise. A sage testified that he saw [the case of] a woman in Rome who gave birth to a child and, after four months, went into labor and gave birth to another child. When they brought her before the Great Church for an explanation, she declared that when she was in her fifth month of pregnancy, she cohabited with her "lover" and, in great passion, became pregnant by him; the first child, she said, is her husband's and the second her lover's. They accordingly "stoned" her. This case was listed in the medical books to show that the retentive power of the womb [can be very strong] and that there are women who, however, are inordinately weak and miscarry.[48]

The second such instance comes from early eighteenth-century Egypt.[49] Like the first, it explains our baraita in terms of the possibility of a second conception but applies it to the advantage of a suspected adulteress:

The baraita says "the pregnant woman [uses a contraceptive] lest her foetus become a *sandal*, etc." But, do we not maintain that a woman cannot conceive while pregnant? [The answer is] *ordinarily (al pi rov)* she cannot, but very infrequently it *can* happen. The baraita therefore is concerned with the remote possibility and hence prescribes a contraceptive so that the existing foetus not become a *sandal*. The practical difference lies in a situation in which a woman whose husband left the country gave birth shortly after his leaving. Then, after a few months she gave birth again. We can assume that the [second] pregnancy began earlier when he was still here and acquit her of any charge of adultery.[50]

An interpretation of our baraita which steers clear of the above debate on superfoetation and is free of the difficulties of either view, was offered by a near contemporary of Rashi and Tosafot whose works were published for the first time in 1962. He is R. Abraham "of the Mountain" (Montpelier,

[48] R. Solomon b. Zemah Duran, descendant of Simon b. Zemah Duran (*Tashbatz*). His responsa are part of *Hut Ham'shulash* which forms Vol. IV of *Tashbatz;* the citation is from No. 49.

[49] R. Abraham B. Mordecai in *Ginnat V'radim*, Vol. I, Section *Gan HaMelekh*, No. 130.

[50] But see *Azulai, loc. cit.*

southern France.)[51] According to him, the "contraceptive" here has the function of keeping the husband from too penetrating an entry; such physical activity could cause a *foetus compressus*. What is significant about this commentary is that the mokh of the baraita would necessarily be used during rather than after *coitus* *contra* Rabbénu Tam in *Tosafot*. Second, the purpose of the mokh is not primarily contraceptive at all, and superfoetation is not the issue. Interestingly, R. Abraham's explication can be compared with what had been written by Soranus, physician in Rome in the early second century, whose *Gynecology* was an authoritative source through medieval days. As quoted by Preuss,[52] he warns of the possibility, through intercourse in the final months of pregnancy, of rupture of the ovarium and premature flow from the amniotic sac. This can result from the husband's penetration; moreover, the exercise involved in coitus is at variance with the uteral contractions close to time of labor. The Talmud itself, in another context,[53] gives the effect of such activity as the reason for prohibiting the marriage of a pregnant widow or divorcee; the second husband, it is suggested, may be less considerate of another man's foetus and may inadvertently damage it through abdominal pressure in intercourse. The Talmud rejects the suggestion;[54] the law's explanation lies in the nursing situation;[55] pregnancy is not the problem. Furthermore, intercourse during pregnancy, especially during the final trimester, is actually recommended for physical or psychological reasons. A curious dictum of the Talmud reads: "During the first three months marital intercourse is injurious (*kasheh*) to the woman and to the child. During the middle three, it is injurious to the mother but beneficial to the child. During the last three months it is beneficial for both the woman and child, since on account of it the child becomes well formed and of strong vitality."[56] Not too much is offered by way of explanation, but the passage follows immediately upon the citation by the Talmud of the aggadic image[57] according to which the embryo moves from the lower "chamber" of the uterus in the first trimester, then higher in the second, and, in the final trimester is in its highest position.[58] Rashi accordingly assumes a relationship between the two passages, although he confesses ignorance as to why intercourse should

[51] *Perush R. Avraham min Hahar* to *Y'vamot* 12b.

[52] *Biblisch-Talmudisch Medizin*, p. 445.

[53] *Yvamot* 36a and 42a.

[54] But Maimonides does not. See *Hil. Gerushin* 11, 25, and *Kesef Mishneh* and *Lehem Mishneh* thereto.

[55] See following section.

[56] *Niddah* 31a. Translation is that of ed. Soncino, but see Rashi, *ad loc.*, on *m'lubban u'm'zoraz*.

[57] *Midrash Aggadah*, Lev. 12, ed. S. Buber, II, 28; *Sefer Y'tzirat HaVlad* in *Beit HaMidrash*, ed. Jellinek, I, 154, 156; and cf. *Lev. Rabbah*, 14:4.

[58] See *Arukh L'Ner* to *Niddah* 31a for an allegorical interpretation.

be avoided during the first trimester.[59] R. Jacob Emden offers an explanation for all three phases, linking the changing position of the embryo to the varying degree of comfort to the woman and safety to the foetus.[60] R. Isaac bar Sheshet (Algiers, 15th Century) makes the matter a point of pride in comparative culture.[61] Now Masters and Johnson, on the basis of controlled investigations, describe, during the final trimester, greater sexual capacity than expected, psychological concern on her part about physical unattractiveness to the husband, and, on the other hand, the possibility of premature labor due to orgasmic contractions near term. The avoidance of coitus near term, "based only upon fear of infection for mother or child," they declare to be "a residual of the preantibiotic days" and now to be negated.[62]

The distinction among trimesters, moreover, seems to be ignored in other Talmudic references to marital relations during pregnancy. Our baraita speaks of contraception during pregnancy without distinction. Similarly, the Talmudic passages—and citations based upon them—that speak of the husband's mitzvah of bringing joy to his wife through onah during pregnancy, also pay scant attention to trimesters.[63] *Ba'alei HaNefesh*, for example, the marital guidebook of twelfth-century R. Abraham ben David, was discussed in this connection in Chapter 4, above. Second highest place is given by that author in his hierarchy of proper motivations for marital sex to the husband's desire to confer the "benefits" accruing to child or wife through intercourse during pregnancy.[64] While he quotes the trimester formula at one point, at another [65] he makes the most, without distinction, of the Talmudic teaching that marital relations during pregnancy is a mitzvah when the husband notices her interest. And the great *Tur* Code which incorporates Ben David's words at length cites only his latter passage about pregnancy in general.[66] No reference to trimesters is made by the *Sefer Mitzvot Katan*, either; this

---

[59] C. T. Javert, *Spontaneous and Habitual Abortion* (New York, 1957), is quoted by W. H. Masters and V. E. Johnson, *Human Sexual Response*, pp. 165, 323, on the possible relation between female orgasmic experience during coition and spontaneous abortion in the first trimester.

[60] *Hagahot V'Hiddushim* to *Niddah* 31a.

[61] *Resp. Rivash*, No. 447. He refers to the final trimester recommendation as an example of the differences between the views of the Talmud and those of Greek and Arabic scholars. The Talmud recommends intercourse during the last three months while the latter say it is harmful. Don't listen to them, he says.

[62] Masters and Johnson, *op. cit.*, pp. 160, 166–67. In a recent article, "Coitus In Late Pregnancy" (*Obstetrics and Gynecology*, II [November, 1953]), W. E. Pugh and F. C. Fernandez report on their studies of 600 women who had had sexual relations during the final weeks of pregnancy. They note the absence of ill effects and urge physicians to reconsider the conventional prescription of abstinence during this time.

[63] *TB P'sahim* 72b.

[64] Ravad, *Ba'alei HaNefesh* (Jerusalem ed., 1955), p. 132. See Ch. 4, Note 60.

[65] *Ibid.*, p. 140.

[66] To *O.H.* 240 and *E.H.* 23.

thirteenth-century Code, we have seen,[67] simply states "Behold how great is this positive mitzvah [v'simmah et ishto]. . . . Even when his wife is pregnant, it is a mitzvah to cause her thus to be happy if he feels she is desirous."[68]

Certainly the fear of superfoetation, or of other such hazards, seems not at all to have enjoyed wide acceptance, even in the Talmud. All the more remarkable that contraception was considered, if not required, for intercourse during pregnancy.

The Nursing Mother

Fear of a different sort attaches to the last of the Three Women, the nursing mother, "lest her child be weaned [prematurely because of the new pregnancy] and die." Twenty-four months is held to be the normal nursing period for an infant, and pregnancy during that time is a serious threat to his wellbeing. So much so, that the practice of coitus interruptus, as we have seen, was actually recommended by R. Eliezer to the husband during this entire two-year period.[69] The recommendation was rejected by the Sages, and the practice is forbidden.[70]

Concern for the wellbeing of an infant who may be prematurely weaned is also given as the reason for a well-established law; a divorcee or widow who is either pregnant or nursing is not permitted to marry until two years have elapsed after the birth of her child. "A man may not marry the pregnant or nursing mother of another [husband]."[71] To the Talmud's question as to how this differs from the case of one's own wife in the same condition, with whom marital relations are permitted, the answer is given that a man may not be as considerate of the welfare of another's child as he is of his own and, although in pregnancy he may be considerate,[72] in the nursing situation he may not take necessary steps to supplement the diet of his stepchild. Regardless of the reason, the law is of such definiteness that divorce is required of him who violates it, and the full twenty-four-month period must elapse before

[67] SMaK, Positive Commandment No. 285. See Ch. 4, Note 75.

[68] Similarly, Sefer Harédim (Ch. 4, above, Note 76); Mitzvat Mosheh (ibid., Note 77); and Igg'rot Mosheh (ibid.). On the other hand, Huppat Hatanim (ibid.); Arokh HaShulhan, O.H. 240, 12; etc. do mention the "final six months." Where the Tur passage omits trimesters, Magen Avraham cites them, without comment.

[69] TB Y'vamot 34b; Tosefta Niddah, Ch. 2, with emendation of Gaon of Vilna.

[70] See above, Ch. 8.

[71] Y'vamot 36b, 42a; K'tubot 60a, b; Even HaEzer, 13, 11 ff. See also Tosefta Niddah, Ch. 2. For the legal extent of the practice, see also Otzar HaGe'onim on Y'vamot 42; Pit-hei T'shuva to E.H., 13 and Otzar HaPoskim, ad loc. Pahad Yitzhak, s.v. m'ubberet havero summarizes: It is known that this is an enactment of the ancient sages, but the Talmud assigns one reason for the pregnant and nursing mother.

[72] See previous section.

the marriage can be resumed. If, however, she had no capacity to nurse or had hired a nurse while her first husband was still with her, the law does not apply. Other circumstances could also set aside the law.[73]

What, now, is the fear that is behind the above law that would, more-over, require contraception during the nursing period according to our ba-raita? One of two: either a second pregnancy—which is likely—may occur and affect her milk; or, her child will be adversely affected or prematurely weaned because of this change. While pregnancy may be inhibited during the actual nursing process,[74] clearly it could not have been assumed to be unlikely during the entire two years. It was because pregnancy was a real probability during this period that R. Eliezer recommended coitus inter-ruptus;[75] he wanted to avoid the consequences for the infant.[76] R. Meir, who called for use of the mokh, knew likewise, although to him the time of risk may have been the period of actual lactation rather than the statutory twenty-four months. We know from another context that, to R. Meir, the time of change in the milk corresponds to the time of temporary cessation of the menses during pregnancy;[77] when nursing stops, be it even after a month, the physiologic situation returns to status quo ante.[78]

This hitherto obscured distinction between the time of actual nursing and the full twenty-four-month period allotted for it may account for the two distinct implications of this baraita for later Responsa. On the one hand, pregnancies certainly occurred during the so-called "nursing period," and the question of attendant risk was the issue. On the other hand, pregnancy is clearly inhibited during actual nursing, and restrictions of the baraita's legal applicability to cases of unlikely pregnancy was the issue.

Representative of one side of this coin is the crucial Responsum of R.

[73] The assumption of the law, according to L. M. Epstein, *Marriage Laws In the Bible and Talmud*, p. 307, is that "there is no substitute for the mother as nurse for the child." If substitution is unavoidable, provision for it becomes our concern. In the early 19th century, R. Barukh Teomim Frankel of Leipnik, Moravia, ruled, in *Resp. Atteret Hakhamim, E.H.*, No. 1, that an unmarried mother could marry a young man who was not the father of her child if he deposited funds for his stepchild's nursing. For references to other such circumstances see, e.g., *Resp. Igg'rot Mosheh*, No. 32, pp. 69–75.

[74] Ovarian-steroid production is completely absent at least during the first four postpartum weeks. See Masters and Johnson, *op. cit.*, p. 162.

[75] See *Resp. Yad Eliyahu, P'sakim*, No. 70.

[76] Noonan, *op.cit.*, p. 50, sees the Talmudic reference to contraception during lactation as a "curious foreshadowing of the stand of some twentieth-century theologians defending the use of progesterone pills during lactation because nature does not intend women to be fertile while they nurse."

[77] *TB Niddah*, 9a.

[78] Ancient women could nurse up to three years to prevent conception every year and to save on costs; mother's milk was cheapest. See H. E. Sigerest, *A History of Medicine* (1951), I, 243.

Hai Gaon of the eleventh century, discussed below,[79] which throws light on the nature of the implied risk:

> As to the suggestion of the Sages that one need only supplement the child's diet with eggs and milk [to avoid risk from premature weaning], you say that "someone tried it" [i.e., without supplementation] in this generation, and the child was not adversely affected. Certainly the Sages spoke of existing conditions and, if this were not true, they would not have said so. Supplementation with milk and eggs [is helpful] for her milk's sufficiency. But, when she uses the mokh to avoid pregnancy she need have no fear, and even this supplementation will not be necessary.[80]

At the opposite extreme, a question was addressed to R. Y'hudah Ayyas of early eighteenth-century North Africa and Italy: May a woman who has become pregnant during her nursing period be permitted an *abortion* to forestall the danger to her existing infant? He answered in the affirmative: The Sages differed with R. Meir on the likelihood of pregnancy at this time; now that that likelihood is a reality, she may take steps to avoid imminent risk.[81]

But perhaps "times have changed," and the risk spoken of in the Talmud no longer obtains, just as R. Hai Gaon's questioner would have it. This very idea was broached by a nineteenth-century Respondent when asked about a woman who gave birth twice "during periods of nursing" and who is now very weak. Could she use contraceptive measures so that her young ones not be weaned?[82] His answer introduces into this context the factor of possible "changed [physiologic] natures"[83] from Talmudic times to our own:

---

[79] See Chapter 11.

[80] *T'shuvot HaGeonim, Y'vamot*, ed. A. Harkavy, p. 167.

[81] *Resp. Beit Y'hudah* (1746), E.H., No. 14.

[82] R. Y. L. Don Yahya in *Resp. Bikkurei Y'hudah*, II, 121.

[83] "*Nishtannu ha-t'va-im*," *op. cit.*, p. 126. The phrase can be traced to the Commentary to the *Shulhan Arukh* by Abraham Gumbiner of 17th-century Poland. In his *Magen Avraham* to *Orah Hayyim* 179:6, he maintains that certain dietetic recommendations of the *Shulhan Arukh* do not apply nowadays, because "now natures have changed." (Similarly, to *Orah Hayyim* 173:1, washing the hands between eating fish and meat he declares no longer necessary, for the same reason.) The *concept* can be traced to *Tosafot, Moed Katan*, 11a, s.v. *kavra*, where it is suggested that medical recommendations of the Talmud no longer apply because they, or times, "have changed"; or to *Tosafot, Avodah Zarah*, 24b, s.v. *parah*, where the age at which animals give birth is empirically observed to differ from what the Talmud maintains, and this difference is ascribed to the fact that "time has changed from what it was in earlier generations." See also *Tashbatz*, Vol. II, No. 101: "I notice that the matter has changed in our generation . . . likewise other matters of nature don't seem to be in accord with what our Sages described." *Resp. Rivash*, No. 447, however, is emphatic in justifying the observations of the Sages.

[Though R. Meir requires a mokh during the nursing period to avert risk] I suspect that natures have changed in this matter . . . for in our times we see many women wean [before the end of twenty-four months], and their children live and thrive. Perhaps then the permission of contraception is not applicable today. Nevertheless, in questions of physical health we cannot depend upon such reasoning because perhaps the majority [of such infants] live while a very small number become thereby weak and die young. . . . [84]

The mother, too, requires protection from the exhaustion of consecutive childbearing, but this does not yet constitute a case of physical hazard which would justify the use of questionable contraceptives, according to many authorities. A less objectionable measure—a spermicide as opposed to the mokh—was permitted by R. Shimon Pollak of Rumania in 1919 on the following grounds: The woman was weakened and had given her children to a nursemaid; the physicians advised at least a year's rest from childbirth; a permissible method of contraception would mean only that the woman was not fulfilling la-shevet for the moment. Yet, even a field is left fallow for a while so that it may the better give forth its produce later; moreover, if she had not been weakened she would not have given her child now to a nursemaid, and if she were nursing now herself she would not become pregnant anyway. Hence, she will not be fulfilling la-shevet any less if she takes advantage of the contraceptive measure! [85]

The mokh itself, according to this point of view, would not yet be permitted for purposes of such "spacing," since only actual hazard makes it legitimate. In this connection, it is interesting to note the reply of R. Mosheh Feinstein in 1958: What you heard in the name of a Rabbi from Lithuania, he writes to his questioner, that the Rabbis there permitted contraception to women for two years after each childbirth, is simply not true. Only cases of genuine physical danger are contemplated in the sanction of mokh. [86]

The illustrious R. Hayyim of Volozhin (d. 1821) is credited with a wryly humorous interpretation of a biblical passage, expressing the despair

---

[84] As to the necessity of weaning because of pregnancy, Dr. Alan F. Gutmacher of Mt. Sinai Hospital, New York, writes: "I am uncertain whether pregnancy during lactation suppresses milk production; it is more likely that the hormonal influence which promotes lactation is already waning sufficiently to release its inhibitory influence on ovulation."—"Traditional Judaism and Birth Control," *Judaism: A Quarterly* (Spring, 1967). Cf. Note 74, above.

[85] *Resp. Shem MiShim'on*, No. 7.

[86] *Resp. Igg'rot Mosheh, E.H.*, No. 64. He, of course, is speaking of precoital mokh. On the other hand, *N'tziv* in *Resp. Meshiv Davar*, No. 88, who permits only postcoital mokh in cases of danger, regards a woman who habitually conceives during nursing as in the category of women in danger.

of those who are visited by births in quick succession. The "curse of Eve" in Gen. 3:16 reads: "I will greatly increase thy pain and thy travail (*itz'vonekh v'heronekh*)." The phrase is called a *hendiadys* by Bible exegetes, namely a phrase in which the conjunction "and" actually serves as a genetive: "Thy pain and thy travail" means "The pain of thy travail [labor]—*itz'von heronekh*," i.e., the pain of childbirth. But R. Hayyim addressed himself to the order of the nouns: When a woman is still in the "pain" of nursing and tending little infants, the "travail" of a brand new pregnancy overtakes her.[87]

Pregnancy during lactation was indeed common, as far as the Responsa are concerned. It is certainly more probable than with the other of the Three Women, says a nineteenth-century Polish Rabbi:

> Pregnancy is very likely in the case of the nursing mother, which is why marriage to one is prohibited. But the Three Women are not all alike: the minor and pregnant woman are not likely to become pregnant, but, because of danger, we take the unlikely into account. The nursing mother, however, is very likely to conceive, but the risk is not great, and the diet might be supplemented, etc.[88]

Hence, he reasons, in cases of greater risk, the mokh is certainly permissible. Or, says a Hungarian Rabbi of the same century, in cases where there is no remedy like the diet supplementation would have been for the nursing mother, contraception is certainly to be sanctioned.[89]

Yet that other side of the coin, that lactation inhibits pregnancy, served the Responsa as a basis for argumentation as well. At least during the time of actual nursing, says R. Mosheh Schick, is conception halted:[90]

> For, observation and experience testify that ordinarily a woman does not conceive during pregnancy. Our women do not use a contraceptive during pregnancy and yet we see they do not conceive then. Also, we see that the nursing mother does not become pregnant at the *time of* nursing—for whatever reason: either the milk changes or the limbs weaken.[91] Either way, experience testifies that pregnancy does not occur during nursing. So also with the minor; although pregnancy is possible for her, it is not usual.[92]

[87] Cited in *Pardes Yosef* to Gen. 3:16.
[88] *Yad Eliyahu, P'sakim,* No. 70.
[89] *Resp. Neta Sorek,* No. 6.
[90] *Resp. Maharam Schick, Hoshen Mishpat,* No. 54.
[91] See *TB Niddah* 9a.
[92] See also *Resp. Neta Sorek,* Nos. 6 and 9; *Resp. Yad Yitzhak,* Vol. III, No. 9.

This phenomenon, theoretically presumed or empirically observed, became the basis for the point made by R. Menahem Shneirson of White Russia, the Lubavitcher Rabbi of the nineteenth century.[93] The unlikelihood of pregnancy during actual nursing was the reason for the demurral by the Sages against R. Meir, whereas in the case of a more likely risk, they would have concurred:

> The Creator so ordained human nature that the Three Women do not ordinarily conceive. . . . However, in cases of ordinary risk [such as in the case before us] the Sages certainly would agree with R. Meir that a mokh must be used. The author of *Hemdat Shlomo* permits a mokh in case of mortal danger.[94] But, according to the way I see it, mokh should be permitted even where risk is only possible, as the text says with regard to the nursing mother: lest she wean and lest he die—which is a double "lest." She may wean [if she becomes pregnant] and yet it may not hurt him; or she may, as the Talmud suggests elsewhere, hire a nurse or supplement his diet. But with danger of another kind, even the Sages would agree with what R. Meir says about the nursing mother; for pregnancy to such a woman [in the case before us] would be much more likely than to a nursing mother.

The words of Dr. John Rock were quoted above, whereby use of the Pill for the benefit of offspring already born was justified on the grounds that it emulated the pattern of nature in preventing a new pregnancy when such would adversely affect an existing foetus. A parallel argument on behalf of the existing infant was advanced by Peter de Ledesma, a Dominican theologian of sixteenth-century Spain: Danger to the foetus in pregnancy was grounds not for contraception but for unilateral refusal of the marital debt. He extended this principle to the lactating mother, on the supposition that her milk would, in a second pregnancy, be "dangerous" to the suckling. And, if such postponement of procreation is allowable for the welfare of offspring, he reasoned, why not such denial of "conjugal dues" to prevent danger to the, say, education of existing offspring? Or, since a man might leave home on business or become a crusader without his wife's consent, why not also abstain against her will for the welfare of his children?[95] Al-

---

[93] *Resp. Tzemah Tzedek (Ha-hadashot), Even HaEzer*, Vol. I, No. 89.

[94] See Chapter 11.

[95] In "Matters Attached to Marriage and the Rendering of the Marital Debt," *Treatise on the Great Sacrament of Matrimony*, quoted by Noonan, *op.cit.*, p. 332.

though he answered his own question with a formal negative, his assumption of danger to the suckling affords an interesting parallel to discussion of the subject in Talmud and Responsa.

A far more intriguing parallel relates to the obverse side of the coin, that of the natural inhibition of pregnancy during lactation. According to "conservative sources within the Vatican,"[96] Pope Paul had been considering approval of the Pill to suppress ovulation for a period of "perhaps two years after each birth," on the grounds that breast-feeding used to serve as a brake on fertility for this period, and it would not be an interference with nature to do by pill what used to be accomplished by lactation.

Our "Three Women," then, comprise three conditions in which a marginal hazard is connected with the pregnancy or with what appertains to pregnancy. Hence R. Meir and the Sages differed as to the extent, reality, or inevitability of the hazard. How the baraita became the springboard for theoretical discussion on so many levels and for determination of myriad practical cases is the subject of our next chapter.

[96] Reported by Barbara Yuncker on August 16, 1966, as part of a series in the New York *Post*. See above, Note 76.

II

The Drama of the Literature

The Debate Surrounding the Baraita

The nature and status of the mokh and the categories of the Three Women have been considered. We can focus now on the many levels of debate as to the meaning of the baraita itself.[1] R. Meir, it will be recalled, taught *shalosh nashim m'shamm'shot*, the Three Women (must or may) use the mokh in their cohabitation; the other Sages, that these carry on their marital intercourse in the usual manner and "mercy be vouchsafed from heaven." As between R. Meir and the Sages, the law (halakhah) follows the Sages,[2] of course, according to the majority-rule principle. But *what* law follows the Sages? What does the baraita mean? By *m'shamm'shot*, does R. Meir mean they "must" or they "may" use a mokh? If he is shown to mean "may," then the other Sages in differing mean they "may not"; if he means "must," then they mean "must not," i.e., need not, but may.

A second level of the debate turns on the kind of mokh usage presumed for the baraita. Is it to be used *kodem tashmish*, before (i.e., during) coitus or after? If after, then the sex act as such is not involved; the question is one of frustration of effect and of a possible technical violation by the woman.

---

[1] The material in this chapter, although apparently detailed, is in fact abbreviated. What is omitted from here can be found in the writer's (Hebrew) thesis, described in Ch. 9, Note 23.

[2] Meiri to *Y'vamot* 12b; *R'mazim* of *Ya'akov ben Asher*, to *Y'vamot*, Ch. 1.

If it is used before, then there are these questions plus that of hash-hatat zera for the man as well—the subject of our main concern. Rashi, the standard Talmudic Commentator, and Rabbénu Tam, an eminent authority of the *Tosafot*, are the principals involved in the debate.

According to the conventional reading of the words of these two chief commentators,

(1) Rashi would say that (*a*) R. Meir means "may" (*mutarot*) and hence the Sages mean "may not" (*asurot*). The law then is that even these Three Women may not; (*b*) the mokh is assumed to be precoital (*kodem tashmish*); hence (*c*) hash-hatat zera is involved here; (*d*) for him as well as for her. Nevertheless, (*e*) R. Meir sought to permit the mokh for these Three Women because of the special circumstances of what to him are potentially dangerous pregnancies—the Sages disagree. (*f*) Other women (*sh'ar nashim*) certainly may not use such a device.

(2) To Rabbénu Tam as reported in *Tosafot:* [3] (*a*) R. Meir means "must" (*tz'rikhot, hayyavot*), hence the Sages, in differing, mean "must not" (need not) but "may" (*mutarot*); (*b*) a precoital mokh is clearly inadmissible; to use one is to "cast one's seed on wood and stones"; hence (*c*) hash-hatat zera would have been involved; (*d*) for him, but technically not for her. If however, the precoital mokh is not used, and the sex act is unimpeded although later rendered nonprocreative by her, then his act does not differ from that of coitus with a barren woman; (*e*) R. Meir would not suggest the precoital mokh even to avoid danger as long as there is a permissible alternative. That alternative is the postcoital mokh, which is what the baraita is talking about. R. Meir requires the use of this mokh for the Three Women; the Sages do not. Being unobjectionable in and of itself, it (*f*) would be permissible to all women (*sh'ar nashim*) even without the justification of potential hazard.

The assumption attributed to Rashi, that the technical violation of hash-hatat zera is applicable to the woman (1*d*), is provisionally supported by this *Tosafot*, which shows where the implication is possible in the Talmud. [4] For itself, *Tosafot* does not concur. [5] The assumption itself, however, may not be correct. Rashi's specification that the mokh be precoital (1*b*), does not require the conclusion that, to him, a postcoital mokh is in any case a violation (1*d*). He may have so stated only because, as a commentator more than

---

[3] To *Y'vamot* 12b, *Ktubot* 39a, both *s.v. shalosh.*

[4] See Ch. 6, above, pp. 123 ff.

[5] A novel objection to this entire approach is raised by R. Pinhas Hurvitz (d. 1802) in *Sefer Hafla'ah* to *K'tubot* 29: The *k'tannah* is not yet *bat onshin*, so how can any violation apply to her alone? Similarly, *Resp. Yad Eliyahu, Psakim,* No. 70: She is not *bat mitzvah*. See on, R. Akiva Eger, etc.

as a decisor, this interpretation is sounder linguistically.[6] Alternatively, he may have specified precoital because he believes the postcoital usage to be of *doubtful effectiveness;* hence, unsafe when pregnancy *must* be avoided.[7] Indeed, Rashi's words elsewhere are held against him in the Responsa of R. Moses Sofer. In defining the mokh usage by the harlot—where the same verbal phrase is used—Rashi clearly describes it as postcoital.[8] All of which may indicate that his commentation is merely *ad hoc:* The harlot does what she does for her reasons, but R. Meir is prescribing what ought to be done to effectively avoid danger.[9] The very existence of unwanted pregnancies testifies, according to R. Aryeh Plotzker, to the unreliability of postcoital efforts.[10] Not because the latter is evil, then, did Rashi specify precoital, but because it is inadequate. If so, we were wrong in inferring (1*f*) that the Sages would not allow the postcoital mokh—to anyone regarding it as safe enough for use.[11]

Nor do the words of Rabbénu Tam go unchallenged. The assumption attributed to him that a precoital mokh is too serious a violation to be set aside by R. Meir (2*e*) is rebutted by "Ri" in another *Tosafot;*[12] he upholds Rashi by pointing to the Talmudic discussion in *reish Niddah,* to which we have referred in Chapter 9,[13] where precoital usage is presumed for mokh. What is more remarkable is that Rabbénu Tam himself in his own writings rather than in *Tosafot's* citations seems to challenge this assumption and, like Ri, offers *reish Niddah* as evidence! In *Sefer HaYashar,* a work by Rabbénu Tam not published until several centuries later, he speaks for himself:

[6] So *Beit Meir* to E.H. 23. *Resp. Tzemah Tzedek E.H.* No. 89: "The language *m'sham'shot b'mokh* clearly points to precoital usage; Rashi's is undoubtedly the correct interpretation" But, *Resp. Hemdat Sh'lomo, E.H.* No. 46, argues the other way: if precoital is meant, the baraita should have read *"im shalosh nashim m'shamm'shim."* Similarly, at least to explain Rabbénu Tam, *K'tav Sofer* compares this phrase to *m'shammeshet b'iddim* which is postcoital. (This Responsum does not appear in *Resp. K'tav Sofer* [1888]; written in 1841, it became part of the correspondence in *Ohel Avraham,* 1895.) Cf. *Torat Hesed,* Note 8, below.

[7] *Beit Meir, loc. cit. (she-lo t'kanneah yafeh yafeh); Resp. R. Akiva Eger (leka vadai shelo tit'abber); Resp. Hatam Sofer,* Y.D., No. 172 *(ein r'fuato b'dukah).*

[8] *Ktubot* 37a. *Resp. Torat Hesed, E.H.,* 42:5, reconciles: *m'shamm'shot—tashmish; ishah m'zannah m'shammeshet—mishtammeshet.*

[9] *Resp. Hatam Sofer, loc. cit.*

[10] *Get M'kushar,* quoted in his *Resp. M'shivat Nefesh,* No. 18.

[11] An unconventional view is set forth by *N'tziv* in *Resp. Meshiv Davar,* Y.D., No. 85: Rashi never meant R. Meir to permit *kodem tashmish,* but *ahar tashmish miyyad. Kodem tashmish* is bad, as indicated in Rashi's words to *K'tubot* 39a: *she-mash-hitot zera; ahar tashmish* is unsafe. At about the same time, Ktav Sofer (see Note 6, above) concluded that Rashi and Rabénu Tam differ only on *hayyavot* and *mutarot.*

[12] To *K'tubot* 39a, *s.v. shalosh.*

[13] See above, pp. 172 ff.

> Three Women, etc. [The meaning is] they must use the mokh to avoid danger. It is wrong to read here "may" ... Even hash-hatat zera, which should make the mokh impermissible to women not in danger, is not involved here, as we see in *reish Niddah* [where precoital mokh is taken for granted]. [14]

Some try ingeniously to reconcile these words of Rabbénu Tam with what *Tosafot* to *Y'vamot* had said in his name. R. Shneur Zalman of Lublin had already sensed many difficulties with the assumption that Rabbénu Tam could have ruled out the precoital mokh, [15] and he therefore concluded that *Tosafot* to *Y'vamot* simply differs with that to *K'tubot*, where *Ri* is cited. [16] What he found in *Sefer HaYashar* confirmed it:

> If I were not afraid, I would say that *Tosafot* to *Y'vamot* did not see what is written in *Sefer HaYashar*, for the latter has no hint of pro-hibiting precoital mokh. I searched the rest of the book and found no other reference to it. [17]

Likewise, R. Issakhar Berish of Bendin discerned that authorities contem-poraneous with Tosafot did *not* assume that Rabbénu Tam forbade the pre-coital mokh. The Talmudic codex of R. Mordecai ben Hillel (d. 1298) relays the words of Rabbénu Tam without reference to precoital or postcoital; [18] so does Nahmanides. [19] R. Berish concludes his analysis:

> Still, although *Tosafot* to *Y'vamot* wrote something contrary to this in the name of Rabbénu Tam, that precoital mokh [is forbidden], thank God my eyes were opened and I saw what is written in Rab-bénu Tam's *Sefer HaYashar*. His words prove ... that his view is as suggested by Ri, Ramban, and Mordecai ... since he concludes

---

[14] *Sefer HaYashar*, ed. Schlesinger (Jerusalem, 1959) to *Niddah* 45a. (Oxford MS., p. 166; Vienna MS., No. 149, p. 19d.)

[15] *Resp. Torat Hesed, E.H.*, No. 44:15, where he raises a strong question: the *next* Tosafot on the same page in *Y'vamot* (*s.v. shemma*) quotes Rabbénu Tam on *hozeret umit'abberet*, where his comment is clearly incompatible with *ahar tashmish*.

[16] *Loc. cit.*, 44:18.

[17] *Loc. cit.*, 44:20.

[18] *Mordekhai* to *Y'vamot*, Ch. 1.

[19] Ramban in *Hiddushei RaN* to *Niddah* 13; and in *Hiddushei Rashba* to *K'tubot* 39.

with "as we see in *reish Niddah.*" *Tosafot* to *Y'vamot* was perhaps telling us how Rabbénu Tam would explain *Rashi*'s view.[20]

Independently of both of the above, R. Yehiel Weinberg, in a Responsum published in 1966, comes to the same conclusion, except that he more boldly disqualifies the report of *Tosafot:*

> What is said in the name of Rabbénu Tam—that the use of a precoital mokh is like "casting one's seed on wood and stones"—is actually *not* the view of Rabbénu Tam. It is the view of Ri in *Tosafot* to *K'tubot.* Rabbénu Tam's true position was stated in *Sefer Ha-Yashar,* bringing evidence from *reish Niddah. Tosafot* to *K'tubot* is correct; in *Tosafot* to *Y'vamot,* the text is in disorder (*ba'u ha-d'varim m'kuta'im*).[21]

Rashi then, did not necessarily specify precoital and Rabbénu Tam postcoital. Their real difference of opinion concerns "may" versus "must"—with its profound legal implications for the Responsa on birth control. It must be remembered, however, that the conventional understanding of the baraita, as described in the beginning of our chapter, continued to predominate in the Responsa. The difference between precoital and postcoital mokh continued to figure, with those of the stricter school allowing the postcoital usage only.[22] Still, the "must" versus "may" controversy was a much more important consideration for determining the law in the case at hand.

[20] *Resp. Divrei Yissakhar* (publ. 1910), No. 138. On the other hand, *Resp. Beit Av,* Vol. VII., No. 12, seeks to restore the position ascribed to Rabbénu Tam, but does so on the strength of a spurious *Tos'fot HaRosh,* on which see below.

[21] *Resp. S'ridei Esh,* Vol. III, No. 14. The author of *Resp. Sitri UMagini* No. 44, had also suggested an emendation of *Tosafot* to *Y'vamot.*

[22] *Resp. Hatam Sofer,* Y.D., 172; *Imrei Esh,* Y.D., 68; *Binat Adam, Beit HaNashim,* 36; *Beit Yitzhak,* No. 91; *Naharei Afars'mon,* Vol. II, No. 47; *Arugat HaBosem,* Y.D., 187; *Neta Sorek,* No. 6; *Zikhron Y'honatan,* No. 3, and many others, permit only postcoital mokh in cases of danger, providing it is effective (see Note 7, above). Some, such as *Avnei Nezer,* No. 81, and *Sitri UMagini,* No. 44, permit it to women in general, in keeping with inference from Rabbénu Tam (2f). See on for special cases of R. Akiva Eger and *Resp. Binyan Tziyyon.* See Ch. 12 for other postcoital usages, such as douche. *Hazon Ish, E.H.* 37 argues that precoital is less of a concession than postcoital, but the bulk of the Responsa clearly assume the contrary. Among the lenient ones permitting even precoital mokh for cases of danger are *Resp. Hemdat Shlomo,* No. 46; *Tzemah Tzedek (Hahadashot)* No. 89; *Torat Hesed, E.H.,* No. 44; *Sdei Hemed, P'at HaSadeh, Ishut,* No. 1; *Marheshet,* Vol. II, No. 9; *Ahiezer,* No. 23; *Or Gadol,* Vol. I, No. 31; *Yismah Lev,* Y.D., No. 4; *Z'kan Aharon,* Vol. I, No. 83; *Ktav Sofer,* No. 26; *Divrei Yissakhar,* No. 138; *Igg'rot Mosheh, E.H.,* No. 63; plus many others. As to precoital mokh for women in general, the most lenient position on birth control, see on, this chapter.

The Early Authorities ("Rishonim"):
The Mitzvah of Avoiding Hazard

The second round of the debate introduces the *Rishonim*, the early authorities before the *Shulhan Arukh*. In the dispute between Rashi and Rabbénu Tam, they take sides, in virtual unanimity, with the latter: "must" as opposed to "may." Some of them are represented in *Shittah M'kubetzet*, a collection of citations from these Sages assembled in the seventeenth century; others, in their own works of commentation or *novellae* on the Talmud. One after another, these *Rishonim* are led by the logic of Rashi's position to reject it: if R. Meir means "may," the other Sages mean "may not" (1a); how can the Sages *forbid* taking precautions to avoid danger? Just because "the Lord preserveth the simple," is she required to place herself in danger?[23] Abstinence, we have seen above (Chapter 4), is not an alternative. Secondly, the child bride before the age of pregnancy would then also, theoretically, come under the prohibition by the Sages; why should they forbid something that will make no difference?[24] The latter objection is met by, among others, R. David ben Zimra, the sixteenth-century heir to Maimonides' seat of authority, who restates the important distinction (above, Chapter 6) between nonprocreative coitus and actual hash-hatat zera.[25] But the former objection of the *Rishonim* stands: if danger exists, the Sages would not prohibit precaution; Rabbénu Tam is right; the Three Women "must," according to R. Meir, and they "need not" but "may," according to the Sages.[26]

This is all well and good as a theoretical exposition of the baraita, but if Rabbénu Tam, on whose authority it rests, is to be followed throughout, the corollary conclusion is that "other women" also may. Such a conclusion was a little too lenient for practical ruling. The aforementioned Ben Zimra, therefore, resisted the tyranny of logic: he rejected Rabbénu Tam's opinion and adopted Rashi's, avoiding its difficulties at the same time:

[23] R. Aharon Halevi and Ritva, in *Shittah M'kubetzet* to *K'tubot*, 39; *Hiddushei Ritva* to *Y'vamot* 12b.

[24] Ritva, Ramban, in *Shittah, loc. cit.; Hid. Ritva, ibid.; Hiddushei Rashba* and *Meiri* to *Y'vamot* 12b; also *Nimmukei Yosef* to *Y'vamot* 12b, who may be the "*Talmid Ha Rashba*" in *Shittah, loc. cit.*

[25] *Resp. Radbaz*, Vol. III, No. 596; *Resp. Binyan Tziyyon*, No. 137. See on, R. Akiba Eger.

[26] R. Menahem Ha Me'iri to *Y'vamot* 12b takes the singular position that this conclusion does not follow with regard to the *k'tannah*. R. Meir means "must"; the Sages, "must not but may sometimes"—such as before the time of danger; after that they too may not. This interpretation, not without its implications in other cases, is called "brand new" in ed. Albeck (Berlin, 1922); in ed. Dyckman (Jerusalem, 1962), we are told that "Ritva so wrote." Cf. *Hid. Ritva, loc. cit.*

The Sages could not be saying that the Three Women *may not* use the mokh. For she can say, "Maybe I don't have enough merit (*z'-khut*) that 'mercy be vouchsafed from heaven.' " Therefore, all agree that the Three Women in fact *may* use the mokh—but others are forbidden. . . . And know that even though Rabbénu Tam holds that . . . mokh is permitted to all women, we shall not rely on him [and permit] this ugly deed (*ma'aseh m'gunneh*) but on Rashi.[27]

His safety clause about her "merit" renders academic the "must" versus "may" debate for the Three Women. Ben Zimra can thus subscribe to Rashi's view, and yet salvage permission for the Three Women (rather than conclude that the Sages *forbade* precaution for them) while denying permission to "other women." The same practical end is attained by the reasoning of another scholar, the eighteenth-century R. Jacob Joshua Falk, in his Talmudic Commentary. He argues that Rashi's "may" actually implies "must": By "may," Rashi means she legally may; since she may, it is her *duty* to take this legal means to avoid hazard![28] Hence she "must," and the Sages mean "must not," but other women still "may not." This variation in inference from the baraita found some support in later writings.[29] In either case, the words of the *Rishonim*, above, figured most prominently in the analyses by later authorities.

Notwithstanding novel variations just described—or even the implications of *Sefer HaYashar*—the majority of Responsa by the Later Authorities (*Aharonim*) assume a conventional reading of the baraita. They presuppose the structure of Rashi versus Rabbénu Tam as to "may" versus "must" and precoital versus postcoital as set forth in the beginning of this chapter. By and large, they accept the logic of the *Rishonim* and side with Rabbénu Tam. However, either because they seek to avoid the consequent leniency of a permission to "other women" to use at least the postcoital mokh, or because they want to secure their argument in favor of permission to women in danger *even* according to Rashi's point of view, they postulate Rashi's view as opera-

[27] *Resp. Radbaz*, loc. cit.

[28] *Pnei Y'hoshua* to *K'tubot* 39a.

[29] The author of *Resp. Ahiezer*, E.H., No. 23, follows Falk, citing Rashi's words in *Niddah* 45a (*takkanatan havvah l'shammesh b'mokh*) as implying prescription rather than permission. Also, *Resp. Divrei Malkiel*, E.H., No. 70, and *Marheshet*, Vol. II, No. 9:2:8. Cf. *Resp. Damesek Eliezer*, E.H., No. 92, who compares this to Ritva (and Meiri) in Note 26, above. *Ahiezer* compares it to *Radbaz*, loc. cit. On the other hand, *Resp. Maharam Brisk*, Vol. I, No. 97, argues that if the view of the Sages is based on consideration of the likelihood of the risk rather than on the likelihood of heavenly mercy in the event of that risk, then we cannot "build upon" the words of *Radbaz*. See on.

tive. They then proceed to delimit the circumstances of its application and elicit a permissive ruling, not for women in general, but only for the imperiled woman whose case has come before them. In the process of doing so, as the following illustrations will show, these Responsa authorities afford us some important and interesting refinements of the Avoidance of Hazard principle in Jewish law. Their final position, upon analysis, is not too far from that of Ben Zimra and Jacob Falk, above, who retained the framework of Rashi but avoided the conclusion of a prohibition of precaution by the Sages. Their method, generally, is to predicate a special kind of hazard implied in the baraita—say, a very *marginal* hazard—which the Sages rightfully discount. From this it could follow that if the danger to the woman before us were less marginal than contemplated by the baraita, that is, were closer to what is usually meant by the term "danger," the Sages, too, would concede that the mokh is indicated.

R. Solomon Lifschutz of Warsaw (d. 1839), for example, sees the Three Women as being exposed to a *very remote danger,* hence the Sages' position:

> How could the Sages permit her to place herself in danger? This is a biblical violation (*v'nishmartem m'od l'nafshoteikhem*), etc. and we are enjoined "not to depend upon miracles." It must be that the danger to the Three Women is very remote, not really requiring safeguards. . . . But where a woman is in clear danger from pregnancy . . . the Sages would agree . . . so that she not be separated from her husband.[30]

"That she not be separated from her husband" reaffirms the relative undesirability of abstinence: that it is "out of the question" under consideration by R. Meir and the Sages; where real danger exists, the mokh is preferable even according to Rashi's reading of the Sages' view. Another writer, R. Malkiel Zvi of Lomza (d. 1901), comes to a parallel conclusion: in order to fulfill the mitzvah of onah, and where the danger is more than *remote by its very nature,* the Sages would have agreed to permit it.[31] R. Issakhar Berish carries the idea forward and adds much explanation of the concepts of protection from hazard.[32] He analyzes the passages in the Talmud wherein "the Lord

---

[30] *Resp. Hemdat Shlomo,* No. 46. Similarly, *Resp. Or Gadol,* Vol. I, No. 31.
[31] *Resp. Divrei Malkiel, E.H.,* No. 70. A Talmudic Commentary *Hina V'Hisda,* to *K'tubot* 39 introduces a new idea; *sh'luhei mitzvah einan nizokin.* But cf. *Resp. Dovev Meisharim,* Vol. I, No. 20.
[32] *Resp. Divrei Yissakhar,* No. 138.

preserveth the simple" is applied,[33] calls them situations where the danger is *at best remote*, and reminds us that the entire Torah is to be set aside to save life—we are not to be told instead "the Lord preserveth the simple"! Even on Rashi's reading, the Sages would not require her to risk real danger.[34] Another such exposition of the baraita comes from R. Menahem Shneirson of Lubavitch in White Russia.[35] The danger to the Three Women may or may not be remote, he says, but it is *unlikely*, for "the Creator so ordained human nature that the Three Women do not ordinarily conceive." Accordingly, in the case of more likely risk, such as the one before him, a permissive ruling is indicated.[36] His contemporary in Hungary, R. Moses Schick, invokes "observation and experience" to testify that the Three Women do *not ordinarily* conceive.[37] Where pregnancy is likely, she must take every precaution to avoid hazard and "not rely on miracles," says still another writer.[38] To the fact of doubtful impregnation, says another, may be added the circumstance that the baraita's situation is *only temporary*.[39] The periods of childhood, pregnancy, or nursing are only for now; where the situation is both more risky and less temporary, the Sages would agree.[40]

In sum, the fact that ordinary illnesses are not mentioned—but the Three Women are—proves the validity of the above arguments, says R. Abraham I. Glick (d. 1906):

> Now we can understand why the Talmud makes no mention of
> the usual sicknesses such as the case before us or before other Responsa

---

[33] *TB Shabbat* 129b; *Y'vamot* 72b; *Avodah Zarah* 30b; *Niddah* 31a.

[34] Another writer, *Resp. Imrei Yosher*, Vol. I, No. 131, quotes *Avodah Zarah* 18a in another context: "I speak to you sensibly (*d'varim shel ta'am*) and you answer me, 'mercy will be vouchsafed from heaven'!"

[35] *Resp. Tzemah Tzedek (HaHadashot)*, E.H., Vol. I, No. 89.

[36] He goes beyond *Resp. Hemdat Shlomo* (Note 29, above) in permitting mokh for possible (likely) risk rather than definite risk. See text of Responsum, Ch. 10, above, p. 192.

[37] *Resp. Maharam Schick*, H.M., No. 54. See Ch. 10, Note 90. Similarly, *Resp. Avnei Nezer*, No. 81: the Three Women do "not ordinarily" conceive. The author of *Bikkurei Y'hudah*, II, 121, says: the dispute between R. Meir and the Sages is not the risk in pregnancy but the likelihood of pregnancy. Where pregnancy is likely, they agree on the risks. Neither rules that abstinence should be practiced.

[38] *Resp. Zikhron Y'honatan*, E.H., No. 3.

[39] *Resp. Damesek Eliezer*, E.H., No. 92.

[40] The Sages should not have permitted taking a chance even on a doubtful risk, except according to the following reasoning, says R. Jacob Ettlinger in *Resp. Binyan Tziyyon, loc. cit.*: In matters of saving life, even the doubtful risk must be considered, but the danger to the Three Women is a *future* danger. One may not interrupt recitation of the Silent Prayer "even if a snake winds itself around his heel," says the Talmud (*B'rakhot* 33)—"but if a scorpion does, he may," for the snake may or may not bite (*Perush HaMishnayot, ad loc.*), but the scorpion will. But even with the snake, how may one take a chance (on a doubtful risk)? It's just that the danger is a future one; there is still time to attend to it. *Resp. Imrei Shefer*, No. 29 demurs: this is untenable; the Sages' reason is that the danger is just unlikely.

writers. It mentions only these Three Women, where pregnancy is anyway unlikely, and hence the Sages demur. But ordinary illnesses, when pregnancy is likely—"there is nothing that stands in the way of saving life." [41]

For, not ordinary sickness is the issue here, but *natural danger*, according to R. Judah Assad. "Every woman in the world" undergoes the natural risks of pregnancy. "But in the case before us where she is stricken with illness and her condition *has been altered* from the natural (*nishtaneit mi-teva ha-olam*), the Sages would agree." [42] Fuller expression of this same idea is offered by R. Mosheh Feinstein: Even though every woman in childbirth sustains risks, we are bidden by the commandments of p'ru ur'vu and onah to enter upon such risk. To the Sages, the Three Women are like everyone else; their danger is a natural one. "But in the case before us," where the danger is *other than a natural one shared in common by all women*, the Sages, too, would agree. [43]

The mitzvah of avoiding physical hazard, then, illumined the ambiguities of our baraita in the eyes of the Responsa authorities. Discerning that abstinence was not suggested by either R. Meir or the Sages, they concluded that some kind of contraception is indicated at least in situations of potential risk. They could do no less. We proceed now to the views of those who would permit even more.

Maimonides' Significant Omission

The principle of avoidance of hazard is accepted with unanimity, but authorities continued to differ on exactly what the baraita permits or does not permit. Much of this wide latitude in theoretical and practical interpretation is due to the all important fact that the major Codes are silent on any possible deduction from this baraita. Perhaps even the sheer number of Responsa on the subject of birth control is due to this silence: each Respondent had to reopen the question and to rely on resources other than codified law. In many cases the resources to which they turned for guidance were the fountains from which the Codes themselves would have drawn. The *Shulhan Arukh*, the standard Code of Jewish law compiled in the sixteenth century by R. Joseph Karo, draws its nurture from many fountains, but three princi-

---

[41] *Resp. Yad Yitz'hak*, Vol. III, No. 9. An intriguing interpretation is suggested by the author of *P'kudat El'azar* (El'azar Lev), namely, that the *p'ta'im* are *y'nokei*, on the basis of Sanhedrin 91b. Preserveth "the simple" refers to the infants—or the *k'tannah*. But risk to an adult mother in the ordinary case of illness or pregnancy hazard, would justify mokh! See his Responsa Nos. 99, 100.

[42] *Resp. Y'hudah Ya'aleh*, Y.D., No. 222.

[43] *Resp. Igg'rot Mosheh*, E.H., No. 63, beg. Cf. No. 64.

pal ones dictate its final conclusions: Alfasi (eleventh century), Maimonides (twelfth), and Asheri (thirteenth), known by their acronyms *Rif*, *Rambam*, and *Rosh*.[44]

The first of these three is of no help for our present purposes. A digest of the Talmud more than a formal Code, Alfasi's work in this case merely relays the baraita bodily, so to speak, without extracting a ruling or even prejudicing the interpretation of the baraita by the manner of his citation thereof.[45]

The second of the three does even less. Maimonides' systematic and comprehensive Code omits entirely any reference to our pivotal baraita. Since his Code is the most substantial of the *Shulhan Arukh's* predecessors and pillars, his omission is of the first importance. It is no doubt the immediate reason for the parallel omission by subsequent Codes—the *Sefer Mitzvot Gadol*, the *Tur*, *Beit Yosef*, and the *Shulhan Arukh* itself, to say nothing of several lesser Codes.[46]

Is it possible that Maimonides saw no practical ruling at all emerging from the baraita; that, to him, the question was a theoretical one on the extent of hazard to the woman rather than on the legality of the mokh? After all, the issue of legality was raised only by the Commentaries of Rashi and Rabbénu Tam—his contemporaries in other lands—and we have no evidence that Maimonides ever made use of these Commentaries in his own Talmudic analyses. References by subsequent writers to his omission are collated herewith so that its implications may be assessed:

(1) Enlisting Maimonides on the side of the rigorists is an eighteenth-century Responsum.[47] Like R. David ben Zimra before him, the author declines to permit even postcoital mokh to "women in general" and takes his support from Maimonides' position against marriage to a minor bride (see above, Chapter 10). Unlike Ben Zimra, however, he is probably the first to add—as if in further support of his nonpermissive view—"Moreover, this baraita is omitted by the Codes."

(2) Also during the eighteenth century, R. Meir Posner of Danzig, in his Commentary to the *Even HaEzer* section of the *Shulhan Arukh*, likewise

---

[44] *Beit Yosef, Introduction.* When these three were insufficiently decisive, *Ramban, Rashba,* and *Ran* were his authorities. For their views, see on.

[45] *Alfasi, Y'vamot,* Ch. 1.

[46] Moreover, Isserles' *Glosses* do not seek, as they usually do, to make good the omission. That *Ein Mishpat*, the small reference-notation to the Codes, indicates their omission by its silence, is confirmed by R. Isaac Arieli, author of *Einayim LaMishpat* to *Y'vamot, ad loc.*, who promises to discuss it in his forthcoming *Hiddushim*.

[47] *Resp. Rosh Mashbir*, Vol. I, No. 69. The author is R. Joseph Samuel Modena, but this Responsum is signed by his son Jacob, and the volume first published in 1821.

arrives at a prohibition of any mokh for women in general.[48] Without referring directly to Maimonides, the author concludes his analysis by an expression of puzzlement:

> But, to my humble knowledge, I do not understand why the Codes omitted any reference to this baraita. For, according to all interpretations, there is a practical difference in law.

(3) To some, the omission is evidence that Rabbénu Tam's view, that the postcoital mokh is permissible to the Three Women and presumably to women in general, is endorsed by Maimonides and the Codes. The first of two nineteenth-century examples comes from a participant in the exchange of correspondence on the subject printed in *Ohel Avraham:*

> Furthermore, Maimonides seems to hold with Rabbénu Tam, for he did not cite the baraita nor did he state a prohibition for women in general. Had he held with Rashi, he should have stated the consequent law and its corollary one that other women are forbidden. . . . Since so many authorities hold with Rabbénu Tam and we have now shown that Maimonides does too, permission should be granted in the case before us.[49]

(4) The second is by R. Mordecai Horwitz of Frankfurt am Main:[50]

> It has already been asked why Maimonides and the Codes entirely omitted this provision. To my mind, their omission is firm evidence that they hold with Rabbénu Tam, meaning that the Three Women "need not" but may. Hence, why should the Codes make any mention of it? By their silence we know that there is no obligation upon the Three Women. And, had the Codes held with Rashi, why would they omit telling us of the consequent prohibition?[51]

(5) Other authorities explain Maimonides' omission by pointing out that there is a principle involved which has already been stated elsewhere. In each of the following three cases, that principle, applied to the mokh question, allows for a lenient ruling:

[48] *Beit Meir* to E.H., 23. See on, for the basis of his prohibition.
[49] *Ohel Avraham*, No. 90 (R. Aharon Cohen, writing to his son R. Mosheh Cohen in 1841).
[50] *Matteh Levi*, Vol. II, No. 31 (1894).
[51] A third example of such reasoning is entertained by *Resp. Imrei Esh, loc. cit.*

(a) Maimonides, *Tur*, and Karo omitted this provision entirely. It is likely, then, that they hold with Rabbenu Tam that no post-coital violation is involved and that therefore there is no prohibition. Nor is there an obligation to use the mokh. And, for cases of [less remote] danger, there was also no need for special mention here by the Codes. The rule has *already been stated* that "nothing stands in the way of saving life."[52]

(b) The question of hash-hatat zera and its applicability to the woman is, I would say, dependent upon the question of *sirus*, of technical castration, and the woman. Maimonides and the Codes have already ruled that *sirus* does not apply to women.[53] The issue, now, of the legality of mokh raised by Rashi reflects the opposite view. Since Maimonides and Karo have already stated their view on *sirus*, we know their view on mokh and hence they omitted specific mention of it.[54]

(c) From the omission by Maimonides, *Tur*, and Karo of this baraita we can conclude that they permit use of even the precoital mokh, because the question is one of *davar she-eino mitkavven*, the good act that results in an unintended evil act.[55] The husband's intention is not hash-hatat zera but prevention of hazard, and since the Codes have already ruled that, in the dispute between R. Shimon and R. Y'hudah, the law follows R. Shimon that such an act is permissible, there was no need to repeat it by citing this baraita too.[56]

(6) In distinctive rhetoric, still another author argues, like the previous one, for the permissibility of even precoital mokh in the name of Maimonides:

Lo, if we scout to view the direction of the Master Teacher—he is Maimonides—we find that he appears to have gone astray in this matter [*na'u ma'ag'lotav bazeh likh'orah*] since he omitted this baraita. Therefore let us betake ourselves to another vantage point; perhaps from there we will discern his tendency.[57]

[52] *Resp. Divrei Yissakhar*, No. 138. Another such example is to be found in *Resp. Y'mei Yosef*, Vol. I, *E.H.*, No. 6.
[53] See on, Ch. 13.
[54] *Marheshet*, Vol. II, No. 9:3:3.
[55] See above, Ch. 8.
[56] *Resp. Hedvat Ya'akov*, Vol. II, No. 37.
[57] *Resp. Damesek Eliezer*, No. 92.

He proceeds to take up Maimonides' view against marriage to a child bride and reminds us that Maimonides opposed such marriage only when this was the man's only wife. Hash-hatat zera, therefore, is not a technical violation to Maimonides, only a neglect of p'ru ur'vu. When the latter is otherwise being fulfilled, the mokh makes no difference.

(7) The mokh is nowhere explicitly forbidden by the Talmud, says another, hence Maimonides' silence:

> Maimonides omitted this, as did *Tur* and Karo. Only Alfasi and Asheri [see on] relayed it, but merely as incidental to the contextual discussion and, since the law follows the Sages there, the Three Women are like all others and no law emerges. Hence, M. made no reference to it . . . nor did he mention any prohibition of mokh, for no explicit prohibition of it is to be found in the Talmud. [58]

(8) Indeed, no law emerges, for the baraita deals with the reality of the hazard rather than the legality of mokh, says still another:

> The dispute between R. Meir and the Sages is one of approach rather than law. R. Meir consistently takes the unlikely into account [*hayish l'mi-uta*], and the Sages do not. Hence Maimonides omits the baraita, which essentially records a difference in outlook as to the extent of danger. So why should Maimonides quote this, when it is not his wont to quote theoretical discussions [*she-ein derekh ha-Rambam l'havi ta'amei halakhah*]? [59]

(9) Our final example sees the omission as evidence that no restrictive law emerges from the baraita, only leniency in each direction. (The author is the grandson of R. Moses Sofer, whose views on our subject will be discussed below.):

> Since the mokh baraita, which appears so often in the Talmud, is omitted by M. and the Codes, apparently they hold with [Rabbénu Tam] that the Three Women—and others, too—may use even the precoital mokh, as other authorities have concluded [see on, Luria, etc.]. Since M. and Karo did not say, "The child bride, the nursing mother, and the pregnant woman must abstain from marital relations," and since they did not say, "These Three Women must use

---

[58] *Resp. Divrei Malkiel, E.H.*, No. 70.

[59] *Resp. Maharam Shick, H.M.*, No. 54.

> the mokh," we can conclude that they hold with the lenient inter-
> pretation, that mokh is permitted under any circumstances, adopting
> the leniencies of both Rashi and Rabbénu Tam . . . [60]

The significance of Maimonides' silence on the implications of our baraita should not be underestimated. More evidence will be adduced later on in this chapter in favor of the contention, implied by some of the authorities just quoted, that no issue of legality of the mokh is, after all, raised by the baraita itself. And if we accept the arguments of those who equate precoital and postcoital mokh, then Rabbénu Tam is actually saying that the baraita's main concern is "must" versus "must not"—which basically reflects a dispute on the extent of hazard rather than the legality of mokh. If so, then Maimonides—and Alfasi before him and the *Shulhan Arukh* after—saw nothing wrong with even precoital mokh for women in general, as our last citation indicated. In other words, no prohibition of birth control, other than the neglect of the positive commandment of procreation and other than coitus interruptus specifically interdicted, can be attributed to the baraita, to Alfasi, to Maimonides, or to the *Shulhan Arukh*. But, the entire story has not yet been told; we must first examine the arguments of the permissive and the nonpermissive schools.

The Permissive School: Asheri and Luria

The last of the three pillars on which the decisions of the *Shulhan Arukh* rest is Asheri, the "Rosh." Having written much more on our subject than Alfasi and Maimonides, his point of view is more amenable to definition. The fact that it, too, is permissive would seem to endorse the above deductions concerning the *Shulhan Arukh's* position.

Asheri's main opus is a Talmudic digest-code much like that of Alfasi. In this work he relays the baraita without legal deduction or other interpretation, again just like Alfasi.[61] Incidentally, Asheri's contemporary, R. Mordecai ben Hillel, compiled a halakhic compendium shortly before Asheri did, which serves as a commentary-code supplementary to Alfasi. This Code [*Mord'khai*] offers some helpful legal authority from that circle and is cited by later permissivists as a source-text. The *Mord'khai* had said:

> Rashi's "may" is unacceptable to Rabbénu Tam, because coitus
> with a nonchildbearing woman is not prohibited and no hash-

---

[60] *Hit'or'rut T'shuvah*, No. 3. The author is at times referred to as R. Shimon Eger-Sofer.
[61] *Rosh, Y'vamot*, Ch. 1.

hatat zera is involved when the act is in the normal manner. Rabbénu Tam therefore reads· "must"; R. Meir is merely offering
"good advice" (*etzah tovah kamashma lan* [against hazard]). This is
also *Rivan's* interpretation.[62]

Rivan is R. Y'hudah bar Nathan, a son-in-law of Rashi, whose running
commentary to part of the Talmud helps to complete the task where Rashi
left off.[63] *Mord'khai* and *Rivan*, then, may be counted as two classic authorities before Asheri who do take sides on the meaning of the baraita, both
aligning themselves with the permissivists.[64] Both assume the Three Women
may—and "other women," without justification of hazard, may also—
use the mokh.[65]

Asheri himself takes his stand, not in his Code, but in a few other places.
In (a) his running commentary to the tractate *N'darim*—where, too, our
baraita is introduced for discussion—his exposition thereof declares for the
permissive side: "[The Three Women] must [*tzrikhot*] . . . "; hence "may"
according to the Sages; hence others also may. And the verb he uses—"to
place"—argues for the precoital usage.[66] (b) Asheri also composed *Tosafot*
of his own to many tractates. In his *Tosafot* to Y'vamot he explains the viewpoint of Rashi and Rabbénu Tam for our benefit without stating his own.
Many later authorities have deduced a permissive stance on his part from
this text as well.[67] (c) Among his many Responsa is the one on coitus interruptus referred to in a previous chapter (8). That Responsum concludes
with a comparison between mokh and interrupted coitus, in favor of the
former;[68] there he even termed mokh usage "coitus in the normal man-

---

[62] *Mord'khai*, Y'vamot, Ch. 1.

[63] See *TB Makkot* 19b: "Our Master's soul left him in purity. He ceased his commentation.
From here on are the words of his disciple, R. Y'hudah bar Nathan."

[64] Luria (see on) assumes their permissiveness for *ahar tashmish* only; *Resp. Divrei Yissakhar*,
No. 138; and *Torat Hesed*, E.H., No. 44:31,32; however, see it for *kodem tashmish* as well.

[65] *Ramban* and *Rashba*, other authorities before Asheri, are likewise enlisted on the side
of the permissivists, on the basis of their interpretation of *reish Niddah*. See, *e.g.*, *Torat Hesed*,
loc. cit., 23, 24.

[66] *Perush HaRosh* to N'darim 35b. Luria (see on) assumes this implies *kodem tashmish*, as do
Torat Hesed, loc. cit., and *Resp. Igg'rot Mosheh* (Note 72, below). *Hina V'Hisda* to K'tubot 39 (p. 198c)
and *Resp. Div'rei Malkiel*, No. 70, dispute that point. Again on the lenient side, *Resp. Ahiezer*,
E.H. No. 23, is representative of the many who assume that this means even "other women"
may. *Resp. K'tav Sofer*, E.H. No. 26, by the way, explains omission by *Tur* and Karo of the baraita
as due to this lenient position of Rosh: "The *Tur* followed the leniency of his father."

[67] *Tos'fot HaRosh* to Y'vamot 12b. With slight variations in style, Rosh's comment here
appears in *Shittah M'kubbetzet* to K'tubot 39, from where it is more commonly quoted. *Resp.
Avnei Nezer* (see on) and *Resp. Beit Av*, Vol. VII, No. 12, place Rosh with Rabbénu Tam; *Hina
V'Hisda*, loc. cit., with Rashi, and those in previous note, with the leniencies of both.

[68] *T'shuvot HaRosh*, Klal 33, No. 3.

ner."[69] In (d) his *Tosafot* to *Niddah*, however, he appears to be saying the opposite: that precoital mokh is forbidden even to the Three Women.[70] This is doubly suprising, since his *Tosafot* here attaches to that same *reish Niddah* context from which many, including Asheri himself, concluded that the legality of mokh is taken for granted.[71] Hence, R. Mosheh Feinstein, who had interpreted Asheri's previous three references in terms of leniency, argues cogently:[72]

> In *Tos'fei HaRosh* [to *Niddah*] which is printed in the Romm [Vilna] editions of the Talmud, we read [as above] . . . But we cannot rely on recently printed editions when they contradict books which were well known to the early authorities. This text must be emended. In place of "this is forbidden *even* to the Three Women," we must read " . . . *except* to the Three Women." Then it accords with what *Rosh* said [in comment to *Y'vamot*] . . . In any case, we ought not to be troubled by this text since it contradicts what *Rosh* says in three places . . . Actually, the language is clearly not his . . . The words are in error—an erring pupil wrote them. For this very spot [*reish Niddah*] is the source of the proof by [*Ri* in] *Tosafot* and by *Rosh* that the precoital mokh is assumed. How could *Rosh* take the position here that precoital mokh is forbidden and not bother to explain how he says so contrary to . . . *Tosafot* and to his own words [elsewhere]?[73]

Other statements of Asheri, adverted to in Chapter 6, above, tell us even more of his permissive point of view.[74]

We come now to the most unequivocal and outspoken of the permissivists. He is R. Solomon Luria, the Polish author (d. 1573) of a Code-Commentary roughly contemporaneous with the *Shulhan Arukh*. In his *Yam Shel Sh'lomo* he precedes the analysis of the mokh baraita with a superscription,

---

[69] *Yad Efrayim* in Addendum to *E.H.*, following *E.H.* 25, is representative of many later authorities who see this as sanctioning precoital mokh. On the other hand, *Resp. Hatam Sofer*, *Y.D.* No. 172, demurs, but *Resp. Torat Hesed*, *E.H.* No. 44:28, removes the objection and points to the evidence of Rosh to *N'darim*, as does *Resp. K'tav Sofer*, Note 66, above.

[70] *Tos'fei HaRosh* to *Niddah* 3b.

[71] In *Tos'fot HaRosh* (and *Sh. M.*) to *K'tubot*, *loc. cit.* For correct reading of reference to *shma'ata kamaita d'Niddah* see *Resp. Divrei Yissakhar*, No. 138.

[72] *Resp. Igg'rot Mosheh*, *E.H.*, No. 63 (p. 161).

[73] Also, *ibid.*, No. 64: "An erring pupil wrote this."

[74] In *Tos'fot HaRosh* to *Y'vamot* he makes a distinction between autoerotic and *ahar she-ne'ekar;* see Ch. 6, Note 101. In *Hilkhot HaRosh* to *Niddah*, Ch. 4, he relays the law that post-coital cleansing that destroys seed is permissible; see Ch. 6, Notes 118, 119.

telling us in advance what his analysis will yield: "The law that all women may use the mokh . . . " Then follows his discussion:[75]

> Rashi assumes women are ordinarily forbidden, since hash-hatat zera is involved . . . Rabbénu Tam sees no violation after the act . . . Hence the three "need not" [according to the Sages] and others too may . . . but only postcoital . . . But it seems to me that although *Mord'khai* represented *Rivan* as holding with Rabbénu Tam[76] and [although] *RaN*, too, so holds,[77] still Rashi's interpretation seems the correct one. Precoital mokh is assumed, and it is not improper; it is still normal intercourse, for one body derives its natural gratifications from the other. It is no different from coitus with a nonchildbearing woman . . . as evidenced by what *Ri* concluded from *reish Niddah* where precoital mokh is taken for granted . . . And I wonder at Rabbénu Tam, how it could have occurred to him to interpret otherwise than is obvious from *reish Niddah*. Still, the [other] point made by Rabbénu Tam is correct, that even "other women" may use the mokh and the Three Women "must" . . . just as Asheri said [to *N'darim*]. It may also be inferred from Asheri's language [and description of the mokh's usage] that precoital mokh is assumed. . . *Reish Niddah* implies also that other women may, for it says, "what about women who are using the mokh . . . ," not "what about the Three Women who are . . . " That any woman may use the mokh is the correct inference (*v'khen ikkar*). The law follows the Sages, that the Three Women "need not" but they and others "may."

Luria's ruling, it may be noted, is founded on several arguments: (a) The plain sense of the Talmud elsewhere where mokh is mentioned, such as *reish Niddah*. We have already shown how other authorities make use of this argument.[78] (b) The precedent in the dicta of predeccessor commentators,

[75] *Yam Shel Sh'lomo, Y'vamot*, 1:8.

[76] *Resp. Torat Hesed, E.H.*, No. 44:31 writes: "I wonder at Luria who says 'although Mord'khai' . . . Mord'khai actually agrees with Luria all the way." So also *Resp. Divrei Yissakhar*, No. 138.

[77] *Resp. Bikkurei Y'hudah*, p. 122d shows that *RaN* agrees with Luria all the way as evidenced by *RaN's* commentary to *N'darim* 35b and in his *Hiddushim* to *Niddah* 3a. The author therefore suggests an emendation, that "and *RaN* too so holds" belongs later, after Luria's position is stated. Curiously, *Divrei Malkiel, E.H.*, No. 70, assumes "*Nimmukei Yosef*" for "*RaN*."

[78] *Hiddushei RaN* and *Hiddushei Ramban* to *Niddah* 3a would endorse the general assumption that "women in general" are presupposed here. *Resp. Zikhron Y'honatan, E.H.* 3 refers it to *nashim p'rutzot; Damesek Eliezer, E.H.* 92 to *shalosh nashim*, and *Divrei Malkiel* to *k'ein shalosh nashim*. *Ahiezer, E.H.* 23 and *Hazon Ish, E.H.* 37:2 endorse Luria all the way. See Ch. 9.

primarily Asheri. In this connection, an interesting challenge was leveled by a nineteenth-century Responsum, where the author writes:

> The law is clear then as Asheri — whose authority we of the Ashkenazi communities follow — wrote, that the Three Women "must," as Rabbénu Tam reads. So ruled Luria. But, what Luria added — even "precoital" and even "women in general" — in this we do not follow Luria, for one of his supports is Asheri, and we know that Asheri wrote in *Tos'fei HaRosh* (to *Niddah* 3b) that precoital mokh is forbidden even to the Three Women. Had Luria known that Asheri is not on his side he would not have presumed to take a singular position without support. The book *Tos'fei HaRosh* was not yet published in Luria's time.[79]

We, however, have seen what R. Mosheh Feinstein has since written about the spuriousness of this *Tos'fei HaRosh* edition, that the text cannot be relied upon and is erroneous in this instance. The objection, then, is overruled, and Luria's support remains intact. Not only Asheri, but *Rivan* and *Mord'khai* and *RaN* are precedent support for the burden of Luria's position, namely that mokh usage is precoital, and that the baraita's point is to require it in special cases; in ordinary cases there is no law one way or the other.

A third foundation of his argument is original with him, namely: (c) the logic of the matter. Luria introduces here his criterion of the integrity of the sex act, that is, of *guf neheneh min ha-guf*, one body deriving normal gratification from the other. In our discussion of the Legitimacy of Sexual Pleasure (Chapter 5, above), Luria's criterion was defined. The integrity of the sex act does not require the possibility of procreation, but it does require the circumstances allowing for normal heterosexual pleasure attendant upon the act.[80] To him, use of even the precoital mokh does not compromise that integrity.

In Luria's bold view, then, no technical violations are incurred either

---

[79] *Resp. Avnei Nezer*, E.H., No. 81.

[80] *Resp. Damesek Eliezer*, E.H., No. 92, takes issue with this specific point:

> Although I am not worthy to dispute Luria, I have come to rescue Rabbénu Tam. Rabbénu Tam called mokh "not in the normal manner, for he thus casts his seed on wood and stones." The two halves of that statement are one, for even though *guf neheneh min ha-guf* and the sexual gratifications are there (*r'evim yisb'u mi-ta-avat nafsham ad l'middai*), still it is not yet "in the normal manner."

Luria, however, also uses both clauses but concludes otherwise.

way. And although his position is arrived at by adopting the leniencies of both Rashi and Rabbénu Tam at one and the same time—"seizing the rope at both ends"[81]—his conclusion is nonetheless in keeping with a respectable body of opinion before and after him. It is also in keeping with the intention expressed in the Preamble to his work, that he would subject all post-Talmudic authorities to critical scrutiny, to determine whether or not they were in accord with the plain sense of the final authority—the Talmud itself.[82] If our conclusions about Maimonides and the *Shulhan Arukh* are correct, he may indeed be representing the true sense of the Talmud.[83] And if the contention of those who make reference to *Sefer HaYashar* is correct—that Rabbénu Tam's *only* point is "must" versus "may," rather than "precoital" versus "postcoital"[84]—then Luria need not have "wondered at Rabbénu Tam" at all; their views actually coincide. The likelihood that these considerations point to the intrinsic validity of Luria's position is enhanced by the extraordinary observation in this connection by the Sage of Bnai Brak: *Hazon Ish* goes so far as to declare that Luria "attained Divine inspiration."[85]

It should, of course, be remembered that only the Talmudic discussions of mokh are under consideration here; the nontechnical questions such as the positive commandment of p'ru ur'vu and the moral justification for birth control, are beyond Luria's immediate concern. *As a method*, he is saying, the Talmud clearly indicates that the mokh is unobjectionable in any circumstances. We shall examine the effect of Luria's teaching upon subsequent Responsa. But first we must sample the literature of the nonpermissive school.

The Nonpermissivists: Eger, Sofer, and Ettlinger

It must be stated at the very outset of our discussion of the nonpermissive school that none of its chief exponents had access, or made reference, to the aforementioned position by Luria. While documentation and assess-

[81] The phrase comes from *Marheshet*, Vol. II, No. 9. The irregularity of adopting "both ends" bothers *Divrei Malkiel, loc. cit.* He writes:

> It seems wrong to rely on Luria . . . for, where do we find that we may take hold of two [contradictory] leniencies (*she-nitpos tartei kulei*) . . . There is just not enough in Luria's words to justify a lenient ruling against both Rashi and R.T.

But see above, Note 60, where *Hit'or'rut Tshuvah* endorses the idea of adopting both leniencies, since the conclusion is warranted.

[82] *Yam Shel Shlomo, Intro. to Bava Kamma.*

[83] See above, p. 208.

[84] See above, Notes 14–17; 20–21.

[85] *Hazon Ish, E.H.* 37:2: "*Kodem tashmish be'emet mutar b'khol ha-nashim . . . v'zeh hakhra'at rabbenu hagadol she-higgia l'ruah hakodesh, maharshal zal.*"

ment of this fact will be offered later, it is helpfully borne in mind at this point.

R. Meir Posner of eighteenth-century Danzig is among the first of the *mah-mirim*, the restrictive school. Not that he would prohibit the postcoital mokh for women in danger of pregnancy hazards, but he certainly would for "women in general."[86] This position is less than what Rabbénu Tam and the *Rishonim* would grant and is arrived at by invocation of another Talmudic discussion to throw light on our baraita.

That discussion is the one referred to in Chapter 6, above, where, in the context of vows imposed by a husband on his wife, the one apparently requiring her to practice postcoital contraception is declared grounds for divorce and settlement due her. This is proof, says *Beit Meir*, that the practice involves a violation; it is no proof, say others, because the sense of the Talmud is that she is being deprived of children against her will, rather than incurring a violation.[87] Proceeding on his assumption, *Beit Meir* declines to go along with Rabbénu Tam and writes: "Whether postcoital mokh is allowable hangs on the dispute between Rashi and Rabbénu Tam, and it is better to rule on the strict side, like Rashi."

The most formidable of the nonpermissivists is R. Akiva Eger of nineteenth-century Posen in Prussia. His keenness of insight and piety of person made his voice influential for most of the European Jewish community. Even those who would challenge his reasoning or evidence in the matter at hand hesitated to rule contrary to his verdict.

In answer to a query about the use of a mokh for a woman plagued with difficult childbirths, he prohibits even the postcoital usage.[88] His discussion continues through two Responsa, and he concludes the second with a relative relaxation of this position; only relative, that is, because he maintains his ban on *effective* postcoital contraception to the end.[89] He bases his opinion on original arguments which are, however, vigorously challenged by his successors.

His first point is, to relay its essence in brief, that the objection of the *Rishonim*,[90] above, which was overcome by granting "must" to the Three Women (and "may" according to the Sages), was made with Rashi's contention in mind, that is, that a postcoital violation of hash-hatat zera is, in fact,

---

[86] *Beit Meir*, to E.H., 23.

[87] See above, Ch. 6, Notes 116–17 for details.

[88] Resp. R. Akiva Eger, No. 71.

[89] *Ibid.*, No. 72.

[90] He focuses his argument on the objection by *Nimmukei Yosef* to *Y'vamot*, Ch. 1, but later equates it with the objection of the *Rishonim* in *Shittah M'kubetzet* to *K'tubot* 39 and *Ritva* to *Y'vamot* 12b.

applicable to women. It is this assumption that the *Rishonim* are working with, not Rabbénu Tam's idea that no violation is incurred by her. Hence, even the postcoital mokh cannot be permitted. He builds his case by citing one of the *Rishonim*—"*Ritva*," R. Yom Tov ben Avraham of fourteenth-century Spain—who in his Talmudic Commentary does speak of two possible violations.[91] But both his (Eger's) argument and his support are effectively disputed by a chorus of successors. That *Ritva* can be used as a support to this position was challenged by the Lubavitcher Rabbi of that (nineteenth) century, among others.[92] That the *Rishonim* grant the existence of a postcoital violation, following Rashi instead of Rabbénu Tam, is set aside by many, some in colorful style as follows:

> (*a*) To me it seems that R. Akiva Eger dreamed this up in some nocturnal vision (*b'hezyon lailah nidmah lo*) from the words of the *Rishonim*, who imply no such thing ... Moreover, all the *Rishonim* ganged up (*nitz'vu k'mo ned*) against Rashi's interpretation ... and argued that the Sages would not spurn safeguards ... and since postcoital mokh is less safe, they would permit the safer precoital usage.[93]

> (*b*) To my mind, I don't understand how he saw this (*mah ra'ah kakhah*) in the words of the *Rishonim*.[94]

> (*c*) Begging his pardon, the *Rishonim* clearly put their question to Rabbénu Tam's position, and their view is identical to his, namely that [postcoital mokh] is permitted to all women.[95]

> (*d*) I am baffled at R. Akiva Eger, for the *Rishonim* clearly imply that precoital mokh is all right in "danger" and postcoital otherwise.[96]

> (*e*) In my humble opinion, the words of the *Rishonim* imply the very opposite of what he suggests.[97]

The next point of evidence adduced by R. Akiva Eger is an inferential argument based on the Talmud's apparently deliberate avoidance of a certain

[91] *Hiddushei Ritva* to *Y'vamot* 12b; *Shittah M'kubetzet* to *K'tubot* 39a.

[92] *Resp. Tzemah Yzedek, loc. cit.* The *N'tziv* in *Resp. Meshiv Davar, loc. cit.*, would emend to *va'afilu lo hayah munah bish'at tashmish* (adding the word "*lo*"). See also *Iggrot Mosheh*, E.H., 63–64.

[93] *Resp. Yismah Lev.*, Y.D., No. 4.

[94] *Resp. Avnei Nezer*, E.H., No. 79.

[95] *Ibid.*, No. 81. Similarly, *Resp. Naharei Afars'mon*, No. 29 and, *idem*, New Series, No. 47.

[96] *Resp. Divrei Malkiel*, E.H., No. 70. Similarly, *Resp. Shevet Sofer*.

[97] *Resp. Zikhron Y'honatan*, E.H., No. 3. Similarly, *Marheshet*, Vol. II, No. 9:2.

answer to an objection. The subject is postcoital cleansing in order to attain the special purity from bodily secretions required for partaking of *T'rumah* or other consecrated foods.[98] To again epitomize:[99] the failure by the Talmud to introduce, as an answer to an objection, the law permitting the kind of postcoital cleansing that destroys seed, is taken by R. Akiva Eger as evidence that this cleansing is unlawful. Unaccountably, he did not advert to the *Tosafot* on the spot which removes his objection and cites the Mishnaic law that explicitly permits postcoital cleansing in such circumstances.[100] In Chapter 6, above, we have alluded to this Mishnaic law and to the subsidiary provision of Asheri (and *Magen Avraham*) concerning postcoital bathing in a manner which destroys seed. R. Akiva Eger accepts Asheri as consistent with his (Asheri's) point of view elsewhere but declines to go along with him.[101] On this point more than on others, R. Akiva Eger was besieged with polite but forceful demurrers. Some examples:

> (*a*) Begging his pardon, R. Akiva Eger did not plumb the depths of the Talmudic discussion (*lo yarad l'omek ha-halakhah*). The *Tosafot* eluded him (*ne'elma me-einei k'vodo*), as did the words of *Ramban*.[102]

> (*b*) I am astonished at what I see . . . How is it that so authentic a genius (*gaon amiti*) should not cast his pure and brilliant eye on the words of the *Tosafot?* . . . On the contrary, the discussion there proves the opposite, that postcoital mokh is permissible. The words of other works by early authorities to the same effect also momentarily eluded the genius . . . I am astonished at his eminent scholarly holiness (*rom'mut k'dushat torato*), for it is the view of all [above] authorities that this is permissible.[103]

> (*c*) All of what R. Akiva Eger says is beyond me, begging his pardon (*kol d'varav bim'hilat k'vodo t'muhim*). [Here the author lists no fewer than six points set forth by Eger that are untenable to him, one of which follows.] If he seeks to prove postcoital mokh forbidden from that Talmudic discussion, it is strange that the words of *Tosafot* and

---

[98] *TB Niddah* 41b. See above, Ch. 6, Notes 118–24.

[99] The objection raised is the contradiction between the rule of "three days" of statutory impurity before eating *t'rumah* and the biblical "until evening" of the same day. The answer was that the former is for the case of *mit'happekhet* wherein seed is expelled, rather than *poletet* because of *kib'dah beitah b'hammin*.

[100] *Mishnah Mikvaot*, 8, 4; *Tosafot* to *Niddah* 41b, *s.v. poletet*.

[101] See Ch. 6, Notes 119 and 124.

[102] *Resp. Yismah Lev.*, *loc. cit.*

[103] *Resp. Torat Hesed*, Vol. II, *E.H.*, No. 43:13, 14, 18.

> *Ramban* escaped him for the moment, and in vain did he challenge *Magen Avraham*.[104]

> (d) I wonder about the Gaon R. Akiva Eger, whose luminous eye momentarily overlooked (*ne'elam me'eino ha-b'dolah l'fi sha'ah*) the words of *Tosafot*, etc. . . . His statement in this matter is unaccountable.[105]

Despite such challenges, R. Akiva Eger's stature lent considerable effect to his ruling. Its restrictive effect, moreover, was heightened by the fact that some were misled by his opening statement into believing that his Responsa dealt with life-threatening danger; that he was forbidding postcoital mokh even for cases of hazardous pregnancy, rather than for "women in general." Even the compiler of Responsa notations attached as a commentary to the *Shulhan Arukh*, R. Abraham Eisenstadt of nineteenth-century Russia, listed Eger in his *Pit'hei T'shuvah* as prohibiting postcoital mokh for cases of danger.[106] But this is both intrinsically impossible and convincingly disproved by at least two eminent authorities of our century. Even though Eger's opening description of the case before him was of "a woman of troubled spirit (*ishah k'shat ruah*) who has difficulty and great pain in each delivery and is always *in the realm of danger (tamid hi bikh'lal sakkanah)*," R. Mosheh Feinstein writes:

> In my opinion, we are compelled to say that R. Akiva Eger's position relates to a woman not in danger but to one of "troubled spirit," etc. Such is considered by Eger in the category of a healthy woman with normal risks . . . This explains why he wrote, "There is no precedent that explicitly permits [precoital or postcoital] mokh," for he himself cites *Rishonim* who do in the case of danger . . . Therefore . . . he is not talking about a case of dangerous pregnancy at all—in which he would probably be lenient like the *Rishonim*. Although, to my mind, he *should* have treated his case—if she has a tendency for danger beyond the ordinary—as a case of danger.[107]

---

[104] *Resp. Divrei Yissakhar*, No. 138. Similarly, *Resp. Beit Yitzhak*, *E.H.*, No. 91: "The proof adduced by Eger is to be discounted." Also, *Resp. Zikhron Y'honatan*, *E.H.*, No. 3.

[105] *Resp. Ahiezer*, *E.H.*, No. 23.

[106] *Pit'hei T'shuvah* to *E.H.*, 23. He equates the case of *Hemdat Sh'lomo*, where life-danger is specified, to *Hatam Sofer* and to *Akiva Eger*, saying *sh'eilah kazo mammash* and *mahmir mammash bazeh*. He is followed by R. M. Tendler, who writes, in *Tradition* (Fall, 1966), p. 11, that R. Akiva Eger "prohibits its use even if life-threatening medical considerations demand contraception."

[107] *Resp. Ig'grot Mosheh, loc. cit.*, No. 63:5.

And the *Hazon Ish:*

> All of what R. Akiva Eger said relates to a woman not in definite
> danger but to one who gives birth in pain, as is evident from all
> he says. It is even more evident from his conclusion of the second
> Responsum, where he concedes that postcoital cleansing which
> removes external seed is all right but not which would remove
> absorbed seed, and he adds, "but I see no use in doing so." If he
> were talking about danger, he would have forbidden coitus *with-
> out* the mokh, or even *with* the kind of mokh usage that he describes,
> which is not effective contraception.[108]

R. Moses Sofer (d. 1839), the famous *Hatam Sofer* of Pressburg who
later became R. Akiva Eger's son-in-law, takes his own tack in analyzing
the subject. Precoital mokh is inadmissible, he rules, and counters some of
the arguments that might prove otherwise. Even postcoital mokh is open
to some question, but in cases of danger it is to be permitted.[109] He adds
the stipulation that the husband's knowledge and permission are important.[110]
As to his arguments, many of them have been touched upon elsewhere,[111]
but a ban on precoital mokh coming from him joined with that of Akiva
Eger to give solidity and authority to that position.

Another estimable voice among the nonpermissivists is R. Jacob Ettlinger (d. 1871) of Altona. In his *Binyan Tziyyon,* he takes the most restrictive
position of all: both precoital and postcoital mokh are forbidden, even in
cases of danger.[112] The burden of his argument is that hash-hatat zera is
serious;[113] that mokh involves hash-hatat zera even when the seed would
not otherwise impregnate;[114] that the case for mokh is just not strong
enough.[115] What should the poor woman do? "Perhaps she can find help
through *kos shel ikkarin*" [an oral contraceptive], which does not pose the
problems that mokh does.[116] But when a precoital impediment exists or a

---

[108] *Hazon Ish E.H.,* 37, 5.

[109] *Resp. Hatam Sofer, Y.D.,* No. 172.

[110] But cf. *Hatam Sofer, E.H.,* No. 20, and below, Ch. 13.

[111] See, e.g., above, Ch. 9, Note 22, where the instance of Esther, which is one of *Hatam Sofer's* more distinctive points, is referred to.

[112] *Resp. Binyan Tziyyon,* No. 137.

[113] See Ch. 6, Note 27.

[114] See above, Note 25.

[115] See Ch. 9, Note 22, for instance of Esther; Ch. 6, Note 117 in the matter of *m'mal'ah v'nofetzet.*

[116] See Ch. 13, Note 52.

postcoital active destruction of seed is indulged in, a violation occurs which is too intrinsically serious to be set aside for any reason.

While Ettlinger's *Binyan Tziyyon* is virtually alone in his extreme stance against mokh usage,[117] countless Responsa have joined R. Akiva Eger and *Hatam Sofer* in their exclusion of at least the precoital mokh.[118] Their position has carried the day ever since.

The Aftermath

What direction, however, would the course of subsequent Responsa legislation have taken if the position of Luria had been known to these fountainheads of the nonpermissive school? That it was in fact not known to them is evidenced in many ways. First, they make no reference at all to him. Second, with regard to precoital mokh even in cases of danger, they state explicitly at the outset, "I have not seen any authority who permits it." [119] An annotator of a later edition of R. Akiva Eger's Responsa, R. Dov Ashkenazi of Lublin, has an entry at this point. He brings Eger's remark up to date by directing our attention to the fact of Luria, "who permits even precoital mokh." Further evidence comes from the circumstance that Luria's volume on *Y'vamot* came gradually to be discussed in the late nineteenth century.[120] Even then, many of those who made reference to him became acquainted with his position only through secondary sources. The writings of one of Luria's disciples, R. Joel Sirkes (*BaH*), was the only source for his words to some Responsa authorities: While R. Solomon Lifschutz of Warsaw (d. 1839) was "shown" the decision of Luria after he had written his own, R. Aryeh Plotzker, in 1849, and R. Judah Assad, in 1873, cite Luria's *Y'vamot* as relayed by Sirkes,[121] while R. Eliezer Deutsch in 1896 finds him through a citation by Azulai.[122] The wide-ranging Responsum on our subject by R. Mosheh Feinstein (1935), though independently permissive on the question of precoital mokh for cases of hazard, omits any reference to Luria in the matter before us, whereas, in a related aspect of the question, he, too, cites only Sirkes, unaware that the latter's original source is

---

[117] *Resp. Maharam Brisk,* Vol. I., No. 97, approximates his position. Curiously, he, too, ends by referring to some kind of *kos shel ikkarin* that he heard about, which would be all right.

[118] See above, Note 22, for examples.

[119] In addition to the above-mentioned nonpermissivists, another, *Resp. Imrei Esh, Y.D.,* No. 68, quotes them and accepts their statement that "no authority has permitted" it. He likewise makes no mention of Luria.

[120] Although *Yam Shel Sh'lomo* to *Y'vamot*, written c. 1563, was first published in Altona in 1739.

[121] *Resp. Hemdat Sh'lomo,* No. 56; *Resp. M'shivat Nefesh,* No. 18 (on kos shel ikkarin); similarly, *Resp. Y'hudah Ya'aleh, Y.D.,* No. 222.

[122] *Resp. P'ri HaSadeh,* Vol. 1, No. 88: "I see that *Birkei Yosef* says . . . in the name of Luria."

Luria.[123] Other Respondents found him quoted on our question of mokh, either in a Commentary to the *Shulhan Arukh* first published in 1828,[124] or in a halakhic compendium from the turn of the century.[125]

The news of Luria's finding was greeted with positive hopefulness by one authority, who was struggling with the law on behalf of an unfortunate woman:

> You write that Luria permitted precoital mokh even to all women. His book is not in my possession, nor did you reveal to me the reasons for his viewpoint. It does seem extreme and more liberal than the *Rishonim* . . . but I cannot judge until I know what he said and why. *Beit Meir,* by the way, is the eminent figure in our generation; he forbade, and never mentioned Luria. . . . O how it would please me to permit the mokh to this poor woman in order to keep her far from any danger, but I have found no explicit permission for precoital mokh. If you feel that Luria has authority in his words (*milei d'sam'- khei hem*), or if you would let me know the essence of what he says, then "I will see and recant" (*az er'eh ashuvah*).[126]

He, however, was writing in 1841, before the Responsa of Eger (d. 1837) and of Sofer (d. 1839) had been disseminated and had taken root. The aforementioned R. Eliezer Deutsch is representative of those who discovered Luria after that fact. In the Responsum dated 1896, he makes no mention of Luria in connection with our subject,[127] whereas in another dated 1906, he does introduce him—and then adds:

> But lo, since many great authorities have forbidden precoital mokh, it is therefore not in our hands to permit it.[128]

---

[123] *Resp. Igg'rot Mosheh,* No. 63, p. 157. After making no reference to Luria, he speaks of *shello k'darkah* according to "Asheri, whose words we know only through *Beit Yosef* and *BaH.*" *BaH,* however, had relayed *Luria's* version of Asheri, verbatim (see p. 157, Note 72, above) whereas in *op. cit.,* No. 64, written 1958, he refers to Luria for the first time.

[124] *Resp. Naharei Afars'mon* No. 29 (and Second Series, No. 47) (c. 1896); and even *Resp. Maharsham,* Vol. I, No. 58 (1902), quoting Luria as found in *Yad Efrayim* by R. Efraim Z. Margolis to *Sh. Ar.,* Addendum following *E.H.,* 25.

[125] *Resp. Yaskil Avdi,* Vol. II, No. 6 (1935), quotes Luria from *S'dei Hemed* (1903), *Ishut,* No. 1, *Asifat Dinim* 32. So does *Resp. Minhat Y'hiel,* Vol. II (1936), No. 22.

[126] R. Tzvi Oppenheim in *Ohel Avraham,* No. 99. As late as 1933, R. Israel Landau of Edelin, Hungary, wrote: "Luria's work is not available here, so I cannot look into it" for you—*Resp. Beit Yisrael,* No. 164.

[127] *Resp. Pri HaSadeh, loc. cit.*

[128] *Idem.,* Vol. II, No. 86.

For, with or without Luria, the authority of Eger and Sofer was so profound and far reaching among the Hungarian Rabbis—and through them to the entire European and world Jewish community—that almost none would make bold to decide against them.[129] The die, says one Respondent, has been cast, and even the discovery of Luria cannot change things:

> But *Hatam Sofer*, Akiva Eger, and *Im'rei Esh* have already closed off that path (*sag'ru alenu ha-derekh*) and have permitted only post-coital mokh.[130]

As does another:

> But *Beit Meir*, Sofer, Eger, and *Binyan Tziyyon* have all forbidden it, and who would [dare] come after them and permit it?[131]

A good number of voices, on the other hand, were duly courageous in their assessment of what Luria's discovery must mean. R. Shalom Schwadron, who, together with his questioner, had apparently seen Luria only in secondary sources, writes:

> Therefore, although *Hatam Sofer* and R. Akiva Eger forbid, as do *Im'rei Esh* and *Binyan Tziyyon* . . . they were unaware of what Luria [and *Radbaz*] had written.[132]

Indeed, if they were "unaware" of Luria, this fact effectively alters the authority of their Responsa. Others, accordingly, express themselves as follows, with varying emphasis:

> (*a*) When I saw that the two luminaries of our generation, Eger and Sofer . . . write . . . "I have seen no authority who permits," I decided at first to leave the matter alone, for who can come after them and permit? Then I reflected and concluded that, since both state their reason as lack of precedent sanction, it is obvious that they were unaware of Luria, who permits in all cases.[133]

---

[129] So, e.g., *Resp. Maharam Schick, H.M.* No. 54 and many others.
[130] *Resp. Naharei Afars'mon*, No. 29. *Im'rei Esh* is based on Eger and Sofer; see Note 119, above.
[131] R. Avraham Ashk'nazi, whose Responsum became No. 5 in *Resp. Yismah Lev* (1878).
[132] *Resp. Maharsham* (see Note 124).
[133] *Resp. Toret Hesed*, Vol. II, No. 44.

(b) You can deduce that *Hatam Sofer* forbade precoital mokh only because, as he says, he saw no precedent-authority who permits it. But we should thank God who has enlightened our eyes and we have found many and honorable authorities [referring to Asheri and Luria] who permit (*mattirim rabbim v'nikhbadim*). Without a doubt had they been revealed before the eyes of *Hatam Sofer*, he certainly would have permitted it easily. *Binyan Tziyyon*, too, overlooked them. . . . [134]

(c) Hatam Sofer wrote that he saw no lenient ruling. But I have found Luria, etc., and he is a firm foundation on which to rely (*y'sod gadol lismokh alav*). Perhaps they never would have differed with him had they seen his words. [135]

(d) It is not my practice to intrude my head among the great mountains, to decide among authorities, but since Luria ruled with such clear leniency . . . he is enough to rely on in this case. [136]

(e) *Hatam Sofer* and Akiva Eger forbade . . . because they could not find precedent. They did not see Luria. Perhaps Luria to *Y'vamot* was not printed yet in their day. [137]

(f) Luria has, after all, permitted this even to "women in general" . . . So in this case where danger is involved we may certainly rely on him. *Hatam Sofer* forbade it, but he did not cite Luria . . . upon whom we can rely. [138]

R. Alter Nebenzahl of Stanislav is an example of one who had published Responsa both before and after exposure to Luria's leniency and whose later work yields to its influence. In 1911 he had cited Eger and others and had concluded nonpermissively. [139] Then in 1936, he tells of Luria and others and declares: "Even though I have written in my [earlier] book prohibiting

[134] *Resp. Yismah Lev*, Y.D. No. 4 (R. Shalom Gagin, 1878).

[135] *Resp. Hedvat Ya'akov*, Second Series, No. 37 (1909).

[136] *Resp. M'lammed L'Ho'il*, Vol. III, No. 18 (c. 1915).

[137] *Resp. Bikkurei Y'hudah*, II, 121 (1929).

[138] *Kiryat Hanah David*, Vol. II, *Ishut* No. 6 (1935). Coincidentally interesting is what Luria himself wrote elsewhere, in the Preface to his Commentary to *Hulin*: "My practice has been to search and investigate . . . every source and quarry of halakhah, with great effort and study and little sleep . . . omitting no authority from my investigations before coming to a conclusion . . . so that no one will later come and say, 'Had this author seen such and such a book or Responsum, he would not have differed with it.' Therefore I have consulted and made mention of all rulings, early, middle, and late."

[139] *P'ri HaEtz U'Minhat Y'hiel*, Vol. IV end, No. 6.

mokh, I have since then looked and found that he who chooses to permit it has a basis in the law and has [authority] upon whom to rely."[140]

Perhaps the most striking indication of what might have been the case had Luria's work been available to, say, *Hatam Sofer*, is afforded in the fact that the latter's own grandson, R. Shimon Sofer of Erlau, so warmly accepted it. We took note above of the latter's statement that Maimonides' omission of the baraita is due to the fact that the baraita teaches no restrictive law; this, says R. Shimon Sofer, is "as Luria ruled," and the mokh is permissible to all under any circumstances, again, "as Luria ruled."[141]

Awareness of Luria's ruling does not, of course, dictate automatic acceptance. In one of those ironies of legal literature, two authorities independently refer to a law by a disciple of Luria, one to prove a leniency, the other to disprove it. R. Joshua Falk, a pupil of Luria's along with Sirkes, is the author of a Commentary to the *Tur* Code, called *D'rishah*. There he relays the provision of his teacher, to the effect that postcoital bathing should not be done during a woman's fertile period, lest she destroy fecund seed.[142] This, says R. Solomon Drimmer of Skola in his Talmudic Commentary, is evidence that Luria "changed his mind" or, rather, "retreated" from his lenient position, for here his close disciple relays an anticontraceptive law in his name.[143] Approaching, however, from another angle, R. Yehiel Weinberg of Montreux is desirous of proving that the law relayed by *D'rishah* is only in the nature of "good advice" to a woman who *wants* to conceive —and he invokes Luria's known leniency as the best proof that this is so.[144]

R. Solomon Drimmer was not alone in resisting Luria's verdict.[145] That same year (1873) in which his work was published in Lemberg, another Talmudic Commentary appeared in Ismir, Turkey, from the pen of R. Yosef Sh'lomo Ardit.[146] He takes note of Luria, disputes the contention that Asheri —on the basis of his *Tosafot* to *Y'vamot*—can be regarded as a precedent for Luria's extreme leniency and declares Luria "alone" in his position.[147] Most notable on this same score is the line of attack pursued by three separate authorities, all, it appears, independently of one another, and whose attack

---

[140] *Resp. Minhat Y'hiel*, Vol. II, No. 22 (see Note 125).

[141] *Hit'or'rut T'shuvah* (see Note 60, above).

[142] *D'rishah* to *Tur*, Y.D., 196.

[143] *Yashresh Ya'akov* to *Y'vamot* 12b.

[144] *Resp. S'ridei Esh*, Vol. III, No. 14.

[145] See *Resp. Div'rei Malkiel* (above, Note 81)—*tartei kulei*; also, *Resp. Tzitz Eliezer*, Vol. IX, No. 51 (1967), who is not sure what to make of *Hazon Ish's* endorsement.

[146] *Hina V'Hisda* to *K'tubot* 39, p. 198b, c.

[147] He is echoed in this attitude by R. Avraham Ashk'nazi (above, Note 131). See also *Resp. Yad Yitzhak*, Vol. II, No. 162—"*da'at yahid hi.*"

has been undermined by a fourth, who, in turn, makes no reference to Luria or to the three who contest him. This remarkable byplay centers on the passage from Asheri discussed earlier, the *Tosfei HaRosh* to *Niddah*. R. Mosheh Feinstein conclusively demonstrated the spuriousness of that passage, where Asheri is supposed to forbid precoital mokh even to the Three Women. Logically, and because it contradicts without explanation what Asheri clearly taught in several other utterances, he declared the passage erroneous, the result of a pupil's or transcriber's error. R. Feinstein did so academically, without reference to the fact that an earlier Responsum (1888) by R. Abraham of Sochachev [*Av'nei Nezer*], had mounted his challenge to Luria on the strength of this *Tos'fei HaRosh;* that since Luria's position had been based on the precedent-authority of Asheri, among other considerations, *Tos'fei HaRosh* to *Niddah* proves that Luria does not have Asheri's support after all. [148] Two others have innocently taken the same tack, unaware that R. Feinstein has removed the basis of *Avnei Nezer's* refutation. This discredited *Tos'fei HaRosh* passage had served R. Avraham Yudelovich of Boston and New York, whose Responsa were published in 1920, as evidence that Luria's conclusion is without support. [149] And, in 1955, R. Mordecai Breisch of Zurich utilized the same passage for the same end, which led him to announce: "Luria's foundation has collapsed." [150]

Unqualified endorsement of Luria's standpoint, on the other hand, was to be found in the writings of eminent Respondents. R. Shneur Zalman of Lublin is among them, by way of his copious and most systematic Responsum. [151] He demonstrates how not only Asheri but other *Rishonim* are all solid support and precedent for Luria's conclusions. R. Menahem Schneirson of Lubavitch adds to his own total endorsement other arguments to further bolster Luria's position, [152] as do R. Issakhar Berish of Bendin and R. Hayyim Ozer Grodzensky of Vilna. [153] All of the above, however, without having to say so explicitly, would attach the important qualification that R. Isaac Halevy Herzog does to Luria's doctrine. In his Responsum (written in 1940, published in 1967), he contends that Luria could only have meant his permissive ruling to apply to one who has already fulfilled the mitzvah of p'ru ur'vu. [154] Taking this even in its rabbinic definition, where

[148] See above, p. 212.

[149] *Resp. Beit Av*, Vol. VII, No. 12.

[150] *Resp. Helkat Ya'akov*, Vol. II, No. 11.

[151] *Resp. Torat Hesed*, Vol. II, No. 43, 44.

[152] *Resp. Tzemah Tzedek, E.H.*, No. 89; see Ch. 8, Note 93.

[153] *Resp. Divrei Yissakhar*, No. 138; *Resp. Ahiezer, E.H.*, No. 23, etc.

[154] *Resp. Heikhal Yitzhak, E.H.*, Vol. II, No. 16.

the duty is ongoing even after the birth of "a son and a daughter," R. Herzog's essential point is unassailable. Luria was speaking of the method itself—and even of motives other than hazard; but he could not have intended his interpretation of the baraita to be used as a negation of the basic mitzvah.

Other Respondents, we have seen, have been more cautious still in utilizing Luria, relying upon his ruling to justify sanction of precoital mokh at least for cases of pregnancy hazard, which happened to be the circumstances of the question addressed to them. But it is simply not correct that Luria himself may be represented—as the otherwise careful scholar R. Immanuel Jakobovitz does in his books—as being "most lenient" for cases "where danger to life may otherwise ensue."[155] Luria wrote quite explicitly in the superscription and in the body of his analysis that "all women . . . "—not just those threatened by danger. Even the authorities who take issue with Luria have acknowledged that this is his clearly stated, if boldly conceived, point of view.

A document that can be said to demonstrate resoundingly the validity of Luria's understanding of our baraita is yet to be introduced. It is dramatic evidence that his interpretation—and that of the other *Rishonim* and Maimonides and the *Shulhan Arukh*, as set forth above—is the nearest to the original meaning thereof. The document is a recently published Responsum by a classic authority, master of the academy at Babylonia Hai Gaon (948–1038). As the one closest to the Talmudic period, his interpretation is the most authoritative. Writing before the period of Rashi and Rabbénu Tam, he manifestly reveals the concern of the baraita to be, as suggested above, the extent of hazard to the woman rather than the legality of the mokh, which is taken for granted. His Responsum provides a theoretic interpretation of the baraita followed by a specific ruling:[156]

> In the matter of the Three Women, the Sages did not forbid them the use of mokh; they merely said they do not have to. Most certainly they are permitted to use it. Women who do not wish to rely on "mercy vouchsafed from heaven"—they and their husbands should use the mokh and there is then no fear at all.
>
> And as to the suggestion of the Sages that one need only supplement the child's diet [to avoid risk from premature weaning], you say that "someone tried it" in this generation and the child was not adversely

[155] *Jewish Medical Ethics*, p. 169; *Journal of a Rabbi*, p. 218.

[156] A. Harkavy, *T'shuvot HaGeonim, Y'vamot* (1959; reprint from Berlin ed., 1887), p. 167: "Of the questions sent from Kabs in the West . . . to the Great Court of all Israel, to the gate of the Academy, before our Master and teacher Hai, head of the Academy, son of our Master and teacher Sherira, etc."

affected. Certainly the Sages, etc. . . . But, when she uses the mokh so that she not become pregnant she need have no fear and even that supplementation will not be necessary.[157]

The baraita, then, has hazard, not legality, as its theme, as was sensed by the great authorities referred to above. Luria thus earns the encomium of *Hazon Ish* upon him in this connection, that he "attained Divine inspiration." [158] His understanding of the baraita can now be said to be confirmed by R. Hai Gaon, as well as by Maimonides, Asheri, and the Shulhan Arukh. Significant new endorsement comes from another hitherto unpublished source, this one of more recent date. R. Abraham Isaac Kuk, Chief Rabbi of the Holy Land until his death in 1935, authored several Responsa on our subject; they were not published until 1969. In one of these, dated 1912, R. Kuk writes that Maimonides and Shulhan Arukh omitted codifying our baraita because they hold that R. Meir "requires," rather than permits, and the Sages "do not require"—meaning that legality or "violation is not the issue" but hazard is.[159] In slightly later Responsa, he declares that R. Akiva Eger had obviously and demonstrably not seen Luria's view; that if he had, he may well have concurred; [160] that, moreover, Eger's cited case is not one of special danger but a near-normal one—as other writers were to observe—and hence his rigorous stand.[161]

This last point helps bring into focus the tendencies traced in this chapter and bridges the two major schools of thought.[162] To the "permissivists," no prohibition issues from our baraita per se. To the others, hash-hatat zera is indeed the question posed by the baraita, at least in Rashi's and Rabbenu Tam's commentation thereto. While this school granted Rashi's assumptions, by and large they limited the Sages' demurral ("may not") narrowly to the Three Women of the baraita. This made it possible even for the nonpermissivists to give situations of real danger the benefit of the baraita's essential concern for hazard. So that, as R. Kuk reassures us, "since abstinence to avoid danger is never commanded," [163] contraception is mandated, when no alternative exists, even by the strictest view. Where Luria's reading is unknown or qualified, it is this stricter view that gave form, substance, and gravity to the pattern of rabbinic legislation on birth control.

[157] *Ibid.*, p. 169, No. 338.
[158] See Note 85, above.
[159] *Resp. Ezrat Kohen* (Mosad Rav Kuk; 1969), No. 34 (p. 135). See pp. 195, 205, above.
[160] *Op. cit.*, Nos. 35 (p. 138), 36 (p. 139 [1925]), and 37 (p. 141 [1933]). See pp. 219–22, above.
[161] *Op. cit.*, Nos. 35, 37 (p. 142). See pp. 217–18, above.
[162] R. Kuk makes other points: *hash-hatat zera* is not applicable where *onah* is mitzvah: Nos. 35, 36, 37. See pp. 76, 153, above. *Shello k'darkah* proves it (*ibid.*)
[163] *Ibid.*, Nos. 35 (p. 138), 36 (p. 139). See pp. 76, 201, above.

12

Variations of
the Mokh Principle

Luria's ruling on mokh effectively removed its usage from the category of hash-hatat zera, at least for situations of pregnancy hazard. But, since awareness—and, to a lesser extent, acceptance—of this ruling was so limited during a period of time when many Responsa were being composed, the critical judgment of these latter was directed to a consideration of available alternatives. New methods of contraception came into being or returned to vogue; queries were now submitted as to their permissibility. Were these methods different from (and hence less objectionable than) the precoital mokh, the tampon? If so, which among them is to be preferred over another? The Talmudic mokh thus becomes the standard against which other contraceptive measures are adjudged, and a hierarchy of relative acceptability emerges.

The Pessary or Diaphragm

Among the measures coming into wider use during the mid-nineteenth century were several forms of pessary: a generic term including the cervical cap and the diaphragm.[1] That a distinction in fact may be made—and that the pessary is free of the objections seen by the Talmudic Commentators in

[1] The cervical cap was first recommended by the German gynecologist F. A. Wilde in 1838 (N. E. Himes, *Medical History of Contraception*, p. 211); the diaphragm was perfected by Wilhelm Mensinga, professor of anatomy at Breslau, in 1880 (*ibid.*, p. 321).

the use of a mokh—is made abundantly clear by a Responsum published in 1934. It is the reply by R. Y'hoshua Baumol of Williamsburg in Brooklyn to a colleague in neighboring Brownsville. He writes:

> Really I don't know why we even need enter into the Debate of Authorities [concerning mokh] now that there is available a new means of contraception, called "birth control," whereby a rubber pessary covers the entrance to the uterus. . . . This is certainly permissible where p'ru ur'vu has been fulfilled and danger exists. *Maharsham* has so stated and thus "the Elder has already ruled." [2]

Maharsham is R. Shalom M. Schwadron of Brezany in Galicia (d. 1911), whose conclusion we have introduced elsewhere: a diaphragm that merely closes the uteral os simulates the "condition of pregnancy when, too, the mouth of the uterus is naturally closed." The use of such a diaphragm is "not at all analogous to mokh," but to coitus during pregnancy. [3] The preeminence of *Maharsham* leads R. Baumol to rely on his decision and to invoke the Talmudic phrase, "the Elder has ruled (*k'var horah zaken*)", [4] and the matter has been settled.

The principle, however, may be said to predate even Maharsham's ruling, for the distinction between tampon and diaphragm in this sense has its own intrinsic logic. Before this type of pessary became available or popular, earlier authorities had made the distinction in principle. We have already seen how R. Hayyim Sofer (d. 1867) differentiated between two types of mokh usage, one which interferes with the sex act and hence is improper, and another which merely closes the uterus to any entry of sperm and would thus not be improper as a method. [5] Others, including R. Mosheh Feinstein, have independently come to the same conclusion through different routes, equating pessary usage with normal coitus; [6] others have relayed and endorsed Maharsham's findings; [7] but some, we shall see, argue otherwise. [8] A significant statement

---

[2] *Resp. Emek Halakhah*, No. 66.

[3] *Resp. Maharsham*, Vol. I, No. 58. In his Responsum cited by *Divrei Yissakhar*, No. 138, he says: "Many Rabbis have agreed with me and I have so ruled many times." Also, in his Responsum appearing in *Tiferet Adam*, No. 74: "not mokh, but pessary."

[4] TB Shabbat 51a; Y'vamot 105b.

[5] *Resp. Mahaneh Hayyim*, E.H., No. 53.

[6] *Resp. Im'rei Shefer*, No. 29; *Resp. Hit'or'rut T'shuvah*, No. 3 (1912); *Resp. Minhat Ha-Kometz*, No. 94 (1934); *Resp. Igg'rot Mosheh*, E.H., No. 63.

[7] *Resp. Zikhron Y'hudah*, No. 246; *Beit Av*, Vol. VII, No. 12; *Resp. Maharash Engel*, Vol. VII, No. 86; *S'ridei Esh*, Vol. III, No. 16.

[8] *Resp. Minhat Yitzhak*, Vol. I, No. 115, disagrees with the theory but would allow the pessary for hazard. For views that hold pessary inferior to other methods, see on.

on the subject takes its place alongside that of Maharsham in making clear the distinction applicable here. R. David Hoffman of Berlin (d. 1921) permits mokh for pregnancy hazard, then tells us:

> After writing the above, the esteemed Rabbi-Physician Hayyim Biberfeld informed me that mokh is not too safe; that pregnancy may occur despite its use. He therefore gave me another suggestion: That the physician or midwife close the uterus with a covering, known to them as an "occlusion." In this I see not the slightest prohibition (*ein ani roeh shum tzad v'nidnud shel issur*), since the seed is not being destroyed; it is merely being prevented from entering the uterus. [9]

The Condom

Unlike the diaphragm, the use of a condom can never be called normal coitus; it is an improper interference. [10] So declares R. Simha Bunem Sofer (d. 1907), a grandson of *Hatam* (Moses) *Sofer* and heir to his seat of authority in Pressburg. [11] At about the same time, our Maharsham ruled similarly: where mokh may be permitted in situations of hazard, the condom is a much worse impediment, one that falsifies the very essence of the act's normal processes. "Therefore," he declares gravely, "he who is lenient in this matter will have to answer for it (*atid liten et ha-din*)." [12] His view, in turn, is seconded by R. Dov Weidenfeld in a Responsum dated 1935: "Maharsham's eminence and his power even to [discover and institute] lenient rulings is well known (*yadua rav heilo v'tokfo b'koah d'heteira*). And if he is afraid to be lenient in *this* matter, so am I". [13]

Others, too, based their restrictive rulings on Maharsham, [14] while still others forbade the condom in their own names: R. Nahum Weidenfeld, a brother of the aforementioned, stigmatizes it simply as "worse than mokh"; [15] so does R. Samuel Engel. [16] But R. Yosef Yonah Horovitz of Frankfurt am

---

[9] *Resp. M'lammed L'Hoil*, Vol. III, No. 18.

[10] The condom is known to be used since the middle of the 17th century (Himes, *op. cit.*, pp. 190–91), but it was the vulcanization of rubber in 1843 that led to wider production and distribution (*ibid.*, p. 227).

[11] *Resp. Shevet Sofer*, No. 2.

[12] *Resp. Maharsham*, Vol. III, *Maftehot*.

[13] *Resp. Dovev Meisharim*, Vol. I, No. 20.

[14] R. Y'hiel M. Leiter in *Resp. Dar'khei Shalom*, Vol. I, No. 2; *Resp. Yagel Ya'akov*, Y.D., No. 66; *Tzur Ya'akov*, No. 141.

[15] *Hazon Nahum*, quoted by *Resp. Im'rei Kohen*, No. 39.

[16] *Resp. Maharash Engel*, *loc. cit.*, and Vol. VIII, No. 90.

Main goes further and adduces the words of R. Hayyim Sofer with respect to the wrong kind of mokh usage. He places the condom in this category too: such usage runs counter to "And he shall cleave unto his wife and they shall become as one flesh."[17]

A measure of flexibility on the matter is reflected in the Responsa of R. Eliyahu Klatzkin of Lublin. He had suggested the pessary in an early Responsum;[18] this evoked further correspondence, to which he addressed himself in a later work: One questioner, writing in 1899, protested that the pessary or diaphragm is much too impractical (it requires the constant assistance of a physician, etc.); could the condom be used? No, he replied, as long as other methods are available, there is no room to permit the condom; leniency in this matter will lead to immorality, etc.[19] Another questioner (1909) claimed that the diaphragm was unsafe, ineffective rather than inconvenient; to him, R. Klatzkin suggests that, when no alternative is available to avoid physical hazard, there may be room to permit it.[20]

The breath of a suggestion here became an articulate statement elsewhere, in the Responsum (1935) of an authority of great renown. R. Hayyim Ozer Grodzensky of Vilna, when asked about a condom for a situation of pregnancy hazard, discussed the matter at some length, found that such usage could also be considered the normal manner of intercourse, and concluded forthrightly: "I therefore concur with my colleague [the questioner] that it is permitted" in such a case.[21] Exception to this singular point of view was taken by R. Mosheh Feinstein: Such usage cannot be called the normal manner at all, for the sperm does not even remain with her; the essence of the act has been basically thwarted. On the theory, however, that those who permit unnatural coitus do so because it is still proper to the heterosexual relationship, even the condom would be permitted. He thus rejects R. Hayyim Ozer's reason but finds it possible to permit it for other reasons. When there is danger and there is no alternative measure available, the theory of these authorities is enough to rely on, especially when *iggun* is threatened and *sh'lom bayyit* is at stake.[22] R. Eliezer Waldenberg of Jerusalem seems to incline toward the same cautious flexibility.[23]

---

[17] In *Rosenheim Festschrift*, p. 108. Cf., R. Ovadia Yosef in *Noam*, Vol. III (1960), where use of a condom is referred to as *darkan shel ba'alei averah . . . etzel n'shoteihem.*

[18] *Im'rei Shefer*, Note 5, above.

[19] *Resp. D'var Eliyahu*, No. 65.

[20] *Ibid.*

[21] *Resp. Ahiezer*, Vol. III, No. 24:5.

[22] *Resp. Igg'rot Mosheh, loc. cit.*, p. 162.

[23] *Resp. Tzitz Eliezer*, IX, No. 51, (p. 218).

Spermicides

Chemical methods of contraception have likewise proliferated in recent years. Foams, tablets that dissolve, and the like, are intended to neutralize the viability of the sperm, without obstructing its normal passage. A major ruling on this subject comes from R. Meir Arik of Buczacz in 1913. Dissolving tablets are much better than mokh, for this measure does not block passage of the sperm, and the coitus is in the normal manner as Luria would have it; that is, the unimpeded contact, with its normal gratifications, still obtains.[24] Parallel to this one, another Responsum by R. Menaham Mannes Babad pronounced spermicides to be "unlike mokh, instead like coitus with a barren woman."[25] Subsequent Respondents quote one or both of these approvingly.[26] R. Sh'lomo Tabak of Sziget introduced the mystic element and pointed out that the evil of insemination "outside the vessel" is thereby avoided.[27] To R. Eliezer Deutsch, the spermicide is fine because it is not obtrusively sensed during the act of coitus (*eino nirgash*);[28] to R. Mosheh Feinstein it is no worse than oral contraception;[29] to R. Y'hudah Leib Zirelson of Kishenev it is to be permitted without question when danger threatens.[30] R. Yosef Rosen of Rogotchev would permit it (because of its indirect mode of operation), for even less than real danger;[31] but two authorities before him forbade it when the contraception was desired for economic reasons.[32] Against the lenient tendency described above, the opposing views will be set forth in our discussion of relative acceptability.

The Douche

Another instrumentality that leaves the sex act alone and requires only a postcoital effort is that of douching. R. Mordecai Winkler of Hungary, agreeing in theory with those who permit spermicides, wants to know why we resort to or take advantage of that measure when douching is possible

[24] *Resp. Im'rei Yosher*, Vol. I, No. 131.

[25] *Resp. Havatzelet HaSharon*, Addendum to *E.H.*, Vol. I.

[26] *Resp. Binyan David*, No. 68; *Helkat Ya'akov*, Vol. II, No. 13; *Resp. Minhat Yitzhak, loc. cit.*

[27] *Resp. T'shurat Shai, Tinyana*, No. 62. He is endorsed by *Atzei Hayyim*, No. 30.

[28] *Resp. P'ri HaSadeh*, Vol. IV, No. 14.

[29] *Igg'rot Mosheh, E.H.*, No. 62.

[30] *Resp. Ma'ar'khei Lev*, No. 66.

[31] *Resp. Tzofnat Pa'aneah* (1935), Vol. I, No. 30; and see also *Resp. Shem MiShimon*, Ch. 10, above.

[32] *Resp. L'vushei Mord'khai*, No. 28; *Resp. Yaskil Avdi*, Vol. II, No. 6.

and which, being postcoital, would qualify even according to *Hatam Sofer*.[33]

In answer to his query, it may be said that several Respondents feared to recommend postcoital douching on the grounds that it was insufficiently effective. R. Yosef Yonah Horovitz says as much: since experience and medical opinion cast doubts on the efficacy of postcoital efforts, he forbore from ruling favorably on it when pregnancy had to be avoided.[34] At about the same time, R. Israel Kuperstok of Poland was writing: "But in these days postcoital douching has been made much more effective [by invention of instrumental aids] and so may be recommended without fear."[35] As a safe method, it would seem to be lawful in itself on the assumption that postcoital hash-hatat zera by the woman is not a violation.[36] Numerous Responsa permit it at least in hazard cases on this assumption;[37] some, in cases without hazard but for ultimate health reasons;[38] and at least one permits it simply because a pregnancy is not desired.[39] Opposing views with respect to this method, too, are seen in the comparative discussion, to which we now turn.

Which Is Better?

A preference for spermicides over the pessary principle is expressed by several Respondents. The aforementioned R. Horovitz (writing in 1932) feels that the pessary, being occlusive, is an improper barrier; it should be resorted to only if chemical means are not a possible alternative.[40] He was seconded by others;[41] among them is R. Mordecai Brisk who opposed the pessary on aesthetic grounds as "unseemly"; spermicides are less direct, less obtrusive, and are definitely to be preferred.[42] The douche, too, is rejected by him on grounds of human directness in removing the sperm.

On the other hand, the opposite point of view has its estimable protagonists. R. Elazar Lev of Hungary (1912) sees the use of a spermicide as no less active or conscious an interference than mokh; he would allow it only for

[33] *L'vushei Mord'khai*, No. 27.

[34] *Rosenheim Festschrift*, end.

[35] *Resp. Ani Ben Pehama*, Y.D., No. 25.

[36] See Ch. 6 (*Hash-hatat zera* and the woman), and Ch. 11 (Rabbenu Tam, etc.).

[37] E.g., *Resp. Av'nei Nezer*, No. 81; *Neta Sorek*, No. 6; *Arugat HaBosem*, Y.D., Vol. II, No. 187.

[38] *Resp. Hedvat Ya'akov*, *Tinyana*, No. 38; *Maharsham*, Vol. IV, No. 132.

[39] *Resp. Sitri UMagini*, No. 44.

[40] *Rosenheim Festschrift*, p. 110.

[41] *Resp. Tzur Ya'akov*, No. 141; *Resp. Maharitz* (Dushinsky), No. 128; *Igg'rot Mosheh*, loc. cit.

[42] *Resp. Maharam Brisk*, Vol. I, No. 97.

hazard.[43] R. Israel Zalmonowitz records in a recent work of his that he had corresponded with the late *Hazon Ish* (R. Isaiah Karelitz, d. 1953) on the matter of spermicides. He reports: "His reply was brief: their use is permissible. Reliable people have since told me that, between the two, he declared the pessary preferable for many reasons."[44] In a Responsum published in 1966, R. Y'hiel Weinberg, a successor to the position of R. David Hoffman, wrote: "The prohibition is with mokh . . . or other chemical means. Therefore, the advice given is to have the uterus closed to entry of sperm, by the occlusion called pessary."[45] And, in a Responsum published this year (1967), R. Eliezer Waldenberg of Jerusalem says:

> Prefer the spermicides? The douche? In my opinion, this is not right. Spermicides destroy the seed immediately upon its entry into the canal, unlike the pessary . . . How can they prefer the others to a pessary where no destruction takes place? Perhaps because they think that spermicides merely neutralize the sperm when actually they destroy it.[46]

Moreover, the preference shown for spermicides is usually predicated on the assumption that no occlusion then takes place. Often, however, they contain a chemical agent that throws up an occlusive sponge, rendering them virtually tampon-like; they immobilize the sperm—in the words of a spokesman for a pharmaceutical corporation—in addition to depriving it of its generative capacity.[47]

Leaving to one side the above point, a simple hierarchy of acceptability does emerge. Contraceptive means that least interfere with the sex act and/or least interfere with the full motility of the sperm towards the end of its natural course are the least objectionable.

The IUCD's

The intrauterine contraceptive devices—the IUCD's—have come upon the scene just yesterday, so to speak. They may have their precursor

[43] *P'kudat Elazar, Resp.*, No. 100. See also *Resp. Da'at Sofer, E.H.*, No. 16, of Akiva Sofer, written Pressburg 1913, published Jerusalem, 1965.

[44] *Hai Nefesh*, I,100.

[45] *Resp. S'ridei Esh*, Vol. III, No. 16.

[46] *Tzitz Eliezer, loc. cit.*, p. 217.

[47] The spokesman writes (letter on file): " . . . To the best of our knowledge, there are none of the first type you mention, i.e., those that would deprive the sperm of its generative capacity without immobilizing it."

in the Graefenberg ring, a ring comprised of silk threads and bound by silver wire, which was invented by Ernst Graefenberg, a Berlin doctor, in 1928. Just how this ring does its work, or how the modern IUCD's do theirs, is not really known. The Responsa do not reflect their usage much—unless a reference to a "ring-like metallic object" by R. Mordecai Winkler is an example of the earlier form.[48] As for the new form, in 1963, R. Immanuel Jakobovitz raised the issue in a halakhic Annual: "A new method, a small ring of silk or plastic with a long silver thread attached" is now in use. The coitus is unimpeded, he points out, but perhaps an abortifacient action takes place.[49] This may still not make it unlawful, as such an act (as we shall see in Chapter 14), is governed by a different set of considerations than is hash-hatat zera. The matter, he concludes, requires further study when the exact mode of operation becomes known. The above-mentioned R. Waldenberg, however, sees this method as "destroying" both sperm and ovum. Why elect to destroy both when, in addition to the uteral inflammations said to be caused this way, the better method of pessary/diaphragm is available?[50]

The legal attitude to still other birth control measures would be derivable by analogy with the foregoing; they are variations of the "mokh" principle. As to "rhythm," the Pill, and other methods in that category, these are more analogous to the principle of an oral contraceptive—subject of our next chapter.

[48] *L'vushei Mord'khai, Tinyana, Y.D.,* No. 110.

[49] *Noam,* VI, 272.

[50] *Tzitz Eliezer, loc. cit.,* p. 218.

13

An Oral Contraceptive

The mokh and its variations take their respective places in the hierarchy of acceptability as contraceptive devices. Over against them all, however, is another instrumentality which, *as a method*, is unobjectionable even to the stricter school. This is an orally administered contraceptive which, by definition, is free of the technical problems of artificial interference with the sex act and hash-hatat zera.

The "Cup of Roots"; Sterilization

The oral contraceptive principle has its basis in the Talmud as a potion or "cup of roots," the *kos shel ikkarin*.[1] The "roots" in that potion may refer to its herbal ingredients (the modern progesterone pill makes use of roots of the Mexican yam), and the mixture, in varying compositions, had many purposes. An alternative to the Talmudic phrase, *kasa d'akarta* [cup of barrenness], may have described the more specifically contraceptive or sterilizing

---

[1] In the Talmud this potion is described as *kos shel ikkarin* in *Mishna & G'mara Shabbat* 109b, 110a; as *kos ikkarin* in *Tosefta Y'vamot*, Ch. 8; and as *kasa d'akarta* in *TB Y'vamot*, 65b. *Kos shel ikkarin* is probably a cup of any medicinally used roots and, in its context, was only secondarily a sterilizing agent. *Kasa d'akarta* is probably more specifically a sterilizing agent, from *akar*, "barren," rather than *ikkar*, "roots," but the *Tosefta* uses *kos ikkarin* perhaps in a double sense. R. Yohanan, in *Shabbat* 110a, enumerates the ingredients of *kos shel ikkarin*, further explained by Preuss, p. 439, but this formula may be not at all identical with that of the *kasa d'akarta*.

potion. But the Codes and Responsa, even when speaking of this specific usage, prefer the generic term, *kos shel ikkarin*.

Potions to induce temporary or permanent sterility are referred to in ancient Greek and Roman sources.[2] References to medicinal drinks of this sort can be found in medieval sources and are even the subject of legislation by the Justinian Code,[3] as well as Church law.[4] Moreover, other-than-contraceptive "potions" of many kinds and purposes are assumed to be effective —or else effective remedies are *called* potions. The Talmud speaks once of an abortifacient potion, like the now-projected abortion pill (*sama d'naftza*);[5] indeed, Maimonides adds the words "by surgery or by drug" in relaying the Talmud's mandate for abortion or embryotomy;[6] and, in a few Responsa concerning the permissibility of abortion, both the question and the answer are phrased in terms of "drinking a potion" to bring it about (*sam ha-mappil*).[7] The *kos shel ikkarin* itself could, in a different dosage or composition, cause fertility rather than sterility, or could cure certain ailments.[8] An inquiry concerning the wife's right to drink a potion that would help her *become* pregnant (*sam l'hit-abber*) was addressed to the eminent R. Solomon ben Adret of the thirteenth century,[9] and his reply became part of the *Shulhan Arukh*.[10] But the most persistent of all is some sort of drug or concoction with real or imagined contraceptive properties.

For, oral contraception, either in principle or in actuality, is a live subject in Jewish legal literature. After the Talmud's mention of *kos shel ikkarin*, both its existence and efficacy are taken for granted in the Codes and Responsa

[2] Pliny, *Natural History*, 20:44, 2, 24:47, 4, etc. quoted by L. Loew, *Lebensalter*, p. 380, Note 160. The Egyptian *Ebers Papyrus* of about 1550 BCE, quoted by I. Jackobovitz, *Jewish Medical Ethics* (New York, 1959), p. 162, Note 65, may also refer to oral contraceptive potions, if not anaphrodisiacs. See also N. E. Himes, *Medical History of Contraception* (New York, 1934, 1963), *passim;* N. Kass, "Birth Prevention in the Talmud," *Hebrew Medical Journal*, 34 (1961), 163 ff.

[3] Lynn Thorndike, *A History of Magic and Experimental Science to 1300* (1923), I, 656; II, 470, 736, 744; *Corpus juris civilis*, ed. Krueger (1928), I, 852, 876, quoted by Jakobovitz, *loc. cit.*

[4] In the *Decretals*, the collection of Church decrees begun under Pope Gregory IX in 1230 and which became part of *corpus juris canonici* in effect until 1915, we read:

> If anyone, to satisfy his lust or in meditated hatred, does something to a man or a woman, or gives something to drink so that he cannot generate, or she conceive, or offspring be born . . .

cited by Noonan, *Contraception . . .* , p. 178. See also *ibid.*, pp. 137, 144, 158–59.

[5] *TB Niddah* 30b.

[6] See Chapter 15, pp. 276–77.

[7] E.g., *Resp. Beit Y'hudah*, E.H., No. 14 (1746). (Women "prepare medicines and potions, known among them, in order to abort the foetus.") See also *Responsa* of Sh'lomo Hasson, E.H., No. 6 (Saloniki, 1720).

[8] See *kos ikkarin* vs. *kasa d'akarta*, Note 1, above.

[9] *Resp. Rashba*, No. 560.

[10] *Yoreh Deah*, 234:74, and see *Be'er HaGolah* and commentators, *ad loc.*

discussed in this chapter. The Codes, up to the most recent,[11] restate matter-of-factly the laws governing its proper use, while the authors of Responsa are asked and reply about something apparently available and effective. In some references, more than "taking for granted" seems to be reflected. Thus, R. Joshua Falk, head of a Talmudic Academy in seventeenth-century Poland, reports that he "saw" the Rabbis permit the "cup of roots" to a woman with childbearing difficulties.[12] The eighteenth-century Italian Rabbi-Physician Isaac Lampronti in his halakhic encyclopedia reports that Jewish physicians ordinarily give (*nohagim latet*) to women a substance called (in Italian) *trifera* "or other pharmaceuticals" which cause sterility.[13] In a famous Responsum dated 1825, R. Moses Sofer of Pressburg discusses the legality of the "cup,"[14] while in a later, lesser-known communication, he expresses his hesitation about its safety; in the interim he had "heard that there is danger in its use."[15] A curious marginal annotation accompanies the Responsum on our subject emanating from Warsaw in 1849:

> In these times in Europe it is forbidden to give one the "cup of roots" to drink, without permission of the medical authorities appointed by the government. . . . [16]

Later, in 1875, also in Poland, when R. Shneur Zalman of Lublin speaks of this "cup of roots" apprehensively, as "despoiling the uterus" (*m'kalkel et heder ha-herayon*), he tells us he learned this fact from "discussion with physicians."[17] But, slightly later in that same century (1894), Rabbi Mordecai Horovitz of Frankfurt am Main says he inquired among the physicians of his community and was told that such a potion is not known to the experts and "must have been forgotten in the course of time."[18] In Galicia of 1906, R. Mordecai Twersky also reports being told by physicians that "today the 'cup of roots' is not given in any form."[19] And in Mad, Hungary, Rabbi Mordecai Winkler writes (in 1912):

---

[11] *Arokh HaShulhan* (c. 1900), *E.H.*, 5, 24. See also *Kitzur Shulhan Arukh* (1864 and reprinted many times later), 191, 5.

[12] *Drishah* to *Tur, Even Ha Ezer* 5:4.

[13] *Pahad Yitzak, s.v. kos ikkarin.*

[14] *Resp. Hatam Sofer, E.H.* No. 20; see on.

[15] *Ibid.*, Vol. VI (*Likkutei Sh'elot Ut'shuvot*), No. 40.

[16] *Resp. M'shivat Nefesh* (not to be confused with later book, same title, same author), No. 18.

[17] *Resp. Torat Hesed*, Vol. II, *E.H.* 44:41.

[18] *Resp. Matteh Levi*, Vol. II, No. 31 (ed. R. Jacob Horwitz).

[19] *Resp. Emek Sh'elah, E.H.*, No. 68.

I find it strange that physicians don't use this means today, unless perhaps no such pharmaceutical is known to them.[20]

Back again in Poland, R. Elijah Klatzkin wrote similarly (in 1915):

Physicians in our time are not able to prepare such a potion which would be safe and effective against pregnancy.[21]

A lengthier essay (1932), again from Frankfurt, offering a comparative analysis of the various contraceptive measures, likewise speaks of the potion as something "not known" now but which teaches us much legal theory.[22] All the more surprising, then, are the questions submitted to R. Obadia Hadaya of the Rabbinical Court of Petah Tikvah, Israel, in 1946. The woman, in one case, claims she was "advised by the physicians to drink the cup of sterility to prevent conception."[23] In the second case, she "already drank the 'cup' but it did not help," and her inquiry now is about alternative methods. Included in his reply is the suggestion that she seek a more "tried and tested" potion at the hands of "more expert physicians."[24]

What manner of contraceptive is actually being referred to in these many instances[25] is difficult to determine. A somewhat helpful judgment on the probable mode of its efficacy is contained in a legal essay on other matters in 1955 by Israel's present Chief Rabbi:

Today we have no idea how this *kos shel ikkarin* worked, for there is no potion today which renders one sterile by drinking . . . . But, very likely, even in those days, the *kos* achieved its effect through functional changes in the nervous system, rather than actual organic means.[26]

Additionally, folk medicine and psychological factors may have played their part alongside the more scientific elements. But the latter are not to be discounted: An American biochemist, pursuing his researches in the primitive island of West Irian, Indonesia, has now isolated a substance from the bark of tall trees growing there. Administered in the form of a drug, the bark

---

[20] *Resp. L'vushei Mord'khai* (First Series), Vol. II, *E.H.* No. 27.

[21] *Resp. D'var Eliyahu*, No. 17.

[22] R. Yosef Yonah Horovitz, in *Rosenheim Festschrift* (1932), p. 111.

[23] *Resp. Yaskil Avdi*, Vol. IV, No. 4.

[24] *Ibid.*, No. 5.

[25] See also references below and especially Notes 63, 64, as well as *Resp. Maharam Brisk*, Vol. I, No. 97.

[26] R. Issar Y Unterman, *Shevet Miy'hudah* (Jerusalem, 1955), I, 285.

substance has demonstrated, in scientifically controlled tests, undoubted contraceptive effects. [27]

Legal Implications of the "Cup"

Our interest here, of course, is not in the medical efficacy of potions but in the legal principles, even theoretical, which they reflect for the rabbinic attitude to any oral contraceptive or sterilizing agent.

No legal inference is drawn in Talmud, Codes, or Responsa—it is surprising to note—from the well-known reference to the "cup of roots" in the Midrashic narrative concerning Lamech, son of Cain. [28] Popularized by Rashi's citation of it in his Commentary to Genesis, [29] the narrative runs as follows:

> The men of the Generation of the Flood used to act thus: each took two wives, one for procreation and the other for sexual gratification. The former would stay like a widow throughout her life, while the latter was given to drink a potion of roots, so that she should not bear, and then she sat before him like a harlot [as it is written, He devoureth the barren that beareth not, and doeth not good to the widow, Job 24 : 21]. The proof of this is that the best of them, who was Lamech, took two wives, Adah [so called] because he kept her away (ya' adeh) from himself; and Zillah, to sit in his shadow (tzillo).

This Midrash may have served as a fine didactic admonition against self-indulgent marital relations; or even less than that, its moral point may be the wrongful neglect of the fruitful wife, who becomes "as a widow in her husband's lifetime." [30] It served the Church, too, through the *Summa Theologica* of Alexander of Hales in the thirteenth century, although its source as a Midrash was later unknown. [31] As for Jewish law, the narrative's

[27] Associated Press report in the Los Angeles *Times*, July 5, 1967.

[28] *Gen. Rabbah*, 23, 3; also *TP Y'vamot* 6 : 5. See above, Chapter 4, p. 66.

[29] To Gen. 4:19; also in his Commentary to Job 24:21.

[30] Preuss (*op. cit.*), p. 480 sees it as a protest against the inconsiderate practice of maintaining concubines in addition to one's fruitful wife.

[31] Alexander of Hales (d. 1245), in his *Summa Theologica* (2–2), derives his definition of "coitus against nature" from the act of Lamech, "who did not intend to procreate . . . to which matrimonial union is specifically directed, but copulated to satisfy his lust." Unaware of this Midrash, our modern authority, Noonan (*op. cit.*) p. 225, wrongly attributes a "slip of the pen" to Alexander, claiming he wrote "Lamech" when he meant "Onan." Yet the Midrash was known even among the medieval Christian scholastics through Rashi or otherwise, as demonstrated by H. Hailperin, *Rashi and the Christian Scholars* (Pittsburgh, 1955). For Alexander of Hales specifically and his knowledge of Jewish literature, see Jakob Guttman, *Die Scholastik des Dreizehnten Jahrhunderts in ihren Beziehungen zum Judenthum und zur Jüdischen Literatur* (Breslau, 1902), pp. 39–46. Alexander's homily, too, fits Lamech rather than Onan.

moral lesson did not render the method per se illegal; and to have made one's only wife barren in such a manner was at worst equivalent to passive neglect of the duty of procreation.

Legal inferences were, however, drawn from the other primary reference, in the Talmud, to this "cup of roots." The wife of R. Hiyya, we are told there, had experienced unusual difficulty in childbearing. She subsequently disguised herself and came before her husband in his official capacity and asked the question: Is the biblical command of "Be fruitful and multiply" incumbent upon the woman, too? No, he said; she then "went and drank the cup of roots." His reaction, although unhappy, indicated that she had incurred no violation. This same R. Hiyya (fourth century) is regarded as the compiler of the separate Talmudic corpus called the *Tosefta*, and there we read:

> A man is not permitted to drink the cup of roots in order to become sterile, but a woman is permitted to drink the cup of roots to become sterile. [33]

From the *Tosefta* and on, such explicit permission is reiterated by all the major law codes without reservation. [34] Some, however, stipulate that there first be unusual difficulty in childbearing, which was actually the case with the wife of R. Hiyya. R. Solomon Luria is the chief protagonist of this stipulation. [35] (His dedication to the pristine Talmudic teaching had led him to a position of bold leniency in the matter of mokh, as we have seen; that same faithfulness now leads him to the stricter side of this question.) His disciple, author of a commentary to the *Tur* Code, [36] gave Luria's formulation wider acceptance. [37]

Before going further, it is important to emphasize that the bulk of the legal discussion surrounding the kos shel ikkarin is based on a crucial assumption, that the sterilizing effect of this potion is permanent. The first of the legal problems incidental to the drinking of the "cup," then, issues from the presupposition that a kind of "castration" is involved in its use. [38]

[32] *TB Y'vamot* 65b.

[33] *Tosefta Y'vamot* Ch. 8.

[34] *SMaG, neg.* 120; *Mai., Issurei Biah,* 16, 12; *Tur* and *Shulḥan Arukh, E.H.* 5, 12; *TaZ* and *Beit Shmuel, ad loc.*

[35] *Yam Shel Sh'lomo, Y'vamot* 6:44. Luria, incidentally, adds another justification for use of the *kos:* "When her children are not proper (*einam hagunim*) and she fears giving birth to more such." This curious provision is without antecedent or subsequent reflection in the sources.

[36] *BaH* to *Tur, E.H.* 5.

[37] E.g., *Arokh Ha-Shulhan, E.H.* 5, 24. *Resp. Yaskil Avdi,* Vol. IV, No. 4, says *BaH* assumes R. Hiyya's wife included the detail of *tza'ar ledah* in her original inquiry, hence the stipulation.

[38] Castration of animals and humans is forbidden by Jewish law in *TB Shabbat* 110b (and *Tosefta Makkot* Ch. 5 and *Tosefta B'khorot,* Ch. 3) based on a wider interpretation of Lev. 22:24 (*uv'artz'khem lo ta-a-su*). See Y. Abramsky, *Hazon Y'hezkel* to *Tosefta Y'vamot,* Ch. 8. See also *Sh. Ar.* and especially *L'vush, E.H.* 5, 11.

Indeed the possibility of *sirus* (castration) in connection with this potion is raised by the Talmud itself[39] but dismissed as technically inapplicable to the woman.[40] The issue was reopened in post-Talmudic times:[41] technical castration *is* applicable to women through the sterilizing potion, and it may therefore be taken by her (as implied above) only for reasons of severe pain in childbirth, for did not Maimonides, who seems to have permitted it unconditionally, rule that *sirus* with regard to women is "unpunishable"— meaning, as that word usually does, unpunishable but forbidden (*patur aval asur*)? At least, therefore, a formal violation is incurred and the practice should not be permitted without sufficient reason. We come full circle as subsequent authorities set aside this argument from Maimonides as well[42] and declare no *sirus* to be involved in her drinking the potion, permitting it, on these grounds at least, unconditionally.[43]

Among the reasons offered for the legal sanction of this drink for women but not for men is—as again suggested by the original story of R. Hiyya's wife—that p'ru ur'vu is not technically addressed to her.[44] Hence we have the social reason as well as the biological. But then this cannot be the essential reason, since no such distinction is made with regard to animals.[45] They certainly do not have to answer to the commandment of p'ru ur'vu either; yet sterilization and castration laws do apply to them. The woman's right to the sterilizing potion, then, is not so much a function of p'ru ur'vu as it is because this medical sterilization does not constitute "castration" in her case but would in a man's case.[46]

But then one more question is raised. May a woman really render herself sterile, though the manner of accomplishing this be "legal"? An obligation of procreation does rest upon her; if not technically through the positive biblical commandment then at least through the more general rabbinic injunction of la-shevet,[47] of contributing to the world's habitation of the

[39] *TB Shabbat* 110b; and *Tosafot, ibid., s.v. v'hatania.*

[40] *Ibid.,* and *Maggid Mishneh* to *Issurei Biah,* 16, 12. See *Hashmatot (Kometz Minhah)* to *Minhat Hinnukh,* No. 559.

[41] By *BaH, loc. cit.*

[42] E.g., *Birkei Yosef* (to *E.H.* 5, 14); and cf. *Beit Shmuel, ad loc. Resp. M'shivat Nefesh* (No. 18) analyzes the question at length and concludes that sirus cannot even technically be applied to women.

[43] See also R. Z. Y. Aloni in *HaPardes,* Vol. 31 (1956–57), *Tishrei* and *Tevet.*

[44] So *Rashi* to *Shabbat* 111a; *Sefer Ha-Hinnukh* 291; *Pahad Yitzhak, loc. cit; Minhat Bikkurim* to *Tosefta, ad loc.*

[45] *Minhat Hinnukh* to *Sefer Ha-Hinnukh, loc. cit.*

[46] So, e.g., *Appei Zutrei,* Comm. to *E.H.* 5 (p. 316). The ban on technical castration for the man, incidentally, makes vasectomy as a birth control measure forbidden in Jewish law.

[47] See above, Chapter 3, pp. 53 ff. Ruling that the "kos" may not be taken by a woman who has not yet fulfilled la-shevet are, e.g., *Emek HaMelekh* to Mai., *ad loc.,* and, possibly, *Resp. Beit Yitzhak, E.H.* No. 91.

species or as partner to her husband in *his* statutory obligations.[48] In a spirited Responsum of R. Moses Sofer (*Hatam Sofer*), this consideration is framed in perspective.[49] True, the obligation of la-shevet applies to her, but unusual pain in childbirth is sufficient reason for her to be exempted from further pursuit of this duty; she need not "build the world by destroying herself." If she already has children and wants to cease conceiving, but her husband wants her to continue—R. Sofer adds, interestingly—she should obtain his approval before drinking the potion. And if the husband refuses permission or a divorce, she is *still* not obliged, by virtue of her marriage contract, to endure unusual pain for his sake!

The above contrasts neatly with *Hatam Sofer*'s more restrictive Responsum on the mokh.[50] Virtually without exception, all who have considered the two methods side by side declare the kos to be free of the legal problems associated with mokh: no mechanical impediment to coitus is interposed; hence no hash-hatat zera is involved; hence the kos, as a method, is permissible.[51] The most notable example of this comparative treatment is the Responsum of R. Jacob Ettlinger of nineteenth-century Altona who, after ruling against the use of a mokh and assuming the most rigorous position on that score, suggests that the unfortunate woman take the kos shel ikkarin as the best solution to her problem.[52] R. Judah Assad, too, declares this potion to be "agreed upon without dissent" as permissible (most certainly in cases of physical hazard) and "therefore the best of all measures to take."[53] So do many others.[54]

Common, then, to the legal attributes of the "cup of roots," as opposed to other contraceptive methods, are two factors. The first is the avoidance of actual hash-hatat zera, which gives the cup its clear preferability over other measures. The second is the assumed permanence of its effect, which accounts for the corresponding concern with sirus and la-shevet as applied to the woman. True, the classic Responsum of R. Shneur Zalman of Lublin admits that the "cup's" effect may be temporary—for which he adduces interesting evidence—and hence is relatively unsafe when pregnancy hazard *must* be

[48] *Beit Mosheh* Comm. to *E.H.* 5, Par. 11; and cf. *Arukh L'Ner* to *Y'vamot* 12b. See Chapter 3, *loc. cit.*

[49] *Resp. Hatam Sofer, E.H.* No. 20. See Notes 14, 15, above.

[50] See Chapter 11, pp. 196, 218 ff.

[51] *Beit Mosheh, op. cit.,* contra *Atzei Arazim* to *E.H.* 5, Par. 22; *Resp. Mar'eh Y'hezkel,* No. 73; *Resp. Beit HaYotzer, E.H.* No. 3; and notes below.

[52] *Resp. Binyan Tziyyon,* No. 137; See Chapter 11, pp. 113, 126, 218 ff.

[53] *Resp. Y'hudah Ya'aleh, Y.D.,* No. 222.

[54] E.g., *L'vushei Mordekhai, op. cit; Resp. Pri Hasadeh,* Vol. 1, No. 88; *Avodat Hashem,* No. 3; *Y'mei Yosef,* No. 6; *Avnei Nezer,* No. 1; *Resp. M'shivat Nefesh,* No. 18; *Resp. Be'er Mosheh* (Danishevsky), No. 12.

avoided.[55] R. Eliezer Deutsch likewise presupposes only a temporary effect in one of his replies.[56] But aside from these, the majority of relevant Responsa assume a permanent sterilization to be involved, and their deliberations take this into account for better or for worse. For better, the two factors give the kos shel ikkarin a double advantage: an acceptable procedure is administered just once, rather than a questionable one being engaged in on a repetitive basis.[57] For worse, this presupposes that the woman's condition is chronic; if she instead wants to avoid pregnancy only for a time, the cup becomes a disadvantage and inferior to other methods. She may soon be healed of what threatens her and then want to resume having children, two Responsa writers reason;[58] now that a presumably temporary method, that of x-ray treatment ("Roentgen rays or radium") has been developed, two later Respondents submit, this is to be preferred to the cup.[59] And not just to be preferred, says R. Yosef Yonah Horovitz, but it renders all other methods forbidden:

> The diaphragm and the douche were permitted because this x-ray treatment was not mastered. Now that it has proven effective and accessible to many women, there is no longer any sanction for the other methods.[60]

The disadvantage of permanency figures in two even more recent decisions on the matter of sterilization. The surgical operation of cutting the Fallopian tubes is to be preferred, we are told, to (the principle of) "drinking the cup," since the former is temporary and the tubes can be rejoined, while the latter is irreversible.[61] A unique contraceptive procedure which is favorably com-

[55] Resp. Torat Hesed, Vol. II, E.H., No. 44:41. He provés his point by citing Seder HaDorot, according to which Zilla, that wife of Lamech who imbibed the potion, conceived and bore a child in her later years. Seder HaDorot is an 18th-century historical work of R. Yehiel Heilperin, based on earlier histories and chronologies of biblical times.

[56] Resp. Pri HaSadeh, Vol. I, No. 88.

[57] Resp. Divrei Malkiel, Vol. I, E.H., No. 70; S'dei Hemed, P'at HaSadeh, Ishut, No. 1; R. Yosef Yonah Horovitz, Rosenheim Festschrift, p. 113. An analogy is offered by the latter to Sh. Ar., O.H. 328:14. There, in the case of feeding the sick on the Sabbath where the choice is between sh'hitah of kosher food for him or having him eat unkosher (n'velah), the former is to be preferred. Although Sabbath violation is more severe (s'kilah) than dietary infractions (lav), the former is a one-time act and the latter is repetitive with each bite!

[58] Resp. Beit Yitzhak, E.H., Vol. I, No. 91; and Resp. D'var Eliyahu, No. 17.

[59] Herman Klein, Geburtenregelung: Eine Halachische Betrachtung (Separatabdruck aus Nachalath Zwi [Vol. I, 1931], Frankfurt am Main); and Y.Y. Horovitz, Rosenheim Festschrift, loc. cit.

[60] Rosenheim Festschrift, loc. cit.

[61] Ezrat Nashim, III, 315 (where, incidentally, the Horovitz [Rosenheim] essay is reprinted in its entirety); and Resp. Minhat Yitzhak, Vol. III, No. 26, 1. (both London, 1955).

pared to the unwanted permanence of the cup is introduced for our information in one recent Responsum (1957): Pregnancy was to be avoided,
according to the "recommendation of the physicians," by "shifting the
uterus to one side" (*l'haziz et ha-rehem litz'dadin*) for the time being, and then
restoring it to its proper position after the danger has passed. R. Obadia
Hadaya declared this novel procedure to be much better than the "cup,"
which "would make her totally barren all her days"; whereas the suggested
measure is both temporary and avoids palpable hash-hatat zera.[62] Again,
the "cup of roots"—or whatever is represented by the phrase—may be more
irreversible than one thinks. One author, writing in Hungary in 1892, declines
to believe the physicians' claim that their treatment (the "drinking of a potion")
will render her sterile only temporarily; he fears it may turn out to be permanent.[63] In fact, a member of the Rabbinical Court of Jerusalem reports in a
work just published (1967) that ". . . a woman came before our Court who
had been assured by the physician that the medicament he was giving her
'to drink' will make her sterile for just three years," but "she has, in fact,
remained sterile forever because her uteral faculties have been shattered"
(*rusak beit rahmah*).[64]

The Pill

But what if our "cup of roots" were temporary—reliably so, and safely
so? Such a combination of desirable properties seems to characterize the
currently popular progesterone pill—known now as "the Pill"—and the
analogy between it and the "cup" was inevitable. Whereas the legal discussions
of the kos do not admit a violation of hash-hatat zera in connection therewith,
but deal rather, as we have seen, with other possible questions; and whereas
this pill likewise allows intercourse to remain natural and unimpeded; and
whereas, moreover, the pill is both temporary and reliable—then this ought
certainly to be permitted *as a method*. True, the active oral ingestion involved
might be considered a conscious interference with the reproductive process
—which is the basis for the present Catholic reservations about the pill.[65]
But on one level the principle has already been established[66] that an orally
administered potion does not constitute an act of active "castration" (*sirus*

[62] *Resp. Yaskil Avdi*, Vol. V, No. 15. The question was addressed to R. Hadaya, then in
Jerusalem, by a rabbi in Kfar Brekhya.

[63] *Resp. Beit HaYotzer*, E.H., No. 3.

[64] *Resp. Tzitz Eliezer*, IX, No. 51, (p. 223).

[65] See J. Rock, *The Time Has Come, etc.*, p. 172, and Noonan, pp. 465–68.

[66] Articulated by *Beit Shmuel, Birkhei Yosef*, and others, cited above. See also *HaPardes*,
loc. cit., Tevet.

b'yadayim) and hence that no offense is incurred on that score. On another
level, a conscious act to prevent conception is blameworthy only if the method
utilized is in itself objectionable, as we have seen. Otherwise, the act is the
legal equivalent of intercourse during pregnancy or of temporary postponement
of procreation, which might still require good and sufficient reason.

Of course, not much has yet been written about the pill itself and its status
in Jewish law. R. Mosheh Feinstein of New York, in a Responsum dated 1961,
discusses the new "pills, recently discovered, which, taken orally, are effective
contraceptives." [67] No "improper emission of seed" is applicable, he admits
from the outset, but they suffer from another drawback: he had been informed
that the use of these anovulant pills causes "spotting" or "breakthrough bleeding" in a majority of cases. This would render the pills unusable for Jewish
women because of *Niddah* laws, according to which the menstrual period must
be determined. In a slightly later Responsum [68] he elaborates: the "new pills"
involve no possible prohibition of hash-hatat zera, but the problem of breakthrough bleeding is a real one, despite the claim that increased dosage decreases
the spot-bleeding. On the other hand, he continues, the woman could make a
proper prior examination over a full month, to determine that there is no bleeding in her case, before beginning normal relations with use of the pill. But then
again, deleterious side effects have been reported among users of the pill. Its
use would then be forbidden on grounds of possible danger to health; such
danger is a weightier consideration than legality.[69] Where these reservations
are eliminated, no halakhic objection would remain; except, of course, that the
mitzvah of p'ru ur'vu is being set aside.[70]

Two articles on the subject have recently appeared in Hebrew journals
by nonrabbinic writers, linking the modern pill to the Talmudic kos shel ikkarin. Dr. Norman Kass of London traces the history of contraceptive usages
in Europe and delineates the trend over the years: orally ingested potions
seemed more popular in antiquity; then came the douche in the sixteenth century (France), and the tampon in the nineteenth century (England); now the
oral contraceptive is back in vogue, and the Talmud's leniency in the matter is
welcome.[71] Similarly, Dr. Jacob Levy of Jerusalem greets the new pill with enthusiasm, as "most of the artificial methods used in the past involved hash-hatat
zera." The pill will prove a boon for women with menstrual difficulties or with
pregnancy hazards. But, he continues, p'ru ur'vu is essential to the Jewish out-

[67] *Resp. Igg'rot Mosheh, Even HaEzer,* No. 65.
[68] *Ibid., Orah Hayyim and Even HaEzer,* Vol. II, *E.H.* No. 17, dated 1962.
[69] *"Hamira sakkanta me-issura,"* TB *Hullin* 10a.
[70] Cf. his Responsum on the "rhythm method," below.
[71] N. Kass, "Birth Prevention in the Talmud," *Hebrew Medical Journal,* 34 (1961),
163.

look and the Jewish future; the pill should be resorted to for grave reasons only.[72]

The latter stipulation is given more emphatic voice by R. Mordecai Breisch of Zurich, replying to a question on "pills discovered by physicians in England." He is eloquent in denouncing birth control for reasons of convenience; but, for reasons of danger or even possible danger, he endorses the pill as being "the best of methods," free of any legal impediment.[73] The return of oral contraception, it seems, has brought the Responsa to a critical turning point, where moral or extralegal objections alone can be adduced. Dr. Immanuel Jakobovitz, now Chief Rabbi of the British Commonwealth, is led to observe that the pill's availability "may well open the way to an entirely new appraisal of birth control in the light of Jewish law." Now that a method permissible in itself is at hand, its sanction could "radically alter the entire pattern of family life and demographic trends. The spirit as well as the letter of the law must be most carefully investigated before such a far-reaching innovation can be evaluated in the light of Jewish teachings." [74] But the "spirit of the law" would embrace the specific imperative—also a law—of ongoing procreation.

The emerging attitude takes shape in recent pronouncements from different circles in Jerusalem. A book on family living, issued by a rabbinical academy there, admits the legal sanction for the pill, but points out the medical hazards, including the possible effect on subsequent children. More important, it declares, the ideal of fruitfulness and its advantages to the family and the mother herself are being forgotten in the "pursuit of luxury and convenience." Despite the legality of the method, women, this book advises, ought not to heed the blandishments of birth control proponents except for good and sufficient reason.[75] "Family Planning in Israel" is the title of a long-ranging article in 1966 by the aforementioned Dr. Levy. He calls for use of the pill not for smaller families but for better spacing for larger families in order to preserve the strength and health of the mother.[75a] And the latest volume of Responsa by R. Eliezer Waldenberg of the Jerusalem Rabbinical Court was published in 1967. He cites the ruling of R. Mosheh Feinstein and tells of his own conversations with physicians on the hazards, apparently diminishing with time, of the anovulant pills. "If they are indeed perfected so that they

[72] J. Levy, "Hormonal Preparations for Women and Religio-Legal Problems," in *Noam, A (Yearly) Forum for the Clarification of Contemporary Halakhic Problems*, 8 (1965), 238.
[73] *Resp. Helkat M'hokek*, Vol. III, No. 62 (1966). Cf., also, the discussion by R. Samuel Huebner in *Ha Darom*, 20 (1964), 42-49.
[74] *Jewish Law Faces Modern Problems* (Yeshiva University, 1965), pp. 67-71.
[75] *Torat HaMishpahah*, by R. Moshe Sternbuch, ed. *Kolel Yad Efraim Fischel* (Jerusalem, 1966), p. 38.
[75a] *HaMa'ayan* (Quarterly, of *Poalei Agudat Yisrael*, 6 (1966), No. 3, pp. 23-33.

do no evil, this will be the best *method* of birth control. They merely prevent sperm and egg from meeting but involve no hash-hatat zera . . ." nor do they cause active or permanent sterilization.[76] Left unsaid but unmistakably implicit in his treatment is the same "but" expressed above—the mitzvah of p'ru ur'vu must be properly fulfilled.

The "Safe Period"

The affinity between the oral contraceptive principle and the "safe period" or "rhythm method" of birth control (both are consciously nonprocreative, but both are free of any mechanical impediment to the sex act) suggests that a word be said here about this analogue to the kos shel ikkarin.

The Talmud refers, in other-than-contraceptive contexts, to periods of greater or exclusive fertility. A woman, we are told, conceives "only" *samukh l'vestah*, that is, immediately prior to the menstrual period, or, according to another view, *samukh lit'vilatah*, right after the purification following the end of the period twelve days after its onset.[77] *Tosafot*, however, pointed out on the basis of other "literary evidence" the essential unreliability of this principle; pregnancy can also occur any time "between purification and her next period."[78] Nevertheless, the observation of the Talmud is made operative in a legal context by a classic fourteenth-century source, the *Maharil* (a compilation of religious practices of the Rhineland communities on the authority of R. Jacob Halevi Moelln of Mainz), where the woman is cautioned against bathing (on the eve of Yom Kippur) in such manner as would cause her to destroy seed (within three days of its implantation). This caution, however, is to apply only to the times mentioned above when fertility is probable.[79] Maharil's provision became part of the larger *Shulhan Arukh* through its citation by an authoritative seventeenth-century annotator thereto, the

[76] *Resp. Tzitz Eliezer*, Vol. IX, No. 51.

[77] *TB Niddah* 31b; *TB Sotah* 27a. The first-century Greek physician Soranos believed the time "when menstruation is ending" as the best time for fruitful intercourse—N. E. Himes, *Medical History of Contraception*, pp. 55, 90; Noonan, *op. cit.*, p. 16. Preuss (p. 435) quotes a medical historian who regarded the biblical requirement of separation during the menses as a birth-limiting device, for "Moses, as physician as well as statesman, sought to curtail the number of children." Preuss calls the idea "pure nonsense." See also H. Sutherland, *Control of Life* (1944), p. 235. For more on the Talmud's observations on the "safe period," see above, pp. 86, 127. See also S. Kardimon, "The Talmud on the Safe Period in the Menstrual Cycle" (Hebrew), in *Hebrew Medical Journal* (1958), I, 91–94. He gives the Talmudic R. Yohanan (and his disciple R. Ami in the parallel passage, *Lev. Rabbah* 14) credit for holding their view of *samukh lit'vilatah* against the prevailing medical error.

[78] *Tosafot* to *Niddah* 10b, s.v. *d'havya;* and to *Sotah, loc. cit.*, s.v. *aliba.*

[79] *Sefer Maharil* (see Ch. 6, Note 123), *Hilkhot Erev Yom Kippur*, p. 44a.

Magen Avraham.[80] In another reference, the Palestinian Talmud exempts the night following purification from the rule [see above, Chapter 3] that calls for sympathetic abstinence in times of famine or widespread sorrow; this same *Magen Avraham* explains the exemption in terms of the greater fertility at that time: p'ru ur'vu rather than the pleasure of marital intercourse is directly involved.[81]

The caveat expressed by *Tosafot* about the dependability of this principle is reflected in those Responsa where attention to cycles of fertility and sterility was entertained as a possible method of contraception. No impropriety is found in that method at all; the far greater concern was that its unreliability made it unprescribable in cases of physical hazard. The dates of the Responsa considering the matter range from 1894 to 1932;[82] the findings of Prof. K. Ogino of Japan and Prof. H. Knaus of Austria, according to which conception can only occur between the twelfth and nineteenth (or sixteenth) day before the onset of the next period—that is, *samukh lit'vilatah*—were promulgated around the year 1931.[83] Despite today's even greater scientific precision in the knowledge of this method, too many variables are involved (time of fertility of ovum, time of ovulation in relation to menstruation or other unpredictable factors, and time of viability of sperm).[84] When pregnancy must be avoided on medical grounds, the "safe period" calculation would just not be sufficient safeguard. For other than medical considerations, a recent ruling condones it only after the basic procreative duty has been fulfilled.[85] By comparison with the pill, however, observation of the "safe period" is on a par with abstinence; it frustrates two positive mitzvot— that of p'ru ur'vu and that of onah—at one and the same time. Oral contraception by pill thus takes its place at the apex of our hierarchy: it enjoys preferred status as the least objectionable method of birth control.

[80] *Magen Avraham* to *Sh. Ar. O.H.* 606, 4. The law was generally taken as *Magen Avraham's;* it was *Resp. Torat Hesed,* II, 43:21 who pointed out its source.

[81] *TP Ta'anit* I,; *Beit Yosef* to *Tur O.H.* 574; *Sh. Ar. O.H.* 574, 4; *Magen Avraham, ad loc.*

[82] *Resp. Matteh Levi,* Vol. II, No. 31 (1894); *Resp. Hedvat Ya'akov,* 2nd Recension, No. 37 (1909); *Resp. Tzur Ya'akov,* No. 167 (1932). The latter explains that *Magen Avraham* spoke of the likelihood (as did the Talmud)—not the exclusive period—of fertility. Other Responsa, too, add the period of lesser fertility as a supplement to contraceptive devices when of questionable permissibility or safety. Thus, *Resp. Maharsham,* Vol. I, No. 58 (1902); *Resp. Emek Sh'elah,* No. 69 (1906); and *Resp Helkat Ya'akov,* No. 13:14. The latter, written in 1955, can be more specific as to the time of the safe period in view of the newer science: "Physicians today concur that a woman cannot conceive after 15 or 16 days after the onset of her period."

[83] Noonan, *op. cit.,* p. 443.

[84] Elizabeth Draper, *Birth Control in The Modern World,* pp. 72–74; John Rock, *op. cit.* pp. 186–87.

[85] *Resp. Igg'rot Mosheh, E.H.,* No. 102.

Part 5

ABORTION

14

The Foetus and Foeticide

Contraception and Abortion

Having concluded that contraception, even where permissible, requires a contraceptive method in itself acceptable, we saw that the problems of technical violation relate to the method rather than to the effect. Granted the moral propriety of limiting procreation in any given circumstance, an act such as coitus interruptus, for example, would remain forbidden as a means to that end, while "the Pill" would be an example of a permitted means. The halakhic concern with methods is a concern with hash-hatat zera; improper methods violate the prohibition against "improper emission of seed." Contraception with licit means, we have seen, is no worse from the standpoint of this consideration than refraining from marriage or from a specific marital act; with licit means, the act itself is normal and unimpeded; hence acceptable in and of itself. The fact of contraceptive *effect* (that the procreational possibility was effectively frustrated) is a separate question responding to another set of considerations. The woman, for example, on biological as well as social grounds, is said not to be involved in the prohibition of hash-hatat zera. The sex act having been completed, her frustration of the seed's reproductive possibility comes under *that* category, of frustrating the seed's effect, rather than the category of "improper emission." Frustration of effect is a moral question—defined in quasi-legal terms by her obligation of la-shevet (see above)—independent of the technical question of hash-hatat zera which appertains to the man and to the sex act itself.

Does the foregoing imply that the woman has a similar right to "frustration of effect" even after the moment of conception? Obviously, still another set of considerations is applicable here, although legal analogies have indeed been proposed between contraception and abortion. To buttress the case in favor of therapeutic contraception, for example, some Responsa writers argued *a fortiori* (*kal va-homer*) from the Mishnah's mandate (see on) for therapeutic abortion. If a developed foetus is to be aborted to save the life of the mother, the argument goes, contraception in such case ought certainly to be allowed, for the sperm has yet "neither life nor creature in it," and "[preventing] the cause should not be more formidable [a problem] than [preventing] the effect." [1] This argument is nonetheless untenable: if abstinence is not to be the alternative where pregnancy would prove dangerous, an acceptable contraceptive method can still be substituted for a questionable one; in the matter of abortion no such option exists.

More to the point of our present chapter, analogies were proposed in the opposite direction: since the hash-hatat zera of contraception, understood here as frustration of the reproductive process as well as an intrinsically improper act, is forbidden, then, *a fortiori*, such an act certainly should be forbidden after conception. R. Ya'ir Bachrach (seventeenth century) suggests such an argument in his classic Responsum on the permissibility of abortion (see on), only to conclude, as we have above, that the autoeroticism of hash-hatat zera makes improper contraception an evil for special reasons, and that the woman incurs no such violation by frustration of effect after the act; her abortive action must be considered separately in other terms. [2] R. Jacob Emden, addressing himself in the next century to the problem of this Respon-

---

[1] *Resp. Torat Hesed, E.H.*, Vol. II, No. 42:1 ("*lo yihyeh hamur hasibbah la-takhlit min ha-takhlit atzmah*"). Also, *Resp. Ahiezer, E.H.*, No. 23 ("*gam ha-zera, d'havei g'rama v'sibbah liy'tzirat hav'lad, lehavei k'rodef*"). Similarly, *Resp. Zikhron Y'honatan, E.H.* No. 3. As to postcoital contraception, there ought certainly to be no doubt of its permissibility, says *Resp. Ani Ben Pehama, Y.D.*, No. 25, since even postconceptional action to save her from hazard is mandated. On another level, if the foetus is declared not a *nefesh*, then the baraita (Chs. 9–11) which allows contraception to prevent damage to an existing embryo, implies that contraception is allowable even in cases other than *sakkanat n'fashot*, according to *Resp. Y'mei Yosef*, Vol. I, *E.H.* No. 6.

[2] *Resp. Havvot Ya'ir*, No. 31. (The relevant portion of this Responsum, dealing with abortion of a foetus conceived in adultery, is strangely missing from the most popular edition of *Havvot Ya'ir*, that published in Sedilkov in 1834. This is probably the result of local censorship; the full text appears in all other editions.) R. Abraham Landàu (d. 1875), in his *Z'khuta D'Avraham*, also proposes the analogy. Aptowitzer, in *Sinai* (see below, Note 20) makes reference to *Havvot Ya'ir's* ruling; then, unaccountably, wonders (*op. cit.*, p. 17, Note 23) why it did not occur to the writers of Responsa to draw an analogy between contraception and abortion!

sum, goes even further in clarifying the special evil of improper contraception: the self-defilement is in a category by itself, apparently more objectionable than technical abortion.[3] In our own century, R. Ben Zion Uziel is among those who have restated the distinction: hash-hatat zera concerns itself with self-pollution or illicit contraceptive methods; after conception, the matter is subject to different laws.[4] Other authorities have similarly confirmed, on these grounds, that no analogies between contraception and abortion can properly be drawn.[5]

The Status of the Embryo

The special set of laws governing the abortion question begins with an examination of the foetus' legal status. For this the Talmud has a phrase, *ubar yerekh imo*,[6] which is a counterpart of the Latin *pars viscerum matris*.[7] The foetus, that is, is to be deemed a "part of its mother" rather than an independent entity. Of course this says nothing about the right of abortion; the designation of the foetus as part of its mother is found only in contexts of far less serious moment than that of abortion, spontaneous or induced. The designation defines ownership, for example, in the case of an embryo found in a purchased animal; that, as intrinsic to its mother's body, it belongs to the buyer.[8] In the regulations of levitical impurity, the principle defines the embryo again as one with its mother;[9] moreover, in the religious conversion of a pregnant woman, her unborn child is automatically included and

[3] *Resp. Sh'elat Ya'avetz*, No. 43. See also the brief reference to this point in *Noam*, VI (1963), 272, in connection with intrauterine devices. In the case cited by *Resp. L'vushei Mord'khai, H.M.*, No. 39 (1913), abortion is permitted to end dangerous pregnancy, but he sees a greater legal problem in preventing future such pregnancies from beginning! See next two notes.

[4] *Resp. Mishp'tei Uziel*, Vol. III, *H.M.* (1940), No. 46. Cf. also, Ch. 6 above, Notes 101–108, citations from *Tos'fei HaRosh, Resp. Mahanei Hayyim*, and *Sefer Marheshet*, etc., on the matter of *zera ahar she-ne'ekar*.

[5] E.g., R. Eliezer Deutsch in *Resp. Pri HaSadeh*, Vol. IV, No. 52 (1912); and now R. Yehiel Weinberg in *Noam*, IX (1966), 207. The legal dissimilarity between the two acts can best be seen by contrasting two Responsa of *Maharash Engel*. In Vol. VI, No. 18, he declares hash-hatat zera to be in the category of *d'oraita*, whereas in Vol. V, No. 89, he had found *harigat ubar* at best *d'rabbanan*.

[6] Lit., "The foetus is the thigh of its mother," *TB Hulin* 58a and elsewhere. Also, "the foetus is regarded as one of her limbs," *TB Gittin* 23b. See *Pahad Yitzhak, s.v. ubar*, and Note 8, below.

[7] Or, *spes animatis*. See sources in Edward Westermarck, *History and Development of The Moral Ideas*, I, 415, Notes 8 and 9.

[8] *TB Bava Kamma* 78a; *Sh. Ar. H.M.*, 220, 10. The principle is accepted—as formulated by "Ri" in *Tosafot* to *Bava Kamma* 47a *s.v. mai* and to *Sanhedrin* 80b, *s.v. ubar*—that *ubar yerekh imo* "applies in all cases but *t'refah*," i.e., if an animal is victim of prey, its foetus does not share this defect, since only the mother was made *t'refah*.

[9] *TB Nazir* 51a. Aptowitzer (see on, Note 20) cites this passage to disprove Leopold Loew's contention that *ubar yerekh imo* applies to animals only.

requires no further ceremony.[10] The foetus' status is further exemplified in the fact that it has no power of acquisition;[11] gifts or transactions made on its behalf[12]—except by its father[13]—are not binding, and it inherits its father only, in a natural rather than transactional manner.[14]

Germane as all of the above information might seem to the question of abortion, it could hardly be sufficient for determining the morality of such action. It merely defines the legal status of the foetus. It tells us, in the words of a modern writer on Roman and Jewish law, that in both systems the foetus has no "juridical personality" of its own.[15]

Slightly more relevant is the factor of "doubtful viability" that attaches to an embryo: it is not reckoned a *bar kayyama* [a viable, living thing] until thirty days after its birth—unless a full nine-month pregnancy is definitely known to have been completed. This accounts for such provisions as the one which declares the laws of mourning, etc. not yet applicable for a child who does not survive until its thirtieth day; a still unborn child, then, is certainly in the category of only "doubtful viability."[16]

Is Foeticide Homicide?

Far more pertinent to our subject and more promising as a criterion for the morality of abortion is the Jewish legal attitude to foeticide as distinguished from homicide or infanticide. The law of homicide in the Torah, in one of its several formulations (Exodus 21:12), reads: "*makkeh ish* . . . " "He who smites a man . . . " Does this include *any* "man," say a day-old child? Yes, says the Talmud,[17] citing another text (Lev. 24:17): *ki yakkeh kol nefesh adam,* [18] "if one smite *any nefesh adam*"—literally, any human person. The "any" is understood to *include* the day-old child (with the presumption in favor of full-term pregnancy), but the "*nefesh adam*" is taken to *exclude*

[10] *TB Y'vamot* 78a. The reason may or may not be *ubar yerekh imo*, but the law is undisputed.

[11] Rashi to *Niddah* 44a, *s.v. v'yesh;* Maimonides, *Commentary to the Mishnah, Niddah* 5, 3; *Sh. Ar. H.M.* 210, 1 (*SMA* vs. *SHaKH*).

[12] *TB Bava Batra* 142a.

[13] *Ibid.,* 142b; *Sh. Ar. H.M.* 276, 5.

[14] The matter of acquisition or inheritance by the foetus is, as admitted by *Beit Yosef* to H.M. 210, complex and elusive. The generalization given here is the substance of an explication offered by Y.K. Miklishanski in *Mishpat Ha-Ubar*, in *Jubilee Volume in Honor of Simon Federbush* (Hebrew) (Jerusalem, 1961), pp. 251–60.

[15] Miklishanski, *op. cit.* (it has no "*ishiyut yuridit*"). Some Responsa, however, such as *Torat Hesed, E.H.,* No. 42, seek to demonstrate a relationship between *ubar yerekh imo* and legal attitudes to abortion. See on.

[16] *TB Niddah* 44b; *Sh. Ar. Y.D.* 344, 8.

[17] *Niddah, loc. cit.*

[18] See *TB Sanhedrin* 84b and correction in *Tosafot, ad loc. s.v. hakhi garsinan.*

the foetus in the womb, for the foetus in the womb is *lav nefesh hu* [not a person] until he is born.[19] In analyzing the foeticide question, Prof. Viktor Aptowitzer of Vienna has sought to prove that the "doubtful viability" status combines with that of "not a [separate] person" to free the guilty one from capital liability;[20] actually Talmudic discussions here and in related questions disregard that factor and consistently presuppose that the foetus is not a person—not a *nefesh adam* nor an *adam*.[21] Only when it "comes into the world" is it a "person."

Delving more deeply into the fundamental issue of capital liability for foeticide, we find more than one jurisprudential question involved. To begin with, the basis for denying capital crime status to foeticide in Jewish law— even for those Rabbis who may have wanted to rule otherwise—is scriptural. The text in Exodus 21:22 provides:

> If men strive, and wound a pregnant woman so that her fruit be expelled, but no harm befall [her], then shall he be fined as her husband shall assess, and the matter placed before the judges. But if harm befall [her], then shalt thou give life for life.

Taking their cue from the *Mekhilta*, the early halakhic Midrash to this verse,[22] Talmudic commentators made its teaching explicit: only monetary compensation is exacted of him who causes a woman to miscarry.[23] The killing of nefesh adam alone is a capital crime, says the *Mekhilta*. (On the principle that exempts a man convicted of a capital crime from payment of monetary damages at the same time,[24] the penalty of paying *d'mei v'ladot* in this case further argues, they point out, against capital liability.) True, a classic Bible exegete, R. Eliyahu Mizrachi (d. 1526) explained, or sought to justify, this apparently lenient ruling in terms of the embryo's "doubtful viability": that

[19] Rashi, *Yad Ramah*, and *Me'iri*, all to *Sanhedrin* 72b; Ramban in *Hiddushim* to *Niddah*, *loc. cit.*; *Resp. Radbaz*, Vol. II, No. 695.

[20] V. Aptowitzer, "Observations on the Criminal Law of the Jews," *Jewish Quarterly Review*, 15 (1924), 111 f; and, in his Hebrew article on the same theme, *Emdat HaUbar B'dinei Onshin Shel Yisrael*, in *Sinai*, 6 (1942), 26 f.

[21] R. Shimshon (Mishantz) makes the point in *Torat Kohanim* to *Tazria, N'ga'im*, 1, with regard to *adam ki yamut b'ohel* which excludes a foetus (*Hulin* 72a); and *N'tziv* makes the point in *Ha'amek Sh'alah* to *She'iltot* 167, No. 17, with regard to *shofekh dam ha'adam* (*Sanhedrin* 57b) and with regard to *adam ki yihyeh b'or b'saro* (*Niddah* 44a).

[22] *Mekhilta* to Exodus, *N' zikin*, Ch. 8. Also *Targum Yonatan* and *Targum Onkelos, ad loc.* Cf. *TB Sanhedrin* 74a, 79a.

[23] Rashi and *Yad Ramah* to *Sanhedrin* 57b and 72b; Ramban and *RaN* to *Niddah* 44b; *HaMe'iri* to *Shabbat* 107b.

[24] "*Kim lei bid'rabbah minei*"—*Gittin* 52b.

the culprit cannot be held capitally liable without *hatra'ah* [formal "warning" in advance; one of the requirements that the Rabbis utilized in order to make capital punishment virtually unenforceable]. Since there cannot be *hatra'ah* where there is "doubt," there can be no capital guilt.[25] To this, a later exegete responds: even if we were certain that the embryo had "completed its months," the law would be the same; the reason remains that the embryo is "not a person" until it is actually born.[26] More to the present point, the standard Commentator to the relevant section of the *Shulhan Arukh* adduces this ruling in a context of practical law to explain why therapeutic abortion is not a case of setting aside one *life* for another.[27] The matter was the subject of a "dialogue" between two eighteenth-century authorities, R. Isaiah (Pick) Berlin of Breslau and R. Ezekiel Landau of Prague; the latter sought to calm the former's doubts and to demonstrate the textual and logical basis for making foeticide a monetary rather than a capital crime.[28] So did R. Tzvi Hirsch of Brody, another luminary of that age, to whom R. Isaiah had also communicated his misgivings.[29]

For, theoretical problems of greater consequence remain. If the crime is merely monetary, what crime is there at all when the woman herself desires the miscarriage, that is, if an abortion is desired? Once homicide is said not to be involved, and all we have is some sort of deprivation, is there any bar to abortion on her request? A weak answer to this question bases itself on the Responsum of a seventeenth-century Turkish scholar, R. Joseph Trani.[30] Emphatically ruling out capital-crime status for induced miscarriage, on the clear teaching of the Exodus passage, Trani uses the self-same passage to label the crime that *has* been committed: The crime is that of *havalah*, of tort or damage to persons or things. If, now, we maintain with Maimonides and the *Shulhan Arukh* that a person has no right to inflict damage even upon himself,[31] abortion on request would be a punishable offense on those grounds —not to speak of the moral offense of thwarting potential life—in the view

[25] *Mizrahi al HaTorah*, to Exodus, *ad loc*. This, in effect, bears strong similarity to the suggestion of Aptowitzer, above, Note 20.

[26] R. Loew of Prague in *Gur Aryeh* to Exodus, *ad loc*.

[27] R. Joshua Falk, *Sefer Me'irat Einayim* to *Sh. Ar. H.M.* 425, Par. 2.

[28] *Resp. Noda Biy'hudah*, Second Series, *H.M.*, No. 59.

[29] *Resp. Tiferet Tzvi*, *O.H.*, No. 14.

[30] *Resp. Maharit*, Vol. I, Nos. 97 and 99. These two Responsa must be taken together; probably a printer's confusion separated and disarranged them.

[31] *Yad, Hovel U-Mazzik*, 5, 1, and *Sh. Ar. H.M.* 420, 6, after *TB Bava Kamma* 90b. *Yad Ramah* and *Tur, H.M., ad loc.*, however, do not hold one to be forbidden to damage himself. On the other hand, *Shulhan Arukh HaRav* (of Habad Hasidism), *Hilkhot Nizkei HaGuf, H.M.* 4, rules it wrong even to strike a person with his permission.

of some authorities.[32] Others, such as R. Aryeh Lifschutz of nineteenth-century Vizhnitz, were unhappy with this approach.[33] Trani must concede, he wrote, that abortion "diminishes God's image" as the Talmud says with regard to him who neglects his duty of procreation;[34] *this* is the offense rather than the material one of self-inflicted torts. Here, and often again as we shall see, the legalities give way to broader considerations, that potential life is, in effect, being thwarted. A modern Responsum by the late R. Mosheh Zweig of Antwerp,[35] for instance, relieves the closeness of his own legal reasoning by citing wider Talmudic attitudes, implied, for example, in the passage where the owner of a barking dog is half-seriously held to account: "A pregnant woman, able to complete her pregnancy, was standing nearby, when a dog barked at her and [frightened her so that] she miscarried."[36] Has not such a one, the Talmud asks, caused the Divine image to be diminished?

The Septuagint and the "Sons of Noah"

Before pressing forward our quest for the source in Jewish law wherein desired abortion should be labeled a crime of any kind, we pause to examine the matter on the historic peripheries, so to speak, of the Jewish community. To begin with, that all-important passage in Exodus has an alternate version in the Septuagint, the Greek translation of the Bible produced in Alexandria in the third pre-Christian century. One word change there yields an entirely different statute on miscarriage. Prof. Viktor Aptowitzer's essays analyze the disputed passage; the school of thought it represents he calls the Alexandrian school, as opposed to the Palestinian—that is, the Talmudic view set forth above.

The word in question is *ason*, which we have rendered as "harm," hence: "if [there be] no harm [i.e., death, to the mother], he shall be fined . . ." The Greek renders the word *ason* as "form," yielding something like: "if [there be] no form [yet, to the foetus], he shall be fined . . . But if [there be] form, then shalt thou give life for life." The "life for life" clause was thus applied to the foetus instead of the mother, and a distinction was made—as Augustine will formulate it—between *embryo informatus* and *embryo formatus*,[37] a

---

[32] E.g., *Resp. Tzofnat Pa'aneah*, Vol. I (Dvinsk, 1934), No. 59; *Resp. Ateret Hakhamim, E.H.*, No. 1.

[33] *Resp. Aryeh D'vei Ila'i, Y.D.*, No. 19. See also *Resp. Binyan David*, Vol. I, No. 47.

[34] *TB Y'vamot* 63b. See Ch. 3, above.

[35] *Noam*, VII (1964), 45.

[36] *TB Bava Kamma* 83a.

[37] St. Augustine, *Questiones in Exodum*, 80, and elsewhere. See·Westermarck, *op. cit.*, p. 416, Note 2. See below, Note 80.

foetus not yet "formed" and one already "formed." For the latter, the text so rendered prescribes the death penalty. Among the Church Fathers, the consequent doctrine of foeticide as murder was preached by Tertullian, in the second century, who accepted the Septuagint, and by Jerome in the fourth, who did not—whose classic Bible translation renders the passage correctly[38] (that is, according to the Hebrew text accepted in the Church). The Didache, a handbook of basic Christianity for the instruction of converts from paganism, follows this Alexandrian teaching and specifies abortion as a capital crime.[39]

Coming closer to the main body of the Jewish community, we find the doctrine accepted by the Samaritans and Karaites[40] and, more important, by Philo, the popular first-century philosopher of Alexandria. Philo's formulation contains the Septuagint base, augmented by his own characteristic philosophizing:

> If one have a contest with a woman who is pregnant, and strike her a blow on her belly, and she miscarry; if the child which was conceived within her is still unfashioned and unformed, he shall be punished by a fine, both for the assault which he committed and also because he has prevented nature—which was fashioning and preparing that most excellent of all creatures, a human being— from bringing him into existence. But if the child which was conceived has assumed a distinct shape in all its parts, having received all its proper connective and distinctive qualities, he shall die; for such a creature as that is a man, whom he has slain while still in the workshop of nature, which had not thought it as yet a proper time to produce him to the light, but had kept him like a statue lying in a sculptor's workshop, requiring nothing more than to be released and sent out into the world.[41]

On the other hand, Philo's younger contemporary, Josephus, bears witness to the Palestinian tradition, in *his* verbal cast:

---

[38] See Aptowitzer, *loci. cit.* (*JQR*, p. 85; *Sinai*, pp. 9–11).

[39] *Ibid.*

[40] *Ibid.*

[41] Philo, *De Specialibus Legibus*, II, 19 (ed. Cohn, V, 180 ff.). Cf. *Zohar*, Exodus 3b: "He who kills an embryo in its mother's womb destroys God's artistic construction." For other Philonic passages on foeticide and their meaning, see S. Belkin, *Philo and The Oral Law*, pp. 130–39.

He that kicks a woman with child, so that the woman miscarry, let him pay a fine in money, as the judges shall determine, as having diminished the multitude by the destruction of what was in her womb . . . [42]

Aside from its textual warrant, the Palestinian (halakhic) tradition, Aptowitzer goes on to argue, is the more authentic, while the other is a later tendency, "which, in addition, is not genuinely Jewish but must have originated in Alexandria under Egyptian-Greek influence."[43] We shall consider the developed Christian view in a separate context below.

In the rabbinic tradition, then, abortion remains a noncapital crime at worst. However, a curious factor with respect to one more periphery of the rabbinic system further complicates the question of the criminality of the act. This is the circumstance that another biblical text, found in Genesis and hence "before Sinai" and part of the Laws of the Sons of Noah (see above, Chapter 3), served as the source for the teaching that foeticide is indeed a capital crime—for non-Jews! Genesis 9:6 reads, "He who sheds the blood of man, through man [i.e., through the human court of law] shall *his* blood be shed." Since the Hebrew (*shofekh dam ha'adam, ba'adam* . . .) allows for a translation of "man, in man" as well as "man, through man," the Talmud records the exposition of R. Yishmael: "What is this 'man in man'? It refers to the foetus in its mother's womb."[44] The locus of this text in Genesis— lacking as it does the qualifying balance of the Exodus (Sinaitic) passage— made foeticide a capital crime for non-Jews in Jewish law. Some modern scholars hold this exposition to be more sociologic than textually inherent, that it represents a reaction against abuses among the heathen. In view of rampant abortion and infanticide, says I. H. Weiss in his history of Jewish tradition, R. Yishmael "forced" the above exegesis out of the Genesis text to render judgment against the Romans.[45] (Leopold Loew had suggested

[42] Josephus, *Antiquities of the Jews*, IV, 8, 33 (ed. Niese, I, 280, 278). In another passage, *Contra Apionem*, II, 24 (ed. Niese, V, 83, 202), Josephus calls both abortion and infanticide akin to murder. Against those who regard this as written for apologetic purposes only, Aptowitzer (*JQR*, p. 87) claims it only to be moral rhetoric rather than a contradictory statement of law. Belkin (*op. cit.*, p. 137) quotes R. E. Goodenough, *Jewish Courts In Egypt*, p. 114, as holding that according to Philo and Josephus the assailant had to pay two fines, one to the husband and another, possibly to charity, for having deprived society of a human being.

[43] *Ibid.*, *JQR*, p. 88, *Sinai*, p. 13. He regards the Alexandrian as a compromise between Plato (the Academy) and the Stoics, the latter holding the foetus to be an independent living being, while the former held it to be dependent upon its mother. (*Ibid.*, *JQR*, p. 114, *Sinai*, p. 28).

[44] *TB Sanhedrin* 57b; and in the name of R. Hanina, in *Gen. Rabbah* 34, 14.

[45] *Dor Dor V'Dor'shav* (1924), II, 21. Jakobovitz (*Jewish Medical Ethics*, p. 180) suggests the ruling was made to check excesses in experiments on foetal anatomy. Belkin (*op. cit.*, p. 139) says the rampant infanticide is the basis of the ruling in *Tosefta Avodah Zarah*, 3, 3, against employing a pagan midwife.

that R. Yishmael's view was a reflection of Roman laws *against* abortion [as a deprivation to the husband[46]]; Aptowitzer counters that this would have been a good "Purim joke" were it not for the fact that such Roman laws do not date from before 200 CE, while R. Yishmael lived a century earlier.[47]) Regardless of its rationale, the doctrine remains part of Jewish law,[48] although this too remains merely theoretical, especially in view of the virtual nonexistence of actual capital punishment in the Jewish court. Maimonides systematically codifies it, albeit in accompanying language that may explain its sternness:

> A "Son of Noah" who killed a person, even a foetus in its mother's womb, is capitally liable . . .
> The Jewish court is obliged to provide judges for the resident alien to adjudicate for them in accordance with these laws [of the Sons of Noah] so that society not corrupt itself. The judges may come either from their midst or from the Israelites.[49]

The Responsum of R. Joseph Trani of early seventeenth-century Turkey, referred to above, takes up a question that results from this doctrine: the question of Jewish participation in abortion for "Sons of Noah." Having made his point that no murder is involved, he extends that lenient conclusion to the non-Israelite as well. Since, however, the latter are under a special ban which renders their act a capital crime, the Jew may not assist them in a violation thereof; to do so would come under the injunction (Lev. 19:14) "Do not place a stumbling-block before the blind," which, in the Talmudic

---

[46] See Westermarck, *loc. cit.*, p. 415, Note 4.

[47] Aptowitzer, *Sinai, loc. cit.*, p. 28, Note 59. See L. Loew, *Lebensalter*, p. 70.

[48] Uniquely interesting is the application by *Maharsha* (to *Sanhedrin* 57b) of this doctrine. He uses it to explain Pharaoh's decree (Ex. 1:15–16) to "the Hebrew midwives" to "look upon the birth stool"—i.e., before the moment of birth—and, "if it be a son, then shall ye kill him, etc." As *Bnai Noah*, the Egyptian midwives are forbidden foeticide; the Hebrew midwives are bound to martyr themselves rather than commit murder—but not foeticide. Hence he instructed them (as suggested in *TB Sotah* 11b) on the indicia of sex determination on the birthstool and commanded them to bring about abortions! (But cf. Bible Commentary of I.H. Hertz: "Hebrew midwives: i.e., Egyptian women who served as midwives to the Hebrews" [after Septuagint and Abarbanel] as Pharaoh would hardly expect them to slay the children of their own.) On the other hand, in relation to Pharaoh's next try, the decree that born Hebrew sons be cast into the Nile, the *Zohar* (Exodus 3b) accounts it to the lasting merit of the Hebrew women that they did not therefore induce an abortion to avoid this fate or "all the more so" not slay them "afterwards."

[49] *Yad, Hil'khot M'lakhim* 9, 4; 10, 11. Incidentally R. Jacob Zvi Jalisch, in his *M'lo HaRo'im* Glosses to *Sanhedrin* 57b, assumes that the "doubtful viability" does not excuse *B'nai Noah*, and the capital penalty applies anyway because of the embryo's potential. On the other hand, see R. Issar Unterman in *Noam*, VI (1963), 8–9.

interpretation means, do not, for example, place wine before one who has taken upon himself a special prohibition of such drink (a "*nazir*"). [50]

Therapeutic abortion is not, of course, included in this Noahide restriction [51] Many have specified, moreover, that an abortion during the first forty days of pregnancy is also not included. [52] A significant Responsum from eastern Europe of the eighteenth century dealt with the matter of *B'nai Noah* in its own way, offering us in the process a fine insight for the modern-day debate on the "human" status of the embryo:

> It is not to be supposed that the Torah would consider the embryo as a person [*nefesh*] for them [Sons of Noah] but not a person for us. The foetus is not a person for them either; the Torah merely was more severe in its practical ruling in their regard. Hence, therapeutic abortion would be permissible to them, too. *Does the matter, then, depend on calling the foetus by the name "person?"* ["*Atu bik'riat shem nefesh talya milta*"] It depends rather on the responsibilities which the Torah has assigned in connection therewith. [53]

Abortion, to sum up the immediately foregoing, is not murder, neither for Israelites nor for "Sons of Noah," except that by special decree, so to speak, capital liability attaches to the latter when the act is done without the justification of saving life. Presumably other justifications, defined below, would likewise be admissible. This now falls into place for our search for the legal basis of the crime of abortion: The very existence of a strong censure against unnecessary abortion for *B'nai Noah* ought to imply some kind of

[50] *Resp. Maharit*, No. 99 and end of No. 97. (See above, Note 30.) The Talmudic source is *TB P'sahim* 22b. Trani's judgment is echoed by his disciple, the compiler of *K'neset HaG'dolah*, to *Tur, H.M.* 425, 6; and by the author of *Pahad Yitzhak* (*s.v. N'falim*) in 18th-century Italy. But R. Aaron Sh'muel Kaidonover (d. 1676), who had heard of Trani's Responsum but not seen it, comes to the opposite conclusion in his *Resp. Emunat Sh'muel*, No. 14, end, that it is not wrong to assist a non-Israelite in this matter, that it is not "placing a stumblingblock." Either way, Jakobovitz (*op. cit.*, p. 187) clearly errs in introducing the idea of a professional fee; it is irrelevant in this connection. R. Issar Unterman (*Noam*, VI, 1963), evidently misled by the wording of Trani's Responsum, confuses assistance in abortion with assistance in fertility and is hard-pressed to resolve (pp. 7–8) a nonexistent difficulty.

[51] See on, *Koah Shor* and *Tosafot*. But cf. *Minhat Hinnukh* to No. 291, who raises theoretical queries. The author of *Mishneh LaMelekh*, in his *Parashat D'rakhim*, No. 2, cites Trani to the effect that B'nai Noah may not risk their lives to perform what is to them a mitzvah, based on *ya'avor v'al yehareg* in *Yad, Y'sodei HaTorah* 5, 4. See also Jacob Ginzberg, *Mishpatim L'Yisrael*, pp. 161–231.

[52] *Resp. Torat Hesed, E.H.*, No. 42:33 (although his line of reasoning requires the conclusion that the foetus has aspects of nefesh after forty days). Also, *Resp. Beit Sh'lomo, H.M.*, No. 132; Zweig in *Noam*, II, 53; Weinberg in *Noam*, IX, 214. On the 40-day time distinction, see below, Notes 79–80.

[53] R. Isaac Schorr, *Resp. Koah Shor*, Vol. I, No. 20 (dated 1755).

similar injunction for Jews. Indeed, on the Talmudic principle that "there can be nothing forbidden to non-Jews [in Jewish law] that is at the same time permitted to Jews," abortion may *thereby* be called unlawful. So *Tosafot* argues in two instances;[54] it proceeds to conclude that (*a*) abortion may be said on this basis to be forbidden to Jews, but the capital liability element does not follow (for reasons described above); and (*b*) the therapeutic abortion required by the Mishnah (see on) extends, at least permissively, to non-Jews as well. The difficulty, however, is created by another *Tosafot* which actually uses the word "permitted," in connection with foeticide, though in a comparative context.[55] Aside from the apparent contradiction, the latter *Tosafot* leads R. Jacob Emden to ask rhetorically in his Glosses to the Talmud: "Who would *permit* killing an embryo without reason, even if there be no death penalty for it?"[56] A Glossator of a century later, R. Zvi Hirsch Chayyes, noted matter-of-factly that, whereas the other *Tosafot* forbade abortion without calling it capital, this *Tosafot* goes further and permits it.[57] Indeed, it serves the lenient school (see next chapter) as clear evidence that no violation is incurred, except deprivation when against her will or anti-procreative when not.[58] Those of the other school will not contest this *Tosafot;* but to them its meaning is governed by the sense of the other *Tosafot:* "permitted" means it is not capital as one might have expected.[59] Some go even further: R. Issar Unterman (whose eloquent argument against abortion as the taking of potential life will be presented later) said of the above: *Tosafot* could not be permitting abortion outright; on the contrary, the Genesis text intimates that a capital issue is involved here, albeit one that, for technical reasons (deriving from the Exodus text), is just not capitally punishable.[60]

Evidence from Sabbath Laws

A firm and direct legal basis in the classic sources has still not been discovered which would unequivocally label abortion on request as impermissible. Perhaps, then, evidence for the existence of at least an implied prohibi-

[54] *Tosafot* to *Sanhedrin* 59a, *s.v. leka;* and to *Hulin* 33a, *s.v. ehad.*

[55] *Tosafot* to *Niddah* 44b, *s.v. ihu.*

[56] *Hagahot Ya' avetz* to *Niddah, loc. cit.*

[57] *Hagahot Maharatz* to *Niddah, loc. cit.*

[58] *Resp. Tzof'nat Pa'aneah* (Note 31, above). Although this *Tosafot* is not their chief source, *Resp. Emunat Sh'muel* (Note 50, above) and *Maharash* Engel (Note 5, above) say that no biblical violation is incurred; perhaps a rabbinic one.

[59] *Mishpatim L'Yisrael* (Note 51, above), p. 228. *Resp. Beit Yitzhak*, Vol. II, No. 162, says *Tosafot* used the word "permitted" imprecisely ("*shigra d'lishna*").

[60] *Noam,* VI (1963), 2, 5.

tion can be deduced from another area of Jewish law. We consider now the evidence from the domain of Sabbath laws and their authorized suspension. Sabbath prohibitions are to be set aside where *life* is in danger. Now, does that include danger to the "life" of a foetus as well? The answer would tell us something about the seriousness of taking such a "life." In situations where the health of the mother is involved with that of the foetus, there is, of course, no question about what may be done.[61] Moreover, where the mother dies when the birth process can be said to have begun,[62] the Talmud specifies that the (surgical) instruments be brought on the Sabbath, in violation thereof, in order to remove the embryo from its mother's body; what is "news" here is that this must be done even though the embryo's present and future viability is in doubt.[63]

The reason for the above provision, however, may be the possible independent survival of the infant; we may thus be dealing with already independent life. What of the earlier stages of pregnancy where—for argument's sake—the welfare of the foetus might, as in the above case, be separable from that of the mother? If the foetus *only* is threatened, that is, may the Sabbath be violated for its sake? May a healthy woman be fed on Yom Kippur, for example, for the sake of her foetus? (The "for argument's sake" is in deference to the view formulated by "Rosh" [Asheri] in this connection: "I don't know what this hairsplitting [*dikdukim*] is all about," he writes. "There can be no danger to the foetus that isn't also a danger to the mother and vice versa"[64]). The answer to our question is doubly instructive: (1) The permission—rather, the requirement—to violate the Sabbath (and Yom Kippur) is derived from Lev. 18:5, where the verse reads, "which, if a man perform them [the commandments of the Torah], he shall live by them." This is interpreted by the Rabbis as indicating "he shall *live* by them and *not die* because of them."[65] Accordingly, since the authorizing text clearly says " . . . if *a man*, etc."—which is interpreted as "if a person" (see above)[66] —then, say some authorities, there is no permission for Sabbath violation

[61] *Mishnah and G'mara, Yoma* 82a and Rashi.

[62] See on ("*kivan d'akar, gufa aharina hu*"). The foetus is then "*k'munah b'kufsa dami*," like something encased in a package and ready for opening. See *Tosafot* to *Niddah* 44b.

[63] *TB Arakhin* 7a.; see *ibid.*, 7b.

[64] *Rosh* to *Yoma* Ch. 8, Par. 13. To which *Korban N'tan'el* responds (*ad loc.*): "I don't know why he doesn't know. Aren't there women who miscarry often without any harm coming to them?" See below, Note 76.

[65] *TB Yoma* 85b.

[66] Ramban, *Torat HaAdam, Sha'ar HaSakkanah*, in the name of "some authorities."

in order to save a foetus.[67] On the other hand, permission to set aside the Sabbath to save a foetus, even in its earliest stages, is indeed to be granted, says the *Halakhot G'dolot*, a Geonic code dating from the ninth century,[68] on other grounds. The basis of the general dispensation, according to the same Talmudic discussion, is the implied imperative, "violate for him *this* Sabbath so that he [remain alive to] keep many Sabbaths";[69] that is, its future viability is the reason for our present concern. Two points, then, are suggested by this exchange: the foetus is not a person, not "a man";[70] but the foetus is indeed potential life and is to be treated as such, which is essentially the teaching that emerges from our other analyses.

The above considerations play an important role for *Tosafot* and the Responsa in determining the criminality of induced abortion. To begin with, we have seen that *Tosafot*, in two separate instances,[71] assumes the existence of some formal ban of foeticide, although that third *Tosafot* makes no such assumption.[72] The latter did try to deduce an implied prohibition from the circumstance that the foetus is evidently "life" enough to warrant a Sabbath violation on its behalf. It succeeded only in concluding that this is yet no warrant for making the crime punishable; no actionable ban can be deduced, only the moral inhibition once again. The point is demonstrated by another Sabbath law: for, argues *Tosafot*, such is the case with him who hastens the death of a dying man; to do so is an offense which is forbidden but unpunishable (*patur aval asur*), and yet the Sabbath may be violated to avoid hastening a dying man's expiration.[73] The Sabbath, that is, may be suspended to save even that "life" which is not protected by capital penalties; the matter of justification for aborting it is left untreated; we can infer nothing from this consideration.

Despite its conclusion, this lenient *Tosafot* became, in turn, one of the central pillars sustaining the theoretical structure of R. Yair Bachrach's Responsum.[74] In reply to a query as to whether an abortion may be induced in, as it happened, the early stages of pregnancy, the author of *Havvot Ya'ir*

[67] Ramban, *Hiddushim* to *Niddah* 44; *Ha'amek Sh'alah* (see Note 21, above).

[68] Cited by Ramban, *Torat Ha Adam, Sha'ar HaSakkanah*: also by *Rosh* and *RaN* to *Yoma*, *ad loc.*, *Ha' amek Sh' alah* (*loc. cit.*) aligns *She' iltot* with *BaHaG*.

[69] *TB Yoma* 85b; Ramban, *loc. cit.* Cf. Weinberg (Note 52, above), p. 200.

[70] Except, perhaps, in the singular view of R. Hayyim Soloveichik who, in *Hiddushei R. Hayyim HaLevi*, p. 95, holds that the foetus may indeed be included in *va-hai ba-hem*, even according to those who see the danger of *ub'rah she-herihah* (*Yoma* 82a) as a danger to the foetus only.

[71] *Tosafot* to *Sanhedrin* and to *Hulin*. See Note 54, above.

[72] *Tosafot* to *Niddah*. See Note 55, above, and Glosses of Emden and Chayes.

[73] *TB Yoma* 84b. See also *Resp. Radbaz*, Vol. II, No. 695.

[74] *Resp. Havvot Ya'ir*, No. 31. See Note 2, above.

assumes that *Tosafot's* argument is built on the Talmudic suspension of the Sabbath for a later-stage embryo only (at the beginning of the birth process, as described above). Apparently, no such suspension is sanctioned for the earlier stages; hence, the foetus at that time, unprotected in this sense, is vulnerable to desired abortion as well. But this syllogism, too, is set aside by a recent essay on the subject, which reestablishes *Tosafot's* distinction between punishability and prohibition, asserts the latter to be in force in the earlier stages, too, and effectively severs the precise nexus between Sabbath suspension and abortion.[75] The principle of potential life may govern both questions, but decisions are to be based on criteria that may apply to one and not the other; we may still infer nothing from one to the other.

An alternative explanation of the reason for tending to the foetus' welfare on the Sabbath yields an argument against abortion in a nineteenth-century Responsum.[76] It is really the mother's wellbeing that is our concern in that Sabbath dispensation, says R. Solomon Drimmer of Skola, for miscarriage at any stage is dangerous for her. Hence, abortion should be disallowed in the case before him on grounds that physical hazard is created thereby. Even her claim that no hazard is involved cannot be accepted against the clear implication of the Talmud that it is.[77] This obstacle is overcome by the knowledge that pregnancy in her case would be *more* dangerous—and he permits the abortion.

Some technical distinctions of separate phases in the gestation of the foetus are, incidentally, brought up in these Sabbath-law discussions. Since they have a wider application, it is important to make note of them at this point: (a) The first distinction is between the foetus *after the birth process* has begun (*yash'vah al ha-mashber*) and the foetus before that time. The foetus in the earlier stage is regarded as *gufah hu* [part of "her body"], which is a more definitive variation of the *yerekh imo* principle above. As soon as the parturition process begins, the foetus is deemed *gufá aharina* [a "separate body"]. It is no longer a dependent part of another's life, but neither is it yet a "person" in its own right; it enjoys the transitional status of a separate entity but not of an independent life. The mandate to bring the instruments on the Sabbath referred specifically to such an embryo. (b) Moving back earlier in the gestational period—farther back from embryotomy to the more usual question

[75] R. Yehiel Weinberg in *Noam*, IX (1966), especially pp. 194–202; and R. Mosheh Zweig in *Noam*, VII (1964), 45–46.

[76] *Resp. Beit Sh'lomo*, H.M., No. 132.

[77] The author of *Resp. L'vushei Mord'khai* (1913), *H.M.* No. 39, independent of the above Responsum, sees an obvious distinction to be made between the miscarriage the Talmud speaks of and an induced abortion. The latter, he says, under good medical auspices, should entail no untoward risk.

of timely abortion—another time distinction is that of *the first trimester*. The
end of the first three months of pregnancy is mentioned in the Talmud (and,
by implication, in such Bible references as Gen. 38:24, *"vay'hi k'mishlosh hodo-
shim"*) as the time when pregnancy is "noticeable" and the foetus' "move-
ments" are about to be discernible to the mother.[78] A recent Responsum
found it relatively simple to permit an abortion to a woman pregnant "several
weeks now," who was in physical danger, because of this distinction, on the
twin grounds that we are not yet dealing with an embryo *and* the danger to
the woman is less now than it would be with an abortion later on.[79] (c) Another
distinction gives *the first forty days* of pregnancy a special status; it is to
this period that *Halakhot G'dolot's* dispensation extended—all the more
notable because the status of so undeveloped a foetus is precarious indeed.
According to one statement in the Talmud, this is the stage of "mere liquid."[80]
The fortieth day is when the embryo "forms," according to other Talmudic
references,[81] just as Aristotle and Roman jurisprudence had assumed.[82]
Responsa dealing specifically with abortion tend to be very lenient in cases
where the pregnancy is not yet that old;[83] one, however, who opposes almost all abortion on grounds of nipping potential life in the bud makes no
such differentiation.[84]

Before leaving the subject of Sabbath laws, another corner of that domain may be found relevant here. In commenting on the Mishnah which
prohibits the killing of insects on the Sabbath, the Talmud wants to know
just what violation is incurred by one who would detach an animal embryo.
The answer is offered that such action comes under the category of "uprooting
something from whence it grows."[85] The fact that the Talmud does not, as

[78] *TB Niddah* 17a, etc.

[79] *Resp. Pri HaSadeh*, Vol. IV, No. 50.

[80] *TB Niddah* 69b (*maya b'alma*).

[81] E.g., *TB Niddah* 15b; *Mishnah and G'mara, Niddah* 30a–b; *Brakhot* 60a (the time of
p'kidat ha-tippah is "forty days before *y'tzirat ha-v'lad"*). In the Codes, *SHaKH* to *H.M.* 210, 1,
and *Mishneh L'Melekh* to *Yad, Tum'ot Met* 2, 1, make the distinction. See Note 52, above, and
next chapter, Notes 19, 20.

[82] Aristotle (*De animalibus historiae*, 7, 3) specified forty days in the case of a male and eighty
days in the case of a female. Westermarck (*op. cit.*, p. 416, Note 4) calls this an "absurd misinter-
pretation" of Lev. 12:2–5, where these time periods are for *after* birth. He notes that the glossarist
of the Justinian Code equalized both at forty days. (See Note 37, above, on Augustine.) The Talmud,
however (*Niddah* 30b), in the name of R. Ishmael, parallels the 40 and 80 days of after birth to those
of after conception. The view of the Sages—that equalizes them at 40 days—prevails.

[83] E.g., *Resp. T'shurat Shai*, Second Series, No. 62; *Resp. Beit Sh'lomo, H.M.*, No. 132;
Ahiezer, Vol. III, No. 65; *Resp. Tzofnat Pa'aneah*, No. 59; Zweig, *Noam* VII, p. 53; Weinberg,
Noam, p. 213; and cf. *Torat Hesed*, Note 52, above, and *Pri HaSadeh*, Note 79, above.

[84] R. Issar Unterman, in *Noam*, VI (1963), 9. He notes (p. 1) that his questioner requested
a speedy reply, having understood that the law would be different after the first forty days.

[85] *TB Shabbat* 107b.

one would expect, classify this as "taking life" (*n'tilat n'shamah*), just as it would the taking of the life of the insects under discussion in that same context, is of significance to the Commentaries and to our subject. While R. Menahem Ha'Me'iri explains the Talmud's answer by saying that "taking of life" cannot be applied to something not yet born,[86] Nahmanides, before him, maintains that causing a miscarriage on the Sabbath is in one sense a case of "taking life" but not self-sufficient life: "The life of the foetus is dependent on the life of the mother," he says. "He who causes it to be aborted takes *its source* of life."[87] These nuances, interesting in themselves, yield no teaching on human foetal life. For the latter, the author of an eighteenth-century Commentary to sections of the *Shulhan Arukh* would say that "taking of life" is certainly involved, for "most" pregnancies eventuate in viable births.[88] But here, too, he is speaking of—in the extralegal terms of our important phrase above—the taking of *potential* life. We have come this far only to find that an identifiable legal prohibition still eludes us. Our quest continues into the following chapter.

[86] *Beit HaB'hirah* to *Shabbat, ad loc.*

[87] Ramban, *Hiddushim* to *Shabbat, ad loc.*

[88] R. Yosef Teomim, *Pri M'gadim* (*Mishb'tzot Zahav*) to *O.H.* 328, 1. But cf. *Resp. Rabdaz, loc. cit.*

15

Warrant for Abortion

The Catholic Doctrine

In the summation of his Responsum on the subject of abortion, one contemporary Rabbi makes respectful reference to the Church's stern and uncompromising stand on the matter and suggests that this fact be taken into positive consideration by the Jewish community as well.[1] Whether or not the Catholic position is consulted for practical decisions, it is important that points of similarity and difference between the two traditions be adequately appreciated.

The authors of an extensive historical study of women in civilization contend that "the distinctive Christian doctrine on abortion is founded neither on Roman law nor Hebrew."[2] Despite the authors' purport, the distinctiveness of the doctrine does not vitiate its integrity; it bases itself on equally distinctive premises. These are, primarily, the entry of the soul into the body and the requirement of baptism.

The teaching of the Pythagorean Greeks that the soul enters the body at conception prevailed in Christianity by way of the third-century Church Father Tertullian, and was confirmed by St. Gregory of Nyssa in the fourth

---

[1] R. Mosheh Zweig, *Noam*, VII, (1964), 56.

[2] H. H. Ploss, and M. Bartels, *Woman* (1935), I, 482 (from the German *Das Weib*).

century.[3] Then, in the fifth century, Augustine introduced the distinction, based on the Septuagint and referred to in the previous chapter, whereby only the killing of a "formed" foetus (one of forty or eighty days) is homicide and consequently that only such a foetus can be said to have a soul.[4]

Although St. Basil (d. 379) had condemned abortion at any stage, the famed Justinian Code in the sixth century exempted abortions before forty days from penalty.[5] Gratian's *Decretum* of 1140, a ruling from Pope Innocent III (c. 1216), and the Decretals of Pope Gregory IX (c. 1241) all reaffirmed the distinction between "vivified" or animated foetuses and those younger than that.[6] A turning point was the bull *Effraenatum* of Pope Sixtus V in 1588, which did away with the forty (or eighty) day rule and declared abortion murder at any stage on penalty of excommunication, even for those who counseled it. His decree was rescinded less than three years later by Gregory XIV. The relaxation of penalties lasted until 1869, when Pope Pius IX re-instituted the doctrine and the sanctions of Sixtus V.[7] This rigorous decree of 1869—further affirmed in the current code of Canon Law which came into force in 1918—is now the reigning doctrine. A contemporary theologian, Bernard Häring, writes: today "almost all theologians believe that conception is the moment when the soul is infused, and that the old rule is no longer a tenable opinion."[8] The original Pythagorean view and the teaching of *Effraenatum* have thus prevailed.

More important than the time of ensoulment is another dogma, namely that the soul is in need of baptism for its salvation—which follows, in turn, from the doctrine of original sin. In his highly esteemed treatise, *De Fide*, written in the sixth century, St. Fulgentius says:

> It is to be believed beyond doubt that not only men who are come to the use of reason, but infants whether they die in their mother's womb, or after they are born, without baptism, in the name of the Father, Son, and Holy Ghost, are punished with everlasting punishment in eternal fire, because though they have no actual sin of their own, yet they carry along with them the condemnation of original sin from their first conception and birth.[9]

[3] *The Catholic Encyclopedia*, I, 46 ff.; J. Needham, *A History of Embryology* (1934), p. 57.

[4] See previous chapter, Notes 37, 82.

[5] Lawrence Lader, *Abortion* (New York, 1966), p. 77.

[6] Noonan, *Contraception* . . . , pp. 88, 91, 232.

[7] *Ibid.*, pp. 362–63. Noonan associates (p. 365) the 1869 decision with biological advances of that time.

[8] *La Loi du Christ*, III, 366, cited by Lader, *op. cit.*, p. 185, Note 9.

[9] *De Fide*, 27; cited by E. Westermarck, *The Origin and Development of the Moral Ideas*, I, 416–17.

Augustine had likewise taught that the embryo is included among those whose souls were condemned to eternal perdition if they died unbaptized.[10] Aquinas later suggested the possibility of salvation for an infant who did not survive until birth,[11] but the original teaching continued its hold.[12] The result was that abortion came to be considered *worse* than murder. The death of a baptized mother is only the beginning of an eternity of salvation, while the death of an unbaptized infant is the beginning of an eternity of perdition. This attitude led logically to the insistence on extraction of the foetus from a deceased mother's womb for purposes of baptism,[13] and to the invention and use in aborted pregnancies of a baptismal syringe for the administration of baptism to a foetus within the womb.[14] The instrument, recommended in 1733 by theologians at the Sorbonne, is mentioned in subsequent moral-theological texts and figures in the novel *Tristram Shandy*.[15] As to current teaching, Canon 747 today requires all living foetuses to be baptized, and the directive for hospital practice reads: "In the event of an operation for the removal of a diseased organ containing a living foetus, the foetus should be extracted and baptized before the excised organ is sent to the pathologist."[16] All of this represents a serious concern with the immortality of the soul of the foetus. Granted its entry at any given time, the concern now is not only that it not be deprived of life in this world but that it not be denied eternal salvation in the next.

Another significant facet to the considerations of baptism and original sin has to do with the role of the mother herself who must continue expiation of the "sin of Eve." As set forth by Father Klarman earlier in this century, original sin is more "manifest in woman, who first disobeyed God"; the grace of her baptism affects her ethical position but not her physical condition, which is still subject to the curse of pain in childbirth; that pain, now, includes the risks and dangers of motherhood as well. Hence, he concludes, even therapeutic abortions are ideologically impossible to justify.[17] (Justification for indirect therapeutic abortion is discussed below.) It must, therefore,

[10] *The Catholic Encyclopedia*, II, 266; Ploss and Bartels, *loc. cit.*

[11] Westermarck, *loc. cit.*

[12] On the horror of death without baptism of infants, born or unborn, see W.E.H. Lecky, *History of the Rise and Influence of the Spirit of Rationalism in Europe*, 1870, I, 360 ff, and his *European Morals*, II, 23; as well as Westermarck, *loc. cit.*

[13] L. Capellman, *Pastoral-Medizin*, p. 24, cited by Jakobovitz, *op. cit.*, p. 310, Note 47.

[14] Needham, *op. cit.*, pp. 182 ff.

[15] An illustration of the baptismal syringe appears in H.W. Haggard, *Devils, Drugs and Doctors* (New York, 1929), p. 4.

[16] *Ethical and Religious Directives for Catholic Hospitals* (St. Louis, 1949), p. 3.

[17] A. Klarman, *The Crux of Pastoral Medicine* (New York, 1905), pp. 209 ff. Cf. J. Fletcher, *Morals and Medicine*, pp. 148–49.

be said that while Christianity's position on abortion has raised the moral level of western civilization in this regard and has succeeded in sensitizing humanity to a greater reverence for life, it is obviously comprised, at the same time, of theological postulates which the Jewish community can not share.

Theories of Ensoulment In Judaism

To begin with, the moment of soul-infusion of the embryo should, it would seem, be of similar importance for the morality of abortion in Jewish law. The extent to which this is or is not so can be gauged from the following examination of the question in the rabbinic system.

A dialogue between the Roman Emperor Antoninus and Rabbi [Judah, compiler of the Mishnah, known simply as "Rabbi"] is recorded in the Talmud:[18]

> Antoninus said to Rabbi: "From when is the soul (*n'shamah*) endowed in man, from the time of conception[19] or from the time of [the embryo's] formation?"[20] Rabbi replied: "From the time of formation." The emperor demurred: "Can meat remain three days without salt and not putrefy?[21] You must concede that the soul enters at conception." Rabbi [later] said, "Antoninus taught me this, and Scripture supports him, as it is said (Job 10:12): 'and Thy visitation hath preserved my spirit (*ruhi*).'"[22]

[18] *TB Sanhedrin* 91b.

[19] Lit., "visitation" [*p'kidah*]. This is explained by Rashi as referring to *Niddah* 16b, according to which the drop of semen is brought by an angel to the throne of God to discuss its destiny. See previous chapter, Note 81, and also *Sefer Y'tzirat HaV'lad* of Jellinek (Ch. 7, Note 1). But *Yad Ramah* to *Sanhedrin* 91b dismisses this as "*div'rei halomot*"; he suggests *p'kidah* is from *pakad et Sarah*, etc.; hence is time of conception for that reason. Hirsch (see on) associates word with *hayyav adam lifkod et ishto*, hence time of coitus is meant.

[20] "*Y'tzirah*." This alludes to the frequently stated idea in the Talmud that embryo begins to "form" on 40th day of gestation. See e.g., *Niddah* 30 a, b; Rashi to *P'sahim* 9a, based on *Mishnah Oholot*, *XVIII*, 7; and see previous chapter, Notes 81, 82. In *TB M'nahot* 99b, R. Yohanan and R. Elazar speak of *n'shamah notz'rah b'arba'im* (as in *Num. Rabbah* 5, 4). Despite Rashi's application of their phrase to *tzurat ha-v'lad*, they imply *n'shamah* at least as much as *tzurah* and hence may be said to oppose Rabbi's ultimate view—as pointed out by R. Moses J. Feldman in unpublished Glosses to the Talmud, *B'rakhot* 60a.

[21] The "three days," suggests Preuss (Note 24, below), refers to the maximum time between coitus and impregnation. The sperm could not last longer than that without something to animate it.

[22] *Maharsha* (*Sanhedrin, ad loc.*) understands the subject and object of this verse to be interchanged: my spirit (i.e., animal soul, or "salt") has preserved my embryo ("thy visitation").

"Visitation" being identified with "ensoulment," the view of Rabbi thus teaches entry of the soul into the body at the very beginning of gestation, at the time of conception. This conclusion is affirmed in the parallel Midrashic version of the dialogue, except that here Rabbi's original view, before his concession to Antoninus, placed ensoulment even later than "formation"—at the time of birth itself:[23]

> ". . . From when is the soul endowed in man; from the time he leaves his mother's womb or from before that time?" Rabbi replied: "From the time he leaves his mother's womb." [Antoninus demurred, etc., and Rabbi agreed: from the time of conception.]

The bearing of these passages on the question of abortion has been debated among modern scholars. Julius Preuss declared at the beginning of this century that such theoretical musings have no relationship to the Talmud's attitude towards the juristic problem of foeticide.[24] Prof. V. Aptowitzer disputes him; Rabbi's juristic decision that the foetus is to be regarded as "part of its mother" is, he claims, a consequence of Rabbi's (original) theological view that the soul enters at a later stage.[25] He further argues for the greater authenticity of the Midrashic version and, accordingly, holds that Rabbi's original view, taken from the Stoics, was that the soul enters at birth.[26] R. Immanuel Jakobovitz discounts the essential relationship, arguing correctly that there is no basis in the Talmud for a connection between views of ensoulment and the legal status of the embryo.[27] W. Hirsch of London, in his recent volume on rabbinic concepts of the soul, rejects Aptowitzer's second point, that of the Midrashic version's relative authenticity. Rabbi, he feels, could never have believed that ensoulment takes place as late as birth.[28] To believe so would have placed him at odds with the various Aggadic teachings about "life" in the embryo: that Jacob and Esau "struggled" with different inclinations in Rebecca's womb;[29] that the child is instructed in Torah and adjured to be righteous before leaving his mother's womb,[30]

---

[23] *Gen. Rabbah* 34, 10.

[24] Julius Preuss, *Biblisch-Talmudisch Medizin*, p. 450.

[25] Viktor Aptowitzer, "The Status of the Embryo in Jewish Criminal Law," *Jewish Quarterly Review*, XV (1924) 115 ff.; and "*Emdat HaUbar B'Dinei Onshin Shel Yisrael*," in Sinai, p. 32.

[26] *JQR*, *loc.cit.*, pp. 69, 115; *Sinai*, *loc.cit.*, p. 29. The Stoics taught that the soul—or "pneuma" —joins the body at birth. See *Encyclopedia of Religion and Ethics*, VI, 56.

[27] *Jewish Medical Ethics*, p. 332, Note 138.

[28] W. Hirsch, *Rabbinic Psychology* (London, 1947), pp. 188–89.

[29] *Gen. Rabbah*, 63, 6.

[30] *Niddah*, 30b; *Sefer Y'tzirat HaV'lad* (see Ch. 7, Note 1).

etc. "What could have induced Rabbi," Hirsch asks rhetorically, "to abandon a general Jewish belief and adopt from Stoicism its materialistic view of the soul?"[31] Clearly he must have assigned "life" to the foetus at least from the fortieth day; the Talmudic version, then, is the authentic one of the two.

The "life" which Rabbi attributed to the foetus, however, may or may not be identical with "soul" as we understand it. The Talmud uses the word "n'shamah" even in connection with the life of animals;[32] moreover, Rabbi and the Emperor Antoninus agreed, in a continuation of the dialogue recorded above, that the *Yetzer HaRa* (see Chapter 5) does not enter until birth.[33] Clearly, *some kind of "life" other than human* is presupposed for the foetus. Indeed, Aristotle distinguished three "ensoulments": the foetus is endowed with vegetative life at conception, with an animal soul shortly thereafter, and with a rational soul on the fortieth day of gestation.[34] "Animation," "life," or "organic life," may describe the stages, but the attribution of life or soul to the foetus at any point does not aggravate the seriousness of abortion. The time of "ensoulment" and the nature of that soul, one could say in summarizing the rabbinic outlook, belong to those "secrets of God." They have no bearing on the practical, jurisprudential issue of foeticide versus homicide. This conclusion is made indisputable by a recently published classic Talmudic Commentary, the *Yad Ramah* of R. Meir Abulafia (d. 1244). He epitomizes the dialogue above as teaching that "the soul" (*nishmat ruah hayyim*) enters at conception,[35] while, in his analysis of the foeticide question, he concludes that the embryo is "not a person" (*lav nefesh hu*) until he is born.[36]

The point of the above becomes clear as we consider another question, one much closer to the Christian concern with the "immortal soul" of the embryo. This is the Talmudic query:[37] "From when does a child enter the World to Come (*Olam HaBa*)?"[38] The time of ensoulment is, after all, irrelevant; "entry into the World to Come" is a concept certainly more analo-

[31] Hirsch, *loc. cit.* The opinion attributed to the Stoics that the soul joins the body after birth is part of their pantheistic system which regards the soul as a material substance, located in the air, and, according to Plutarch, caught with the first breath of the newborn child.

[32] *TB Shabbat* 107b. See previous chapter, Note 85.

[33] *Sanhedrin, loc. cit.; Gen. Rabbah*, 34, *loc. cit.*

[34] *De animalibus historiae*, VII, 3. Actually, he posited the 40th day for the male embryos and the 80th for females, but the period was equalized for legal purposes in Roman law. See previous chapter, Note 82.

[35] *Yad Ramah* to *Sanhedrin* 91b.

[36] *Ibid.*, to *Sanhedrin* 72b.

[37] *TB Sanhedrin* 110b. Also, *TP Shvi'it*, 4, end; *Yalkut* to Psalms, No. 689.

[38] *RaN* to *Sanhedrin, ad loc.*, understands the question to refer rather to resurrection than immortality. He may have support for this view in the language of *TP, loc. cit.*, where the question is "From when does a child live [again]?"

273

gous to the crucial Christian idea of the soul ascending to heaven. For, despite Rabbi's view that the soul enters at conception, a variety of answers are proposed in the Talmud for when the "child" (*katan*) can "come to *Olam HaBa*": he is ready to do so according to these various views either at (*a*) conception,[39] (*b*) birth, (*c*) circumcision; or when he is (*d*) able to speak or (*e*) to respond "Amen." Clearly the body's endowment with a "soul" or "animation" is not the same as its endowment with immortal life; clearly, too, the Rabbis' answers to this query remain conjectural and indeterminate dicta; they remain "the secrets of God" with no doctrinal and certainly no legal binding force. Paradoxically, in fact, the farther back the time of endowment with immortality is set, the less serious the crime of abortion should be. For, as has been suggested in another (Christian) context, the "soul-embryo's relationship to God would not be affected whether it matured to childhood or died, as presumably a soul is not enlargeable or reducible."[40] And, if not affected, the difference can only be the extent of the perpetrator's guilt, of whether "murder" has been committed or not.

Indeed, lacking the problem of original sin and the consequent need for baptism, the soul's ascent to heaven is untouched by this entire matter; abortion would not interfere with the immortal rights or destiny of the foetus. In the Aggadic narrative of how the father of Moses wanted to refrain from having children because of Pharaoh's decree that "all male children" not be allowed to survive, the young Miriam is said to have reproved her father: "Pharaoh decreed against male children; you decree against male and female; Pharaoh decreed against their life in this world; you against their life in this and the next world."[41] On the one Talmudic assumption that immortality is endowed at conception,[42] full-term birth would not be necessary for "life in the next world"; on the other assumptions that immortality can begin at various stages after conception or after birth, early infanticide would be no worse. This is because, in either case, "*n'shamah she-natata bi t'horah hi*" ["the soul with which Thou hast endowed me is pure"[43] and untainted from the beginning]. The conclusion is inescapable that these Aggadic or theo-

---

[39] "*Zera ya'avdenu*" in Psalms 22:31 is interpreted in *Midrash T'hillim*, *ad loc.*, as "seed" in its fulfilled sense of a born child as opposed to a (naturally or artificially) aborted embryo. *Yalkut* to Psalms, end of No. 688, relays this, but *ibid.*, No. 689, relays TB and TP of Note 37, above, where zera implies conception and allows for immortality from then on.

[40] *Position Statement on Therapeutic Abortion* (unpublished; The Episcopal Diocese of Albany, New York, Jan., 1967), p. 3.

[41] TB Sotah 12a. See above, Ch. 3, Note 13.

[42] Sanhedrin, *loc. cit.*, and TB K'tuvot 111a; and see Ch. 3, above, *ad she-yikhlu ha-n'shamot she'baguf*.

[43] TB B'rakhot 60b; Morning Service, Daily Prayer Book.

logical reflections—or the actual spiritual destinies of the foetus—have no bearing on the abortion question. The Responsa accordingly omit them from consideration.[44] With the soul's immortality as much irrelevant as the time of its endowment, the earthly court must concern itself with the human problem of murder and deprivation of life in this world. For the earthly court, the law is defined: before birth, the embryo is not a person; from the moment of birth and on, it is; the disposition of the soul, being pure to begin with, is unaffected. The Jewish and Catholic doctrines have once again parted company.

The Foetus as Aggressor: Therapeutic Abortion

We come now to another field of discussion, one which promises much more enlightenment on the morality of abortion. Its focus is a provision in the Mishnah which permits—nay, requires—an abortion (actually an embryotomy or craniotomy) to save the life of the mother:

> If a woman has [life-threatening] difficulty in childbirth, one dismembers the embryo within her, limb by limb, because her life takes precedence over its life. Once its head (or its "greater part") has emerged, it may not be touched, for we do not set aside one life for another.[45]

The first half of this provision is very much in keeping with the general principle of saving existing life. The second half, however (the child's inviolability after its head has emerged), was challenged in another Talmudic context. There the principle of "pursuer" or "aggressor" [*rodef*], whereby one in pursuit of another to kill him may be killed by an onlooker to save the victim, is extended to apply to the case of a young child as well. That is, just as an adult in pursuit may be killed without benefit of "due process" or court procedures, such as *hat-ra'ah* (the formal "warning" which must have been given and acknowledged prior to a murder or else the court cannot execute), so may a child whose actions endanger another. To this it is

---

[44] Again despite Rabbi's conclusion, *Resp. Pri HaSadeh*, Vol. VI, No. 50, describes a foetus in existence "several weeks now" as one in which "the living soul has not yet begun to be sparked." And, *Resp. Mahaneh Hayyim, E.H.*, No. 53: " . . . now that conception has occurred, the Divine Image will, in the course of time, take shape . . ." Endowment with immortality is also omitted from legal consideration, except for incidental reference in the Responsum by R. Mosheh Zweig, *op. cit.*, p. 47; and in *Resp. Igg'rot Mosheh, E.H.* No. 62, in a context other than abortion.

[45] *Mishnah, Oholot* 7, 6. (The phrase "its head, etc.," appears in some parallel texts [*Tosefta Y'vamot* IX and *TB Sanhedrin* 72b]. The alternate, "its greater part" [*TP Shabbat*, 14, 4] or "its head or the greater part thereof" [*TP Sanhedrin* 8, end] also occurs.)

objected: Why should not the same principle be applied to the above Mishnah of the woman in difficult labor, which forbids us to set aside one life, even that of a child, for another? Why not let the infant there be considered pursuer-aggressor? The answer: "That case is different. She [the mother] is being pursued 'from Heaven'"; that is, the aggression is not from the innocent infant but can be said to be an "act of God."[46] Or, in the words of the parallel discussion in the Palestinian Talmud, there is no way of determining, when mother and child "move" involuntarily against each other, "who is pursuing whom."[47] The argument of aggressor, then, cannot apply to the babe a-borning; and it *need* not be applied to the foetus before birth because, says Rashi in keeping with what we have seen so far, the foetus is just not a person.

The matter would have ended right there except for the language in Maimonides' Code. His wording, its implications, and the efforts by others to reconcile these with Rashi and the Talmud gave rise to a substantial literature which, in turn, yielded new insights for the entire matter and became the basis of more stringent legislation concerning abortion in some Responsa. Where all other avenues had failed to lead to a designation of foeticide as capital, or to limit its permissibility to life-threatening situations, an analysis of Maimonides' language did point at least to the latter position. In "Laws of Homicide and Preservation of Life" in his Code, the Mishnah's provision appears as follows:

> This, too, is a [Negative] Commandment: Not to take pity on the life of a pursuer. Therefore the Sages ruled that when a woman has difficulty in giving birth, one may dismember the child in her womb—either with drugs or by surgery—*because he is like a pursuer seeking to kill her.* Once his head has emerged, he may not be touched, for we do not set aside one life for another; *this is the natural course* of the world.[48]

Introducing the "pursuer" argument to justify therapeutic abortion before the moment of birth is apparently a distinct departure by Maimonides from the sense of the Mishnah. And it brings in tow a second question about his formulation: Why deny application of the same argument to the moment after birth? The Mishnah's mandate for therapeutic abortion was based simply on the premise that her life takes precedence because, in Rashi's explanation,

[46] *TB Sanhedrin* 72b.

[47] *TP Shabbat* XIV, 4; *TP Sanhedrin* VIII, 9.

[48] *Yad, Hilkhot Rotzeah USh'mirat Nefesh,* 1, 9.

the foetus is not a person.[49] The argument of "pursuer," however, implies that only for that reason, that is, only to save her life from attack, is abortion permitted. A lesser urgency would not place the foetus in the special category of aggressor and hence would not be sanctionable. This surprising position of Maimonides—followed, incidentally, by some subsequent Codes[50]—is at theoretical variance with the Talmud and has important practical implications. Hence, it occasioned a series of attempted explanations, some of which we can profitably scan at this point, however briefly:

(1) R. Yair Bachrach (d. 1702), in his volume of Responsa, explains:[51] Maimonides does agree with Rashi that the foetus is not a person; yet, since the case in the Mishnah happens to deal with a life-and-death matter, Maimonides implicitly limits it to that *and* makes use of the pursuer idea to justify it. For, although the foetus has no human status, additional justification, such as the saving of her life, is necessary, from Maimonides' standpoint, to make *its* life forfeit.[52]

(2) R. Isaac Schorr (d. 1776), in his Responsa:[53] Maimonides agrees with Rashi; he introduces the factor of pursuer not to limit abortion to life-saving situations, implicitly or otherwise, but to further define the law. A detail of the pursuer principle is listed elsewhere by Maimonides: one who kills a pursuer when he could have stopped him in his tracks by merely disabling him is not liable. The foetus now is like a pursuer in that this detail, too, applies—which, by the way, explains the curious addition by Maimonides of the words "with drugs or by surgery."[54] Maimonides, whose phrasing is always deliberate and precise, is saying: first we try to relieve the situation by drugs; if that does not work, then surgery to dismember the entire foetus is indicated, because the unborn child is to be *treated* in this respect *as a pursuer*, and stopped by whatever means necessary.

(3) R. Jacob Schorr, in a Responsum appearing in an eighteenth-century collection:[55] Another feature of the law of homicide gives the above a slightly different twist. In connection with a court execution, the injunction "Love thy neighbor as thyself" is applied by Rabbi Akiva to the judges of

---

[49] See previous chapter.

[50] *SMaG*, Neg. 164; *Sefer HaHinnukh*, No. 600; *Shulhan Arukh*, H.M. 425. On the other hand, *Arokh HaShulhan* to H.M. 425, 2, Par. 7, takes issue with such a position.

[51] *Resp. Havvot Yair*, No. 31 (see previous chapter, Note 2).

[52] Cf. also Zweig, *Noam*, *loc. cit.*, p. 38, and Notes 58-59, below.

[53] *Resp. Koah Shor*, No. 20.

[54] A "drug" for abortion, incidentally, is mentioned in the Talmud, *Niddah* 30b: "*samma d'naftza*." It was a "scattering drug" given by Cleopatra to her pregnant bondwomen. See Ch. 13.

[55] *Resp. Geonim Batra'i*, No. 45. Preuss (p. 490, Note 4) mistakenly attributes this Responsum to another authority, whose name belongs to the previous unit.

the court, as instructing them to "choose for the convicted criminal the easiest possible death." Just as the pursuer is, of course, not entitled to this nicety, so should the foetus be *treated as a pursuer* in this respect, too, and stopped by whatever means necessary.

(4) Two contributions, one only apparently similar to what has been suggested already, another in fact similar, may be mentioned in passing. (a) Joseph Teomim (d. 1792), in his Commentary to the *Shulhan Arukh*:[56] He is *like* a pursuer; the designation is used figuratively but not actually. Actually, the mother is being pursued "from Heaven," as the Talmud says in the postnatal case.[57] (b) R. Ezekiel Landau (d. 1793), in the dialogue with R. Isaiah (Pick) Berlin, recorded in his Responsa:[58] As Bachrach implies, the pursuer idea must be *combined* with the inferior status of the embryo to render abortion permissible.[59]

(5) R. Yekutiel Teitelbaum (d. 1875), in his Responsa:[60] A pursuer or attacker may be killed in defense or self-defense even when disabling him *may* do the trick. Just as the law of pursuer applies even when such doubt exists, so a foetus whose threat to the mother's life is only doubtful (that is, the physicians see a strong *possibility* that her life is in danger), may, according to this reading, be aborted.[61]

(6) R. Shneur Zalman of Lublin (d. 1902), in his Responsa:[62] Light is shed on the problem by another specific reference to the pursuer concept in the Talmud itself. If a donkey, or inanimate objects such as baggage, are aboard a boat that is in danger of sinking, they are to be regarded "as a pursuer" and may be sacrificed.[63] In Maimonides' codification this law reads:

> A boat is about to sink from the weight of its load. One passenger [with no baggage of his own] steps forward and jettisons the baggage of another to ease the boat's load. He is not liable [to make restitution], for the baggage is *like a pursuer* seeking to kill them; he performed a great mitzvah by throwing the baggage overboard and saving the passengers.[64]

[56] *Pri M'gadim* (*Mishb'tzot Zahav*) to *Sh. Ar.*, *O.H.* 328, 1.
[57] That Maimonides said "*k'rodef*" and not "*rodef*" is offered as a solution by still others, notably R. Yonatan Eibeschuetz in *Urim V'Tumim*, No. 30:103.
[58] *Resp. Noda Biy'hudah*, Second Series, *H.M.*, No. 59.
[59] Cf. Also *Resp. Beit Yitzhuk*, Vol. II, No. 162, and others.
[60] *Resp. Avnei Tzedek* (1886), *H.M.*, No. 19.
[61] See Note 95, below.
[62] *Resp. Torat Hesed*, Vol. II, No. 42.
[63] *TB Bava Kamma* 117b.
[64] *Yad, Hovel U'Mazzik* 8, 15. See, especially, *Migdal Oz* thereto.

The purpose of the law of pursuer, continues the author of this Responsum, is not *punishment;* if it were, "warning," witnesses, and the rest would be necessary. Its purpose is to *save the victim* in time. Still, the danger in the boat would not justify throwing a human being overboard, for one of the bases of the law against homicide and against "setting one life against another" is the Talmudic rationale, "What makes you think that your blood is redder [that is, your life more precious] than the next man's?"[65] Only the position of pursuer renders a man's life forfeit, by virtue of his deliberate intent. The donkey or the baggage in this instance are not responsible or deliberate; yet, not enjoying human status, they may be jettisoned to save the others. A foetus is also like a pursuer in that, despite its innocence and because it is not yet a person, it must be sacrificed to save its victim.[66] After its birth it has equal claim, just as no humans may be cast overboard. Thwarting a pursuer, moreover, is fulfillment of a mitzvah; hence Maimonides' distinctive citation of the commandment "not to take pity on the life of the pursuer" in the matter of the foetus.[67] This dovetails with his judgment here—also distinctive—of "mitzvah" in saving the passengers.

(7) R. Issar Zalman Meltzer (d. 1953), in his Commentary to Maimonides' Code: This author also compares our case to that of the overloaded boat, but refines the additional element wherein both mother and foetus are "pursuers" one against the other. In blocking exit of the foetus, the mother, too, is an aggressor. Of the two equally guilty pursuers, the claim of the foetus is to be *subjugated*, like the donkey or other load on the boat. After the moment of birth, its claim is equal.[68]

(8) R. Hayyim Soloveitchik (d. 1918), in his Commentary to Maimonides' Code:[69] In what is by far the strictest theoretical construction of the matter, this author resolves the problem by assigning near-human status to the foetus. The same law of *pikkuah nefesh* [of setting aside the entire Torah to save life] applies on behalf of the foetus as a potential person just as it does on behalf

---

[65] *TB Sanhedrin* 45b.

[66] Cf. also Resp. *Pri HaSadeh*, Vol. IV, No. 50 (*l'tovat ha-nirdaf*); and *Resp. Tiferet Tzvi*, O.H., No. 14, (*l'sallek et ha-gorem*).

[67] The specific biblical text from which the law of pursuer is derived is important. Our Talmud locates it in Lev. 19:25 [*lo ta'amod al dam re'ekha*] (*TB Sanhedrin* 73a). The *halakhic Midrash*, however, the *Sifrei* to Deut. 25:12, derives it from *lo tahos einekha*. Maimonides utilizes the *Sifrei's* exegesis—a fact pointed out by *Ravad, ad loc.* The latter's purpose of comment is not to "locate sources" for Rambam, says *Resp. Torat Hesed, loc. cit.*, 42:19, but to set off Rambam's special emphasis here which makes attacking the foetus to save the mother a fulfillment of *v'katzota et kappah* (*lo tahos einekha*) a definitive commandment. See also *SMaG*, Neg. 165, and *Resp. Galya M'sekhta* 91c. Ravad takes issue with Rambam in the matter of the boat as well.

[68] *Even HaAzel* (1935) to *Yad, ad loc.*

[69] *Hiddushei R. Hayyim HaLevi* (1936) to *Yad, ad loc.*

of the mother.[70] The Mishnah's provision, therefore, that her life be preferred, does not derive from consideration of her *pikkuah nefesh*, because the foetus would equally be entitled to such consideration. It derives from the special scriptural decree rendering the life of a pursuer forfeit.

(9) R. Hayyim Ozer Grodzenzky (d. 1940), in his Responsa:[71] The discussion applies only to the special circumstances of the Mishnah's case—namely an embryotomy near the moment of birth. We have already seen that the foetus assumes a new status at that moment. It leaves the status of "part of its mother" but is still not in the category of "person"; it enjoys that intermediate status of *gufa aharina*, a separate body awaiting birth. Only the pursuer factor can justify an embryotomy. Prior to these stages, even Maimonides would not apply the argument of pursuer.[72]

(10) Chief Rabbi Ben Zion Uziel (d. 1954), in his Responsa: The foetus is a pursuer when birth is fatally difficult because the foetus, Maimonides would say, is fighting *not* to be born, that is, is struggling *against* the birth process. After birth begins, however, he obviously is fighting to *live;* this proves retroactively that not he but other factors were "pursuing" her.[73]

(11) Chief Rabbi Issar Unterman, in his legal essays: The pursuer forfeits (a) his claim to our protection; *and* (b) the status which makes killing him murder. The unintentional pursuer (one following the "natural course") forfeits the first but not the second. The foetus before birth similarly need not be protected *and* his status renders abortion not murder; after birth he may not be "touched." The "natural course" means that all babies are born through a struggle; the difficulties derive from the mother; at best we cannot establish just who the pursuer is. Rashi and Maimonides do not agree; the latter would require "pursuit" of her life before abortion can be permitted.[74]

(12) R. Mosheh Zweig of Antwerp (d. 1965), in a Responsum appearing in a legal journal: Maimonides' formulation comes to teach us that therapeutic abortion is *required* rather than permitted. That the foetus may be attacked to save its mother's life is obvious; but if out of love for her potential child or because of her husband's objections she may *choose* to die so that it may live— this, Maimonides is saying, she may not do. The foetus is a pursuer, and we are under *obligation* to protect the mother; the obligation derives from the

[70] He interprets danger to foetus as independent of danger to mother in discussion above, previous chapter.

[71] *Resp. Ahiezer*, Vol. III, No. 23.

[72] The solution offered by Jakobovitz, *op. cit.*, p. 185, largely corresponds to this one.

[73] *Resp. Mishp'tei Uziel*, Vol. III, *H.M.* No. 46.

[74] *Shevet Miy'hudah*, pp. 26 ff. Also, in *Noam*, VI (1963), 6–7.

(Negative) Commandment "not to take pity on the life of a pursuer." That obligation ceases the moment the baby is born.[75]

(13) R. Yehiel Weinberg of Montreux (d. 1966), in a Responsum as above:[76] Still another law in Maimonides' Code is apposite. A man forced, on penalty of death, to surrender money belonging to another must make restitution.[77] Although he is not required to endanger his life in order to safeguard another's money, he must nevertheless make good later. Such is Maimonides' ruling, following the view that the injunction against theft is suspended by the duty to save one's life, but the "theft" must be restored. Opposing him is his critical annotator R. Abraham ben David, who holds the view that no theft is involved, and he need not make good. Maimonides, in keeping with his own position, then means: the foetus is like a pursuer who forfeits its right to live *and even* any subsequent indemnification to the husband.

Of the foregoing representative expositions of Maimonides' formulation, that of R. Hayyim Soloveitchik (No. 8) yields the most stringent theoretical position, that only the pursuer argument can deprive the foetus of its inviolability, and that of Rabbi Unterman (No. 11) yields the most stringent practical conclusions: only life-threatening circumstances are adequate warrant for abortion. All the others understand Maimonides' use of the pursuer merely as a means of defining and applying details of the law of pursuit to the mother-foetus situation—not to derive from his language that only extreme gravity justifies[78]—and, at that, probably only at the final stages of pregnancy. Indeed, the point made in *Ahiezer* (No. 9) that the entire discussion presupposes an embryotomy when labor has already begun would seem to place the question of earlier abortion outside the realm of this discussion altogether. Rabbi Unterman does not think so; his views will be discussed further.

One noteworthy corollary of the assumption that "pursuit" is necessary to justify abortion is that a life-threatening situation in pregnancy emanating from causes *other* than the foetus would make an abortion to relieve this situation *unjustifiable*. The author of the eighteenth-century encyclopedic *Pahad Yitzhak*, R. Isaac Lampronti, makes this point:

[75] *Noam*, VII (1964), esp. pp. 49–53.

[76] *Noam*, IX (1966), esp. pp. 202–204.

[77] *Yad, Hovel UMazzik* 8, 4.

[78] The ample Responsum in *Tzitz Eliezer*, Vol. IX, No. 51:1, although it makes reference to only two or three of the above expositions, concludes: no authority sees Maimonides as implying capital crime status for abortion.

> It follows that we may not induce an abortion . . . to save her
> from a disease deriving from . . . other "fevers" . . . in the sixth
> month of her pregnancy . . . for only a pursuer may be killed in
> self-defense or for defense of another . . . but this foetus is no
> pursuer . . . We must save her by other treatments . . .[79]

If "other treatments" are not an effective alternative, the author would presumably rule otherwise. As it stands, however, his stringency here coincides with a leniency in the Catholic position. For, although the "pursuer" principle is to be found there as well—Thomas Aquinas, in the century following Maimonides, had granted one the right to protect his life even, if necessary, at the expense of the aggressor's life[80]—it was not applied to the mother-foetus situation. Even to save the life of the mother, any "surgical operation which is directly destructive of the life of the foetus" was expressly forbidden by Holy Office decrees of 1884 and 1888[81] and again in 1895.[82] Something of the "aggressor" idea was then suggested for *indirect* abortion: it should make possible at least the alleviation of an ectopic gestation. In this pathological condition, a fertilized ovum is lodged in a Fallopian tube (or abdominal cavity or ovary) and threatens death to both embryo and mother. The foetus in this case, it was argued, "not in a position in which it had a right to be," should be regarded as a "materially unjust aggressor" and vulnerable to at least indirect expulsion.[83] The argument, nonetheless, did not carry the day; only the treatment of an illness could be sanctioned—such as removal of a cancerous uterus, though an abortion does in effect result—and that on the principle of double effect.[84] And ectopic pregnancies have recently been designated as such an illness and included within the scope of this permission.[85] An attack on the pathological condition, now, but never on the foetus itself as the cause of the difficulty, is sanctioned. This is in neat contrast to the techni-

[79] *Pahad Yitzhak, s.v. n'falim.*

[80] *Summa theologica* 2, 2a. 64 a. 7.

[81] A. O'Malley and J. Walsh, *Essays In Pastoral Medicine* (1906), pp. 49 ff. See also *Catholic Encyclopedia*, I, 47.

[82] G. Kelly, *Medico-Moral Problems* (1950), Part I, pp. 10 ff.

[83] O'Malley and Walsh, *op. cit.*, p. 26.

[84] See above Ch. 8, end; and Fletcher, *op. cit.*, pp. 112–15. (If a good and evil end will simultaneously result from an action, but the good end is desired and the evil end is not desired, the action may be taken.)

[85] Fletcher, *op. cit.*, p. 153, quotes the *Homiletic and Pastoral Review* for October, 1945: "Medical men today are quite commonly agreed that tubal pregnancy constitutes a pathological condition and is as much a threat to the mother's health as a cancerous uterus. The theologians of the last century who held that it is gravely sinful to remove an unruptured tube containing a living foetus, because such a procedure is direct killing, were right in their principle but wrong in their facts . . . it is not direct but indirect killing."

cality raised by Lampronti above, according to which the difficulty *must* come from the foetus if he is to qualify as "pursuer."

The latter, too, becomes entirely academic in the Responsa. R. Isaac Schorr, for instance, entertains such a question—whether abortion is lawful when the difficulty derives from something other than the foetus—only to dismiss it as a valid question only for those who take Maimonides literally. Actually, he says, the sense of the Talmud is that the foetus is not a person, and Maimonides (to be understood as in No. 2 above) would agree with Rashi in permitting abortion whatever the source of her difficulty.[86] Other Responsa before and after Lampronti and Schorr conclude that therapeutic abortion by all means is indicated by Talmudic law generally and by our Mishnah in particular.[87]

There is yet another facet to the "pursuer" factor, this one having to do with the second half, the "postnatal" one, of the Mishnah. How far do we carry the principle of "not setting aside one life for another"? Does it include not setting aside one life for *two* lives when, for example, both mother and baby may die? R. Meir of Eisenstadt (d. 1744) is the first to raise this question. He answers that sacrificing the life of a child aborning when the alternative is the death of both,[88] is permissible, although he adds cautiously that the matter requires more deliberation.[89] His conclusion is cited by R. Akiva Eger in his Commentary to the Mishnah,[90] while another standard Commentator thereto argues the matter anew and has less doubt about its permissibility.[91] The point at issue is that while the principle of self-defense might operate in the mother's case, a third party, that is, the physician, must still abide by the principle of not setting aside one life for another (since the *born* foetus does not qualify as a pursuer). Indeed, R. Hayyim Sofer says of such a case, "Who appointed him [the physician] a 'ruler and judge' [after Exodus 2:14] in this matter?"[92] (to decide between two lives when neither

[86] *Resp. Koah Shor*, No. 20. H.J. Zimmels, *Magicians, Theologians, and Doctors* (1952), p. 212, Note 79; and Jakobovitz, *op. cit.*, p. 335, Note 173, both misrepresent this important Responsum for they quote only its first phase (the *hava amina*, as it were), neglecting to observe that it proceeds to reject the question-and-answer as valid only in terms of what to Schorr is an unacceptable interpretation of Maimonides, etc. (as above), and hence inadmissible.

[87] *Resp. Maharit* Nos. 97 and 99 (See previous chapter, Note 29); *Resp. L'vushei Mord'khai*, Second Series, *Y.D.*, No. 87; and others in this chapter.

[88] Question 35 replied to by the Holy Office (March, 1902), affirms that direct abortion is forbidden even though the embryo will be destroyed anyway if it is allowed to proceed and destroy the mother. See Fletcher, *loc. cit.*

[89] *Resp. Panim M'irot*, Vol. III, No. 8.

[90] *Tos'fot R. Akiva Eger* to *Oholot, ad loc.*

[91] *Tif'eret Yisrael* (*Boaz*, No. 10), to *Oholot, ad loc.*

[92] *Resp. Mahaneh Hayyim*, Vol. II, *H.M.* No. 50. The *rishon* he refers to is *Ba'al Hashlamah*. See now *Me'iri* to *Sanhedrin* 72b.

is a pursuer), although a colleague, with whom he consulted, declined to go along with such reasoning.[93] The theoretical problem is in any case solved by having the woman appoint the physician as her *agent* to act for her "defense." [94] Subsequent Responsa assume an attack upon the emerging infant where the alternative is sure death to both [95] to be unequivocally permitted.[96]

Abortion Other Than Therapeutic

Having seen that therapeutic abortion—that is, to save her life up to the moment of birth, or to save her life even after the moment of birth when death to both is the alternative—is mandated by the Mishnah, we can proceed to the implications that follow therefrom and to a discussion of cases of less severe gravity. First, from all indications, the above can be said to apply only to the terminal stage of pregnancy, when the operation is more commonly known as an embryotomy or craniotomy. The more timely "abortion" in the earlier stages, is very likely not even contemplated in the Mishnaic law. What generalizations, then, can be made about the rabbinic attitude to abortion at any time? It can best be described as bifurcating into two directions, both of which will presuppose that the foetus is not a person; yet one approach builds *down* and the other builds *up*. The first can be identified especially with Chief Rabbi Unterman, who sees any abortion as "akin to homicide," and therefore permissible only in cases of corresponding gravity, such as saving the life of the mother.[97] It then builds *down* from this strict position to embrace a broader interpretation of life-saving situations which include a threat to her health, for example, as well as a threat to her life.[98] The other viewpoint (identifiable with the late Chief Rabbi Uziel and others, and to which we shall return), assumes no real prohibition against abortion at any time, except perhaps during the most advanced stage of pregnancy, and builds *up* from this lenient position to safeguard against indiscriminate abortion.

(1) Rabbi Unterman bases his exposition on a literal understanding of the passage in Maimonides discussed above. He dismisses Trani who had con-

[93] *Resp. Maharam Schick*, Y.D., No. 155.

[94] *Resp. Beit Yitzhak* (Smelkes) Vol. II, No. 162.

[95] In circumstances of doubt, *Resp. Avnei Tzedek, H.M.*, No. 19 is inclined to permit the action as well but suggests *shev v'al ta'aseh* (allow nature to take its course) might be more proper. He and authorities in next note emphasize importance of securing only the most expert and deliberate medical opinion.

[96] *Resp. M'lammed L'Ho'il*, Vol. II, No. 69; *Resp. Binyan David* (Meisels), Vol. I, No. 47; *Resp. She'elat Yitzhak* (Oelbaum), No. 64.

[97] I. Y. Unterman, *Shevet Miyhudah* (1955), pp. 26–30; 49; 50; *Noam*. VI (1963), 1–11. *Resp. Divrei Yissakhar*, No. 168; *Resp. Tzur Yd'akov*, No. 141; and now *Mishpatim L'Yisrael* (p. 226) would side with R. Unterman in seeing a kind of *sh'fikhat damin* involved here.

[98] For the woman whose pregnancy is considered medically dangerous following, as it does, three Caesarean deliveries, abortion is easily permitted by R. Obadia Yosef in *Resp. Yabbia Omer*, Vol. IV, *E.H.*, No. 1 (Jerusalem, 1964).

cluded that no homicide is involved at all (*ein nidnud klal shel ibbud n'shamot*); he wonders why Trani and *Ahiezer* see no problem with Maimonides. Not that Rabbi Unterman claims actual homicide to be involved; only its peripheral "appurtenances" (*abizraihu*) mentioned in the Talmud are, embracing borderline situations "akin to homicide."[99] For, after all, murder is an offense so grave that it requires martyrdom rather than its commission. He cites an actual incident from the time of the German occupation of Poland and Lithuania during the First World War. A Jewish girl had become pregnant by a German officer and insisted that he assume responsibility for the child's upbringing. The officer sought out a (Jewish) doctor and ordered him at gunpoint to perform an abortion.[100] Unterman says that the doctor would not have been required to undergo martyrdom rather than accede, even according to *his* point of view. Nevertheless, potential life is involved and Judaism's reverence for that life bespeaks only the most serious warrant for abortion. He gives an edge to his argument by making reference to the Mishnaic formula for "scaring" the witnesses who come to testify in capital cases. The Mishnah has the judges recite the following exhortation to the witnesses: Know ye that a life hangs in the balance. If your testimony comes from conjecture or hearsay or carelessness, know that the life of a man and that of his descendants after him will be on your hands. For, when Cain slew Abel, God said to Cain, "the sound of your brother's bloods (*kol d'mei ahikha*) cries out to me from the earth." Not "blood" but "bloods," for, by killing Abel, Cain killed his would-be descendants after him as well.[101] So, implies this author, any termination of pregnancy invariably snuffs out a viable potential life and the would-be offspring of that life.[102] Although most persuasive, this argument is not intended as an identification of abortion with homicide. For, the same moral or metaphysical judgment could be applied to every act of marital relations that does not take place. Even the postponement of marriage from, say age eighteen to age twenty could be construed as destructive of potential life in this sense. True, one is more "active" a deed than the other, but life has been declared to begin with birth, and all stages prior thereto are part of "the secrets of God."

In broadening his interpretation of life-threatening situations, Rabbi Unterman does include *extreme mental anguish* as well. Suicidal tendencies are a threat to her life and, as such, also constitute adequate warrant. In another

---

[99] R. Jacob Rosin of Rogatchov in *Resp. Tzofnat Pa'aneah* (Dvinsk, 1934), No. 59, also uses the term "akin to homicide." The query addressed to him was whether one could divorce his wife against her will because she would induce abortions. She should not do this; it is "akin to homicide." But it is not a real enough homicide or offense to make her divorcible against her will.

[100] *Noam, loc. cit.*, p. 5.

[101] Mishnah, *Sanhedrin*, 4, 3 (37a).

[102] *Noam, loc. cit.*, p. 10.

article prepared for members of an Israeli hospital medical staff,[103] he delineates in full what does and does not fall into the category of *pikkuah nefesh* [danger to life]. Insanity alone is not a life-threatening situation, he writes, for the insane are protected by the same instinct for self-preservation as the rest of us. Insanity, however, that carries with it *suicidal tendencies* or attacks of hysteria does constitue a life-and-death matter, because a person so afflicted can do physical harm to self or others, and so on. Precedent for equating mental health with physical health comes from a late-seventeenth-century Rabbi who was asked whether nonkosher chicken soup could be given to a man who believed it to have therapeutic properties; and was in danger of going out of his mind unless he had some. On the basis of Talmudic teaching,[104] R. Israel Meir Mizrachi argued that serious danger to mental health (*tiruf da'at*) is tantamount to risk to one's physical wellbeing, and issued a permissive ruling.[105] It is cited by other authorities as significant legal precedent;[106] more important for our purposes, at least one Responsum (dated 1913)[107] applied it specifically to the matter of abortion:[108]

> Mental-health risk has been definitely equated to physical-health risk. This woman who is in danger of losing her mental health unless the pregnancy is interrupted, therefore, would accordingly qualify.[109]

---

[103] "The Law of Pikkuah Nefesh and Its Definition," in *HaTorah V'HaM'dinah*, IV (1952), 22-29.

[104] *TB Yoma* 82a, 83a, b.

[105] *Resp. Pri HaAretz*, Vol. III (Jerusalem, 1899), Y.D., No. 2.

[106] E.g., *Resp. Admat Kodesh*, Vol. I, No. 6; *Birkhei Yosef* to Y.D., 155 (not included in the excerpts appearing in standard *Yoreh Deah* editions).

[107] *Resp. L'vushei Mord'khai*, H.M., No. 39.

[108] This application is, in turn, endorsed by Hermann Klein in his comprehensive treatment in *Nachlat Zvi*, reprinted as *Anhang zum Artikel Geburtenregelung, Separatabdruck aus Nachlath Zvi* (Frankfurt am Main, 1931), p. 234. The principle was applied to the more formidable legal problem of contraception. *Resp. Binyan David*, No. 68; *Minhat Yitzhak*, Vol. I, No. 115; and *Igg'rot Mosheh*, E.H., No. 65, would allow the contraceptive mokh when pregnancy would create a serious mental-health risk.

[109] This renders superfluous the attribution of the psychiatric principle—incorrect in any case—to "Rabbenu Tam" in *Therapeutic Abortion*, ed. Harold Rosen (New York, 1954), pp. 169, 171. There we are told that he is "quoted in the *Shulhan Arukh* which is widely accepted as the standard guide to traditional Jewish practice" to the effect that any impairment of any limb or organ of the body is a threat to life—and the source is given as "*Tur Shulhan Arukh, O.H.*, 328." The inadmissible deduction is then made that danger to the mind is danger to a limb, etc. But, R. Jacob Ba'al Haturim is meant, not Rabbenu Tam; the *Tur* is not the *Shulhan Arukh*; the source is actually neither, but the Talmud itself (e.g., *Avodah Zarah* 28a) where danger to a limb is equated to danger to life; moreover, the idea of mental risk can hardly be deduced from impairment of other limbs! This many-faceted error is unwittingly relayed and compounded in L. Lader, *Abortion* (New York, 1966), p. 98. The "psychiatric principle" is more firmly grounded and more logically structured in Jewish law, as set forth in Notes 104–108, above. That laws of *pikkuah nefesh* apply to mental-health danger as well as to physical hazard, was again affirmed in a recent Responsum by R. Nathan Friedmann of B'nei Brak in his *Netzer Matta'ai*, No. 8 (1957).

Whether danger to the health of *an existing child* is also contemplated in this stricter interpretation of abortion law was answered in the affirmative in a recent Responsum. Asked whether a woman whose milk was affected by her pregnancy and whose infant could not substitute formula feeding, as attested by the physicians, R. Yitzhak Oelbaum replied that an abortion would be justified to protect the health of her child.[110] He was preceded in this regard by R. Yehudah Ayyas of two centuries earlier.[111]

In one Responsum, termination of a pregnancy resulting *from rape* is dealt with—or, at least, postcoital contraception in such a case. The matter at hand was the permissibility of mokh (Chapter 11, above). The author, R. Yehudah L. Perilman of Minsk, cites the Talmudic case of the victim of rape who according to R. Yosei there need not wait the statutory period of three months (*havhanah*) before marriage—usually required for establishment of paternity if she were to conceive immediately—because she presumably used the postcoital mokh (Chapter 9, above). Even if a woman were forbidden to "destroy seed" postcoitally, our author says, this Talmudic presumption indicates that in the case of rape, she certainly may do so. The reason she may is that while woman is said to be a vehicle for reproduction (*karka olam*), as a human being she differs from "mother earth" in that she need not nurture seed implanted within her *against her will;* indeed, she may "uproot" seed illegally sown.[112] (Interestingly, Catholic teaching gives the victim of rape the benefit of the doubt at least for the first several hours. The "medicinal or artificial sterilization of the *semen virile post copulam*" is, of course, forbidden under ordinary circumstances.[113] Yet, in the hours immediately following rape, a medical douche is permitted because, "it cannot be said with certainty how soon conception takes place after sexual congress; it may be hours or days."[114] In cases other than rape, the probability of *immediate* conception is invoked; for rape, that of *delayed* conception is invoked; after that moment, abortion cannot be sanctioned.) More specific references to abortion of a conceptus resulting from rape seem to be lacking in the available Responsa. What the Rabbis would have ruled, however, can safely be surmised from the sentiment reflected here and, more assuredly, from that expressed in the following decisions.

[110] *Resp. She'elat Yitzhak*, No. 64.

[111] *Resp. Beit Y'hudah*, E.H., No. 14 (see Ch. 10). The difference is that this author sees no legal bar to abortion in any case, whereas the previous one does—as do *L'vushei Mord'khai, Beit Sh'lomo*, and *Binyan David*, all *loci. cit.*

[112] *Resp. Or Gadol*, No. 31 (1891).

[113] A. Koch and A. Preuss, *Handbook of Moral Theology* (St. Louis, 1925), V, 475, quoted by Fletcher, *op cit.*, p. 91.

[114] Henry Davis, S.J., *Moral and Pastoral Theology*, II (New York, 1943), 171.

(2) We turn now to the second of the two viewpoints on the subject: the position whereby no homicide or express offense is committed by the execution of an abortion, but which builds *up* from there, which stipulates that adequate warrant be present before such a step—for it is a serious one —be taken. The tradition begins with R. Joseph Trani (sixteenth century) who discounted any homicidal element, but nevertheless spoke only of abortion "for need" or "for the mother's cure."[115] It continues with Bachrach (seventeenth century), whose famous Responsum saw no legal bar to abortion but would not permit it in the case before him.[116] The case was one of a pregnancy conceived in adultery; the woman, in "deep remorse," wanted to destroy the fruit of her sin. The author begins by declaring no distinction to obtain between bastard and legitimate fruit; he proceeds to demonstrate from the sense of Talmudic laws that no clear prohibition really exists; but he concludes by refusing to sanction the abortion because of what it might lead to—that it will open the door to immorality:

> Therefore, according to what we have shown, strict Torah law would permit what you ask, were it not for the practice among us and among them to seek to curb immorality ... Whoever assists [in making the abortion possible] gives a hand to transgressors.[117]

His verdict was challenged by the next in line in this permissive tradition, R. Jacob Emden (eighteenth century), who offered many reasons why a foetus conceived in adultery may be aborted. To these he added the significant aside:

> With legitimate fruit, too, there is room to permit abortion for "great need"; as long as the birth process has not yet begun, even if the reason is not to save her life—even if only to save her from

[115] *Resp. Maharit,* No. 99. Among the permissivists, aside from those referred to below, are: *Resp. Hayyim V'Shalom,* Vol. I, No. 40, and *Maharash Engel,* Vol. V, No. 89, both of whom see here at most a *d'rabbanan. Resp. Emunat Sh'muel,* No. 14, in an incidental reference, sees even less, as do those discussed below.

[116] *Resp. Havvot Ya'ir,* No. 31. *Resp. Tzur Ya'akov,* No. 141, mistakenly represents him as forbidding even *l'khat'hillah.*

[117] His conclusion is relayed in a later work, *Kuntres Aharon* to *Lehem HaPanim,* No. 19: "Drugs may not be administered to a woman to abort her foetus conceived in adultery [as ruled by] *Havvot Ya'ir,* No. 31."

> the "great pain" it causes her. But the matter requires further deliberation.[118]

And, at the turn of this century, R. Yosef Hayyim ben Eliyahu replied coyly to a similar question. He announced he was giving no answer of his own, yet relayed the words of Bachrach, Emden, and Trani, and then added:

> Evidently there is room to permit when disgrace is involved, which can be called a matter of "great need." But I have already said that I am issuing no ruling, merely placing the above before you for consultation with [another] sage.[119]

'This brings us to Chief Rabbi Ben Zion Uziel (d. 1954) who, in his turn, takes up the question of interrupting a pregnancy conceived in adultery by a now contrite woman. He provides even more reason why the abortion should be permitted;[120] however, it is his treatment of the larger question—in the immediately preceding unit in his Responsa[121]—which is of much more significance for the exposition of the permissive school. For an understanding thereof, we return to the Talmud, to a precedent-narrative there which we have reserved for now. A piquant law of the Mishnah provides as follows:

> [In the case of] a woman [convicted of a capital crime] who goes forth to be executed [and who, after the verdict was returned, is found to be pregnant], we do not wait for her to give birth.[122]

Tosafot explains that *innui ha-din* is the reason for this; that in keeping with the duty of the court to avoid unnecessary suffering for the convicted criminal, the execution must follow directly upon conviction.[123] If her pregnancy was known beforehand, the *trial* would, of course, be postponed;[124] after the trial, a delay is *innui* [suffering]. A further provision is recorded in the name of R. Samuel in the Talmud: if she is going to be executed while preg-

[118] *She'elat Ya'avetz*, No. 43.

[119] *Resp. Rav P'alim*, Vol. I, *E.H.*, No. 4.

[120] *Resp. Mishp'tei Uziel*, Vol. III, *H.M.*, No. 47. He declines, however, to grant the same permission to an unwed mother.

[121] *Ibid.*, No. 46.

[122] Mishnah, *Arakhin*, I, 4 (7a).

[123] *Tosafot* to *Arakhin*, 7a, *s.v. yash'vah; Yad, Hilkhot Sanhedrin*, 12, 4.

[124] See the above and S. Belkin, *Philo and the Oral Law* (New York, 1940), p. 134, Note 128. See also *Sifrei Zutra*, ed. Horowitz, p. 334, and Aptowitzer, *Sinai*, pp. 18–19.

nant, an abortion should be brought about beforehand so that the execution does not cause the extrusion of a foetus, to the disgrace (*nivvul*) of the woman.[125] To prevent her *innui* or *nivvul*, her (nonphysical) suffering or disgrace, then, abortion is prescribed.

But the above law still seems cruel, it may be argued, for why execute a pregnant woman under any circumstances? Prof. Aptowitzer, in the two essays already referred to,[126] offers the following apologia: It is a mistake to compare this law unfavorably to the Roman, Greek, and Egyptian laws which require postponement of execution for a pregnant woman.[127] The fundamental difference between Jewish law and their laws is obvious here. Jewish law is ethical; Greek and Roman law is political. Politics subjugates the good of the individual to the good of the state; to ethics, the individual is supreme. The political state knows military units and taxpayers; the ethical state knows persons. To the former, persons are members of a state; to the latter, the state is a collection of persons, etc. In the political entity, the convicted woman is only a part of the machine that has become rusty and useless and must be cast to the wasteheap, while the foetus within her womb is a brand new cog in the machine and is therefore jealously guarded. In the ethical community, even the convicted woman is a person, entitled to compassion and consideration. Roman, Greek, and Egyptian societies, built on political foundations, are the very ones which indulged in infanticide and exposure of weak children who had lost their value *to the state*. The unfortunate woman has no claim to pity; she must merely do her duty to the state by delivering it a new citizen. The law of Israel, just as it requires that the foetus be sacrificed to save the mother's *physical* life, likewise requires that it be sacrificed to save her *spirit* from torture and suffering. And there *is* suffering, we may at least assume, for a woman who must daily await her execution. Prof. Aptowitzer continues in this vein, adducing other legal examples to make his point,[128] all of which should be viewed against the further circumstance that capital punishment was more theoretic than actual.

To return to our Responsum of Rabbi Uziel, we find this Talmudic teaching being given full play. He then summarizes the entire matter by saying:

---

[125] *TB Arakhin, loc. cit.*, and Rashi, *ad loc.*

[126] Note 25, above; and Note 20, previous chapter.

[127] See sources cited by Aptowitzer, *Sinai*, p. 20, Notes 34, 35. See also *Tosefta Niddah* 4, 17 and Belkin, *loc. cit.* (and *TB Niddah* 30a).

[128] *JQR, loc. cit.*, pp. 98–101; *Sinai, loc. cit.*, pp. 19–34.

It is clear that abortion is not permitted without reason. That would be destructive and frustrative of the possibility of life. But for a *reason*, even if it is a *slim reason (ta'am kalush)*, such as to prevent her *nivvul*, then we have precedent and authority to permit it.

The tradition personified by Rabbi Uziel, especially its emphasis on avoidance of pain for the woman, is carried forward by others as well. R. Mosheh Zweig of Antwerp does so at least in principle.[129] He introduces, from "left field" so to speak, another law from Maimonides' Code, one dealing with the husband's obligations for the support of his wife and the special circumstance of pregnancy cravings:

> If a certain amount was set aside for her support, but she has a desire to eat more, or to eat "other foods" because of the sickness that comes from her craving, she may eat whatever she wants. Her husband may not [try to] stop her, saying, if she eats too much or eats wrong food she might miscarry; for her physical pain [the pregnancy cravings] is to be considered first *(tza'ar gufah kadim)*.[130]

Assuming, for the moment, that pregnancy cravings are as serious as suggested here and assuming the unlikely situation of a woman who would care more about such pain than about the health or life of her foetus, a principle is enunciated here. It proves, says our author, that the woman's pain "comes first"; that it is to be considered ahead of the husband's interest in his future child *and* ahead of the potential life of the child itself. It is entirely consonant, he says, with the Talmudic laws of the condemned woman![131] But then, he continues, how does one measure pain? And, more important, *Tosafot* elsewhere[132] declares that *shame* is the greatest pain. If a woman may have an abortion to preclude shame, the door is opened to a great "stumbling block." Our author, without reference to R. Yosef Hayyim's similar guardedness, thus stops short of carrying his argument to its conclusion.[133]

The principle that a mother's pain "comes first," however, is the most pervasive of all factors in the consideration of the abortion question. It produces the *following fundamental generalization:* if a possibility or probability exists that a child may be born defective and the mother would seek

[129] *Noam*, Vol. VII (1964), pp. 36–56.
[130] *Yad, Hilkhot Ishut* 21, 11.
[131] *Noam*, loc. cit., pp. 47–48.
[132] To *Shabbat* 50b, *s.v. bishvil*.
[133] *Noam*, ibid., p. 54.

an abortion on grounds of pity for the child whose life will be less than normal, the Rabbi would decline permission. Since we don't know for sure that he will be born defective, and since we don't know how bad that defective life will be (in view of the availability of prosthetic devices, etc.), and since no permission exists in Jewish law to kill born defectives, permission *on those grounds* would be denied. If, however, an abortion for that same potentially deformed child were sought on the grounds that the possibility is causing severe *anguish to the mother,* permission would be granted. The foetus is unknown, future, potential, part of "the secrets of God"; the mother is known, present, alive, and asking for compassion.[134]

That this is a valid statement of the Jewish attitude is evidenced by at least the following Responsa: (a) The first was published in Rumania in 1940 and deals with the case of an epileptic mother who wants to interrupt her pregnancy for fear that her child, too, will be epileptic.[135] The author discusses the question of whether epilepsy is hereditary, quotes the Talmud which advises against marrying into a family of epileptics, but dismisses this as meaning merely that that family is unlucky. Then in a reference to world history highly unusual in such a Responsum, he writes:

> For fear of possible, remote danger to a future child, that maybe, God forbid, he will know sickness, how can it occur to anyone to actively kill him because of only a possible doubt? This seems to me very much like the laws of Lycurgus, King of Sparta, according to which every blemished child would be killed . . .
>
> Whatever the author of *Resp. L'vushei Mord'khai* wrote in order to permit an abortion was only because of fear of mental anguish for the mother. But for fear of what *might* be the child's lot—"the secrets of God are none of your business."

(b) Rabbi Unterman's Responsum, discussed above, dealt specifically with the question of rubella (German measles); he rules out an abortion, saying, "We have no law that permits us to deny life to one who is 'wounded.' " [136]
(c) Rabbi Jakobovitz makes a similar point with regard to "thalidomide babies"; since physical or mental defects in no way compromise the claim to life or make a difference in the laws of murder, he writes, it follows that

---

[134] Exceptions to this point, basing the abortion on probable birth defects, appear in two recent works. R. Saul Yisraeli of the Jerusalem Court of Appeals, in *Resp. Amud HaY'mini,* No. 32 (1966), rules that in thalidomide cases abortion is a favor to the potential child as much as a relief for mother's anguish. (Cf. Weinberg, Note 139, below.) Also, R. Eliezer Waldenberg, in *Resp. Tzitz Eliezer,* Vol. IX (1967) permits (No. 51:3:9) abortion to prevent birth of a defective since, simply, no legal bar exists, especially during the early stages.
[135] *Resp. Afr'kasta D'Anya,* No. 169.
[136] *Noam,* VI, p. 9.

no such legal distinction can be made for foeticide either. A fear, however, that continuation of the pregnancy would have "such debilitating effects (psychologically or otherwise)" on the mother would justify abortion.[137] (*d*) Rabbi Zweig's Responsum, quoted frequently herein, also was addressed to the thalidomide question, in the wake of the celebrated Liege trial in his country, in which a Belgian mother who killed her child born with deformities caused by that drug was acquitted. He turns to the question of an abortion in such a case. During the first forty days of pregnancy, there does not seem to be much standing in her way, and he is inclined to permit; after that an abortion is sanctioned only for the health of the mother.[138] (*e*) German measles, once again, is the occasion for still another Responsum on abortion; that of R. Yehiel Weinberg of Montreux, written in 1950 to the Rabbinate of England and published in 1966. There the problem was complicated by the government law requiring abortion in such cases after three months; the doctor who made the inquiry feared the penalties for noncompliance as well. The author has less doubt than our previous one about the first forty days; no prohibition against abortion can be said to exist then. He cites Emden (above) who would permit an abortion at any time during the pregnancy to save the mother pain, and concludes:

> The proofs I have adduced to permit an abortion to save the mother pain are only in accordance with those authorities [*rishonim*] who differ with Maimonides on the matter of "pursuer" ... But since these authorities are *in the majority*, it is possible to permit the abortion as Emden did.[139]

One more citation, actually from a context other than abortion, must be brought here to complete the picture. It comes from R. Moses Sofer (d. 1839), the famous *Hatam Sofer* of Pressburg. The question addressed to him was from a woman who sought to render herself sterile because her childbearing had been unusually painful. His answer is that her husband's permission must be sought; if he refuses, let her go ahead anyway, for she is not so beholden to him that she must undergo unusual pain for his sake. True, she does have a duty to bring forth children but, he says in what can be called characteristic of all of the above, no woman "*is required to build the*

---

[137] *The Jewish Review* (London, 1962), quoted in *Jewish Law Faces Modern Problems* (New York, 1965), pp. 74–76.

[138] *Noam*, VII, *loc. cit.*

[139] *Noam*, IX (1966), 193–215; also published in *S'ridei Esh*, Vol. III (1966), No. 127.

world by destroying herself."[140] This, of course, does not mean that ordinary pain, and certainly not economic or social inconvenience, would come under this manifesto. The Bible prescribes that an offering be brought to the sanctuary by the woman following childbirth (Lev. 12:6). Its purpose, explains the Talmud, is to atone for a vow never meant to be kept:[141] When birth pangs were severe, she presumably vowed "never again"; a while later she would forget that oath; satisfaction had dispelled anxiety.

Abortion, then, for ephemeral pain or for capricious reasons is clearly not intended here; in such cases the legal "warrants" and the extra-legal attitudes of reverence for life play their part. They may even save a woman from herself, so to speak, from sacrificing ultimate blessing to the apprehensions of the moment. Apposite here in a related sense is the narrative in *Sefer Hasidim* about the husband who wanted to avoid another pregnancy for his wife, but when she did give birth and the child took sick, he was beside himself with fear of losing the child.[142] Abortion for less than a serious reason can be a serious mistake, and even the permissive Responsa are weighted with a solemn awareness of the potential life involved. Yet, "the judge can rule only on the evidence before his eyes"[143]—the situation of the woman before him. The Rabbis relied on her maternal instinct and on the safeguards which they instituted; beyond that, their humane compassion for the welfare of the woman, alive and actual, moved them to be guided by the principle, "her pain comes first."[144]

---

[140] *Resp. Hatam Sofer, E.H.*, No. 20.

[141] *TB Niddah* 31b; *Sh'vuot* 8a.

[142] *Sefer Hasidim*, No. 520.

[143] *TB Sanhedrin* 6b.

[144] Another treatment of the subject by R. Jakobovits appeared after the above was written and in press. Entitled "Jewish Views on Abortion," it comprises Ch. 6 of *Abortion and the Law*, edited by David T. Smith (Cleveland: Western Reserve University, 1967). In this article, Dr. Jakobovits takes a severe stance, making no reference to most of the lenient sources presented here. Abortion is to be sanctioned only to save the life—and the health, physical or mental—of the mother. Pregnancy resulting from adultery or incest may not be terminated, because this removes a necessary deterrent to sin; a foetus conceived through rape may also not be aborted, because every foetus, including this one, has a right to be born and society must assume the burden of its care. But R. Jakobovits offers no support from Jewish sources for his argument of "title to life." The rabbinic position is grounded in the mother's welfare, not at all in "title to life" of an unborn foetus. Incidentally, Dr. Kenneth J. Ryan, Professor of Obstetrics and Gynecology at Western Reserve University, contributed Ch. 3 to the aforementioned volume. The substance of his position is that "fetal indications can be a hazardous basis for moral or medical arguments on abortion . . . For this reason, the author favors an abortion law . . . on the premise of protecting the mother's health" (*op. cit.*, pp. 66, 67). This coincides remarkably with the generalization deduced here from rabbinic Responsa.

Part 6

POSTSCRIPT

16

The Jewish View
of Birth Control

"Permitted" or "forbidden" in the final judgment of Jewish law codes tells only a small part of the story of Judaism's attitude towards birth control. Much more significant material for the Jewish philosophy of marriage, sex, and moral decisions emerges from the process of the law, with its discussion of principles and analysis of factors involved.

The law and its rationale are to be found in Talmud and Commentaries, Law Codes and their Commentaries, the mystic literature, moral tracts and, above all, Responsa literature. The latter applies legal theory and principles, blended with practical understanding, to specific questions put to the rabbinic authorities. Coming from diverse countries, cultures, and centuries, this rich literary and human treasure makes a substantial contribution to the development of the law and philosophy of our subject.

Against the backdrop of a culture in which marriage was regarded as a concession to man's weakness and the marital act justified because of its procreative end, the Jewish tradition was nurtured on a radically different set of presuppositions. Marriage is an imperative for human happiness and for the procreation of progeny; it is a mitzvah, a religious duty. Talmud, Midrash, and Zohar celebrate the blessings of marriage in passages of uplifting beauty. An unmarried man is only half a man, abiding without joy, without peace, without good.

The duty of bringing forth progeny is at the core of the mitzvah of marriage. Technically defined as to minimal fulfillment, the duty of procreation is nonetheless an ongoing one, as various legal and extralegal considerations combine to make that minimum largely academic. But another mitzvah, that of sexual responsibility, devolves upon the husband with respect to his wife's other-than-procreational needs. This mitzvah, too, is defined in terms of minimal fulfillment as to frequency and quality, but the legalistic framework is declared an "estimate" of proper fulfillment; the husband must be alert to her mood and gestures beyond the "statutory" requirements as well.

A paradigm in which the above factors are counterpoised with others is the foundation upon which the Jewish view of birth control is built. With marital sex integral to the relational side of marriage—to *sh'lom bayyit*, that is—as well as to the procreational, a threat to the wife's health in connection with pregnancy must be balanced against these factors. If the hazard of pregnancy were to be avoided by sexual abstinence, both purposes or functions of marriage, instead of just one, would be subverted. Where the conception of children must be prevented, it would be wrong to subvert the mitzvah of marital sex as well. Hence, contraception is mandated.

But a fourth factor in the paradigm stands against these three, namely the evil of possible hash-hatat zera, destruction or improper emission of generative seed. Two facets are discernible in the Talmudic, Zoharic, and other pronouncements on the subject: one, that such an act is self-defiling and immoral in and of itself; another, that it destroys would-be life. Since, however, nonprocreative intercourse with barren, sterile, or pregnant women, or with those too young or too old for childbearing, is clearly permissible and at times encouraged, logic dictated that the destruction of would-be life is not the essence of the evil of hash-hatat zera. The evil is in the self-defiling abuse of the generative faculties by improper, nonheterosexual semination. When properly heterosexual, the act has its own self-sufficient value and purpose other than procreation. The burden of condemnation by the mystic and moralistic literatures is directed at the autoerotic rather than the nonproductive, while the halakhic norms yield the same teaching; even the halakhah with regard to deviations from the ordinary manner of coitus seeks to safeguard the heterosexual principle. Within that principle, moreover, a concept evolves whereby the seed itself has the same dual purpose as the sex act; its normal passage through its course is an essential element in the physical gratifications of coition. In accordance with our paradigm, therefore, the method of contraception chosen should be one that avoids palpable hash-hatat zera—from actual coitus interruptus to the use of devices that may be described as tantamount thereto; it should least interfere with the normal processes of the sex act.

The token by which the various contraceptive measures are judged is that of the Talmudic mokh, referred to in a context that allows for multiple interpretation as to both its nature and the circumstances of its legality. Incidental to his analysis of the Talmudic discussion of mokh, R. Solomon Luria offers us a criterion for the integrity of the sex act, which further refines the definition of hash-hatat zera for our paradigm. Not the "natural law" of procreative possibility determines that integrity, but the naturalness of a heterosexual act with its attendant gratifications. The Talmudic phrase he introduces is *guf neheneh min ha-guf*, referring to the mutual physical satisfactions appropriate to the marital act. Whether the mokh usage qualifies, as Luria claimed, or not, his criterion stands. Least interference with the normal course of the act means least diminution of its proper satisfactions.

The elements of sheer drama are to be found in the history of legal rulings on the subject of contraception itself; a drama of legal structure, of literary dependence, of schools of thought evolving because of the availability or nonavailability of crucial literary links in the sturdy chain of Jewish law. The Talmud, which is both the primary legal basis for the Responsa and, at the same time, the final court of appeals for their inherent validity, may actually betray an indifference to the legality of most acts of contraception. Its discussions, however, of coitus interruptus, of irregular practices, of the positive mitzvah of procreation and of onah, and, above all, its references to mokh, have lent themselves to much more cautious interpretation. The mokh baraita is the *locus classicus*, the crucial text that serves as the springboard for volumes of Responsa and their disquisitions on the matter of birth control. While the major law codes before and after Maimonides, but that of Maimonides preeminently, omitted any legislation based on this passage because—as is suggested—they found no legal implications therein at all, his contemporaries in other lands, Rashi and Tosafot, did find such implications. Their Talmudic commentation helped center the discussion of hash-hatat zera on the mokh baraita; and subsequent literature sought to analyze and determine what legal guidance the baraita might yield. Is the baraita proscriptive or prescriptive? Are the Three Women of the baraita being given permission or the obligation to practice contraception; if the first, then it follows that other women generally lack that permission; if the second, this does not yet follow. Is the baraita speaking of, and hence limiting its applicability to, a certain kind of contraceptive usage, such as a precoital absorbent-tampon, which would mean that other devices, less obtrusive or less objectionable for one reason or another, are not included in these restrictive implications? What, in any case, is the extent of these restrictions, seeing that the baraita does concern itself with the avoidance of hazard? Since abstinence in such case is not contemplated, what circumstances of hazard and, in the hierarchy of comparative objectionability, what contraceptive usages are indicated?

Following the first round of debate on these moot questions in the writings of Rashi and Tosafot, a second round was joined by the Rishonim, those master authorities in the earlier days before the Shulhan Arukh. The principle of Avoidance of Hazard was refined by them as the debate itself took on new dimensions. But the ordinarily definitive decisors, Alfasi, Asheri, Maimonides, and the Shulhan Arukh, extracted no law from our baraita, leaving the matter wide open, so to speak, for individual interpretation by later Talmudists and Respondents. They examined cross-Talmudic discussions, analyzed the rulings of the great decisors in related issues, and drew their conclusions. Outstanding among the latter was the verdict of this same R. Solomon Luria who, on the basis of literary and logical analysis, affirmed that the prima facie meaning of the Talmudic source is that no restrictive inference could be made; the Talmud is teaching that the Three Women, or other women in circumstances of hazard, are required to practice contraception even if by precoital mokh—the method generally taken to involve hash-hatat zera—and all other women are free to do so if they choose to. Of course, the mitzvah of p'ru ur'vu must be fulfilled; the permission is expressed with regard to any individual sex act and with regard to this questionable method.

The authority that Luria commanded might have been sufficient to dictate a more lenient trend in subsequent legislation. Instead, his writings were insufficiently available and other commanding authorities were unaware of their existence. Without his permissive lead to guide them, luminaries such as R. Akiva Eger, the Hatam Sofer, and others, analyzed the matter on their own and came to cautious conclusions because "I have seen no precedent authority that permits." Their own influence and prestige being so substantial in Hungary, in Europe, and in the Jewish world generally, a nonpermissive school arose that inspired such statements as "How can I permit, seeing that Eger and Sofer have forbidden?" With the discovery of Luria's bold analysis, based as it was on both precedent and logic, such statements began to give way to others, as "Had Eger and Sofer seen what Luria wrote, they never would have forbidden."

Some striking generalizations are nevertheless available to us on the basis of the Responsa as they now stand. Even the nonpermissivists would agree to the conclusions about the mitzvah of marital sex and that its preservation is as important as the avoidance of possible hash-hatat zera. They would join in the unanimous affirmation that abstinence is not an admissible alternative and, with methods that avoid the questionable properties of mokh, such as, for example, an oral contraceptive, the lenient school would find the others in agreement about the legitimacy of contraception—in keeping, that is, with the general imperative of p'ru ur'vu.

Having said this much in recapitulation of what emerges from the foregoing chapters, some additional reflections, which were left for now, may herewith be essayed.

The notion that the Jewish view of birth control is determined by economic-historic factors, that leniency or restrictiveness depended upon external environmental causes, finds no support at all in the pages of this literature. The only history at work here is literary history and, if you will, underlying spiritual determinants. The Rabbis consulted legal precedent and found it applicable or not; they were in possession of lenient precedents, such as those of Luria, or of nonpermissive ones, such as those of Eger and Sofer. Onto this framework was added another literary-historic determinant: that of the Zohar and its spiritual descendants, with their conscious or unconscious influence upon the Respondent. As to external or environmental factors, the Responsa seem to take cognizance of them by ruling in spite of them.

The matter of avoidance of physical hazard is much more significant than would appear at first glance. Once again, comparison with the Christian exegetical tradition helps us understand. Whereas the mandate for therapeutic contraception is the one universal and unanimous principle in the many-faceted discussion of birth control in Talmud, Codes, Commentaries, and Responsa, the opposite is true in classic Catholic legislation. Prof. Noonan's exhaustive survey of the history of the Church's rulings on contraception shows only two instances wherein the question of therapeutic contraception was posed, one in the twelfth century[1] and the other in the seventeenth century: Is contraception permissible when the woman's life is at stake? The answer in both cases is "no." Paul Laymann, an authoritative Jesuit moralist of the seventeenth century, explains: "If in some cases such permission to prevent conception were given to women, it would be wonderfully abused with great loss to human generation."[2] This point of view, of course, follows logically from Catholic premises concerning marriage, the function of sexual relations, and the licitness of contraception to begin with. In the Jewish system, the values of marriage and marital sex are on an entirely different plane, although the horror of hash-hatat zera is no trifling matter. True, martyrdom is

---

[1] Noonan, *op. cit.*, p. 177: Peter Cantor, 12th-century theologian, ruled that it is "prohibited in every case."

[2] *Ibid.*, p. 370.

asked of the Jews by their Rabbis rather than the transgression of the three cardinal sins: murder, adultery, and idolatry. Short of that, the operative principle is "nothing stands higher than saving life [or health]." To those who saw no hash-hatat zera to be involved at all because it was "nullified" by the context of proper marital relations, the principle of *sakkanah* or *pikkuah nefesh* [danger to health] did not even have to be invoked. The authorities who did invoke it, however, are making a significant point: As morally questionable as contraception may be, *pikkuah nefesh* determines not that abstinence be resorted to, but that these inhibitions be set aside. This speaks volumes for the value system.

Yet, this same matter requires another moment of reflection. After all, one Mishnah speaks of the "sins for which women die in childbirth," and the Talmud explains the phrase as taking cognizance of the fact that childbirth is a time of danger.[3] If a woman is lacking in merit and is doomed to die for her sins, childbirth is the precarious—or logical—moment for her fate to overtake her. Theologically speaking, then, a kind of humble resignation to fate should have been the case; yet, as in so many other areas, the Rabbis legislated with a this-worldly humaneness. The "curse of Eve" beset women with the pain of childbirth; when anesthesia became available, however, the Rabbis did not hesitate to recommend it. "In pain shalt thou give birth" is a curse for Eve, but not a commandment to be implemented by her descendants. The tradition of humaneness and compassion for "that poor woman" motivated the entire thrust of Jewish law on birth control and, as we have amply seen in the last chapter, on the perplexing question of abortion as well. The Rabbis seem, in fact to betray a discernible prejudice in favor of the woman, affirming the principle that consideration of "her pain comes first" and seeking whatever legal leniencies they can muster on her behalf.

While the Catholic and Jewish traditions part company in this complex of value judgments, with contrasting doctrines resulting in contrasting legislation, the two traditions heartily agree on one relevant aspect. A corollary of the halakhic principle of avoidance of hazard is that of the economic factor. The question must arise: If physical risk is to be eschewed, if a duty exists to take whatever means are necessary to avoid physical hazard, then why not to avoid financial risk as well? If support of another child will incur a hardship—a severe hardship, let us say, not just an ordinary one—do not the same principles of attention to self and its legitimate interests come into operation? This question is answered with the same unanimity of legal opinion, but in the opposite direction: The economic factor is simply not admissible!

[3] *TB Shabbat* 32a.

Precaution against physical threat is a mitzvah; as to financial exigency, the very idea of allowing it to figure in considerations of birth control seems unworthy. True, the contraceptive methods available to those who sought rulings from the writers of Responsa were questionable from the standpoint of Jewish law and tradition; the motive for birth control had to be good enough to overcome these legal inhibitions. With methods now available that do not entail a technical violation, and with the acknowledgment of Luria's authority, the matter of method will cease to be the obstacle it has been. But even before the Pill entered the picture, the classic Respondents, finding a particular method unobjectionable in itself, would make it clear that the permissive ruling was being granted because physical danger was involved. One is not to take advantage of this sanction, they would say, in order to be spared the inconveniences of child-rearing or the difficulties of economic hardship. [4] Here the Jewish and Christian spiritual traditions meet: both would underwrite the essential religious message implied thereby, that material considerations are highly improper in connection with something as spiritual and selfless as the bearing and raising of children. In the words of Talmud and Midrash, man in this world is a "revolving wheel, being rich today and poor tomorrow, or poor today and rich tomorrow." [5] The human experience of procreation, with its responsibilities discharged, its personal fulfillment, and the special joys inherent in parenthood are just not to be reckoned by the coin of material circumstance. And, since the vast majority of the relevant Responsa come from times and places where poverty was the rule, and affluence or much less than that was the exception, this value judgment is all the more eloquent. Admittedly, the Jewish community was so structured as to provide charitable assistance when necessary; the Talmudic concern with proper nourishment for the suckling child argued a responsible realism. But much more pertinent is the fact that the "wantedness" of the child was greater than the desire for—and hence compensated for the lack of—material comfort. Transcending, then, the legalities of "permitted" and "forbidden," the collective voice of the Responsa speaks with

---

[4] *Resp. L'vushei Mord'khai,* No. 28: "But for those who would do so without reason, just because it is better for them without children, or because they lack faith, or have worries of support, Heaven forbid that they should be permitted," etc.

Resp. Yaskil Avdi, Vol. II, No. 6: "Where there is no fear of physical danger, just to avoid poverty, all would agree that it is not permitted."

An exception is R. Sinai Schiffer of Karlsruh, in his *Resp. Sitri UMagini,* No. 44. The very wording is out of keeping with the rest of the Responsa: He speaks of those who "don't want to worry that they might have more children" and proceeds to apply the leniencies that derive from logical interpretation of the baraita.

[5] *TB Shabbat* 151b; *Exodus Rabbah* 31, 4 and 14.

unmistakeable clarity in setting guidelines for moral decision in these matters. It offers another paradigm, as it were, for balancing the material, spiritual, personal, and social considerations.

The component parts of our paradigm do shift and realign themselves by virtue of the Pill, if not in acknowledgment of Luria's reading. With the heterosexual essence of conjugality declared intact, any given contraceptive act is relieved of its erstwhile odium. Not that the shift calls for a betrayal of the above guidelines, according to which communal responsibility or the burden and joys of parenthood dare not be subordinated to material consider-ations. It does, however, allow for "family planning" in a manner consistent with the mitzvah of p'ru ur'vu as an ideal and as a programme. As marriage may be postponed for practical or romantic reasons while p'ru ur'vu yet awaits its fulfillment, [6] so may other considerations within marriage defer, but not subvert, the completion of this mitzvah. While no justification for momentary postponement is actually required according to this point of view, the monetary factor remains least worthy as a reason for doing so, while other factors, such as sh'lom bayyit and the like, stand as high as p'ru ur'vu itself—as no less a mitzvah, no less a spiritual value.

It must be repeated here that the "population explosion" has nothing to do with the Responsa, and vice versa. The Rabbis were issuing their analyses and their replies to a specific couple with a specific query. These couples were never in a situation where they might aggravate a world problem; on the contrary, the Jewish community was very often in a position of seeking to replenish its depleted ranks after pogrom or exile. It is very much in such a position today. As to the problem of the world at large, we might imagine that the advice of the classic Rabbis, if it were solicited, would read some-thing like the following: Personal morality and the holiness of the individual human being demand that sexuality not be abused; that man's heterosexual nature be preserved and properly expressed. Moreover, a this-wordly spiritual orientation requires the application of both idealism and enlightened respon-sibility. It would be just as recklessly self-indulgent to overbreed as to refrain from procreation, especially if steps are not taken to provide for the proper nurture of the posterity to whom we give life. But self-indulgence in the opposite direction is the target of rabbinic efforts at hallowing life. This sacred goal they pursued through the spiritual-moral disciplines embodied in the legal tradition.

[6] See Ch. 2, Note 35.

Bibliography

PRIMARY HEBREW SOURCES

The principal texts are followed by the Commentaries thereon, which are indented and listed chronologically.

BIBLE AND COMMENTARIES

Mikraot G'dolot. New York: Pardes Publishing Co., 1951. (Hebrew text of the Bible, with Targum and Commentaries of Rashi, Ibn Ezra, and Ramban, identified below, printed alongside on the page.)
    Saadiah Gaon (d. 942). *Perush RaSaG al HaTorah*. Edited by J. Kapah. Jerusalem: Mosad Kook, 1962.
    Rashi (R. Solomon Yitzhaki, d. 1105).
    Abraham ibn Ezra (d. 1167). Also in ed. Mantoba, 1559.
    Rashbam (R. Samuel ben Meir, d. 1174). Breslau, 1881.
    Yosef B'khor Shor (fl. 12th century). Jerusalem: Kiryat Sefer, 1957.
    Abraham ben HaRambam (d. 1237). *Perush L'Sefer Breshit Ush'mot*. London: Sasson, 1958.
    Moshav Z'kenim (of *Ba'alei HaTosafot*, 13th century). London: Sasson, 1959.
    Ramban (R. Moses ben Nahman, Nahmanides, d. 1270). Also in edition of C. Chavel. Jerusalem: Mosad Kook, 1962.
    Joshua ibn Shuaib (early 14th century). *D'rashot al HaTorah*. Cracow, 1778.
    Bahyah ben Asher (d. 1340). *Midrash Rabbenu Bahya al HaTorah*. Amsterdam, 1746.
    Samuel ibn Seneh (d. 1343). *M'kor Hayyim*. Mantoba, 1559.
    Jacob ben Asher (d. 1343). *Perush al HaTorah*. New York, 1956.
    ———. *Ba'al HaTurim*. In many editions of the Bible by Hebrew Publishing Co., New York.
    Ralbag (Levi ben Gerson, d. 1344). *Perush al HaTorah derekh Beur*. Venice, 1547.
    Isaac Aboab (d. 1492). *Ramban im Perush Isaac Aboab al Perusho*. Venice, 1548.

Isaac Arama (d. 1493). *Akedat Yitzhak*. Jerusalem: HaIvri, 1961.
Isaac Abravanel (d. 1508). *Abravanel al HaTorah*. Amsterdam, 1768.
Elijah Mizrachi (d. 1526). *Mizrachi al HaTorah*. Jerusalem: Horeb, 1950.
Moses Alsheikh (d. 1600). *Rom'mot El*. Zalkva, 1764.
Loew of Prague (d. 1609). *Gur Aryeh*. Printed with *Mizrachi al HaTorah*.
Hayyim Yosef David Azulai (d. 1806). *Homat Anakh*. New York: Feldheim, 1960.
Samuel David Luzzato (d. 1865). *Perush ShaDaL*, Tel Aviv: Dvir, 1965.
Meir Leib ben Y'hiel Michael (d. 1879). *Malbim*. Vilna, 1922.
Naftali Tz'vi Y'hudah Berlin (Ntziv, d. 1893). *Ha'amek Davar*. Tel Aviv: Dvir, 1961.
David Hofmann (d. 1921). *Sefer Vayyikra*. Jerusalem: Mosad Kook, 1953.
Barukh HaLevi Epstein (d. 1942). *Torah T'mimah*. New York: Hebrew Publishing Co., 1925.
Menahem M. Kasher. *Torah Sh'lemah*. Jerusalem: Torah Sh'lemah Institute, 1938.
Meir Me'iri. *Torah Me'irah*. I. London, 1948.

TARGUM, MIDRASHIM

Targum (Onkelos, 2nd century, Aramaic translation—paraphrase of Bible). *Mikraot G'dolot*.
Targum Jonathan (c. 7th century). *Mikraot G'dolot*.
Midrash Rabbah. Vilna: Romm, 1921.
    Matt'not K'hunah. Issakhar ben Naftali HaKohen (16th century).
    Perush Maharzu. Z'ev Wolf Einhorn (19th century).
Tanhuma. Berlin: Horeb, 1927.
Mekhilta. Edited by Lauterbach. Philadelphia: Jewish Publication Society of America, 1949.
Sifrei Zutta. Edited by S. Horowitz, Breslau, 1917.
Midrash HaGadol. Edited by Margaliot. Jerusalem: Mosad HaRav Kook, 1947.
Midrash Lekah Tov. Vilna: Romm, 1880.
Midrash Sekhel Tov. Edited by S. Buber. Berlin, 1900.
Midrash Shoher Tov. Warsaw, 1893.
Mishnat Rabbi Eliezer. Edited by H. Enelow. New York: Bloch, 1934.
Tanna d'vei Eliyahu. Edited by M. Friedmann. Vienna, 1902.
Yalkut. Vilna, 1898.
Midrash Aggadah. Edited by S. Buber. Berlin, 1910.
Pirkei Rabbi Eliezer. Venice, 1608.

TALMUD AND COMMENTARIES, INCLUDING VOLUMES OF NOVELLAE

Mishnah. New York: Pardes Publishing Co., 1963.
    Commentary to the Mishnah. Moses ben Maimon (Maimonides, d. 1204). In *Babylonian Talmud*.
    Tos'fot Yom Tov. Yom Tov Lippman Heller (d. 1654).
    Tos'fot R. Akiva Eger (d. 1837).
    Tiferet Yisrael. Israel Lipschutz (d. 1860).
Tosefta. Printed with Code of *Alfasi*. Vilna: Romm, 1911.
    Glosses of R. Elijah Gaon (d. 1797).
    Minhat Bikkurim. Samuel Avigdor of Slonimo.
    Tosefet Rishonim. Saul Lieberman. Jerusalem: Bamberger and Wahrmann, 1937–39.
    Hazon Y'hezkel. Y'hezkel Abramsky. Jerusalem: Mosad Kook, 1944.
Babylonian Talmud. Vilna: Romm, 1895.
    Rishonim [Early Authorities].
        Rashi (see above). Printed in all editions of the Talmud.
        Tosafot (of various Franco–German Talmudists of the 12th–13th centuries). Printed in all editions of the Talmud.
        Sefer HaYashar. Rabbenu (Ya'akov) Tam (d. 1171). Edited by Schlesinger. Jerusalem: Kiryat Sefer, 1959.

Perush L'Massekhet Kallah Rabbati. Abraham ben Nathan HaYarhi (12th–13th centuries). Edited by Toledano. Tiberias, 1906.

Yad Ramah. Meir Abulafia (d. 1244). To *Sanhedrin.* Salonica, 1798.

Tos'fot RiD. Isaiah da Trani (13th century). To *Y'vamot.* Jerusalem: Zuckerman, 1931.

Perush Avraham Min HaHar. Abraham of Montpelier. To *Y'vamot.* Edited by Blau. New York, 1962.

Beit HaB'hirah. Menahem HaMe'iri of Perpignan (d. 1306). New York, 1930.

Hiddushim [Novellae] of 13th–14th century Spanish Talmudists.

    Ramban (see above). Jerusalem, 1928.

    Rashba (R. Solomon ben Adret, d. 1310). Warsaw, 1902.

    Ritva (R. Yom Tov ben Abraham Ishbili, d. 1340). Warsaw, 1902.

    RaN (R. Nissim Gerondi, d. 1380). New York: Feldheim, 1946.

    RaH (R. Aaron HaLevi, 14th century).

    Others cited in *Shittah M'kubetzet,* below.

Tos'fei HaRosh, Tos'fot HaRosh. Asher ben Y'hiel (d. 1327). To *Y'vamot* and *K'tubot,* Leghorn, 1776; to *Niddah,* in later editions of the Talmud.

Aharonim [Later Authorities]

    Maharsha. Samuel Edels (d. 1631). *Hiddushei Halakhot Va'Agaddot.*

    P'nei Y'hoshua. Jacob Joshua Falk (d. 1756). Lemberg: Grossman, 1809.

    Glosses of Ya'avetz. Jacob Emden (d. 1776).

    Sefer Hafla'ah. Pinhas HaLevi Hurwitz (d. 1802). Lemberg: Grossman, 1816.

    Petah Einayim. Azulai (see above). To *Niddah.* Jerusalem: Weinberger, 1961.

    Glosses of Maharatz Chayyes. Zvi Hirsch Chajes (d. 1855).

    Turei Even. R. Aryeh Leib HaKohen (d. 1785). To *M'gillah.* Metz, 1781.

    Yashresh Ya'akov. Solomon Drimmer (19th century). Lemberg, 1863.

    Arukh L'Ner. Jacob Ettlinger (d. 1871). To *Y'vamot,* Pietrkov: Zederbaum, 1914; to *Niddah,* 1924.

    Hina V'Hisda. Isaac ben Sh'lomoh Ardit. To *K'tubot.* Izmir, 1873.

    Elazar Mosheh Hurwitz (19th century). In *K'vutzei M'far'shei HaShas.* No title page.

    Me'lo HaRo'im. Jacob Zvi Jalisch. Warsaw, 1911.

Palestinian Talmud. Vilna: Romm, 1922.

    P'nei Mosheh. Moses Margolis (18th century).

    Korban HaEdah. David Fraenkel (18th century).

CODES AND COMMENTARIES

Sh'iltot d'Rav Ahai Gaon (d. 670). Vilna: Romm, 1861.

    Sh'elat Shalom. Isaiah Berlin (d. 1799).

    Ha'amek Sh'alah (N'tziv, see above).

Halakhot G'dolot. Simon Kaira (9th century). Edited by Hildesheimer. Berlin, 1892.

Sefer HaMitzvot L'RaSaG. Saadia Gaon (d. 942). Warsaw, 1914.

    Beur. Yeruham Perla.

Alfasi. Issac Al–Fasi (d. 1103). Vilna: Romm, 1911.

    RaN (see above).

    Nimmukei Yosef. Joseph Habib.

    Shiltei HaGibborim. Joshua Boaz (d. 1557).

Even HaEzer. Eliezer ben Nathan (d. 1165). Prague, 1610.

Sefer HaMitzvot LaRambam. Maimonides (see above). Lemberg, 1860.

Mishneh Torah (or *Yad HaHazakah*). Maimonides. Vilna: Rosencrantz, 1900.

    Hassagot of Ravad. Abraham ben David (d. 1198).

    Hagahot Maimuni. Meir HaKohen (13th century).

    Maggid Mishneh. Vidal of Tolosa (14th century).

    Kesef Mishneh. Joseph Karo (d. 1575).

    Kiryat Sefer. Moses ben Yosef Trani (d. 1580). Venice, 1553.

    Lehem Mishneh. Abraham di Boton (d. 1609).

Mishneh LaMelekh. Judah Rozanes (d.1729).

Sha'ar HaMelekh. Isaac Belmonti (d. 1774). Salonica, 1771.

Emek HaMelekh (early 19th century). Lemberg, 1808.

Hiddushei R. Hayyim HaLevi. Hayyim Soloveitchik (d. 1918). Vilna: Grossberg, 1920.

Even HaAzel. Issar Zalman Meltzer (d. 1953). Jerusalem: Halvri, 1934.

Sefer HaT'rumah. Barukh of Worms (d. circa 1250). Venice, 1523.

Or Zarua. Isaac of Vienna (d.1260). Zhitomir, 1862.

Torat HaAdam. Nahmanides (see above). Warsaw, 1840.

Mord'khai. Mordecai ben Hillel (d. 1298). Printed with *Alfasi.*

Torat HaBayit. Rashba (see above). Vienna, 1811.

Sefer Mitzvot Gadol. Moses of Coucy. Venice, 1522.

Sefer Mitzvot Katan. Isaac of Corbeil. Ladi, 1805.

Asheri. Asher ben Yehiel (d. 1327). Printed with Babylonian Talmud.

    Kitzur Pis'kei HaRosh. Jacob ben Asher (see *Tur,* below).

    Korban N'tanel. Nethaniel Weill (18th century).

    Ma'adanei Melekh. Yom Tov Lippman Heller (d. 1654). Printed with text in many editions.

    Lehem Hamudot. See *Ma'adanei Melekh.*

    Hagahot HaBaH. Joel Sirkes (d. 1640).

Sefer Adam V'Havvah. Yeruham ben Meshullam (d. 1340). Venice, 1553.

Sefer HaHinnukh. Attributed to R. Aaron HaLevi of the 14th century. Vilna, 1912.

    Minhat Hinnukh. Joseph Babad (d. 1874).

Kol Bo. Author uncertain (14th century). Fiorda, 1782.

Tur (Arba'ah Turim). Jacob ben Asher (d. 1343). Vilna, 1900.

    Beit Yosef (and *Bedek HaBayit*). Joseph Karo (d. 1575).

    Dar'khei Mosheh. Moses Isserles (d. 1572).

    D'rishah and *P'rishah (Beit Yisrael).* Joshua Falk (d. 1614).

    Bayit Hadash (BaH). Joel Sirkes (d. 1640).

    K'neset HaG'dolah (on *Tur* and *Beit Yosef*). Hayyim Benveniste. Izmir, 1731.

Sefer Abudraham. David Abudraham (d. 1345). Amsterdam, 1726.

Agudah. Alexander Susslein (d. 1349). Cracow, 1571.

Sefer (Likkutei) Maharil. Jacob HaLevi Moelln (d. 1427). Lvov, 1860.

The *Shulhan Arukh.* Joseph ben Ephraim Karo (d. 1575). Vilna: Romm, 1911.

    Glosses of RaMA. Moses Isserles (see *Tur* above).

    Erekh Lehem. Jacob Castro (d. 1610). Constantina, 1718.

    Be'er HaGolah. Moses Rivkes (d. 1671).

    Magen Avraham. Abraham Gumbiner (d. 1683).

    Sefer Me'irat Einayim. Joshua Falk (see *Tur,* above).

    ShaKH (Sif'tei Kohen). Shabb'tai HaKohen (d. 1662).

    TaZ (Turei Zahav). David HaLevi (d. 1667).

    Beit Sh'muel. Samuel ben Uri (d. 1698).

    Elyah Rabbah. Composed primarily as a commentary on the *L'vush* below. Elijah Shapiro (d. 1712). Sulzbach, 1757.

    Beit Meir. Meir Posner (18th century). Lemberg, 1836.

    Bir'khei Yosef. Azulai (see above). Vienna, 1860.

    Beur HaGRA. Elijah Gaon (d. 1797).

    K'reti Uf'leti. Jonathan Eyebeschuetz (d. 1767). Lemberg, 1860.

    Yad Aharon. Primarily on *Tur* and *Beit Yosef.* Aaron Al-Fandari (d. 1774). Salonica, 1755.

    Mor Uk'tziah. Jacob Emden (d. 1776). Altona, 1768.

    P'ri M'gadim (Mishb'tzot Zahav and *Eshel Avraham*). Joseph Teomim (late 18th century).

    Atzei Arazim. Noah Hayyim Zvi Berlin (18th century). Fiorda, 1790.

    Appei Zutrei. Jacob Pardo (late 18th century). Venice, 1798.

    Beit Mosheh. Moses Epstein (19th century). Zamosch, 1848.

    Yad Efrayim. Ephraim Zalman Margoliot (d. 1828). Printed with his *Tiv Gittin.* Vilna, 1849.

    Pit'hei T'shuvah. Abraham Zvi Eisenstadt (d. 1868).

Ezer MiKodesh. Abraham David of Buczacz (19th century).
Y'shuot Ya'akov. Jacob Orenstein (d. 1839). Zalkva, 1809.
Av'nei HaEfod. David Pipano (d. 1912). Sophia, 1912.
Hazon Ish. Isaiah Karelitz (d. 1953). B'nai B'rak, 1958
Yam Shel Sh'lomoh. Solomon Luria (d. 1573). To *Bava Kamma*, Prague, 1715; to *Y'vamot*, Altona, 1739.
L'vush(im). Mordecai Jaffe (d. 1612). Venice, 1620.
Shulhan Arukh HaRav. Shneur Zalman of Ladi (d. 1812). Zhitomir, 1847.
Hokhmat Adam. Abraham Danzig (d. 1820). Warsaw, 1908.
Kitzur Shulhan Arukh. Solomon Ganzfried (d. 1886). Leipzig, 1933.
Arokh HaShulhan. Yehiel Michael Epstein (d. 1908). Warsaw, 1900–12.

EXTRALEGAL LITERATURE: MORALISTIC, PHILOSOPHIC, AND MYSTIC

Ba'alei HaNefesh. (Ravad; see Mishneh Torah above). *Sha'ar HaK'dushah.* Jerusalem: Masorah, 1955.
Ben Yohai. Moses Konitz. Vienna, 1815.
Emek B'rakhah. Abraham HaLevi Hurwitz. Sedilkov, 1834.
Emunot V'Deot. Saadiah Gaon (d. 942). Edited by Judah ibn Tibbon. Constantinople, 1562.
HaZera L'Minehu. H.L. Zuta. Jerusalem, 1909.
Huppat Hatanim. Raphael Meldola. Venice, 1737.
Iggeret HaKodesh. Ascribed to Nahmanides. Bound with *Ba'alei HaNefesh.*
Magen Avot. Simon ben Tzemah Duran (d. 1444). Leghorn, 1785. This served as a long introduction to his briefer *Magen Avot* on *Pirkei Avot,* Leghorn, 1763.
Menorat HaMaor. Isaac Al Nakawa (d. 1391). Edited by H. G. Enelow. New York: Bloch, 1932.
Menorat HaMaor. Isaac Aboab (d. 1492). Jerusalem: Mosad Kook, 1961.
Midrash Talpiyyot. Elijah HaKohen of Izmir (d. 1729). Smyrna, 1736.
Mitpahat S'farim. Jacob Emden. Altona, 1786.
Moreh N'vukhim. Maimonides. Warsaw, 1872.
Reshit Hokhmah. Elijah de Vidas. Vilna, 1900.
Sefer HaB'rit. Pinhas Elijah ben Meir. Bruen, 1797.
Sefer Harédim. Elazar Azkari. Venice, 1601.
Sefer Hasidim. Judah HeHasid. Edited by Reuben Margoliot. Jerusalem: Mosad Kook, 1964.
    M'Kor Hesed. Reuben Margoliot.
Sha'arei T'shuvah L'Rabbenu Yonah. Yonah HeHasid of Gerona. Jerusalem, 1961.
Sh'nei Luhot HaB'rit. Isaiah Hurwitz (d. 1626). Fuerth, 1764.
Siddur Beit Ya'akov. Jacob Emden. Zhitomir, 1880.
Tokhahat Hayyim. Hayyim Pallagi (d. 1869). Salonica, 1873.
Tola'at Ya'akov. Meir ibn Gabbai. Constantina, 1560.
Y'sod Yosef. Yosef HaDarshan. Frankfurt am Oder, 1679.
Zera Kodesh. Moses Prager. Fiorda, 1696.
Zohar. 5 vols. Edited by Reuben Margoliot. Jerusalem: Mosad HaRav Kook, 1960.
    Nitzoztzei Zohar. Reuben Margoliot.

RESPONSA

Rishonim
    Hai Gaon. In *T'shuvot HaGeonim,* Edited by Harkavy, 1887, 1949.
    T'shuvot HaRambam. Edited by Freimann. Jerusalem: 1934.
    T'shuvot HaRashba (see Ben Adret above). Several editions.
    T'shuvot HaRosh. Asher ben Yehiel. Zalkva, 1803.
    Rivash. Isaac Bar Sheshet (Barfat, d. 1408) Lemberg, 1805.
    Tashbatz. Simon ben Tzemah Duran (d. 1444). Amsterdam, 1739.
    Mahari Mintz. Judah Menz (d. 1509). Fiorda, 1766.
    Binyamin Ze'ev. Binyamin ben Mattityahu (d. 1540). Venice, 1539.

Oholei Tam. Tam ibn Yahya (d. 1542). Printed in *Tumat Y'sharim.* Venice, 1622.
Responsa of Joseph Karo (d. 1575). Salonica, 1598.

Aharonim
    Admat HaKodesh. Moses Mizrahi. Constantina, 1742.
    Afarkasta D'anya. David Sperber. Satmar, 1940.
    Ahiezer. Hayyim Ozer Grodzensky. I, Vilna, 1922; III, New York, 1946.
    Alehu Ra'anan. Isaac Silverberg. Warsaw, 1936.
    Akiva Eger. New York, 1945.
    Ani Ben Pehama. Israel Kuperstok. Jerusalem, 1928.
    Arugat HaBosem. Moses Grunwald. Szolyva, 1912.
    Aryeh D'vei Ilai. Aryeh Lifschultz. Vishnitz, 1850.
    Ateret Hakhamim. Barukh Teomim Frankel. Josephov, 1886.
    Av'nei Nezer. Abraham Bornstein of Sochachev. Pietrkov, 1926.
    Av'nei Tzedek. Yekuthiel Teitelbaum. Sziget, 1886.
    Avodat HaShem. Samuel Matalon. Salonica, 1893.
    Be'er Mosheh. Moses Danishevsky. Slabodka, 1905.
    Be'er Sh'muel. Samuel Rosenberg. Cracow, 1923.
    Beit Av. Abraham Yudelovich. VII, New York, 1920.
    Beit HaYotzer, Yoel Tzvi Roth. Muncacz, 1896.
    Beit Shelomoh. Solomon Drimmer. Lemberg, 1878.
    Beit Ya'akov. Jacob ben Samuel. Dyrenfuerth, 1696.
    Beit Y'hudah. Judah Ayyas. Leghorn, 1746.
    Beit Yisrael. Israel Landau. Buenos Aires, 1954.
    Beit Yitzhak. Isaac Schmelkes. Premszl, 1875.
    Big'dei K'hunah. Meshullam HaKohen. Fiorda, 1807.
    Bikkurei Y'hudah. Judah Don Yahya. II, Tel Aviv, 1939.
    Binyan David. David Meislich. Ohel, 1935.
    Binyan Tziyyon. Jacob Ettlinger. Altona, 1868.
    Da'at Sofer. Akiva Sofer. Jerusalem, 1965.
    Damesek Eliezer. Abraham Perlmutter. Pietrkov, 1905.
    Div'rei Malkiel. Malkiel Tanenbaum. Vilna, 1901.
    Div'rei Yissakhar. Yissakhar Berish. Pietrkov, 1910.
    Dovev Meisharim. Dov Weidenfeld. Jerusalem, 1956.
    D'var Eliyahu. Elijah Klatzkin. Lublin, 1915.
    Emek Halakhah. Y'hoshua Baumol. New York, 1934.
    Emek Sh'elah. Mordecai Twersky. Horonostopol, 1906.
    Emunat Sh'muel. Aaron Ben Sh'muel Kaidonover. Lemberg, 1884.
    Ezrat Nashim. Meir Me'iri (Feuchtwanger). III, London, 1955.
    Geonim V'radim (a collection). Turka, 1764.
    Ginnat V'radim. Abraham ben Mordecai. Constantinople, 1717.
    Hatam Sofer. Moses Schreiber (Sofer). Vienna, 1855.
    Havatzelet HaSharon. David Menahem Mannes Babad. Bilgoray, 1931.
    Havvot Yair. Yair Bachrach. Lemberg, 1896.
    Hayyim V'Shalom. Hayyim Pallagi. Izmir, 1862.
    Hazon Nahum. Nahum Weidenfeld. New York, 1951.
    Hedvat Ya'akov. Tzvi Meislich. Second series, Pietrkov, 1919.
    Heikhal Yitzhak. Isaac HaLevi Herzog, II, Jerusalem, 1967.
    Helkat Ya'akov. Mordecai Breisch. II, London, 1959; III, Bnei Brak, 1966.
    Hemdat Sh'lomoh. Solomon Lifschutz. Warsaw, 1836.
    Heshev HaEfod. Hanokh Padwa. Jerusalem, 1963.
    Hinnukh Beit Yitzhak. Isaac Glueck. St. Peter, 1870.
    Hit'or'rut T'shuvah. Simon Eger–Sofer. Muncacz, 1912.
    Igg'rot Mosheh. Mosheh Feinstein. E. H. II, New York, 1961; E. H. and O. H., New York, 1961.
    Im'rei Esh. Meir Eisenstadt. Lemberg, 1852.
    Im'rei Binah. Meir Auerbach. Jerusalem, 1869.

Im'rei Shefer. Elijah Klatzkin. Muncacz, 1913.
Im'rei Yosher. Meir Arik. Bucacz, 1925.
Kiryat Hanah David. David Sekli. Jerusalem, 1935.
K'tav Sofer. Abraham Sofer. Pressburg, 1873.
Koah Shor. Isaac Schorr. Kolomea, 1888.
L'vushei Mord'khai. Mordecai Winkler. First series, Mad, 1913; Second series, Budapest, 1922.
Ma'ar'khei Lev. Judah Leib Zirelsohn. Kishinev, 1932.
Mahaneh Hayyim. Hayyim Sofer. Pressburg, 1882.
Maharam Brisk. Mordecai Brisk. Tashnad, 1939.
Maharam Rotenberg. Meir of Rothenberg. Berlin, 1891.
Maharam Schick. Moses Schick. Muncacz, 1881.
Maharash Engel. Samuel Engel. I–VII. Bardiov, 1926 and on.
Maharit. Joseph of Trani. Lemberg, 1861.
Maharitz. Joseph Tzvi Dushinsky. Jerusalem, 1956.
Maharsham. Sholom Mordecai Schwadron. I, Warsaw, 1902; III, Brezany, 1910; IV, Pietrkov, 1917.
Maharya. Judah Assad (*Y'hudah Ya'aleh*). Pressburg, 1880.
Mar'eh Y'hezkel. Ezekiel Panet. Sziget, 1875.
Marheshet. Hanokh Agus. II, New York, no date.
Matteh Levi. Mordecai Horowitz. II, Frankfurt am Main, 1932.
Me'il Tz'dakah. Jonah Landsofer. Sedilkov, 1835.
Meshiv Davar. Naftali Tzvi Berlin. Warsaw, 1894.
M'lammed L'Ho'il. David Hofmann. Frankfurt, 1932.
M'shivat Nefesh. Aryeh Leib Plotzker. Warsaw, 1849.
Mima'amakim. Ephraim Oshry. II, New York, 1959.
Minhat HaKometz. Klonymos Zuckerman. Kolomea, 1937.
Minhat Y'hiel. Alter Nebenzahl. II, Stanislav, 1936.
Minhat Yitzhak, Isaac Weisz. London, 1955.
Mishp'tei Uziel. Benzion Uziel. Tel Aviv, 1935.
Naharei Afars'mon. Jacob Tannenbaum. First series, Putnok, 1898; Second series, Muncacz, 1901.
Neta Sorek. Shraga Tannebaum. Tchatèh, 1897.
Netzer Matta'ai. Nathan Friedmann. B'nei Brak, 1957.
Noda Biy'hudah. Ezekiel Landau. Vilna, 1904.
Ohel Avraham. Abraham Karpeles (containing the Responsa of many others, in a kind of symposium).
Or Gadol. Y'ruham Perilman. Vilna, 1924.
Or Yisrael. Israel Lipschutz. Cleves, 1770.
Panim Me'irot. Meir Ashkenazi. III, Sulzbach, 1738.
P'kudat Elazar. Elazar Lev. Satmar, 1931.
P'nei Y'hoshua, Joshua of Cracow. Lemberg, 1860.
P'ri HaAretz. Israel Meir Mizrahi. Constantinople, 1721.
P'ri HaEtz UMinhat Y'hiel. Alter Nebenzahl. IV, Stanislav, 1928.
P'ri HaSadeh. Eliezer Deutsch. Pacz, 1906.
Rav P'alim. Yosef Hayyim Ben Eliyahu. Jerusalem, 1905.
Rosh Mashbir. Joseph Modena. Salonica, 1840.
Sha'arei Deah. Hayyim Yehudah Leib. Lemberg, 1878.
Sh'elat Ya'avetz. Jacob Emden. Altona, 1739.
Sh'elat Yitzhak. Isaac Oelbaum. Prague, 1931.
Shem MiShim'on. Simon Pollak. Satmar, 1932.
Shevet M'nasheh. Menasheh Grossberg. Berlin, 1896.
Shevet Sofer. Simhah Bunem Sofer. Vienna 1915.
Shoel UMeshiv. Joseph Saul Nathansohn. Lemberg, 1868.
Shmat'ta D'RaVA. Barukh Avraham Mirsky. Mir, 1901.
S'ridei Esh. Yehiel Weinberg. III. Jerusalem, 1966.

Sitri UMagini. Sinai Schiffer. Tirnau, 1932.
Tiferet Tz'vi. Tz'vi Hirsch of Brody. Warsaw, 1711.
Torat Mord'khai. Mordecai Rabinowitz. Bilgoray, 1909.
Torat Hesed. Shneur Zalman of Lublin. Jerusalem, 1909.
T'shuvah L'Marei Dakhya. Mordecai Silberer (also containing a symposium). Vienna, 1875.
T'shurat Shai. Solomon Judah Tabak. Sziget, 1905.
T'shuvah Sh'lemah. Hayyim Fischel Epstein. Pietrkov, 1914.
Tsemah Tzedek (Hahadashot). Menahem Mendel Schneirson.
Tzitz Eliezer. Eliezer Judah Waldenberg. IX, Jerusalem, 1967.
Tzofnat Pa'aneah. Joseph Rosen of Rogachev. Dvinsk, 1931.
Tzur Ya'akov. Abraham Jacob Horowitz. Provzna, 1932; Jerusalem, 1955.
Yad Eliyahu. Elijah Rogoler. Warsaw, 1900.
Yad Yitzhak. Isaac Glueck. Satmar, 1908.
Yaskil Avdi. Ovadiah Hadayah. II, Jerusalem, 1935; IV, 1948.
Yismah Lev. Shalom Gagin. Jerusalem, 1878.
Y'mei Yosef. Yosef Mordecai Y'did. Jerusalem, 1913.
Zikhron Y'honatan. Jonathan Abelman. Vilna, 1904.
Zikhron Y'hudah. Judah Grunwald. Satmar, 1913.
Z'kan Aharon. Aaron Walkin. II, New York, 1951.

OTHER WORKS OF HALAKHAH OR COMMENTATION

Books

Hai Nefesh. Israel Zalmonovitz. Tel Aviv: Dvir, 1960.
Iggeret Bikkoret. Jacob Emden. Zhitomir, 1867.
Lehem HaPanim. Moses Yekuthiel Kaufmann. With code–like *Kontres Aharon* appended. Wilmarsdorf, 1726.
Otzar HaPoskim. Vol I, Jerusalem: Otzar HaPoskim Institute, 1962; IX, 1965.
Pahad Yitzhak. Isaac Lampronti (d. 1756). Lyck, 1846.
Pardes Yosef. Joseph Pachanovski. Lodz, 1900.
S'dei Hemed. Hayyim Hizkiyah Medini. Warsaw, 1903–07.
Shevet Miy'hudah. Issar Y'hudah Unterman. Jerusalem, 1955.
Shittah M'kubbetzet. Betzalel Ashkenazi.
Yosef Ometz. Joseph Hahn. Frankfurt am Main, 1723.

Articles

Aptowitzer, Viktor. "Emdat Ha-Ubar B'Dinei Onshin Shel Yisrael, "*Sinai,*" IV (1952), 26ff.
Heschel, Abraham J. "R. Nahman Mi–Kossov, etc. *Wolfson Jubilee Volume* (Hebrew Section). Jerusalem: American Academy for Jewish Research, 1965.
Horwitz, Yosef Yonah. "M'ni'at Herayon." *Rosenheim Festschrift* (Hebrew Section). Frankfurt am Main, 1932.
Huebner, Samuel. "M'niat Herayon al y'dei G'lulot" *HaDarom.* New York: Tishrei, 1965.
Jakobovitz, Immanuel. "Sh'elot B'inyanim R'fu'iyim Shonim," *Noam:* A Forum for the Clarification of Contemporary Halakhic Problems (Jerusalem), VI (1963), 272.
Klein, Hermann. "Geburtenregelung: Eine Halachische Abhandlung" (Hebrew) *Separatab-druck, Nachalath Zwi* (Berlin), I (1931).
Miklishanski, Y.K. "Mishpat Ha–Ubar." *Simon Federbush Jubilee Volume.* Jerusalem: Mosad Kook, 1961.
Unterman, Issar Y'hudah. "Mitzvat Pikkuah Nefesh Ug'darehah," *HaTorah V'haM'dinah* (Tel Aviv), IV (1952), 22–29.
———. "B'Inyan Pikkuah Nefesh Shel Ubar," *Noam,* VI (1963), 1–11.
Weinberg, Yehiel. "Happalat Ubar B'Ishah Holanit," *Noam,* IX (1966), 193–215.
Yosef, Ovadiah. "B'Din Esher Ish HaNe'eseret LaBa'al V'LaBoel," *Noam,* III (1960), 162–166.
Zweig, Mosheh Yonah. "Al Happalah M'la'akhutit, " *Noam,* VII (1964), 36–56.

SECONDARY HEBREW SOURCES

Beit HaMidrash. Jellinek, A. Leipzig, 1853.
Dor Dor V'Dor'shav. Weiss, I.H. Vienna, 1871.
Kit'vei HaRamban. Chavel, C. Jerusalem: Mosad HaRav Kook, 1965.
Mishpatim L'Yisrael. Ginzberg, Jacob. Jerusalem: Harry Fischel Institute, 1956.
Mitzvot HaBayit. Epstein, Joseph. New York: Balshon Press, 1966.
Otzar Dinim UMinhagim. Eisenstein, Judah David. New York: Hebrew Publishing Co., 1917.
Tol'dot HaPoskim. Tchernowitz, Chayim. 3 vols. New York: Va'ad HaYovel, 1946.
Torat HaMishpahah. Sternbach, Moses. Jerusalem: Harry Fischel Institute, 1966.
Yad Mal'akhi. Cohen, Malachi. Leghorn, 1759.

OTHER SECONDARY SOURCES- JEWISH AND GENERAL

BOOKS

Abrahams, Israel. *Jewish Life in the Middle Ages.* Philadelphia: The Jewish Publication Society of America; New York: Meridian Books, 1961.
Bailey, Derrick Sherwin. *Sexual Relation in Christian Thought.* New York: Harper and Bros., 1959.
Bakan, David. *Sigmund Freud and the Jewish Mystical Tradition.* New York: Schocken Books Inc., 1965
Baron, Salo W. *A Social and Religious History of The Jews.* (2nd ed.) Philadelphia: JPSA, 1958.
Belkin, Samuel. *Philo and the Oral Law.* Cambridge, Mass., 1940.
Birmingham, W. (ed.). *What Modern Catholics Think About Birth Control.* New York: Signet ed., 1964.
Bromley, D.D. *Catholics and Birth Control.* New York: Devin–Adair, 1965.
Cole, W.G. *Sex in Christianity and Psychoanalysis.* New York: Galaxy ed., 1966.
Falk, Ze'ev. *Jewish Matrimonial Law in the Middle Ages.* Oxford University Press, 1966.
Finkelstein, Louis. *Jewish Self-Government in the Middle Ages.* New York, 1924.
Fletcher, Joseph. *Morals and Medicine.* Boston: Beacon Press, 1960.
Freehof, Solomon. *The Responsa Literature.* Philadelphia: JPSA, 1955.
Garrison, F.H. *Introduction to the History of Medicine.* Philadelphia: W.B. Saunders, 1914.
Ginzberg, Louis. *On Jewish Law and Lore.* Philadelphia: JPSA, 1962.
Haggard, H.W. *Devils, Drugs and Doctors.* New York: Harper and Row, 1929.
Himes, N.E. *Medical History of Contraception.* New York: Gamut Press, 1934, 1963.
Hirsch, W. *Rabbinic Psychology:* The Soul in Rabbinic Literature. London: Goldston, 1947.
Jakobovitz, Immanuel. *Jewish Medical Ethics.* New York: Bloch, 1959.
———*Journal of a Rabbi.* New York: Living Books, Inc., 1966.
Katz, Jacob. *Exclusiveness and Tolerance.* New York: Schocken Books Inc., 1962.
Kerns, Joseph E. *The Theology of Marriage.* New York, 1964.
Lader, Lawrence. *Abortion.* New York: Bobbs–Merrill Co., 1966.
Lecky, W.E.H. *History of European Morals.* 2 vols. London: Longmans, Green and Co., 1911.
Liber, M. *Rashi.* Philadelphia: JPSA, 1926.
Loew, Leopold. *Die Lebensalter in der Juedischen Literatur.* Szegedin, 1875.
Mace, D. and V. *Marriage East and West.* New York: Dolphin ed., 1955.
Masters, W.H., and Johnson, V.E. *Human Sexual Response.* Boston: Little, Brown, and Co., 1966.
Moore, George Foot. *Judaism in the First Centuries of the Christian Era.* Cambridge, Mass.: Harvard University Press, 1927.
Noonan, John T., Jr. *Contraception: A History of Its Treatment by the Catholic Theologians and Canonists.* Cambridge, Mass.: Harvard University Press, 1965.
Patai, Raphael. *Family, Love and the Bible.* London: Macgibbon and Kee, 1960.
Ploss, H.H., and Bartels, M. *Woman.* New York: W. Heineman, Ltd., 1935.
Preuss, Julius. *Biblisch–Talmudische Medizin.* Berlin, 1911.

Rock, John. *The Time Has Come; A Catholic Doctor's Proposal to End the Battle Over Birth Control.* New York: Alfred A. Knopf, 1963.

Rosen, Harold (ed.). *Therapeutic Abortion.* New York: Julian Press, 1954.

Scholem, Gershom. *Major Trends in Jewish Mysticism.* New York: Schocken Books Inc., 1954.

Sigerist, H.E. *A History of Medicine.* New York: Oxford University Press, 1951.

St. John Stevas, N. *Birth Control and Public Policy.* Santa Barbara: Fund for the Republic, 1960.

Steiman, Sidney. *Custom and Survival.* New York: Bloch, 1963.

Sutherland, H. *Control of Life.* London: Burns and Oates, Ltd., 1944.

Thielecke, Helmut. *The Ethics of Sex.* New York: Harper and Row, 1964.

Twersky, Isadore. *Rabad of Posquieres: A Twelfth–Century Talmudist.* Cambridge, Mass.: Harvard University Press, 1962.

Waxman, Meyer. *A History of Jewish Literature.* 4 vols. New York: Bloch, 1948.

Westermarck, E.W. *The Origin and Development of the Moral Ideas.* 2 vols. London: Macmillan, 1906.

Wouk, Herman. *This is My God.* New York: Dell ed., 1964.

Zimmels, H.J. *Magicians, Theologians and Doctors.* London: Goldston, 1952.

ARTICLES

Aptowitzer, V. "Observations on the Criminal Law of the Jews," *Jewish Quarterly Review* (Philadelphia and London), XV (1924), 111ff.

DuBarle, A.M. "La Bible et les peres, ont–ils parlé de la contraception?" *La vie spirituelle,* Supplement (1962), 575ff.

Feldman, David M. "Sefirah, Lag BaOmer and Mourning Observances, " *Proceedings of the Rabbinical Assembly* (1962), 201–224.

Jakobovitz, Immanuel. "The Cost of Jewish Survival," *Judaism: A Quarterly* (Fall, 1966).

———"Thalidomide Babies," *The Jewish Review* (London, November, 1962). Reprinted in his *Jewish Law Faces Modern Problems.* New York: Yeshiva University Press, 1965.

Kardimon, S. "The Talmud on the Safe Period in the Menstrual Cycle," *Hebrew Medical Journal,* XXXII (1958), with English resume.

Kass, N. "Birth Prevention in the Talmud," *Hebrew Medical Journal* (New York), XXXIV (1961), with English resume.

Lauterbach, Jacob Z. "Birth Control—A Responsum," *Yearbook* of the Central Conference of American Rabbis, XXXVII (1927).

Twersky, Isadore. "The Shulhan Arukh—Enduring Code of Jewish Law," *Judaism: A Quarterly* (Spring, 1967).

Weisner, L. "Kindersegen und Kinderlosigkeit in altrabbinischem Schrifttume," *Monatsschrift fuer Geschichte und Wissenschaft des Judenthums* (Breslau), LRVI (1922).

Index

The function of a Glossary is encompassed by this Index: italicized numbers indicate pages where non-English phrases are defined.

Subjects listed in chapter headings or subheadings are omitted here.

Gershom, R., 7, 38 ff
Gerson, Levi ben, 138
Glick, Abraham, 202
Glueck, Isaac, 154
G'mara, 6, 30
Gnostics, 51, 145
Grandchildren, 49, 51
Grodzenzky, Hayyim Ozer, 224, 230, 280, 281, 285
Guf, 49
Guf neheneh min ha-guf, 104, 129, 212, 299
Guide for the Perplexed, 99, 150*n*

Hadaya, Obadia, 123*n,* 244
Hadrian, 51
Hai Gaon, 7, 189, 225
Halakhah, 4, 7, 194
Halakhah l'Mosheh mi-Sinai, 4n, 113
Halakhot G'dolot, 6, 264 f
Halitzah, 150n
HaMe'iri, Menahem, 10, 56*n,* 58*n,* 87, 199*n*
Hananel, R., 7
Häring, Bernard, 147, 269
Harlot, 66, 171, 177, 196. See also *Zonah.*
hash-hatah, 77, 78, 165
Hash-hatat zera, 65, 68, 76, 79, *109 ff,* 143, 156, 175, 195, 207, 218, 235, 298; factor in birth control, 109, 115, 131; as obverse of *p'ru ur'vu,* 112; as homicide, 115, 119 ff; and homunculus, 121 f; as autoerotic, 114, 122, 124 f, 298; involuntary, 117; in mythology, 117 f; consequences, 116 ff; definitions, 109 f, 122, 125, 128 f, 131, 157, 177; annulled by onah, 76, 129; as related to *shello k'darkah,* 156 f; as related to oral contraception, 242, 245 f; as related to abortion, 251 f
Hasidism, 82 f, 118, 256*n*
Hat-ra'ah, 256, 275
Havalah, 256
Hav-hanah, 170, 287
Hayyim of Volozhin, 190 f
Hazard, avoidance of, 52, 77, 162, 199 ff, 300. See also *Pikkuah nefesh; Sakkanah*
Hazon Ish, 125, 139, 174, 198*n,* 213, 218, 226, 233
Heller, Yom Tov, 14, 139, 160
Helpmeet, 28 f, 33
Hertz, I. H., 51, 260*n*
Herzog, Isaac, 110*n,* 123, 163, 224
Heschel, A. J., 118*n*
Hezekiah, 52
Hillel and Shammai, 37*n,* 48, 63, 172

Hinduism, 81
Hirsch, W., 272 f
Hiyya, R., 240
Hizz'kuni, 149n
Hoffman, David, 50, 97*n,* 140*n,* 160*n,* 229, 233, 284*n*
Homicide, 56; law of, 254 f; onanism as, 112, 119 f, 147
Homosexuality, female, 125
Homunculus, 121
Horvitz, Yosef Yonah, 229, 232, 243
Horowitz, Abraham, 77
Horwitz, Mordecai, 205, 237
Hurwitz, Elazar M., 157*n*
Hurwitz, Isaiah, 17, 159
Hysterectomy, 80

Ibn Ezra, Abraham, 87, 95, 97, 113, 135
Ibn Seneh, Samuel, 95, 97
Ibn Shuaib, Joshua, 90*n,* 101, 116, 137
Iggeret Bikkoret, 51, 76*n*
Iggeret HaKodesh, 11, *73 f,* 99 f, 137*n*
Iggun, 39n, 44, 230. See also *agunah.*
Immersion, ritual, 127
Impotence, 120, 155*n*
Imrei Esh, 219*n,* 221
Incest, 36, 151
Innui, 161
Innui ha-din, 289
Insanity, 286
Intent, 154 f, 163 ff
Intercourse, objectives of, 92, 95 ff. See also marital relations.
Intercourse, unnatural, 89, 149, 155 ff, 239*n;* as sin of Onan, 149; legal-moral attitude, 155 ff
Isaac Elhanan (Spector), 45
Isaiah, 52, 114
Isserles, Moses, 13, 27*n,* 42, 44, 68, 159

Jacob, 34*n,* 37, 46, 115, 117*n;* and Esau, 272
Jaffe, Mordecai, 14, 29, 160, 178
Jakobovits, Immanuel, 52*n,* 53*n,* 54, 183*n,* 225, 234, 246, 261*n,* 272, 283*n,* 294*n*
Janssens, Louis, 26
Jerome, 23, 82, 133, 145, 181, 192, 258
Jerusalem, 31, 155
Joseph, 117*n*
Josephus, 181, 258 f
Joshua, R., 48, 50
Judaeo-Christian sex ethic, 89 f, 102 f
Judah, 8, 97*n,* 144 ff, 150, 171
Judah, R. ("Rabbi"), 4, 66; and Antoninus, 271 ff
Justinian Code, 236, 269